Contemporary Diplomatic and Consular Relations

Paraskevi Naskou-Perraki
Editor

Contemporary Diplomatic and Consular Relations

Selected Aspects

Springer

Editor
Paraskevi Naskou-Perraki
Department of International Studies
University of Macedonia
Thessaloniki, Greece

ISBN 978-3-031-99242-1 ISBN 978-3-031-99243-8 (eBook)
https://doi.org/10.1007/978-3-031-99243-8

This work was supported by International Federation of Consular Corps and Associations (FICAC)

This Springer imprint is published by the registered company Springer Nature Switzerland AG
The registered company address is: Gewerbestrasse 11, 6330 Cham, Switzerland

To Diplomats and Honorary Consuls all over the world

Diplomatie:
«L'art d'exprimer l'hostilité avec politesse,
l' indifférence avec intérêt
et l'amitié avec prudence»
André Maurois
Tribune de Genève (14-15 Avril 1956)

Job Description of a Diplomat

"An ambassador
should be a trained theologian,
should be well versed in Aristotle and Plato,
and should be able at a moment's notice to
solve the most abstruse problems
in correct dialectical form;
He should also be an expert in mathematics,
architecture, music, physics, and civil and
canon law.
He should speak and write Latin fluently
and must also be proficient in Greek, Spanish,
French, German, and Turkish.
While being a trained classical scholar, a
historian, a geographer,
and an expert in military science,
he must also have a cultured taste for poetry.

And above all he must be of excellent family,
rich, and
endowed with a fine physical presence"
By Ottavianno Maggi,
Venetian Diplomat, 1596

Foreword

Dear Distinguished Colleagues and Esteemed Readers,

It is with profound honor, as President of the Federation Internationale des Corps et Associations Consulaires (FICAC)—the World Federation of Consuls—that I present this volume. In a world where borders may seem ever more visible, the work of diplomacy builds bridges that transcend them, fostering peace, understanding, and cooperation.

In our rapidly evolving global environment, the practice of diplomacy has undergone fundamental transformations. The rise of digital communication, the growing importance of non-state actors, the emergence of new security challenges, and the increasing complexity of international trade have all contributed to a dramatic expansion of diplomatic and consular functions. Traditional frameworks of diplomatic relations, while still foundational, must now accommodate new forms of engagement and novel channels of international cooperation.

Thus, the time has come to reassess and expand our understanding of diplomatic engagement. Authored by respected academics, this volume emerges as both a response to these demands and a guide to the evolving landscape of international relations. Unlike existing works that often address diplomacy from a singular perspective, this volume unites traditional and forward-looking approaches, creating a comprehensive guide that reflects the true complexity of modern diplomacy.

Under the expert editorial guidance of ret. Professor Paraskevi Naskou-Perraki, this volume brings together seventeen carefully curated sections, each addressing crucial aspects of modern diplomatic practice. The work begins with a historical foundation, essential for understanding the evolution of diplomatic relations, before moving through various dimensions of contemporary practice.

The selection of topics reflects the multifaceted nature of modern diplomacy. From the foundational aspects of diplomatic and consular law to emerging fields such as energy diplomacy and health diplomacy, each chapter provides both theoretical insight and practical guidance. The inclusion of specialized areas such as judicial diplomacy and entrepreneurial diplomacy acknowledges the expanding scope of diplomatic engagement in the twenty-first century.

Our distinguished contributors, leading scholars in their respective fields, bring together decades of academic research and practical experience. Their analyses not only illuminate current practices but also point toward future developments in diplomatic relations. This combination of theoretical rigor and practical insight makes the volume valuable for both scholars and practitioners.

As an organization that has evolved from seven member nations in 1982 to encompass more than 100 Consular Corps and Associations worldwide, FICAC has witnessed and participated in the transformation of diplomatic practice. Our commitment to championing peace, safeguarding consular rights, and promoting the implementation of the Vienna Convention on Consular Relations, aligns perfectly with the scholarly mission of this volume.

Our organization's dedication to educational partnerships with universities and business schools finds expression in this publication. By offering this work online, free of charge, to consuls worldwide and the academic community, we aim to strengthen the bridge between diplomatic practice and scholarly research. This initiative reflects our broader mission of enhancing understanding and cooperation in international relations.

The challenges facing modern diplomacy are complex and evolving. Climate change, technological disruption, global health crises, and shifting geopolitical dynamics require innovative diplomatic approaches while maintaining respect for established principles and practices. This volume provides both the theoretical framework and practical insights necessary for understanding and navigating these challenges.

FICAC's motto, "BRIDGING THE WORLD," takes on special significance in the context of this publication. As consuls work to connect nations and peoples, this academic work serves to connect theory and practice, tradition and innovation, in the service of more effective international relations.

We are particularly proud to announce that this volume is published by Springer Publishing, one of the world's leading academic publishers specializing in scientific, technical, and medical content. Springer's reputation for academic excellence and their global reach ensure that this work will meet the highest standards of scholarly publication and reach the widest possible audience.

This book will be available online free of charge. Springer Publishing will distribute the digital version to more than 1000 academic libraries worldwide, ensuring that scholars, practitioners, and students across the globe can benefit from the insights contained within these pages.

We hope this volume serves as a valuable resource for you, whether you are a scholar, a practitioner seeking to deepen your expertise, or a student preparing to enter the world of international relations, as well as anyone interested in the complex workings of modern diplomacy.

Thessaloniki, Greece — Nikolaos K. Margaropoulos

Major Sponsors

1. Hon. Madhusudan Agrawal, Honorary Consul of the Republic of Uganda in Mumbai
2. Hon. Arvind Gupta, Honorary Consul of the Republic of North Macedonia in India
3. Hon. Ebrahim Dawood Mamoon (Imran), Honorary Consul of the Republic of Ghana in Bangladesh

Sponsors

1. Association of Honorary Consuls in Bulgaria
2. Honorary Consular Corps of Cyprus
3. Consular Corps of Israel
4. Association des Consuls Honoraires de Monaco
5. Hon. Asif Chowdhury, Honorary Consul of Chile in Bangladesh
6. Mr. Amit Goyal, Managing Director, India Sotheby's International Realty
7. Hon. Pawel Michalak, Honorary Consul of the Republic of Albania in Poland
8. Hon. Karim Elyas Qubain, Honorary Consul General of Japan in Honduras
9. Hon. Dias Suleimenov, Honorary Consul of Portugal in Kazakhstan
10. Hon. Vikram Viswanath, Honorary Consul of Peru in India
11. Hon. Michail Xynos, Honorary Consul of Sri Lanka in the Hellenic Republic

Preface

Diplomacy, as a science or an art or both, is as old as international society. Over time the practice of diplomacy has acquired enduring, uniform institutional features and contributed to a more rational organization of international relations.

Customary rules on interstate diplomatic relations were initially codified to some extent by the Congress of Vienna (1815), yet codification of this field became completely global only in the era of the United Nations (1945–). The rules on diplomatic and consular relations are now enshrined in emblematic multilateral acts, such as the Vienna Convention on Diplomatic Relations (1961), the Vienna Convention on Consular Relations (1963), and other related instruments which have been adopted at the universal or regional level.

In the twenty-first century, diplomacy also continues to develop in the framework of international institutions which operate all over the world. As a result, a new era for diplomacy has emerged and institutional developments are observed in various subject-specific areas, including diplomacy of international organizations, the EU, climate, sports, cultural, energy, health, judicial diplomacy, economic and entrepreneurial, parliamentary diplomacy.

This collective work attempts to highlight some of the above institutional developments and also refer to the practice of the Hellenic Republic in various aspects of diplomatic and consular law. However, the views expressed here represent only those of the authors.

I wish to thank all the eminent authors who have kindly contributed to this collective work. I am particularly indebted to the President of FICAC Mr. N. Margaropoulos for supporting our effort and to Emerita Professor Kalliopi Koufa (Faculty of Law, Aristotle University of Thessaloniki) for giving permission to include here her article on consular judicial immunity.

The chapters of this book are a translation from P. Naskou-Perraki & N. Zaikos, Diplomatic and Consular Law, Sakkoulas Publications, 2022 (in Greek). I wish to thank Associate Professor Nikolaos Zaikos (University of Macedonia) for his kind permission to include parts of his text (Chapter IV 1–4 and 8–10 and Chapter VI) for this volume.

Thessaloniki, Greece
February 2025

Paraskevi Naskou-Perraki

I. Foundation and Early Years (1982–1992)

In the autumn of 1982, a transformative vision for international consular relations took shape in Copenhagen, Denmark. On October 2, 1982, the Federation Internationale des Corps et Associations Consulaires (FICAC), also known as the World Federation of Consuls, was established through the visionary leadership of Consul General Vagn Jespersen of Denmark and a small group of dedicated consuls.

The founding meeting brought together representatives from seven nations:

- Denmark
- Finland
- Greece
- Iceland
- Italy
- Norway
- Sweden

These founding nations shared a common commitment to establishing a platform that would enhance consular status and promote the role of consuls in the international arena. This initiative marked a watershed moment in consular history, and FICAC was soon recognized by Royal Decree in Belgium as an International Non-Profit Association (AISBL).

The organization's early years were characterized by careful deliberation and strategic planning. Two crucial meetings were held in Copenhagen in 1984 and 1986, during which the founding members worked to develop the Copenhagen Statutes. These statutes established a robust constitutional framework that would guide FICAC's growth and development in the years to come.

FICAC was conceived as a forum where consuls could:

- Share experiences
- Exchange best practices
- Collaborate on issues impacting their profession
- Address the evolving demands of diplomacy
- Respond to increasingly complex global interactions

This period of thoughtful foundation-building set the stage for FICAC's emergence as a respected voice in international diplomacy. As the organization's reputation grew, new consular associations and corps from around the world began joining FICAC, extending its reach across continents and establishing it as a truly global organization.

II. International Recognition and Growth (1993–2009)
United Nations Recognition

A pivotal moment in FICAC's history came in 1993 when it achieved recognition as an NGO by the United Nations with ROSTER ECOSOC status. This status was later elevated to SPECIAL ECOSOC Status in August 2018, marking a significant milestone and affirming the organization's growing influence and contributions to global diplomacy.

Expanding International Presence

FICAC's recognition by other international bodies soon followed. The Organization of American States (OAS) and other international bodies acknowledged FICAC as an NGO, expanding its ability to advocate on behalf of consuls globally. This institutional support underscored FICAC's mission of bridging cultural and diplomatic divides, promoting mutual understanding and working to protect the rights of consular officers worldwide. These recognitions enhanced FICAC's ability to influence international policies, particularly those addressing consular privileges and immunities, thereby strengthening the effectiveness and security of consular work.

Development of Congress Structure

One of the most notable aspects of FICAC's structure is its triennial World Congress of Consuls. First held in Vienna in 1988, these congresses have become landmark events in the consular community. Each congress provides a forum for representatives from across the globe to convene, discuss key issues, share insights, and elect new leaders. Some of these gatherings have been held under the patronage of global figures, such as the 10th Congress in Monaco, which was hosted by H.S.H. Prince Albert II.

Regional Conferences Initiative

Beginning in 2007, FICAC expanded its global outreach through the establishment of regional conferences. These conferences, held at least twice yearly across different continents, serve several crucial purposes:

- Address specific regional challenges and opportunities
- Foster closer cooperation between neighboring consular corps
- Enable more frequent interaction between members between the triennial World Congresses
- Build stronger regional networks while maintaining global connectivity
- Provide platforms for discussing region-specific diplomatic initiatives

III. Strategic Partnerships and Modern Development (2010–Present)
Key International Collaborations

In 2010, FICAC formalized its collaboration with the Prince Albert II Foundation of Monaco, focusing on environmental and climate change issues. The organization has established meaningful partnerships with notable organizations, including:

- ASCAME (Association of the Mediterranean Chambers of Commerce)
- RASIT (Royal Academy of Science International Trust)
- INTERLEGAL (global network of law firms)
- PAM (Parliamentary Assembly of the Mediterranean)
- PCCI (Philippines Chamber of Commerce)
- ICC (International Chamber of Commerce)
- KAZCIC (Chamber of International Commerce of Kazakhstan)

These collaborations have enabled FICAC to extend its work into diverse areas, from legal and environmental advocacy to supporting trade and economic development.

Educational Initiatives

Education stands as a cornerstone of FICAC's mission. The organization has formed partnerships with universities worldwide to promote education in diplomacy, peace, and conflict resolution. Partner institutions include:

- International Hellenic University (Greece)
- Dubrovnik and Nişantaşı Universities (Turkey)
- University of Environmental and Sustainable Development Somanya (Ghana)
- ANUPRIH (Asociación Nacional de Universidades Privadas de Honduras)
- Vrije Universiteit Brussel (Belgium)
- National University of the Philippines
- Yasar University (Izmir, Türkiye)
- Nazarbayev University (Astana, Kazakhstan)
- Università LUM Giuseppe Degennaro (Bari, Italy)

Through these initiatives, FICAC supports the academic growth of future consuls and diplomats, fostering a spirit of service and international cooperation among students and scholars.

IV. Contemporary Programs and Activities

Digital Engagement and Webinars

FICAC has embraced technology to expand its reach, hosting webinars featuring distinguished speakers including:

- Former President of Croatia, H.E. Kolinda Grabar-Kitarović
- Former President of Malta, H.E. Marie-Louise Coleiro Preca
- Minister of Foreign Affairs of Ghana and Secretary of the Commonwealth, H.E. Shirley Ayorkor Botchwey
- Mr. Kailash Satyarthi, Nobel Peace Prize Laureate
- H.E. Mrs. Yadira Gómez, Minister of Tourism of Honduras
- H.E. Mrs. Juliette Handal de Castillo, Ambassador in Political process against violence against women in Honduras at UN

Energy Diplomacy

In September 2023 and 2024, FICAC organized the 1st and 2nd Energy Diplomacy Forum in collaboration with the International Hellenic University. These groundbreaking events brought together experts, distinguished guest speakers from around the world and policymakers to discuss the challenges facing the energy sector and to explore solutions that promote clean and affordable energy. The forums provided a unique platform for exchanging knowledge and best practices, contributing to the global effort to achieve Clean and Affordable Energy, with a focus on innovative technologies and sustainable practices. Topics such as renewable energy, energy efficiency, and international energy policies were at the forefront of the discussions.

Women in Diplomacy

The Women in Diplomacy Committee has become one of FICAC's most active bodies. Notable initiatives include:

- In 2023, the Women in Diplomacy Committee in collaboration with the Culture and Art Committee organized an inspiring event titled "Art Exhibition and Charity Auction: Healing Through Art," at the prestigious Pera Museum in Tepebaşı, Istanbul. The primary objective was to promote gender equality and raise funds for young women pursuing postgraduate studies in Peaceful Resolution of State Disputes. A distinguished selection of talented and globally recognized women artists generously donated their artwork for this noble cause. Their diverse expressions and styles enriched the exhibition, showcasing the transformative power of art.
- The "Women and Children's Book" initiative. The project aimed at finding a meaningful and long-lasting solution to a well-known and delicate issue faced by thousands of women and children across the globe. This initiative's main goal would translate into constructing multiple long-term solutions:
  - Professionally and psychologically empowering women and children
  - Help locally installed "sheltering" infrastructures gain further recognition and more means of action
  - Allocate more funds for women to re-integrate the professional workforce
  - Highlight the benefits of artistic expression for at-risk children (through writing and drawing)
  - Provide further psychological, health, and educational support for at-risk children
  - The Acknowledgment of local stories of personal resilience

- United Nations Women's Commission Engagement:
  In 2024, FICAC achieved another significant milestone with its participation in the 68th session of the United Nations Commission on the Status of Women in New York. The FICAC ECOSOC Committee, working in conjunction with the FICAC Women in Diplomacy Committee (WIDC), organized a parallel event focused on "Directed Diplomacy: Women's Leadership—Key to Fiscal Success." This event provided a unique platform for honorary consuls, who serve as both diplomats and leaders in the private sector, to share their perspectives and catalyze change in gender equality and women's leadership in diplomacy.

United Nations Engagement

FICAC maintains active engagement with the UN. In January 2024, FICAC President Hon. Nikolaos K. Margaropoulos and Board members met with:

- H.E. Rabab Fatima, Under-Secretary-General & High Representative for LDCs, LLDCs & SIDS
- H.E. Paula Narváez, President of the 79th Economic and Social Council

Humanitarian Initiatives

FICAC has championed numerous social causes, including:

- Partnership with UNICEF to raise funds for children affected by HIV/AIDS
- Establishment of scholarships in peace and conflict resolution studies
- Various humanitarian programs supporting international cooperation, such as providing support for the Türkiye earthquake victims in 2023.

V. Leadership and Recognition

Presidential Succession

FICAC's leadership history reflects its international character:

- Consul General Vagn Jespersen (Denmark, until 1995)
- Consul General Andreas Mavrommatis (Cyprus)
- Consul General Peter Gad Naschitz (Israel)
- Consul General Roland Dahlman (Sweden)
- Consul General Arnold Foote (Jamaica)
- Consul General Aykut Eken (Türkiye)
- Consul Nikolaos K. Margaropoulos (Greece, current)

Each president has contributed uniquely to FICAC's development, from expanding membership to initiating new programs, ensuring the organization remains responsive to the evolving landscape of global diplomacy.

The FICAC Gold Star

FICAC's highest honor, the FICAC Gold Star, has been awarded to incumbent Heads of State/Government who have demonstrated exceptional commitment to international cooperation and diplomatic excellence. Recipients include:

- H.E. P.J. Patterson, Governor General of Jamaica
- H.E. Abdullah Gul, President of the Republic of Turkey
- H.S.H. Prince Albert II of Monaco
- H.E. Herman van Rompuy, President of the European Council
- H.E. Benigno Simeon Aquino III, President of the Philippines
- His Holiness Pope Benedict XVI
- H.E. Tomislav Nikolic, President of the Republic of Serbia
- H.E. Borut Pahor, President of Slovenia
- His All Holiness Bartholomew, Archbishop of Constantinople, New Rome and Ecumenical Patriarch
- H.E. Danilo Medina Sanchez, President of the Dominican Republic
- H.E. Bidhya Devi Bhandari, President of the Federal Democratic Republic of Nepal

- His Holiness Pope Francis
- H.E. Nicos Anastasiades, President of the Republic of Cyprus
- H.E. Governors of Jamaica and San Kitts and Nevis
- H.E. Nana Addo Dankwa Akufo-Addo
- H.E. Iris Xiomara Castro Sarmiento, President of the Republic of Honduras

VI. Future Vision and Ongoing Mission

FICAC's growth over the years has transformed it into a dynamic organization with a multifaceted mission. "*Working Hard to Serve You Better*" is a motto that embodies its commitment to providing consular professionals with the support they need while advocating for diplomatic integrity and mutual respect among nations. Its structure includes specialized committees focusing on:

- Climate change & Environment
- Security and Consular Privileges Protection
- Education and Relations with Universities
- Culture and Art
- Charitable Agreements and Events, World & Regional Conferences
- Women in diplomacy
- Trade and Economic Development
- Maritime affairs
- Health
- Mediation

From its modest beginnings with seven member nations, FICAC has grown to encompass more than 100 consular corps and Associations worldwide. This remarkable expansion reflects the universal recognition of the organization's value and the growing importance of consular services in an increasingly interconnected world.

As FICAC looks to the future, it remains committed to innovation, adaptability, and dedication to its founding principles. Through its extensive work in advocacy, education, and humanitarian efforts, FICAC continues to underscore the essential role of consuls in bridging divides, fostering trust, and promoting the ideals of peace and justice on a global scale.

6. Convention on the Prevention and Punishment of Crimes Against Internationally Protected Persons, including Diplomatic Agents

Adopted in New York on December 14, 1973; entered into force on 20 February 20, 1977.Text: UNTS 1035, p. 167et seq.

7. Vienna Convention on the Representation of States in their Relations with International Organizations of a Universal Character

Adopted in Vienna on March 14, 1975.Text: UNDoc.A/CONF.67/16; has not entered into force.

8. Convention on the Safety of United Nations and Associated Personnel

Adopted by UNGA Res. 49/59 (December 9, 1994); entered into force on January 15, 1995. Text: UNTS 2051, p. 363 et seq.

9. UN Convention on the Law of the Sea

Adopted by the Third United Nations Conference on the Law of the Sea, Montego Bay, Jamaica, (1982), Text: 1833 UNTS 3.

10. Vienna Convention on the Law of Treaties

Adopted by the United Nations Conference on the Law of Treaties, entered into force 27 January 1980, Text: UNTS vol. 1155, p. 331.

11. UN General Assembly Rules of Procedure

Adopted by the General Assembly, Text: A/520/Rev. 20 (2020).

B. **Council of Europe**

1. Statute of the Council of Europe

Adopted in London 5 V. 1949, Text: ETS No. 001.

2. General Agreement on Privileges and Immunities of the Council of Europe

Adopted in Paris 2.IX.1949, Text: ETS No. 002.

3. European Convention on Consular Functions

Paris, December 11, 1967; entered into force on June 9, 2011. Text: European Treaty Series No. 061.

3a. Protocol to the European Convention on Consular Functions concerning the Protection of Refugees

3b. Protocol to the European Convention on Consular Functions relating to Consular Functions in respect of Civil Aircraft

Both protocols adopted in Paris, December 11, 1967. Text: ETS 061A and 061B respectively; have not entered into force.

4. European Convention on the Abolition of Legalization of Documents executed by Diplomatic Agents or Consular Officers

Adopted in London, June 7, 1968; entered into force on August 14, 1970. Text: ETS 63.

C. **European Union**

1. Treaty on the European Union (Consolidated version 2016)

OJ EU C 202, 7.6.2016.

2. Treaty on the Functioning of the European Union (Consolidated version 2016)

OJ EU C 202, 7.6.2016.

3. Protocol No. 7 to the Treaty on the Functioning of the European Union on the Privileges and Immunities of the European Union

OJ EU C 202/266.

3. **Decision 95/553/EC** of the Representatives of the Governments of the Member States, meeting within the Council, of 19 December 1995 regarding protection for citizens of the European Union by diplomatic and consular representations, OJ L 314, 28.12.1995, p. 73.

4. **Decision 96/409/CSFP** of the Representatives of the Governments of the Member States, meeting within the Council of 25 June 1996 on the establishment of an emergency travel document, OJ L 168, 6.7.1996, p. 4-11.

5. **Council Regulation (EC) No 1/2003** of December 2002 on the implementation of the rules on competition laid down in Articles 81 and 82 of the Treaty, OJ EU L 001/04/01/2003.

6. **Council Regulation (EU) No 267/2012** of 23 March 2012 concerning restrictive measures against Iran and repealing Regulation (EU) No 961/2010, OJ L 88, 24.3.2012, p. 1–112.

7. **Council Directive (EU) 2015/637 of 20 April 2015** on coordination and cooperation measures to facilitate consular protection for unrepresented Union citizens in third countries and repealing Decision 95/553/EC, 24.4.2015, L 106/1.

8. Council of the European Union; Treaty on Stability, Coordination and Governance in the Economic and Monetary Union, Brussels, 02/03/2012, T/SCG/

9. **Council Directive (EU) 2019/997 of 18 June 2019** establishing an EU Emergency Travel Document and repealing Decision 96/409/CFSP, OJ EU L 163/1.

10. **Council Regulation (EU) 2022/576** of 8 April 2022 amending Regulation (EU) No833/2014 concerning restrictive measures in view of actions by Russia destabilizing the situation in Ukraine, OJ EU L 111/1.

11. **Council Regulation (EU) 2022/577** of 8 April 2022 amending Regulation (EC) No765/2006 concerning restrictive measures in view of the situation in Belarus and Belarus' involvement in Russia's attack against Ukraine, OJ EU L 111/67.

12. **Council Decision (CFSP) 2022/578 of 8 April 2022** amending Decision 2014/512/CFSP concerning restrictive measures in view of actions by Russia destabilizing the situation in Ukraine, OJ EU L 111/70.

13. **Council Decision (CFSP) 2022/579** of 8 April 2022 amending Council Decision 2012/642/CFSP concerning restrictive measures in view of the situation in Belarus and Belarus' involvement in the Russian aggression against Ukraine, OJ EU L 111/81.

14. **Commission Implementing Decision (EU) 2022/2452** of 8 December 2022 laying down additional technical specifications for the EU Emergency Travel Document established by Council Directive (EU) 2019/997 (SECRET UE/EU SECRET non classifiée en l'absence de la partie II de l'annexe/when detached from Part II of the Annex—non-classified.) (notified under document C(2022) 8938) C/2022/8938, OJ L 320, 14.12.2022, p. 47–53.

15. **Council Regulation (EC) No 1/2003** of December 2002 on the implementation of the rules on competition.

D. **Organization of the American States**

1. Multilateral Agreement on privileges and immunities of the Organization of American States

Adopted at Washington on 15 May 1949.

E. **Organization of Africa Unity**

1. General convention on the privileges and immunities of the organization of Africa Unity

Adopted at Accra, Ghana on 25 October 1965.

Contents

Contributors

Elisavet Athanasia Alexiadou International Hellenic University, Thessaloniki, Greece
Open University of Cyprus, Hellenic Open University, Patras, Greece
Aristotle University of Thessaloniki, Thessaloniki, Greece

Despoina Anagnostopoulou Department of International and European Studies, University of Macedonia, Thessaloniki, Greece

Maria N. Bozoudi Phd Department of International and European Studies, University of Macedonia, Thessaloniki, Greece

Stelio Campanale Libera Università Mediterranea-LUM Giuseppe Degennaro, Casamassima - Bari, Italy
Universiteti Katolik "Zoja e KëshillittëMirë", Tirana, Albania

George Dikaios Department of Political Science and Public Administration, National and Kapodistrian University of Athens, Athens, Greece

Emmanuella Doussis Department of Political Science and Public Administration, National and Kapodistrian University of Athens, Athens, Greece

Dimitrios Gargalianos Department of Physical Education, Democritus University of Thrace, Komotini, Greece

Styliani Gerani PhD Department of International and European Studies, University of Macedonia, Thessaloniki, Greece

Emmanouil Kalaintzis Hellenic Court of Audit (Supreme Financial Court), Athens, Greece

Theodosios Karvounarakis Department of International and European Studies, University of Macedonia, Thessaloniki, Greece

Komninos Komnios International Hellenic University, Thessaloniki, Greece

Konstantinos D. Magliveras Department of Mediterranean Studies, University of the Aegean, Rhodes, Greece

Nikolaos K. Margaropoulos Honorary Consul of the Philippines in Thessaloniki, President of FICAC, the World Federation of Consuls Thessaloniki, Thessaloniki, Greece

Paraskevi Naskou-Perraki Department of International Studies, University of Macedonia, Thessaloniki, Greece

Antonia Zervaki Department of Political Science and Public Administration, National and Kapodistrian University of Athens, Athens, Greece

List of Abbreviations

A/	(General) Assembly (UN)
A/AC.10	Committee on the Progressive Development of International Law and its Codification
A/C.6	General Assembly/Sixth Committee
A/CN4	Commission 4 (International Law Commission)
ADD.	addendum
ADR	Alternative Dispute Resolution
AEAJ	Association of European Administrative Judges
AELCJ	Association of European Competition Law Judges
AFDI	Annuaire Français de Droit International
Art.	article
ASIL	American Society of International Law
AU	African Union
BIS	Bank of International Settlement
BYIL	British Yearbook of International Law
CBDR	Common But Differentiated Responsibility
CoE	Council of Europe
CEM	Clean Energy Ministerial
CEPEJ	Commission for the Efficiency of Justice
CETS	Council of Europe Treaty Series
CJEU	Court of Justice of the European Union
CIJ	Cour International de Justice
CIS	Commonwealth of Independent States
COCON	Consular Affairs Working Party
COMP.	Compiled by
CONF.	Conference
COPs	Conference of the Parties
CCJE	Consultative Council of European Judges
CCEP	Consultative Council of European Prosecutors
CEPI	Coalition for Epidemic Preparedness Innovations
CEPEJ	Commission for the Efficiency of Justice
DEIK	Foreign Economic Relations Board of Turkey
DIR.	Director/Directeur

Doc.	Document
EAJ	European Association of Judges
EBRD	European Bank for Reconstruction and Development
EC	European Commission
ECHR	European Convention of Human Rights
ECtHR	European Court of Human Rights
ECOSOC	Economic and Social Council
ECOWAS	Economic Community of West African States
ECtHR	European Court of Human Rights
Ed(s)	Editors
EEAS	European External Action Service of the EU
EJIL	European Journal of International Law
EJN	European Judicial Network
EJTN	European Judicial Training Network
EMEM	European Mediterranean Gas Forum
EMU	European Economic and Monetary Union
EPPO	European Public Prosecutor's Office
ERA	European Round Table
ESM	European Stability Mechanism
ETS	European Treaty Series
ETDs	Energy Travel Documents
ETO	Extraterritorial Obligations (Consortium)
ERT	Academy of European Law
EU	European Union
EUFJE	EU Forum of Judges for the Environment
EvrHYIEL	Evrigenis Hellenic Yearbook of International and European Law
FCTC	Framework Convention on Tobacco Control
FICAC	Federation Internationale des Corps et Associations Consulaires
GA	General Assembly
GAOR	Official Records of the General Assembly
GCC	Gulf Cooperation Council
GDP	Gross Domestic Product
GEMME	European Association of Judges for Mediation
GYIL	German Yearbook of International Law
HICLR	Hastings International and Comparative Law Review
HRIR	Hellenic Review of International Relations
Hrsg.	Herausgeben
IAEA	International Atomic Energy Agency
IAJ	International Association of Judges
IARMJ	International Association of Refugee and Migration Judges
IATJ	International Association of Tax Judges
IAWJ	International Association of Women Judges
ICAO	International Civil Aviation Organization

ICC	International Criminal Court
ICCPR	International Covenant on Civil and Political Rights
ICESCR	International Covenant on Economic, Social, and Cultural Rights
ICJ	International Court of Justice
ICJ Reports	International Court of Justice, Reports
ICLQ	International and Comparative Law Quarterly
IFIs	International Financial Institutions
IFPP	INTOSAI Framework of Professional Pronouncements
IHRs	International Health Regulations
ILC	International Law Commission
ILO	International Labor Organization
IMF	International Monetary Fund
INTOSAI	International Organization of Supreme Audit Institutions
IOM	International Olympic Committee
IPCC	Intergovernmental Panel on Climate Change
ISSAI	International Standards of Supreme Audit Institutions
LGBTI	Lesbian, Gay, Bi, Trans, and Intersex people
LON	League of Nations
LONHO	League of Nations Health Organization
MEDEL	Magistrats Européens pour la Démocratie et les Libertés
MINERS	Ministers and Senior Officials Responsible for Physical Education and Sports
MFN	Most-favored Nation
NOC	National Olympic Committees
OAS	Organization of American States
OECD	Organization of Economic Cooperation and Development
OIHP	Office International d Hygiene Publique
OSCE	Organization for Security and Cooperation in Europe
p.	Page/pages
PAM	Parliamentary Assembly of the Mediterranean
para.	paragraph
PCIJ	Permanent Court of International Justice
PIP	Pandemic Influenza Preparedness
Recueil des Cours	Recueil des Cours de l' Academie de Droit International de La Haye
RBDI	Revue Belge de Droit International
Res.	Resolution
REEEP	Renewable Energy and Energy Efficiency Partnership
RGDIP	Revue Générale de Droit International Public
Roc	Republic of Cyprus
SAIs	Supreme Audit Institutions
SCN	Superior Courts Network
SR	Summary Records

T.	Tome
TFEU	Treaty for the Functioning of European Union
UANI	United Against Nuclear IRAN
UN	United Nations
UNCITRAL	United Nations Commission on International Trade Law
UNESCO	United Nations Educational, Scientific, and Cultural Organization
UNFCCC	United Nations Framework Convention on Climate Change
UNGA	United Nations General Assembly
UNSC	United Nations Security Council
UNTS	United Nations Treaty Series
VJTL	Vanderbilt Journal of Transnational Law
WB	World Bank
WHO	World Health Organization
WTO	World Trade Organization
YILC	Yearbook of the International Law Commission
YJIL	Yale Journal of International Law

Diplomacy: A Historical Overview

1

Theodosios Karvounarakis

Abstract

Since antiquity, diplomacy has always been a constant in relations between human societies. By the eighteenth century, it had assumed most of the features of its modern form. Initially a European creation, the modern diplomatic system gradually expanded to the rest of the world. Multilateral diplomacy received a major boost by the two World Wars. New institutions, new functions, and functionaries have been introduced. Diplomacy has been decisively affected by the historical process although in its main features it remains unchanged.

Diplomacy is as old as the human race. Even when violence and conflict were the result of contact between human groups, some compromise had to be reached to attain common goals. For instance, a truce had to be negotiated so that rival parties could collect their dead and injured, or a longer cessation of hostilities so that both sides could tend to their fields. Later, when states were established, the need to negotiate and compromise to achieve mutually beneficial goals was institutionalized as diplomatic interaction. The basis of this was the realization by rulers that nobody was strong enough to achieve their full goals, according to their wishes. Some give

---

This chapter is based on the author's book *The Art of Diplomacy and Its Artisans* (in Greek), Thyrathen Publications, Thessaloniki, 2013, which includes a more extensive bibliography. A few useful titles are listed as follows:

M.S. Anderson, *The Rise of Modern Diplomacy, 1450–1919*. Longman, London, 1993.
G. R. Berridge, *Diplomacy. Theory and Practice*. 3rd Edition. Palgrave, NY, 2005.
K. Hamilton, R. Langhorne, *The Practice of Diplomacy*. Routledge, London, 1995 and 2011.
H. Nicholson, *The Evolution of Diplomacy*. Collier Books, NY, 1966.
Roberts, *Satow's Diplomatic Practice*. 6th Edition. Oxford University Press. Oxford, 2012.

T. Karvounarakis (✉)
Department of International and European Studies, University of Macedonia, Thessaloniki, Greece
e-mail: theokar@uom.gr

P. Naskou-Perraki (ed.), *Contemporary Diplomatic and Consular Relations*,
https://doi.org/10.1007/978-3-031-99243-8_1

and take had to occur. A diplomatic system, i.e., continuous diplomatic contact, involving a number of states with certain rules and procedures, first emerged in the kingdoms of the Middle East (in Anatolia and Mesopotamia) in the third millennium B.C. However, the diplomatic system developed by the Greek city states in classical times (around the fifth century B.C.) is better documented and easier to decipher. The Greek diplomats "πρέσβεις" (elderly men) were members of ad hoc missions sent by one Greek state to another. They did not negotiate but simply presented their case to the ruler or the assembly of the city they were sent to. By this time, respect for the life and safety of the envoys had been established, which is also one of the principles of present-day diplomacy. The Greek diplomatic system, aided by the common language and culture of its participants, was effective in maintaining communication among the Greek city states and limiting conflict, although war was a constant phenomenon in their relations.

The diplomacy of Rome evolved with the fortunes of this great city. While Rome was relatively weak, and therefore vulnerable, it made compromises and negotiated treaties with neighboring cities. This was not necessary when it came to be the greatest military power of its time. With its powerful army, it could impose its will on anyone. It therefore mostly negotiated the terms of surrender by the cities and lands it conquered. It did that to avoid the destruction and therefore the reduction of the value of its target, if that was to be taken violently, as well as to avoid the costs of deployment of its very efficient but very costly army. Rome's contribution to diplomacy was the introduction of legal forms and concepts developed by Roman law in the writing and the interpretation of the treaties, which made them a more effective diplomatic instrument.

Because of its vulnerable position and constant challenge to its borders, Byzantium had to adopt a different approach. Its resources and its military were not sufficient to ignore the danger posed by its many potentially hostile neighbors. Therefore, it frequently tried to placate rather than confront them. It distributed money to foreign rulers and tried to impress them with the riches of its capital, Constantinople, and the splendor of the Empire's civilization. It tried to convert them to Christianity, sent its princesses as brides and turned them against each other. It put together an important system of informants and spies and appointed a government official to supervise information gathering. The systematic collection of intelligence, another element of modern diplomacy, can first be observed in the diplomacy of Byzantium.

Until the fifteenth century, no resident envoys were employed by the states in their diplomatic communications. Ad hoc missions visited foreign capitals and departed once their job was done. The first permanent missions can be observed in the Italian city states around 1450. In the Middle Ages the Italian city states, aided by their common culture and immunity from outside invaders up to the end of the fifteenth century, had developed an international system akin to that of ancient Greece. However, their small size, contested legitimacy of some of their rulers and therefore vulnerability to the rivals' designs, required constant communication to find common cause with others, as well as information gathering to constantly assess the very unstable environment in which they existed. A resident envoy was therefore found to serve such purposes. In the beginning, their main function was to carry messages from their masters and gather information. Gradually, they were entrusted with the conclusion of minor treaties. Major diplomatic businesses were conducted by ad hoc missions consisting of high-ranking members of the aristocracy. As the quality of the permanent envoys improved though (initially commoners or even persons of dubious reputation made up their ranks) and more tasks were assigned to them, ad hoc missions were limited to the conclusion of peace treaties.

In Renaissance Europe, on the basis of reciprocity, the envoys' safety and property were protected by the receiving state. The inviolability of the resident embassy was a different matter and was achieved gradually. An important step was toleration of chapels on the embassy grounds of a religious dogma different from the prevailing one in the receiving state, which became common by the beginning of the seventeenth century.

A problem that states and diplomats had to tackle up to the beginning of the nineteenth century was precedence, i.e., the ranking of the diplomatic representatives in state functions, the order in which they were announced, sat, or received by the sovereign, and the order in which they signed international treaties. This symbolized the relevant international status of the sovereign they represented and was therefore treated as a matter of utmost importance. Many disputes, some of them with serious diplomatic complications, can be traced to this matter. Precedence was finally determined at the Congress of Vienna in 1815 on the basis of the relevant seniority of the ambassadors in the country to which they were accredited. Three years later at Aix-la-Chapelle (Aachen), it was decided that international treaties would be signed in alphabetical order of the signatory states following the French alphabet.

Another major development in the evolution of diplomatic practice was the establishment of a separate government department responsible for the conduct of foreign affairs. The first such ministry was established in France in 1626 when Cardinal Richelieu was in charge of the affairs of the state. Up to that point, different government departments shared in the conduct of foreign affairs. However, Cardinal Richelieu considered this area of government activity so important as to deserve its own bureaucracy. Gradually, the new ministry took over most diplomatic functions, although it was not until the next century that ministries with such competences became the norm in Europe.

The diplomatic system that took shape in Europe during the seventeenth and eighteenth centuries is known as the French Diplomatic System. After the 30 Years' War (1618–1648), France became the best organized and most powerful European state. To serve its complex international activities, it developed and advanced a sophisticated diplomatic system which, aided by the preponderance of the French culture and universal use of the French language as the language of Europe's elite, came to dominate the European states system. Its main characteristics were the establishment of permanent diplomatic missions, the use of professional diplomats, a certain protocol in the conduct of diplomatic business, secrecy of negotiations, and honesty in statements made and obligations undertaken. To this day, the French System defines the parameters of bilateral interstate relations.

than a means to achieve mutually beneficial results. They stalled, prevaricated, even conducted a form of "war of nerves" by insisting on the minutiae of the issues examined, using aggressive language or going back on positions they seemed to have accepted, to exhaust their counterparts and make them accept their views. Their credibility was undermined, as in some cases they seemed to be encouraging the activities of Comintern, an organization aiming at world revolution that Moscow controlled, against the very government with which they were trying to engage diplomatically. This mentality bred distrust and impeded cooperation with the Western democracies against Nazi Germany.

Hitler's approach was very different. He pretended to respect the rules and norms of conventional diplomacy to allay his opponents' suspicions and achieve his goals without interference. He retained in their positions all diplomats including the Minister of Foreign Affairs appointed by the previous government. However, the diplomats' authority was constantly eroded by Nazi cadres who, with Hitler's approval, assumed diplomatic duties, including the conclusion of international agreements. Eventually, in 1938, Hitler, feeling strong enough to defeat his opponents, put Joachim Von Ribbentrop, the most influential of the Nazi "diplomats," at the helm of the foreign office, ushering in the final and openly aggressive phase of his foreign policy. Characteristic of Hitler's approach to diplomacy as a mere expedient to achieve his expansionist goals was his total disregard for international commitments. The nonaggression pacts he signed with Poland in 1934 and Russia in 1939 to last for 10 years were violated in 1939 and 1941, respectively.

As far as diplomacy was concerned, the Second World War was largely a repetition of the first. Major decisions were made by the allied leaders, while foreign ministries, certainly in the United States and USSR, played a secondary, subordinate role. In the United States, Secretary of State Cordell Hull was eclipsed by Harry Hopkins, President Roosevelt's trusted advisor and special envoy. Again, government departments established direct contact with their allied counterparts, further eroding the influence of foreign ministries.

The Second World War brought in its wake a major reorganization of the world institutions. The League of Nations had proven incapable of stopping another major war and had to be replaced. In April 1945, the United Nations Organization was established as an improved version of the League, better endowed to fulfill its mission of maintaining world peace and security. The League's cumbersome unanimity rule in decision-making was replaced with majority voting and Security Council decisions were made mandatory for the member states. Political initiative was assigned to the Secretary General, whereas the Soviet Union and the United States, the most powerful countries in the world in the aftermath of WWII, were both founding members, with a permanent, influential position in the Security Council. Additionally, a nexus of specialized agencies and International Governmental Organizations (IGOs) tied to the United Nations was created to deal with problems such as health, food security, and economic development to promote the well-being of the world's population, facilitate international cooperation and therefore limit the causes of world friction.

Under the UN system, multilateral diplomacy expanded. More bilateral contacts were also made possible in the context of the new constitution since permanent diplomatic missions in New York could conduct bilateral business with those of other states, even when no former relations existed between the two countries or none was officially represented in the other.

Membership in the United Nations vastly increased with decolonization, since ex-colonies considered joining the organization as confirmation of their newly acquired independent status. By 1960, former colonies were numerous and powerful enough to obtain an overwhelming majority for General Assembly Resolution 1514, which called for an end to colonial rule.

The appearance of so many new and unpredictable actors on the world scene (some of the new states had openly revolutionary and anti-Western ideologies) was one of the reasons why more established states expedited the conclusion of the Vienna Convention on Diplomatic Relations (1961). This instrument codified the rules of bilateral diplomatic relations, making intercourse among states more secure and predictable. It was thought that if such a set of rules was presented to and accepted by the new states, the functioning of diplomacy would not be disturbed by their arrival. On the whole, Third World countries showed no wish to disrespect the established rules and norms of the international system.

The Cold War had an adverse effect on diplomacy. The world was divided in two hostile camps that limited communication and increased adversarial behavior. Great power competition infected the United Nations, turning it into a theater of confrontation rather than cooperation. Suspicion was widespread and embassies were turned into instruments of destabilization and covert operations. Diplomats were hampered in the execution of their duties. At the same time, new diplomatic techniques were invented to confront problems as they arose: proximity talks, shuttle diplomacy, interests sections.

Since WWII, multilateral diplomacy has expanded. The world community is more willing to tackle problems affecting everyone such as terrorism, drugs, disease, food security, and climate change—and for this purpose, collective action is required. The world has shrunk due to the digital information revolution. Diplomatic business can be conducted online and meetings of officials or Heads of State are easier, either through improvement of the means of transport or online. Such developments had undermined the position of the Residence Embassy. Critics argue that nowadays any government official, including diplomats, can communicate with his/her counterpart in another country online or, if need be, easily travel to a meeting. Information gathering is possible via the vast media networks that operate on the internet. Face-to-face diplomatic business is easy to conduct in the multiple multilateral fora. The maintenance of residence embassies is a costly affair and, on some occasions, it exposes its employees to great safety risks. However, a resident ambassador still possesses irreplaceable qualities: extensive knowledge of the country where they are accredited as well as their ability to gather information from sources not accessible to journalists or ordinary spies, to offer advice to their government, to initiate or expertly contribute to negotiations, to maintain constant and intimate contact with their host states' government, to promote the image of their country, and to communicate their government's wishes with precision and clarity. For these reasons, their future and that of the Resident Embassy's seem secure. Some changes had to be made. Representatives from government departments other than the foreign ministries had to be included in the resident missions, the promotion of trade was made a higher priority, security measures increased, as well as the hiring of local personnel for administrative positions. Budget cuts have resulted in fewer available resources, the downsizing or even closure of permanent diplomatic missions. On the whole, the Ministry of Foreign Affairs faces competition from other government departments such as defense, trade, or the economy, which claim their share in their countries' foreign policy, and its influence many times depends on the wishes of the head of government.

At the same time, diplomacy has not ceased to evolve. New diplomatic actors other than the sovereign states have emerged, such as International Governmental Organizations (e.g., the International Monetary Fund has representatives in a number of countries around the world and the United Nations as a separate entity participates in multilateral negotiations). International Non-Governmental Organizations negotiate with sovereign governments the terms of cooperation in the field and participate in international conferences on issues such as the environment. Multinational corporations, some of them with enormous economic power, negotiate business deals and terms of operation with governments, often from a position of strength. Distinguished individuals may act as intermediaries between states or promote a cause that involves lobbying or direct consultation with a government. Cultural diplomacy, the promotion of a country's cultural heritage to increase its international appeal, has become a higher priority. Summits of all kinds, including institutionalized ones, such as G7, G20, and ASEAN, have become more numerous and more consequential. Diasporas, potentially a tool in the exercise of foreign policy, have attracted the attention of many foreign offices, sometimes leading to the creation of specialized directorates.

In a complex, dangerous world, diplomacy, the dialogue between states, is a most valuable tool in the pursuit of security, peace, and prosperity. More than that, it is an institution that enables the world community to maintain its cohesion and work toward achieving common goals. Its judicious practice and theoretical understanding must be a vital goal for every responsible government.

Theodosios Karvounarakis is Professor of Diplomatic History at the University of Macedonia in Thessaloniki. He holds a law degree from the University of Athens and an MPhil and a PhD from Cambridge University. His interests include diplomatic history, the history of diplomatic practice, and the history of the foreign relations of the United States. His publications include books and articles on a number of topics, such as Anglo-Greek relations, Transatlantic relations, the Cold War, and the evolution of diplomatic practice.

The Law of Diplomatic Relations: Diplomacy and Its Legal Framework

2

Paraskevi Naskou-Perraki

Abstract

The notion of diplomacy, its roots, and some historical data bring the practice back to ancient Greece, to Roman times, to Byzantium, and its evolution in the rest of Europe. Contemporary diplomacy is the main instrument for conducting a state's foreign policy, covering legal and political issues in particular, now extending thematically to areas such as the economy, industry, trade, ecology, sports, culture, energy, etc., on an ongoing basis. Modern diplomacy comes in many forms, based on the sources of international law, as international treaties and international customs.

2.1 On Diplomacy: General Remarks

The term "diplomacy" is multifaceted. Depending on the author or the thematic context in which it is used, the word "diplomacy" may denote the science, art, technique, practice, institution, or process of handling the foreign affairs of a state.[1]

According to Sir Ernest Satow, diplomacy is "the use of intelligence and tact to the conduct of official relations between governments of independent states."[2] It follows that diplomacy is an efficient way for rapprochement between states; in this

[1] E. Plischke, Introduction, in E. Plischke (Ed.), Modern diplomacy—The art and the artisans, American Enterprise Institute for Public Policy Research (American Enterprise Institute—Studies in Foreign Policy), Washington D.C., 1979, p. 10.

[2] E. Satow, A guide to diplomatic practice, fourth edition, edited by Sir Neville Bland, Longmans Green, London, 1957, p.1, as quoted in E. Plischke, Modern diplomacy—The art and the artisans, Cambridge University Press, New York, 2011, pp. 1–4.

P. Naskou-Perraki (✉)
Department of International Studies, University of Macedonia, Thessaloniki, Greece
e-mail: perraki@uom.edu.gr

P. Naskou-Perraki (ed.), *Contemporary Diplomatic and Consular Relations*,
https://doi.org/10.1007/978-3-031-99243-8_2

predominant position until the end of World War I and the signing of the Treaty of Versailles in 1919, when the English language found its place on an equal footing with French. However, French retained its primacy in oral diplomatic communication for many years thereafter.

The First World War also catalyzed changes in diplomacy by abolishing the culture of secrecy among diplomats, which was deemed responsible for the deterioration of relations between states. The establishment of the League of Nations facilitated the expansion of multilateral diplomacy, fostering dialog between states and introducing partial oversight of foreign policy by public opinion and the parliaments of democratic nations.[11]

2.3 Contemporary Diplomacy

Diplomacy is the main instrument for conducting a state's foreign policy.[12] However, the foreign policy of states should be distinguished from diplomacy, as the former consists of selecting objectives, while the latter consists of implementing them.

Although politicians conduct diplomacy within the framework of their institutional responsibilities, diplomatic agents, by virtue of their position, have no political power. Diplomatic agents are intermediaries, have no political initiative, and are under the direction of the ministries of foreign affairs, whose instructions they carry out.

As is evident from the aforementioned, diplomacy is a process through which entities acting at the international level—in particular, but not only, states—establish and maintain permanent relations. Traditionally, diplomacy is a technique of persuasion aimed at making the policy of the diplomat's government understood and, if possible, accepted by other governments. To be practiced successfully, diplomacy requires knowledge of history and culture, as well as of the political, economic, technological, and social conditions of the society in which the diplomat serves. However, although states maintain specialized institutions for the training of diplomats, it is perhaps the long-term experience that ultimately makes a diplomat an expert in their field. Above all, the diplomat has to be level -headed, well-informed, and polite.

Although diplomacy has never been a simple affair, in the twenty-first century it has become particularly complex because of the exponential growth in the number of states and the increasing complexity of international problems. In 1900 there were

[1111] Th. Karvounarakis, The Historical Evolution of Diplomacy from antiquity to 'New Diplomacy', in Th. Karvounarakis (ed.) Diplomacy in the twenty-firstcentury, Proceedings of Conference 23–24 May 2013, University of Macedonia Publications, Thessaloniki, 2014, p. 9 (in Greek).

[12] S.E. Nahlik, Development of Diplomatic Law, Recueil des Cours de l'Académie de Droit International de La Haye, vol. 222, 1990, p. 201 et seq.

45 states on earth, by 1945 and the creation of the United Nations had increased to 64, and today they are 193 equal to member states of the United Nations.

Alongside the traditional powers appear the names of new states such as São Tomé and Príncipe, Tuvalu, Comoros, Nauru, and Cape Verde.[13]

Moreover, while diplomacy has traditionally covered legal and political issues in particular, it is now extending thematically to areas such as the economy, industry, trade, ecology, sports, culture, etc., on an ongoing basis.[14]

2.4 Forms of Diplomacy

Modern diplomacy comes in many forms. The most typical are the following:

- **Traditional diplomacy** is a bilateral cooperation implemented through the embassy located in a state. The diplomatic mission is in constant contact with the relevant ministries of the state where it is accredited, informs the sending state of any developments and, depending on the instructions received, promotes areas of cooperation and the interests of the state.
- **Multilateral diplomacy** is an important form of diplomacy involving multiple states and seeks to meet the new requirements of foreign policy as expressed at the multilateral level. Issues of economy environment and security are some of the issues discussed in the context of multilateral diplomacy as that of international organizations.
- **Parliamentary diplomacy**, where various issues are discussed at the level of international organizations and where parliamentary representatives are sent on diplomatic missions in support of the government's policy.
- **Summit diplomacy**, a practice that first appeared in the form of informal meetings of heads of states and governments, is now institutionalized and widespread, playing an important role in the regulation of national and international issues.
- **Cultural diplomacy**, a new form of diplomacy aimed at promoting a state abroad. It is important for all states, especially small ones, because through this diplomacy they have the opportunity to show the world their history and their culture, and to cooperate with other states and through cultural centers and cultural events.
- **Economic diplomacy** attempts to highlight important issues through economic routes, trade, development, financial aid, energy resources, and more.

[13]See also E. Plischke, Microstates: Lilliputs in world affairs, The Futurist 12, February 1978, pp. 19–25, as republished in E. Plischke, Modern diplomacy—The art and the artisans, op. cit., pp.92 et seq.

[14]See B. Sen, A diplomat's handbook on international law and practice, op. cit., p.56 et seq.

In some cases, and depending on the political context, other types of diplomacy are also present in diplomatic practice, such as "ping-pong diplomacy,"[15] which initiated relations between the United States and China in 1971, "**backward diplomacy**" or "**shuttle diplomacy,**" which the United States initiated in the 1970s in an attempt to resolve the Middle East crisis.

2.5 Diplomatic Law

2.5.1 Sources

Diplomacy is a process regulated by law. Diplomatic law is defined as the set of legal rules governing the external relations of the subjects of international law.[16] The sources of diplomatic law are as follows.

2.5.2 International Custom

International rules on diplomatic relations originate in customary law.[17] According to theory, in order to form an international custom, it is required that two elements converge:

(a) practice—the so-called essential element, which consists of acts repeated in a general and uniform manner; and
(b) the belief in law (opinion juris sive necessitatis)—the so-called psychological element, i.e., the belief that repeated acts correspond to a legal obligation.[18]

[15] It was named after the American ping-pong team that first visited China to participate in the Beijing Ping Pong Games, thus providing the opportunity to open relations between China and the United States. It is worth noting that until 1972, China was represented by the government of Nationalist China that had fled to Taiwan when in 1949 the Chinese Communists under Mao Zedong took control of mainland China. For more details, see K. Antonopoulos, in P. Naskou-Perraki, K. Antonopoulos, M. Sarigiannidis, International Organizations, third edition, Sakkoulas, Athens-Thessaloniki, 2024, p. 108 et seq. (in Greek).

[16] Ph. Cahier, Le droit diplomatique contemporain, Publications de l Institute des Hautes Etudes Internationales, No 40, Droz, Geneve, 1964, pp. 5–6.

[17] See, for example, A.-V. Papakostas, Law of Diplomatic and Consular Relations, Ant. N. Sakkoulas, Athens, 1989, p. 36 et seq. (in Greek) and Ph. Cahier, Le droit diplomatique contemporain, ibid., p. 29 et seq.

[18] See, from the Greek bibliography, E. Roukounas, International Law, fourth edition, Nomiki Bibliothiki, Athens, 2021, pp. 77–78. See also K. Antonopoulos—K. Magliberas, The Law of International Society, third edition, Nomiki Bibliothiki, Athens, 2017, pp. 65–78 and K. Hatzikonstantinou, M. Sarigiannidis, Ch. Apostolidis, Fundamental Concepts in International Law, second edition, Sakkoulas, Athens–Thessaloniki, 2014, p. 250 et seq. (in Greek).

Through the customary law-making process, rules have been established on the exchange of permanent diplomatic agents and on the privileges and immunities of diplomats—rules which, because of their customary nature, apply to all states.

International custom is differentiated from mere habit. Custom is the source of law and is therefore binding. By contrast, custom in the field of diplomatic relations—and not only—are acts of courtesy that are not binding, such as, for example, the choice of the language used at diplomatic receptions and in correspondence or the protocol for accepting gifts.[19]

2.5.3 International Treaties

2.5.3.1 Global Conventions

In contemporary international society, the law concerning diplomacy could not remain unwritten. Since the nineteenth century, it has been decided by international scientific bodies and states to document various areas of international law in order to promote "legal certainty" in international relations.

The formation of modern international law regarding diplomatic and consular relations is attributed to the arduous preparatory work of the United Nations International Law Commission,[20] which consists of thirty-four (34) distinguished legal experts and diplomats from all corners of the globe, with balanced geographical representation. Its main task is to draft treaty proposals concerning various aspects of international relations. The Commission has drafted treaty proposals for diplomatic and consular relations, which have been approved within the framework of international conferences.[21] In 1952, the Commission was authorized to codify the Convention on Diplomatic Relations, and in 1959 it requested the UN Secretary-General to convene a conference for the adoption of the Convention. The Conference took place in Vienna in 1961. The new Convention concerns only relations between states and not international organizations; however, it can be applied to them as well as to entities that do not possess state characteristics, e.g., the Palestine Liberation Organization (PLO).

Thus, contemporary international law on diplomatic and consular relations is recorded in a series of multilateral international conventions adopted at both universal and regional levels. These written international rules are supplemented by various

[19] J. Salmon, Manuel de Droit Diplomatique, Bruylant, Brussels, (Précis de la Faculté de Droit—Université Libre de Bruxelles), 1994, p. 10.

[20] K. Economides, Inviolability and immunity of diplomatic officials with reference also to consular officials' detainees (Analysis of the Vienna Conventions of 1961 and 1963), Athens, 1975, p. 36. 2 (in Greek).

[21] N. Zaikos, United Nations International Law Commission—Contribution to the study of the codification and progressive development of international law, Sakkoulas/Institute of International Public Law and International Relations (Contemporary Studies of International Law and International Relations 3/Directorate: Professor K. Koufa), Thessaloniki, 2002, pp. 124 et seq. (in Greek).

resolutions and decisions of international organizations that have diverse thematic content.

From a universal perspective, today exist the following international conventions regulating various aspects of diplomatic and consular relations:

- The Vienna Convention on Diplomatic Relations of 1961,[22] supplemented by the Optional Protocol Concerning the Compulsory Settlement of Disputes.[23]
- The Vienna Convention on Consular Relations of 1963.[24]
- The Convention on Special Missions of 1969.[25]
- The Convention on the Prevention and Punishment of Crimes against Internationally Protected Persons, including Diplomatic Agents of 1973.[26]
- The Convention on the Representation of States in their Relations with International Organizations of a Universal Character of 1975.[27]

Furthermore, the codification of the status of the diplomatic postman and the diplomatic bag, which is not accompanied by a postman, has been attempted.

2.5.3.2 Regional Conventions

An early attempt to establish a set of rules for diplomatic relations at the regional level was the Convention on Diplomatic Agents, adopted by the Sixth Pan-American Conference in Havana on February 20, 1928.[28]

More recently, international instruments relating to diplomatic privileges and immunities within the Council of Europe have been adopted, such as:

1. The European Convention on Consular Functions of 1967.[29]
2. The Protocol to the European Convention on Consular Functions concerning the Protection of Refugees.

[22] It was adopted on April 18, 1961, entered into force on April 24, 1964, and was published in UNTS 500. Greece ratified it by ND 503/1979, Government Gazette A'108.

[23] It was adopted on April 18, 1961, entered into force on April 24, 1964, and was published in UNTS 500. Greece has not ratified it.

[24] It was adopted on April 24, 1963, entered into force on March 19, 1967, and was published in UNTS 596. Greece ratified it by Law 90/1975, Government Gazette, Series I, No 150.

[25] Adopted in New York on December 8, 1969, entered into force on July 21, 1985, and was published in UNTS 1400. Greece has not ratified it.

[26] It was adopted in New York on December 14, 1973, entered into force on February 20, 1977, and was published in UNTS 1035. Greece ratified it by Law 1368/1983, Government Gazette, Series I, No 89.

[27] It was adopted in Vienna on March 14, 1975, and has not yet entered into force. Greece has not ratified it.

[28] See S. E. Nahlik, Development of Diplomatic Law, op. cit., p. 210 et seq., where reference is made to other encoding projects of a private or transnational nature from the nineteenth century onward.

[29] Adopted in Paris, December 11, 1967, entered into force on June 9, 2011, and was published in ETS 061. Greece ratified it by Law 1363/1983, Government Gazette, Series I, No 79.

3. The Protocol to the European Convention on Consular Functions relating to Consular Functions in respect of Civil Aircraft.[30]
4. The European Convention on the Abolition of Legalisation of Documents executed by Diplomatic Agents or Consular Officers[31]s

2.5.3.3 Bilateral Conventions

In addition to multilateral treaties with broad participation concerning various aspects of diplomatic law, states are free to negotiate bilateral conventions regarding their mutual diplomatic relations.

2.5.4 Domestic Law

International diplomatic activity is, of course, influenced by the relevant national legislation of particular states. For example, the jurisdiction of any state includes rules regarding the immunity of diplomatic agents.

Additionally, each state organizes its diplomatic service with specific laws that provide, for example, the terms of entry into diplomatic service for any individual.[32]

Dr. Dr.h.c Paraskevi (Paroula) Naskou-Perraki, ret. Professor of International Law and International Organizations, Department of International and European Studies, University of Macedonia, Thessaloniki (1994–2014). She has served for 20 years at the Law Faculty of Democritus University of Thrace, in Komotini (1974–1993). She has been teaching International Law, International Organizations, Diplomatic Law and Human Rights in different universities in Greece, Europe, and the USA, recently at the Masters Programme "On Human Rights and Migration Studies," University of Macedonia (2019–2025). Founder and Director of the UNESCO Chair on Intercultural Policy for an Active Citizenship and Solidarity (2004–2014), she was a representative of the Greek Ministry of Foreign Affairs at the Conference held in Brussels (2003) and then Tehran (2004) between Iran and the EU on Human Rights and in 2003 at the conference held in Beijing between China and the EU on Human Rights. She was awarded as Dr. Honoris Causa from the Faculty of Law and History of Neofit Rilski University in Blagoevgrad, Bulgaria, in 2003. She was member of the Scientific Committee of International Law at the Ministry of Foreign Affairs (2016–2019), President of the board of the Institute of Balkan Studies (2019–2021), Director of the Hellenic Institute for UN Affairs (2017-), Vice-President of the Board of the UNESCO Center for the Women and Peace in the Balkans (2012–2020), Secretary General of the board of CIEEL, Secretary General of the Kalliopi Koufa Foundation for the promotion of International Law and the protection of Human Rights, (2015–2019). Ad Hoc Judge of the European Court of Human Rights (ECtHR) (2011–2013), Awarded with the title F.U.N.—Friend

[30] Both the above Protocols were adopted in Paris on December 11, 1967, published in ETS 061A and 061B, respectively, and have not entered into force.

[31] It was adopted in London on June 7, 1968, entered into force on August 14, 1970, and was published in ETS 63. Greece ratified it by Law 844/1978, Government Gazette, Series I, No 227.

[32] As regards Greece, see Law 4781/2021 (Government Gazette, Series I, No 31), 'Organization and Operation of the Ministry of Foreign Affairs, Council for Hellenes Abroad, Regulation of international development cooperation and humanitarian aid and other provisions. See also Presidential Decree 23/2017 (Government Gazette, Series I, No 43).

President) shall nominate, and by and with the advice and consent of the Senate, shall appoint ambassadors, other public ministers, and consuls."[3]

3.2 Legislation on the Conduct of Foreign Policy of Greece

According to the Constitution of Greece, the guidelines for the country's foreign policy are as follows:

(a) the principle of international peace, justice, and friendly relations among peoples and states (Article 2, paragraph 2 of the Constitution);
(b) participation in the processes of European integration (Article 28, paragraphs 2 and 3 of the Constitution);
(c) the principle of welfare for Hellenes abroad (Article 108 of the Constitution).

Greek legislation concerning the Ministry of Foreign Affairs, which is responsible for the conduct of Greece's foreign policy, is codified in Law 4781/2021,[4] "Organization and Functioning of the Ministry of Foreign Affairs, Council of Hellenes Abroad, regulation of issues of international development cooperation and humanitarian aid and other provisions," intended to build on the positive elements of the preceding laws.

Noteworthy is the fact that the first Statute of the Ministry of Foreign Affairs was published in 1877 by Charilaos Trikoupis and was based on two Laws, HNZ'/1877 and HNs'/1877, which concerned the operation of the Ministry of Foreign Affairs, and the activities of consular authorities abroad, but above all the first attempts to staff the Ministry with professional diplomats were made during that time. The second Statute, Law 4952/1931, was adopted under the government of Venizelos in order to lay the foundations of the diplomatic service and to contribute to the promotion of the country's foreign policy. It contained innovative regulations, many of which are still in force today. Following the restoration of the Republic in 1974 and the ratification of the Vienna Convention on Consular Relations by Greece, the third Statute was adopted by Law 419/1976 with the objective of fully modernizing foreign policy. This Law also provided for the creation of the Centre for Diplomatic Studies for the selection and preparation of future diplomats. Subsequently, Law 2594/2001 (Government Gazette A′ 293), with its many innovative provisions, made the Ministry of Foreign Affairs the sole body for the formulation of the country's foreign policy. A minor restructuring was attempted in 2002 concerning the Diplomatic Academy and the transfer of economic diplomacy from the Ministry of Finance to the Ministry of Foreign Affairs. In 2007, Law 3566 adopted the Statute, which sought to codify the amendments that had occurred in the meantime and to contribute toward a more active participation of the MFA in

[3] J. Salmon, Manuel de Droit Diplomatique, op. cit., pp. 57 et seq.
[4] Law 4781/2021, Government Gazette, Series I, No 31, 28 February 2021.

international and European affairs. Under Law 4451/2017 (Government Gazette A 16), an attempt was made to amend the previous Law in order to ensure the necessary infrastructure and to improve the efficiency of the MFA's operations. In accordance with this Law, the International Development Cooperation Service (IDC) was created, as well as the Office for Greek Candidacies in International Organizations, the position of Deputy Secretary-General for International Ecumenical Relations and Development Cooperation, while emphasis was given to the improvement of the functioning of the Diplomatic Academy, on issues related to economic diplomacy, etc.[5]

In addition, the new Law 4781/2021 restructures the organization of the Ministry of Foreign Affairs, specifically its mode of operation, and regulates a number of issues related to the Council of Hellenes Abroad, International Development Cooperation and Humanitarian Aid. The purpose of the new Law is to make Greece's foreign policy more effective in order to promote national interests, which are intended to be achieved by reforming the structures and operation of the MFA.[6] The objectives, responsibilities, internal organization, operation, service, and legal status of the employees of the Ministry of Foreign Affairs are governed by this Statute.

According to the new Law, the mission of the Ministry of Foreign Affairs includes the following[7]:

1. The conduct of the foreign policy of the Hellenic Republic and the promotion of international legitimacy in cooperation with other states and the international community.
2. The Ministry of Foreign Affairs seeks:
   (a) the security and integrity of the country as dictated by the Constitution,
   (b) regional and international stability and peace,
   (c) the protection of human rights,
   (d) the upgrading of the role and presence of the country in the European Union and the international system,
   (e) the contribution to the consolidation of international legitimacy,
   (f) the promotion of the political and economic interests of the country at bilateral and multilateral levels,
   (g) the projection of the Greek spirit and culture abroad,
   (h) the promotion and protection of the rights and interests of Greeks abroad, as well as the maintenance and strengthening of ties with expatriates around the world,

[5]G. Koptsidis, Historical elements of the structure and operation of the Ministry of Foreign Affairs, in Th. Karvounarakis (ed.) Diplomacy in the twenty-first century, op. cit., p. 11 et seq.

[6]In accordance with Article 1 of Law 4781/2021.

[7]In accordance with Article 3 of Law 4781/2021.

(i) the promotion of economic, commercial, maritime, tourist, and other Greek interests abroad, as well as facilitating access to international markets for domestic businesses and attracting foreign direct investment,
(j) the improvement of Greece's international image abroad through the practice of public diplomacy.

Whereas the responsibilities are as follows[8]:

"(a) the promotion and protection of the rights and compliance of the obligations of the Hellenic Republic, as well as the support and promotion of national interests in foreign states, international organizations, international institutions, and conferences,

(b) monitoring bilateral and international political, economic, cultural, and other issues, as well as international security issues, informing the government and making suggestions on them,

(c) informing foreign states, international organizations, and international public opinion, as well as providing information on Greek positions and issues of national interest,

(d) participating in international cooperation, negotiating, and ensuring the conclusion, monitoring and implementation of international treaties and other international instruments,

(e) the representation of the Hellenic Republic before foreign states, international organizations and other international bodies and conferences, as well as its representation before the International Court of Justice in Hague and any other international court, the courts of the European Union, the European Court of Human Rights or any other international tribunal,

(f) representing the country in the European Union and formulating policy on the institutional development of the Union and European integration, in cooperation with other ministries and bodies,

(g) coordination of the ministries and agencies in the planning, implementation, and evaluation of the European and foreign policy of the country in general,

(h) the diplomatic support of the institutions of the state, legal persons governed by public law, public enterprises, and organizations, as well as political parties and members of the Parliament, when conducting their international contacts,

(i) the promotion and protection of the rights and interests of Greeks abroad, as well as issues related to expatriate Greeks and repatriation, as in the maintenance and strengthening of the ties between Greece and expatriates around the world and the provision of services to them and to expatriates, through the Centre of Service and Information for Citizens and Expatriate Greeks (K.E.P.P.A.E.),

(j) intervention in international and regional economic cooperation institutions for the service of the national economy, in the context of the progress of technology, information and communication, the development of intercultural relations, the

[8] Article 4 of Law 4781/2021.

internationalization and the intensification of the interdependence of national economies and the supranational arrangements promoted by international and regional cooperation institutions,

(k) the promotion and protection of Greek interests in cyberspace,

(l) the diplomatic and consular assistance of Greek citizens, of recognized social groups and of private organizations in their international activities, provided that these are not contrary to national interests,

(m) the development of the international political, economic, and cultural relations of the Hellenic Republic, through the provision of information, mobilization and influence on international public opinion and the public opinion of other states, for the purpose of attaining the objectives of extroversion, the management of the national image and the support of national interests,

(n) the international promotion of Greece, the Greek spirit and culture and the improvement of the international image of Greece abroad through the practice of public diplomacy,

(o) the monitoring of issues related to the protection of human rights and humanitarian action at the international level,

(p) monitoring issues arising from the implementation of international treaties for specific groups of the country's population, in cooperation with other competent ministries,

(q) the supervision and control of recognized educational institutions and associations abroad,

(r) monitoring the community, educational and ecclesiastical affairs of Greeks abroad,

(s) matters related to national and other bequests, donations, and contributions in favour of the state or charitable purposes abroad,

(t) matters relating to the general personal situation of Greeks abroad, matters related to Greek citizenship and their passports, as well as the custody of the inheritances of Greeks who died abroad,

(u) issues related to legal aid, the service of indictments, the execution of court decisions and investigative orders abroad, as well as the extradition of criminals subject to applicable international agreements binding the Hellenic Republic,

(v) the diplomatic correspondence of the President of the Hellenic Republic,

(w) formality and etiquette, matters of awarding Greek Orders of Excellence and permission to receive foreign honours,

(x) granting diplomatic and service passports,

(y) the relations of the Hellenic Republic with the Ecumenical Throne, the other Patriarchates, the Autocephalous Orthodox Churches, as well as matters concerning other Christian denominations, religions, and international ecclesiastical organizations abroad,

(z) the political administration of Mount Athos,

(aa) the authentication of documents of the Greek authorities intended for Greek and foreign authorities abroad and the authentication of the signatures of the authorized bodies of the diplomatic and consular authorities in Greece in respect of documents intended for the Greek services, (bb) matters relating to diplomatic and consular authorities' duties, in accordance with the provisions of the relevant articles of this Law,

(cc) informing the members of the Hellenic Parliament on matters within its competence,

(dd) any other competence related to the international relations of the country that has not been entrusted to any other public authority."

3.3 Conditions for Admission to the Diplomatic Service of Greece

The diplomatic service in Greece is staffed by persons who successfully pass the examinations of the Ministry of Foreign Affairs.

The recruitment of Foreign Ministry officials is governed by the principles of meritocracy, transparency, and equal opportunities. For the recruitment of new diplomats, the Ministry of Foreign Affairs, under the responsibility of the Directorate of Personnel, announces an invitation to tender at least once a year, provided that there are vacancies for Embassy Attachés. The invitation is issued by the Minister for Foreign Affairs.[9] Those who successfully complete the examination process may be accepted into the Diplomatic Academy of the Ministry of Foreign Affairs (as candidates for Embassy Attachés).

According to the legislation in force, candidates for the diplomatic service must have the following qualifications:

General qualifications[10]:

"(a) Have Greek citizenship. In case of acquisition of Greek citizenship by naturalization, three (3) years must have passed since the date of naturalization. Contract employees of the Foreign Service Authorities may be also foreigners.

(b) Have reached the age of twenty-one (21) years. For the purpose of attaining the minimum age for appointment, the date of birth shall be deemed to be the first of January. Proof of age shall be provided by identification card and, in case of dispute, by a birth certificate drawn up within ninety (90) days of birth. If no such document exists, age shall be proved by the male registers for men and by the General Register of Citizens (civil register) for women. If more than one records exist in the relevant register, the first record shall prevail. Verification of age or correction of the registration, by any other means, shall under no circumstances be accepted.

(c) Have completed their military service or have been legally discharged from military service and have not been convicted of desertion.

(d) Have not been deprived of their civil rights as a result of a conviction.

(e) Not have been convicted of a felony, as well as any sentence for theft, embezzlement, fraud, extortion, forgery, lawyer's disloyalty, unlawful collection or collection of rights of the state, bribery, unfaithfulness, when it is directed against

[9] Article 48.1 of Law 4781/2021.

[10] Ibid, Article 319.

the Greek state, local authorities or any other legal person under public law, dereliction of duty, slander, as well as for any crime against sexual freedom or economic exploitation of sexual life. Furthermore, any person who has been irrevocably prosecuted for a felony or for one of the misdemeanours referred to in the preceding subparagraph, even if the statute of limitations has expired. Restitution and pardon shall not remove the above disqualification unless the order issued pursuant to para. 1 of Article 47 of the Constitution shall also remove this bar.

(f) Not be subject to deprivation of liberty or subsidiary legal aid.

(g) Not be liable to the penalty of definitive dismissal or have not had their contract of employment terminated for good cause attributable to the fault of the worker, unless five years have elapsed since the dismissal or termination.

(h) be physically fit and healthy enough to perform their duties.

1. The staff member under appointment must not suffer from serious cardiovascular or serious respiratory or nephrological or infectious diseases, or serious diseases of the nervous system.

2. The recruitment of employees of the Ministry of Foreign Affairs is governed by the principles of meritocracy, transparency, and equal opportunities. No person may be excluded from the relevant examinations, provided that he or she fulfils the legal requirements for participation thereto.

3. The conditions for appointment of employees of the Ministry of Foreign Affairs must be fulfilled both at the time of submission of the relevant applications and at the time of appointment or, in the case of employees of the Diplomatic Branch, at the time of admission to the Diplomatic Academy."

Specific qualifications[11]:

"(a) degree from a Greek University or an equivalent foreign degree or a duly recognized diploma at undergraduate level from a foreign country,

(b) Fluency in English and French. On the subject of languages, the new Law reintroduces French as the main language for the qualification examinations, from 2023."

In accordance with paragraph 2, article 48, the time spent studying at the D.A. is counted as pensionable, since the provisions of Part B and Part C of the Civil Service Code apply to D.A. students during their studies and they are counted as cadet civil servants from the time of their admission, with all the relevant duties, restrictions, and rights, as well as full insurance coverage, upon payment of the relevant contributions. By order of the Director of the D.A., students may be assigned, as part of their training, duties within the Directorates of the Ministry of Foreign Affairs.

Pursuant to paragraph 3 of the same article, students attending the Diplomatic Academy shall receive during their training a salary equal to the total salary of an Embassy Attaché and shall continue to receive such salary after their graduation and until their appointment as Embassy Attachés.

[11] Ibid, Article 48,1, a.

assist the operation of the Diplomatic Academy, there is also a six-member Education Council[19] with a term of office of 3 years.

The Education Council (EC) consists of:

"(a) the Director of the D.A., as its President, with his/her deputy in the same capacity,

(b) one (1) Professor or Associate Professor of a University, with a subject related to the responsibilities of the Ministry of Foreign Affairs or an employee of the Scientific Staff of the Ministry of Foreign Affairs or of the Experts Branch, holding a doctoral degree, with his/her deputy in the same capacity,

(c) one (1) diplomatic official with an ambassadorial rank, with his/her deputy in the same capacity,

(d) the Director of Studies of the DA, with his/her deputy in the same capacity,

(e) one (1) representative from the world of letters and arts, with his/her deputy in the same capacity,

(f) one (1) economist with at least a postgraduate degree, with his/her alternate in the same capacity.

3. The Director of Studies of the D.A. shall serve as the rapporteur of the EC and the secretary of the EC along with his/her deputy thereof shall be appointed as a Ministry official."[20]

The responsibilities of the Education Council are defined as follows[21]:

"1. The Education Council shall advise on:

(a) the adoption of the decrees provided for in par. 2 of Article 49, concerning issues of admission, attendance and graduation at the Diplomatic Academy, the method of grading and passing order, the procedure for training of MFA employees and any other issue relating to the organization and operation of the Diplomatic Academy.

(b) the curriculum of diplomatic trainees,

(c) the preparation of the training programs for Ministry of Foreign Affairs officials,

(d) the teaching staff of the Diplomatic Academy,

(e) its operating regulations, which are drawn up by order of the Minister of Foreign Affairs.[22]

(f) the terms and conditions regarding accreditation and recognition of certification of professional skills, as well as the establishment of the list of acceptable certifying bodies in Greece and abroad.

2. For the affairs of par. 1 the Director of the Diplomatic Academy shall submit a recommendation to the Minister of Foreign Affairs.

[19] Article 46 of Law 4781/2021. The Secretary of State has the possibility to increase the members of the EC to nine; see Article 46.4.

[20] Article 46 of Law 4781/2021.

[21] Article 47 of Law 4781/2021.

[22] Article 49.3 of Law 4781/2021.

3. The Education Council, following a relevant recommendation of a three-member committee of professors from a domestic or foreign university with a subject related to the skills to be certified, which is formed by a decision of the Minister of Foreign Affairs, issued on the recommendation of the Director of the Diplomatic Academy, shall determine the subject matter of the examinations for the certification of the professional skills of employees of the Diplomatic Branch and other branches of the Sub-secretariat of Foreign Affairs."[23]

Following the successful completion of the examination, the Embassy Attaché candidates undergo a 12-month training period at the Diplomatic Academy. During the first 9 months, they are taught a series of courses on the structure and functioning of the MFA, on issues of Public Administration, Diplomatic and Consular Practice, and Negotiation Techniques, on Issues of Formalities, on the European Union, International Law, and International Relations, and on Economic, Political, and Cultural Diplomacy.[24] In the following months, the Embassy Attaché candidates undertake educational trips and fact-finding visits to other authorities and services and participate in international training programs.[25] At the end of their studies, the Embassy Attaché candidates undergo a written and oral test and are then appointed to Embassy Attaché posts.[26]

As is generally apparent from the criteria for admission to the diplomatic service in Greece, in order for a diplomat to carry out his/her mission in an effective manner, he/she should possess a wide range of knowledge: he/she should know the language of the country where he/she is serving, if possible, he/she should be familiar with its culture, geography, history, economy, and politics, he/she should be up to date with current international political developments, and, of course, he/she should continually deepen and broaden knowledge of the country where he/she is serving.[27]

Those appointed to the diplomatic service commence their career at the entry level ("Embassy Attaché") up to the highest rank (Minister Plenipotentiary of the First Class or Ambassador). In addition to diplomatic staff, who are admitted to the service following the standard examinations, there are also a number of people who are recruited from the ranks of public figures: these are persons who are awarded diplomatic status by virtue of their work and prestige in areas such as scientific research, military service, economic life, and so on.[28]

Dr. Dr.h.c Paraskevi (Paroula) Naskou-Perraki, ret. Professor of International Law and International Organizations, Department of International and European Studies, University of Macedonia, Thessaloniki (1994–2014). She has served for 20 years at the Law Faculty of

[23] Article 47 of Law 4781/2021.

[24] Article 17 of Presidential Decree 17/1999, Government Gazette, Series I, No 10.

[25] Article 16 of Presidential Decree 17/1999, Government Gazette, Series I, No 10.

[26] Articles 349 and 350 of Law 4781/2021.

[27] P.H. Cahier, Le droit diplomatique contemporain, op. cit., p. 162 et seq.

[28] K.I. Skaltsas, The Diplomatic Representatives in the context of International Relations and International Law, op cit. p 30 et seq.

Democritus University of Thrace, in Komotini (1974–1993). She has been teaching International Law, International Organizations, Diplomatic Law and Human Rights in different universities in Greece, Europe, and the USA, recently at the Masters Programme "On Human Rights and Migration Studies," University of Macedonia (2019–2025). Founder and Director of the UNESCO Chair on Intercultural Policy for an Active Citizenship and Solidarity (2004–2014), she was a representative of the Greek Ministry of Foreign Affairs at the Conference held in Brussels (2003) and then Tehran (2004) between Iran and the EU on Human Rights and in 2003 at the conference held in Beijing between China and the EU on Human Rights. She was awarded as Dr. Honoris Causa from the Faculty of Law and History of Neofit Rilski University in Blagoevgrad, Bulgaria, in 2003. She was member of the Scientific Committee of International Law at the Ministry of Foreign Affairs (2016–2019), President of the board of the Institute of Balkan Studies (2019–2021), Director of the Hellenic Institute for UN Affairs (2017–), Vice-President of the Board of the UNESCO Center for the Women and Peace in the Balkans (2012–2020), Secretary General of the board of CIEEL, Secretary General of the Kalliopi Koufa Foundation for the promotion of International Law and the protection of Human Rights, (2015–2019). Ad Hoc Judge of the European Court of Human Rights (ECtHR) (2011–2013), Awarded with the title F.U.N.—Friend of the United Nations for her contribution in the dissemination of the work of the Organization through the UN Models (2007). Since 2016 she has been responsible for the "Students as Diplomats," an annual Model UN addressed to Greek high school students, on issues concerning the work of UN Human Rights Committees. Editor in Chief of Evrigenis Yearbook of International and European Law, published by Ant. N. Sakkoulas, Athens (issues 2019–2023) she has published in Greek, English, and French.

Diplomatic Relations Between States in Contemporary International Law

4

Paraskevi Naskou-Perraki

Abstract

Diplomatic relations are based in the Vienna Convention on Diplomatic Relations of 18 April 1961, and Additional Protocols. The Convention is dealing with state practice as well as the jurisprudence of the International Court of Justice (ICJ), in the Hague. A big part is dedicated to the diplomatic relations between states, members, and structure of the diplomatic mission, the size and the obligations in the receiving state, their privileges and immunities, and the status of their families and staff, together with the termination of their duties.

4.1 States and the Right of Legation

4.1.1 On Statehood

The right of legation (jus legationis), i.e., the sending of diplomatic agents abroad, has historically been linked to the sovereignty of the state. States have the right of legation ipso jure by virtue of a customary rule of international law.[1]

Since antiquity there have been harbingers of the concept of "state," in the sense in which it is perceived today, i.e., as a geographical area inhabited by a group of people subject to a common authority. However, it is generally accepted that the nexus of international instruments of the Peace of Westphalia (1648) was the starting point, not only for the formation of the contemporary concept of state but also of

[1] K. Th. Efstathiadis, International Law, I, Athens, 1977, p. 281 (in Greek).

P. Naskou-Perraki (✉)
Department of International Studies, University of Macedonia, Thessaloniki, Greece
e-mail: perraki@uom.edu.gr

P. Naskou-Perraki (ed.), *Contemporary Diplomatic and Consular Relations*,
https://doi.org/10.1007/978-3-031-99243-8_4

international law as a set of legal rules governing relations between sovereign states.[2]

According to customary international law, three elements must converge to create a state: a permanent resident population, territory, and sovereign political power. To some extent, one additional element must also be present: the ability to participate in international relations (e.g., concluding international treaties, exchanging diplomatic agents, joining international organizations). Nevertheless, the criterion of participation in international relations raises the question of the recognition of states and is ultimately only a consequence of statehood. In contemporary international reality, however, the question of whether a territorial entity is a state is resolved in practice by admission as a member state of the United Nations. As of 2022, the United Nation had 193 member states.[3]

It should be noted that since 1964 the Holy See has been a "permanent observer state" within the UN framework.[4] Also, since 2012, the Palestinian National Authority has been a "nonmember observer state" under the UN General Assembly,[5] has the capacity to be a party before the International Court of Justice,[6] and is recognized by 138 states.[7]

According to a clear rule of customary international law, territorial entities formed by an occupying power on occupied territory with the intention to be recognized as supposedly independent states constitute unlawful creations.[8] Third states are obliged not to recognize such heterogeneous entities, which are called "puppet states."[9] For this reason, the so-called "Turkish Republic of Northern Cyprus" is not a state under international law, but an occupied territory of the Republic of Cyprus, recognized as a state only by the occupying power of Turkey.[10]

---

[2] L. Gross, The Peace of Westphalia, 1648–1948, The American Journal of International Law, 42/1, 1948, p. 20–41.

[3] United Nations, Member States, https://www.un.org/en/about-us/member-states (Retrieved: 28.6.2024).

[4] A/RES/58/314 (Participation of the Holy See in the work of the United Nations) (Adopted on July 1, 2003).

[5] See Status of Palestine in the United Nations, A/RES/67/19 of 29 November 2012.

[6] International Court of Justice, States not parties to the Statute to which the Court may be open, https://www.icj-cij.org/en/states-not-parties (Retrieved: 28.6.2024).

[7] For the constituent elements of the state and the statehood of territorial entities that have declared independence and are often described as de facto states, but are not UN Member States; see N. Zaikos, Territory and acquisition of territorial sovereignty, in K. Antonopoulos & K. Magliveras, The law of international society, third edition, Nomiki Bibliothiki, Athens, 2022 (in Greek).

[8] Cf. the provisions of Articles 42–56 (Section C "On military authority in the country of the belligerent state") of the Hague Convention on the Laws and Customs of War on Land (18.10.1907).

[9] N. Zaikos, International law and cooperation with the enemy. The legal nature of the "dummy" governments of the Second World War from the point of view of International law, Stamoulis, Thessaloniki, 2006, pp. 35 et seq. (in Greek).

[10] D. Richter, Illegal States? in: W. Czapliński and A. Kleczkowska (Ed.), Unrecognized subjects in International Law, Scholar Publishing House, Warsaw, 2019, pp. 19 et seq. Especially for Cyprus,

It should be noted that for the aforementioned reason, states such as Belgium, for example, never established diplomatic relations with the "Turkish Republic of Northern Cyprus," as well as the so-called "bantustans" established by South Africa and Southwest Africa (now Namibia) during the apartheid period.[11]

4.1.2 The Right of Legation

The institution of legation has an active and a passive aspect: i.e., the sending of a diplomatic agent (the so-called "active legation") corresponds to an obligation to accept a diplomatic agent from the other state (the "passive legation") and vice versa.[12]

The freedom of the state to maintain or not maintain diplomatic contacts with other states is the foundation of diplomatic law. There is no rule of international law requiring states to send diplomatic agents to other states, nor to accept diplomatic agents of other states. Consequently, the establishment of diplomatic relations between states is a political choice: it is left to the discretion of each state and is based on mutual consent.[13] In particular, as regards reciprocity, Dimitrios Evrigenis wrote: "mutuality means exchange and reciprocity in human relations and, in the last place, analyses equality. It means compensating for the conduct of one subject of the social relationship by a similar or analogous behaviour of the other subject."[14] However, in contemporary international relations, the maintenance of diplomatic relations is imposed de facto, as otherwise the state would be led to international isolation.[15]

The recognition—i.e., the unilateral act by which a state declares ("recognizes") that a territorial entity has the elements of a state—does not automatically imply the establishment of diplomatic relations between them, in the sense of a direct exchange of diplomatic agents. For example, when the United States of America recognized the State of Vanuatu in 1980, it expressed its willingness to establish diplomatic

see J. Ker-Lindsay, H. Faustmann, F. Mullen (Ed.), An Island in Europe. The EU and the Transformation of Cyprus, I.B. Tauris, London, 2011, p. 15.

[11] J. Salmon, Manuel de Droit Diplomatique, Bruylant, Bruxelles, 1994, pp. 41 et seq.

[12] K. P. Economides, Public International Law, Vol. A (University Lectures), Ant. N. Sakkoulas, Athens-Komotin, 1989, pp. 140 and E. Roukounas, International Law, III, University Lectures—Diplomatic and Consular Relations—Recognition—Immunity—Liability—Succession—International Organizations, Ant. N. Sakkoulas, Athens, 1983 (in Greek).

[13] See Article 2 of the Convention on Diplomatic Relations.

[14] D. Evrigenis, On 'diplomatic' and 'legislative' reciprocity. Contribution to the jurisprudence of the law of international relations, Armenopoulos (1959), p. 757 et seq., as republished in Annales - Periodical of the Department of Law of the School of Law and Economics, Volume Three, Papers of Dimitrios I. Evrigenis, Issue Two, Thessaloniki, 1992, p. 877 et seq. (in Greek).

[15] For information on Greece's bilateral diplomatic relations, see the website of the Ministry of Foreign Affairs, http://www.mfa.gr/dimereis-sheseis-tis-ellados.html (Accessed: 28.06.2024).

relations with the then-newly established state—which happened in 1986, when Vanuatu consented.[16]

On the contrary, the establishment of diplomatic relations is one of the ways in which states are recognized. In fact, the existence of diplomatic relations is not conceivable without mutual recognition.[17]

In addition to states, there are a number of bodies of international activity with international legal status—that is to say, entities subject to international law—which are recognized as having the right of representation. This category includes intergovernmental international organizations, which have the capacity of international representation, in principle and in accordance with the conditions laid down in their statutes. In addition, sociopolitical developments within the United Nations Organization have led to the recognition of the right of representation for so-called recognized patriotic liberation movements. As Constantinos Economides had pointed out, these are peoples who are turning against colonial or racialist regimes or illegal foreign occupation in the context of the implementation of the right of the principle of self-determination.[18]

Nevertheless, from a historical perspective, the institutional framework of diplomacy developed on the basis of relations between sovereign states, and it is precisely the interstate diplomatic relations that are governed primarily by international law—customary and conventional.

4.2 The Contemporary International Legal Framework of Interstate Diplomatic Relations: The Vienna Convention on Diplomatic Relations (1961)

From ancient Greek "consulates" and "embassies" to the emergence of the contemporary state and up to the present day, diplomacy has been a constant current through international relations. As a channel of communication, diplomacy is vital to the service of state aspirations and the stability of international society.[19]

The general and uniform practice of states in matters of diplomatic exchanges gradually led to the development of customary, i.e., unwritten, legal rules around the diplomatic profession—and a rare phenomenon in international relations, and these rules were clear, unambiguous, and accepted by all states. Since the early nineteenth century, the substance of diplomacy has been systematized in written, legally binding acts with a multilateral scope.

[16]E. Denza, Diplomatic Law - Commentary on the Vienna Convention of Diplomatic Relations, fourth Edition, Oxford University Press, Oxford, 2016, p. 24–27.

[17]K.P. Economides, Inviolability and immunity of diplomatic officials, op. cit., p.19 et seq.

[18]See, inter alia, K.P. Economides, Public International Law, op. cit., pp. 172–174; J. Salmon, Manuel de Droit Diplomatique, op. cit., p.33 et seq.

[19]S.E. Nahlik, Dévelopment of Diplomatie Law, Recueil des Cours de l'Académie de Droit International de La Haye, vol. 222 (1990), p. 201 et seq.

However, the most decisive impetus in the development of diplomatic law came after the Second World War with the establishment of the United Nations. Political leaders then decided that the consolidation of international peace and security required closer interstate cooperation and, consequently, an upgrading of the role of law in international relations, both in the sense of codification—i.e., the undertaking of the written recording of previously unwritten or scattered normative material, and its progressive development—i.e., the adoption of new law.[20]

Ultimately, according to the UN Charter, none of the bodies of the organization has legislative power over all states.[21] In this respect, not only was no innovation introduced in relation to the League of Nations period but the deliberative nature of international law was further underlined.[22]

Nevertheless, the establishment of the International Law Commission was decided upon.[23] This Commission is a permanent subsidiary body of the United Nations General Assembly with general competence in the field of codification and progressive development of international law.[24] The first group of 15 members of the Commission were elected on November 3, 1948—among whom was the Greek Professor of International Law Ioannis Spyropoulos—and their first session was held on April 12, 1949.[25] It was the first time in the history of international relations that states had agreed to undertake the recording and development of the law of international relations on a permanent and global basis.[26]

The International Law Commission today consists of 34 jurists and diplomats from all over the world with a balanced geographical distribution. The Commission prepares drafts of international conventions on various aspects of international

[20]For the establishment of the United Nations Organization, see K. Koufa, 'The United Nations forty years after their establishment', Armenopoulos 39/10, 1985, pp. 818 et seq. For the reflection on the codification and progressive development of international law in the early stages of the United Nations Organization, indicative sources are P. C. Jessup, 'Development of international law by the United Nations', AJIL 39/4, October 1945, pp. 754–757, and R. B. Potter, Crucial problems in the development and codification of international law, AJIL 41/3, July 1947, pp. 631–634.

[21]K. Koufa, Evolution of International Law: International Legislation through the United Nations, Thesaurus Acroasium Vol. XVI—The evolution of International Law since the Creation of the U.N. with Special Emphasis on Human Rights, Institute of International Public Law and International Relations of Thessaloniki, 1986, p. 263–286.

[22]C. Tomuschat, International law as the constitution of mankind, International law on the eve of the twenty-first century: Views from the International Law Commission, New York: United Nations (Sales No. E/F.97.V.4), 1997, p. 45.

[23]G.A. Res. 174 (II) (21.11.1947).

[24]Article 1 § 1 of the Statute of the International Law Commission.

[25]C. Eagleton, First session of the International Law Commission, AJIL 43/4, October 1949, p. 758–762.

[26]See C.-A. Fleischauer, The United Nations and the progressive development and codification of international law," I.J.I.L. 25/1, (1985), p. 2.

relations, which are submitted to the consideration of states and, if approved, lead to multilateral conventions.[27]

The Commission's legislative work is admittedly monumental. In particular, its contribution to ensuring that diplomatic practice is translated into accessible legal texts has led to outstanding results with a global reach.[28]

The contemporary international law of diplomatic relations is codified in the Convention on Diplomatic Relations, adopted in 1961 in Neue Hofburg, Vienna, by the United Nations Conference on Diplomatic Relations and Immunities.[29]

The substantive content of the Convention on Diplomatic Relations is based on a draft prepared by the International Law Commission.[30]

The Convention consists of 54 articles, entered into force on April 24, 1964, and has universal application. It is one of the most effective international conventions in the history of international law, as by mid-2022, 191 UN member states, plus the Holy See and the state of Palestine, which have observer status within the universal organization, were bound by its provisions. The only UN member states that have not ratified the Convention are Palau and South Sudan.[31]

The scope of the Convention covers diplomatic relations between states but not the right of representation of other subjects of international law (e.g., international organizations). The provisions of the Convention codify customary international rules on diplomatic relations and, at the same time, introduce new provisions of a non-customary nature, which constitute a "progressive development" of international law.[32] However, the Convention does not crystallize the entirety of the

---

[27] For the current work of the Commission, see the official website https://legal.un.org/ilc/ (Accessed: June 28, 2024). For an analysis of the Commission's work, see, for example, N. Zaikos, The International Law Commission of the United Nations. A Contribution to the Study of the Codification and Progressive Development of International Law: Sakkoulas, Thessaloniki, 2002, and N. Zaikos, The International Law Commission at 70. Thoughts on law-making in the framework of the United Nations, in: Th. Karvounarakis (Ed.), The University of Macedonia Master's in International Public Administration Book. Essays on the Functioning of the World Community, University of Macedonia Publications, Thessaloniki, 2018, pp. 39–60.

[28] K.P. Economides, Inviolability and immunity of diplomatic officials, op. cit., p.36, note 2.

[29] Adopted on April 18, 1961, entered into force on April 24, 1964. Text: UNTS 500, p. 95. Greece ratified the Convention on Diplomatic Relations on July 16, 1970, by Law No. 503 of April 13, 1970, Government Gazette A′, 108 of May 15, 1970.

[30] See Articles on Diplomatic Relations and Immunities with commentary in Y.I.L.C. 1958-II, pp. 89–105 (U.N. Doc. A/3859).

[31] For the numbers of ratifications of multilateral conventions on diplomatic relations, see Multilateral Treaties Deposited with the Secretary-General, https://treaties.un.org/Pages/ParticipationStatus.aspx?clang=_en (United Nations Treaty Collection. Status of Treaties) (Accessed: June 28, 2024).

[32] K.P. Economides, Inviolability and immunity of diplomatic officials, op. cit., p.37f, and Denza, Diplomatic Law, op. cit., p.2 .

customary law of diplomatic relations, which remains in force simultaneously, binding states by custom.[33]

The Convention reflects in a most authoritative, responsible, and comprehensive manner the existing law on diplomatic relations[34] and has been the model for subsequent international conventions on other aspects of diplomatic and consular relations.[35] In accordance with the jurisprudence of the International Court of Justice,

"[T]he Vienna Conventions, which codify diplomatic and consular relations, set forth principles and rules essential to the maintenance of peaceful relations between states and accepted throughout the world by nations of all beliefs, cultures, and political systems."[36]

The United Nations General Assembly has underlined the importance of the Diplomatic Relations Convention in a special resolution on the occasion of the 25th anniversary of its adoption.[37]

Along with the Convention on Diplomatic Relations, Optional Protocols on Acquisition of Nationality and Compulsory Settlement of Disputes have been adopted. Both entered into force on April 24, 1964, and number total fifty-one (51) and seventy (70) contracting parties respectively. Greece has not ratified either of the aforementioned Protocols.

4.3 The Establishment of Diplomatic Relations Between States: The Agrément of the Head of Mission

Traditionally, the first step in establishing diplomatic relations between two states is the establishment of an international convention.[38] Such international conventions often introduce detailed arrangements for the regulation of the mutual diplomatic relations of the contracting states. Subsequently, the procedure for appointing the head of the diplomatic mission and the other staff of the mission is as follows: one state confidentially submits the name and curriculum vitae of the head of the diplomatic mission to the government of the other state. The proposed person should be identified by the authorities of the state where he/she is to serve as persona grata.

[33] Indicatively G. Schwarzenberger—E. D. Brown, A manual of International Law, sixth Edition, Professional Books Ltd., London, 1976, p. 79.

[34] K.P. Economides, Inviolability and immunity of diplomatic officials, op. cit., p.12.

[35] S. E. Nahlik, "Development of Diplomatic Law, op. cit., p. 214 et seq. f.

[36] United States Diplomatic and Consular Staff in Tehran, Merits, Judgment of 24 May 1980, I.C.J. Reports, 1980, p. 24, para. 45.

[37] A/RES/41/79, Twenty-fifth anniversary of the Vienna Convention on Diplomatic Relations, 3 December 1986.

[38] A/RES/41/79, Twenty-fifth anniversary of the Vienna Convention on Diplomatic Relations (3 December 1986).

"Elizabeth the Second, by the Grace of God of the United Kingdom of Great Britain and Northern Ireland and of Her other Realms and Territories Queen, Head of the Commonwealth, Defender of the Faith, &c., &c., &c.

To the President of the Republic of Z. Sendeth Greeting!

Our Good Friend! Being desirous to maintain, without interruption, the relations of friendship and good understanding which happily subsist between Our Realm and the Republic of Z.,

We have made choice of Our Trusty and Well-beloved X.Y. to reside with You in the character of our Ambassador Extraordinary and Plenipotentiary.

Envoy Extraordinary and Minister Plenipotentiary.

The experience which We have had of X.Y.'s talents and zeal for Our service assures Us that the selection We have made will be perfectly agreeable to you; and that he will discharge the important duties of his Mission in such a manner as to merit Your approbation and esteem, and to prove himself worthy of this new mark of Our confidence.

We therefore request that You give entire credence to all that X.Y. shall communicate to You in Our name, more especially when he shall renew to You the assurances of the lively interest which we take in everything that affects the welfare and prosperity of the Republic of Z.

And so, we commend You to the protection of the Almighty.

Given at Our Court of St. James, the ...... day of ...... One Thousand Nine Hundred and ......, in the ...... Year of Our Reign.

Your Good Friend,
(signed)
ELIZABETH R."

4.4 Additional Information on the Establishment of Interstate Diplomatic Relations

Following the issuance of the credentials, the embassy sends a letter of formal notice to all diplomatic missions of the state announcing the accreditation and expressing the wish for cooperation and the strengthening of friendly relations. The diplomatic missions respond with a letter of formal notice, followed by a personal visit (courtesy call) by the Head of Mission to his/her colleagues, who then reply. In this way, the members of the Diplomatic Corps get to know each other.[49]

Each state is free to determine the rank of the Head of Mission to be sent to another state. It is customary for representatives of the same class to be mutually accredited.[50]

It should be noted that it is possible for a single diplomatic agent to represent a state to several states, provided that none of these states objects.[51] For example, before World War II, the ambassadors of Japan, Sweden, Norway, and Denmark in Ankara were also accredited in Athens.[52]

[49] K. I. Skaltsas, Diplomatic representatives in the context of international relations and international law, op. cit., p. 42 (in Greek).

[50] K. Th. Efstathiadis, International Law, op. cit., p. 283.

[51] Article 5 of the Convention on Diplomatic Relations.

[52] K. Th. Efstathiadis, International Law, op. cit., p. 283.

In addition, it is not uncommon for several states to accredit the same person as Head of Mission in another state, provided the latter does not object.[53] For example, in 1965, Niger, Upper Volta, Ivory Coast, and Dahomey were jointly represented in Israel by a single diplomatic agent.[54]

The other members of the mission holding diplomatic status shall be appointed by each state without requiring the prior consent or acceptance of the receiving state and shall not be granted credentials.[55] Their appointment shall be notified to the Ministry of Foreign Affairs of the accrediting state or other competent ministry. The same procedure shall apply to the administrative, technical, and service staff of the mission.[56]

However, each state shall be free at any time to designate a member of the diplomatic staff of the mission as persona non grata and a member of the administrative, technical, and service staff of the mission asnon acceptable, even before their arrival in the state. In this respect, the principles applicable to the Head of Mission shall apply accordingly.[57]

It should be noted that, in particular, military, maritime, and aviation attachés may be required to submit their names for prior approval in a similar procedure to that of the Head of Mission.[58]

4.5 Members and Structure of the Diplomatic Mission

4.5.1 Members

In contemporary international reality, diplomatic missions are exchanged not only between states but also between other entities subject to international law. In general, a diplomatic mission is an instrument of a subject of international law, which is charged with the conduct of diplomatic contacts and activities with another subject of international law.[59]

More specifically, in terms of diplomatic relations between states, a diplomatic mission is defined as the state's body permanently established in another state with the primary purpose of representing the delegating state in which it is established.[60]

[53] See Article 6 of the Convention on Diplomatic Relations and indicatively B. Sen, A diplomat's handbook on international law and practice, op. cit., p. 21.

[54] Inter alia, J. Salmon, Manuel de Droit Diplomatique, op. cit., p. 155.

[55] See Articles Άrticle 8§ 2 and 3 of the Convention on Diplomatic Relations regarding the case where the diplomatic agent has the nationality of the state where the accreditation is carried out or the nationality of a third country.

[56] Article 10§ 1 of the Convention on Diplomatic Relations.

[57] K.P. Economides, Inviolability and immunity of diplomatic officials, op. cit., pp. 72–73.

[58] Article 7, paragraph b of the Convention on Diplomatic Relations and K.P. Economides, Inviolability and immunity of diplomatic officials, op. cit., p. 73.

[59] See P.H. Cahier, Le droit diplomatique contemporain, op.cit., p. 55.

[60] C. P. Economides, inviolability and immunity of diplomatic officials, op. cit., p. 21 et seq.

The diplomatic mission consists essentially of diplomatic staff—i.e., persons having diplomatic status—and nondiplomatic staff—which includes administrative and technical staff and auxiliary staff.[61] Members of the mission shall enjoy in principle the nationality of the accrediting state and may not be selected interchangeably between nationals of the state where they are accredited other than with the consent of the latter, which may be withdrawn at any time.[62] Diplomatic staff shall consist of the Head of Mission and the members who have diplomatic status. The Head of Mission is in charge of the mission and shall be the highest in rank. According to the rules in force, the Heads of Mission are divided into three ranks:

1. Ambassadors or nuncios[63] accredited before Heads of State and other Heads of Mission of equivalent rank,
2. Envoys, Ministers, or Ministers-in-Charge accredited before Heads of State,
3. Chargé d'affaires accredited[64] before Ministers of Foreign Affairs.[65]

As previously noted, the appointment of a Head of Mission requires the approval of the state[66] where he/she is to serve, and he/she presents his/her credentials[67] before the Head of State in a special ceremony (or, in the case of a staff member before the Minister for Foreign Affairs).[68] In the event of refusal, however, the state is not obliged to state the reasons for refusing to accept him/her.[69] A typical example is Greece's refusal in 1977 to accept Mr. William Schaufele as the US Ambassador in Athens because of his comments on Turkey's claims in the Aegean during a meeting of the Senate Committee on International Affairs.[70]

The remaining members of the diplomatic staff bear the title:

1. Embassy Counsellor A and Embassy Counsellor B.
2. Embassy Secretary A, B, and C.
3. Embassy Attaché.

---

[61] See, instead, K. P. Economides, inviolability and immunity of diplomatic officials, op. cit., p. 57 et seq.

[62] Article 8(1) and (2) of the Convention on Diplomatic Relations.

[63] They are the emissaries of the Pope, having a lead over the ambassadors of the states.

[64] See Article 19 of the Convention on Diplomatic Relations.

[65] See Article 14 of the Convention on Diplomatic Relations.

[66] As early as 1932, the Harvard draft Convention adopted the principle of acceptance, prior to the appointment of the head of mission, as an illustration of modern customary international law that contributes to the best possible functioning of diplomacy. See E. Denza, Diplomatic law commentary on the Vienna Convention on Diplomatic Relations, fourth edition, Oxford University Press, 2016, p.38 et seq.

[67] Article 4(1) of the Convention on Diplomatic Relations.

[68] Article 18 of the Convention on Diplomatic Relations.

[69] Article 4(2) of the Convention on Diplomatic Relations.

[70] See Revue General De Droit Internationale Publique, 1977, p. 827.

Diplomatic staff may also include persons entrusted with specific tasks, such as legal, economic, commercial, commercial, educational, military, or press attachés. In regard to military, maritime, or aviation attachés, the accrediting state may request that the names of these persons be submitted in advance to the receiving state for approval.[71,72]

In the event that the position of Head of Mission has not been filled or is prevented from performing his/her duties, the Head of Mission shall temporarily act as "ad interim chief of staff"; the Minister of Foreign Affairs of the state where the accreditation was granted shall be notified of this.[73]

The nondiplomatic staff of the mission includes:[74]

1. Administrative and technical staff (e.g., secretaries, stenographers, typists, archivists, accountants, translators, interpreters); and.
2. Support staff (e.g., car drivers, doormen, janitors, gardeners, cooks).

In addition to the mission staff, two additional categories of persons exist for which specific international arrangements are introduced:

1. Members of the family of diplomatic, administrative, and technical staff of the mission[75]; and.
2. Private servants (i.e., private servants of members of the mission who are not employees of the represented state).[76]

4.5.2 Structure

As noted, the diplomatic mission is a multi-member state body with complex tasks, composed of diplomatic and nondiplomatic officials. A diplomatic mission may have the following structure[77]:

1. A high secretariat or chancellery:
   This is the main body of the diplomatic mission, headed by the person hierarchically next in command to the head of the diplomatic mission

[71] Article 7 of the Convention on Diplomatic Relations.

[72] Ibid.

[73] K. Th. Efstathiadis, International Law, I, op.cit., p. 285 (in Greek).

[74] For these categories of persons, see, in detail, K. P. Ekonomides, inviolability and immunity of diplomatic officials, op. cit., p. 73 et seq.

[75] Article 37 (1) and (2) of the Convention on Diplomatic Relations.

[76] Article 1 of the Convention on Diplomatic Relations.

[77] For example, see B. Sen, A diplomat's handbook on international law and practice, op. cit., p. 44 et seq.; Cahier, Le droit diplomatique contemporain, op. cit., pp. 70–76; A. V. Papakostas, Justice and Diplomatic and Consular Relations, op. cit., p. 59 et seq.

(EmbassyCounsellor or First Secretary). It is responsible for assisting the Head of Mission, coordinating the work of the individual offices or sections of the mission, and handling matters such as the issuing and renewal of passports and the issuing of certificates.

2. *Economic and commercial office*, which shall be coordinated by the Commercial Attaché.
3. Military Office, coordinated by a military, maritime, or aviation attaché (ranging in rank from lieutenant to general). The mission of the military office is to collect military information, promote exchanges of military equipment and foster military cooperation. The office is supervised by the Head of Mission and/or the state's Ministry of Military Affairs.
4. *Press office*, whose mission is to study the country's press attitude on bilateral or international issues, to inform the local population about the state, and to publish a newsletter. It is headed by the press attaché.
5. *Office of cultural attaché*, whose mission is to promote artistic and educational exchanges, such as the conclusion of educational agreements and the granting of scholarships, the conduct of book exhibitions, and the overall promotion of friendship through cultural encounters.
6. Diplomatic missions may also have an immigration office and a Consular Chief Secretariat or Chancellery, and may be staffed, for example, by a doctor or a priest.

4.6 The Size of the Diplomatic Mission

The size of the diplomatic mission, in the absence of specific agreement, may be determined by the state sending the diplomatic mission itself. In the case of an excessively large diplomatic mission, the receiving state may request that the mission be kept within "reasonable" and "normal" limits in view of the state's general circumstances and the needs of the mission.[78]

In some cases, the question of reducing the number of members of the diplomatic mission arises, as occurred, for example, on October 26, 1983, when Suriname requested from Cuba to recall its ambassador and reduce its diplomatic staff. Within 14 days, more than 20 diplomatic staff and 80 advisers had departed.[79] The receiving state, according to article 11, 2, may refuse to accept officials of a particular category.

[78] Article 11 of the Convention on Diplomatic Relations.

[79] B. Sen, A diplomat's handbook on international law and practice, op.cit., p. 38 et seq.

4.7 The Diplomatic Corps

By Diplomatic Corps (Corps diplomatique) is meant the total number of diplomatic agents serving in a state. The Diplomatic Corps is not a legal entity but an informal association of independent persons. The longest serving ambassador is elected by the Corps as a Dean. The Dean is the head of the Corps and defends the rights of the "diplomatic family."[80]

The seniority of the Heads of Mission is determined according to the day and time of their assumption of office and the rank to which they belong.[81]

It should be noted that the Ministry of Foreign Affairs of each state periodically publishes the Diplomatic List, which is a form containing the names of persons belonging to the diplomatic staff. In order to be included in the Diplomatic List, a person must hold a diplomatic passport and a declaration must be made that the holder of the diplomatic passport is a member of an embassy. The inclusion of the name of the diplomatic agent in the Diplomatic List is important because it informs the persons concerned about the diplomatic status of a person,[82] and the granting of diplomatic protection. A typical case is that of an individual by the name of Vivianu, an economic counsellor at the Romanian Embassy in Bern. Vivianu was accused of illegal actions in violation of Swiss law and following an investigation it was revealed that he had not registered as a member of the Romanian mission and therefore did not have diplomatic status and could not enjoy diplomatic immunity.[83]

4.8 Functions of Diplomatic Agents

According to the classic quote of Sir Henry Wotton, British Ambassador to Venice in 1604, "legatus est vir bonus peregre missus ad mentiendum Respublicae causa," which translates as "the envoy (ambassador) is a good man sent abroad to lie for the sake of the republic he represents."[84] However, Wotton's advice a few years later became somewhat simpler and more direct: "Tell the truth."[85]

[80] See, among others, J. Salmon, Manuel de Droit Diplomatique, op.cit., p.88 et seq.

[81] Article 16 of the Convention on Diplomatic Relations.

[82] K. P. Economides, Inviolability and immunity of diplomatic officials, op. cit., pp. 70 et seq.; K. I. Skaltsas, Diplomatic Representatives in the context of international relations and international law, op. cit., pp. 29–30 and 41–42 (in Greek).

[83] L. Oppenheim, International Law, eighth edition, vol. I, Lauterpacht, Longman, London, 1955, p. 784.

[84] H. F. Eilts, Diplomacy—Contemporary Practice, (Lecture, US Army War College, Carlisle Barracks, Pennsylvania, August 31, 1973, in E. Plischke, Modern diplomacy—The art and the artisans, op. cit., p. 3–18, p. 3.

[85] Th. Bailey, Advice for the Diplomat, in The Art of Diplomacy—The American Enterprise, Appleton—Century—Crofts, New York, 1968, p. 5, as referenced in E. Plischke, Modern diplomacy—The art and the artisans, op. cit., p. 223 et seq., pp. 234–235.

4.10 Privileges and Immunities of Diplomatic Agents

4.10.1 General Remarks

Under international law, state bodies of international relations, including diplomatic agents, have always been surrounded by a special protective legal status.[101] Indeed, part of the public believes—falsely—that diplomats have such extensive relative protection that they remain outside the scope of law, policing, and tax obligations.

The protective legal status of diplomatic agents goes back to the origins of modern diplomacy,[102] formed by custom[103] and consisting, in particular, of a series of privileges and immunities. The term "privileges" refers to a series of rights linked exclusively to diplomatic functions. When reference is made to immunities, it is implied that the power of the state's bodies does not extend to diplomatic agents.[104]

The customary (unwritten) international rules concerning the special treatment of diplomats were codified and progressively developed in the Convention on Diplomatic Relations. This Convention provides for a series of immunities and privileges for the head of the diplomatic mission. The relevant framework also covers mission staff, as well as members of the diplomat's family, subject to certain conditions.

4.10.2 Basis of Justification for Diplomatic Privileges and Immunities

Three theories have been developed to justify the privileged status of diplomatic agents.[105] According to the theory of extraterritoriality (exterritorialité), privileges and immunities are justified because the location of the embassy and the place where the diplomatic agent is located form an extension of the territory of the sending state in accordance with the law. In other words, it is assumed that diplomatic agents do

[101] G. Schwarzenberger—Brown, A manual of International Law, ibid., p. 79 and, from the classical Greek literature on the privileges and immunities of diplomats, see S. Seferiades, Lectures in Public International Law, Book I, International Public Law in Peace, Athens, 1925, pp. 488 et seq. (in Greek) and I. Spyropoulos, Public International Law, System of the theory and practice of Public International Law, Athens, 1933, pp. 205 et seq. (in Greek).

[102] Do Nascimento e Silva, Diplomatic Law, op. cit., p. 90 et seq.

[103] See A.-V. Papakostas, The Immunity of Diplomatic Agents, second edition, Athens, 1971, p. 3 (in Greek) and, in particular, on the customary character of diplomatic immunity, and K.P. Economides, Inviolability and immunity of diplomatic officials, op. cit., p.9 et seq.

[104] S. E. Nahlik, Development of Diplomatic Law, op. cit., pp. 218–219.

[105] K. Koufa, Aspects of consular relations between Greece and the United Kingdom: Considering consular amenability to local jurisdiction in the light of customary international law, the Consular Convention between the United Kingdom and Greece and the Vienna Convention on Consular Relations, Hellenic Review of International Relations Vol. I, No. II (1980), p. 382 et seq. and K.P. Economides, Inviolability and immunity of diplomatic officials, op. cit., p.44 et seq.

not remain within their state of origin and are outside the state in which they serve (fingitur esse extra territorium).[106]

Conversely, in the theory of representation (théorie du caractère représentatif de l'agent diplomatique), privileges and immunities are granted because the person of the diplomatic agent is associated with the sovereign ruler of the foreign state they represent. According to Montesquieu's maxim, diplomatic agents "constitute the voice of the ruler who sends them and, therefore, that voice must be free."[107] Furthermore, according to a classic axiom of international law expressed in the phrase "par in parem non habet imperium" ("equally not subject to equal authority"), the diplomatic agent of a sovereign state is prohibited from being subject to the jurisdiction of another sovereign and equal state.

The aforesaid theories have now been wholly or partly abandoned or superseded.[108] The prevailing justification of privileges in modern theory and practice is that of functional theory (théorie de l'intérêt de la fonction), according to which the privileges and immunities of diplomats are provided to facilitate the exercise and effective accomplishment of diplomatic duties.[109] Consequently, the protective net covers acts that fall within the official functions of the mission but not acts outside the scope of diplomatic function.[110] The theory of functional needs provides not only the justification but also the necessary evaluation of diplomatic privileges and immunities. As has been maintained by the Greek courts, "these may be sued before the Greek courts in the case of a dispute unrelated to the functions."[111] Accordingly, illegal acts that are not functionally linked to official duties should entail the personal accountability of the diplomatic agent.[112]

According to subparagraph (d) of the Preamble of the Convention on Diplomatic Relations, the purpose of privileges and immunities is not to favor specific individuals but to ensure the effective fulfilment of the functions of diplomatic missions "as representatives of States." In view of this wording, it may be inferred

[106] The problem of extraterritoriality in relation to a refugee applying for asylum in an embassy was an issue before the ICJ in a number of cases, as the Haya de la Torre, in early 1950. See, among others, K. Ioannou-St. Perrakis, Introduction to International Justice, vol, 2 Ant N Sakkoulas, Athens-Komotini 1984, pp. 10 et seq.

[107] Referenced by R.-J. Dupuy, International Law, Que. sais-je? No 131, p. 41.

[108] For a detailed analysis of the theories in historical perspective, S. E. Nahlik, Development of Diplomatic Law, op. cit., pp. 221ff.

[109] J. Basdevant (Ed.), Dictionnaire de la terminologie du droit international, Sirey, Paris, 1966, p. 322, « Pour remplir leur mission et pendant sa durée, les agents diplomatiques jouissent de certains privilèges que l'on désigne sous le nom d'immunités diplomatiques ».

[110] B. Sen, A diplomat's handbook on international law and practice, op. cit., p. 96 et seq.

[111] See No. 1481/1972, Nomiko Vima, vol. 20 (1972), p. 1222–1223. See also Athens. Court of Appeal 5917/1973, Hellenic Law Journal vol. 41, p. 586 (in Greek).

[112] See I. Brownlie, Principles of Public International Law, second edition, Clarendon Press, Oxford, 1973, op. cit., pp.344–345, on the difficulties of defining the acts that fall within official duties.

that the Convention adopts a combination of functional and representational theory.[113]

The International Court of Justice in the Immunities and Criminal Procedures case (Equatorial Guinea v. France, December 11, 2020) ruled that the justification for privileges and immunities is to safeguard and promote friendly bilateral interstate relations.[114]

Also, as ruled by the Greek justice system, "the purpose of the peaceful immunities is... to ensure the effective fulfilment of the duties of diplomatic missions in their capacity as representatives of the States."[115]

4.10.3 Inviolability

The customary rule of inviolability covers the staff and premises of diplomatic missions.[116] The inviolability of the person of diplomatic agents has been an international custom with universal scope since the era of Grotius.[117] According to this, the state must provide specialized and enhanced protection by means of preventive measures to deter any kind of offense against the person of diplomatic agents by private and state bodies. The authorities of the state must treat diplomats with due respect and prevent any insult to their person, freedom, and dignity. Diplomatic agents are not subject to coercive measures such as arrest, detention, extradition, or expulsion. Therefore, the freedom of the diplomatic agent cannot be restricted in any way by the authorities of the state or by any individual. Inviolability is absolute and covers not only the official acts of diplomatic agents but also matters relating to privacy.[118]

If the diplomatic agent holds the nationality of the state in which he/she is employed, the inviolability shall cover only official acts in the performance of their duties, unless otherwise agreed between the state of origin and the host. The inviolability of the diplomatic agent is waived when he/she acts in self-defense or

[113] K. Koufa, Aspects of consular relations between Greece and the United Kingdom..., op. cit., pp. 379, 388–389, E. Roukounas, International Law, op. cit., p. 29 and M. Akehurst, A modern introduction to International Law, fifth ed., George Allen and Unwin, London, 1984, p. 113, referring to "double basis for diplomatic immunities." See also J. S. Parkhill, Diplomacy in the modern world: a reconsideration of the bases for diplomatic immunity in the era of high-tech communications, HICLR Vol. 21, No. 2 (1998), pp. 565–596.

[114] L. A. Sisilianos, Foreword" in I. Iakovidis, Judicial Immunities and Human Rights, Nomiki Bibliothiki, Athens, 2021, p. VII (in Greek).

[115] See Opinion of Athens Court of Appeal, Nomiko Vima, vol. 17, 1969, p. 368.

[116] Article 22 of the Convention on Diplomatic Relations.

[117] Inter alia, J. Salmon, Manuel de Droit Diplomatique, op. cit., p. 291 et seq.

[118] Article 22 of the Convention on Diplomatic Relations.

voluntarily engages in activities involving an element of danger (e.g., driving while intoxicated or engaging in encounters).[119]

The inviolability consideration also covers the "premises of the mission," archives, and documents.[120] "Premises of the mission" refers to buildings or parts of buildings and contiguous property used for diplomatic purposes, regardless of their owner, as well as the residence of the head of mission.[121]

The inviolability of the premises of the mission means that no state body may enter without the consent of the head of mission.[122] The premises, furniture, and items of the mission shall not be subject to search, requisition, attachment, or execution.[123]

The state should ensure that it refrains from occupying the premises of the mission, causing damage, disturbance of the peace of the mission, or impairment of its dignity.[124] Finally, the inviolability protects the archives, documents of the mission,[125] and diplomatic correspondence.[126] The inviolability applies even in the event of fire, epidemic, or other emergency situations.

4.10.3.1 Cases Related to Inviolability

In times of great political tension between certain states, violations of the rules regarding inviolability have been observed. For example, in early 1963, a crowd stormed the British Embassy in the Congolese city of Léopoldville due to the British stance on the rebellion in Katanga province. The crowd caused significant material destruction, including the destruction of furniture and the hurling of the Embassy's archive from the windows. Following a protest by Embassy authorities, the Congolese Prime Minister expressed regret for the incident, granted compensation, and pledged to bring those responsible to justice.[127]

The issue of the inviolability of mission premises was also raised during the war in the former Yugoslavia when US aircraft mistakenly bombed the Chinese embassy in Belgrade. The US apologized and attributed the incident to a malfunction of the navigation systems, which provided incorrect coordinates to the bombers. Additionally, the United States committed to restoring all damages by paying US$ 28 million to the relatives of the victims and US$ 4.5 million for the material damage from the bombing, after signing an agreement with the Chinese government. In response,

[119] J. Salmon, Manuel de Droit Diplomatique, op. cit., p. 292. J. Salmon, op. cit., p. 295, citing Revue Générale de Droit International Public (1988), p. 1004, refers to the case of the arrest of an armed diplomat from the former Yugoslavia threatening the crowd in Stockholm.

[120] Article 29 of the Convention on Diplomatic Relations.

[121] E. Denza, Diplomatic Law, op. cit., p. 112 et seq.

[122] Article 22 § 1 of the Convention on Diplomatic Relations.

[123] Article 22 § 3 of the Convention on Diplomatic Relations.

[124] Article 22 § 2 of the Convention on Diplomatic Relations.

[125] Article 24 of the Convention on Diplomatic Relations.

[126] Article 27 of the Convention on Diplomatic Relations.

[127] S. E. Nahlik, Development of Diplomatic Law, op. cit., p.322.

China agreed to pay US$ 2.8 million to repair damages to the US embassy in Beijing and the consulate in Guangzhou, which had been targeted in retaliation for the bombing of the Chinese embassy in Yugoslavia.[128]

4.10.3.2 The Case of the United States Diplomatic and Consular Staff in Tehran (ICJ, USA v. Iran, 1980)

In relation to the inviolability of the person of the diplomatic agent and the premises of the mission, the decision of the International Court of Justice in the case of the United States Diplomatic and Consular Staff in Tehran (US v. Iran) was a milestone. This case was the most pronounced case in which the issue of diplomatic immunity emerged in the entirety of the twentieth century.

In 1979, after two long years of demonstrations and protests, armed groups succeeded in overthrowing the Shah, who fled the country after all offers of compromise fell on deaf ears. A revolutionary government of fundamentalist Islamists took power. Even after his removal from the country, the situation remained unstable and unrest prevailed, leading to serious incidents.

On November 4, 1979, demonstrations were held outside the American embassy in Tehran and the consulates in the cities of Tabriz and Shiraz demanding the extradition of the former monarch and his wife, who immediately fled to various countries after his overthrow before being admitted to the United States, where he was hospitalized in a New York clinic. Some violent gunmen, who called themselves "Muslim students, followers of the Imam," stormed the embassy and, at gunpoint, took hostage those inside. The American hostages were subjected to degrading treatment at gunpoint, kept tied up for hours or in solitary confinement and were not allowed to stand or talk to each other. At the same time, they were constantly threatened that they would be tried as spies and possibly executed. It should be noted that Ayatollah Khomeini, the leader of the revolution, congratulated the occupiers, issued a decree calling the US embassy a "centre of espionage and conspiracy" and stated that "those who plot against our Islamic movement should not be accorded international diplomatic respect."[129]

Following pressure from Washington, on November 18–20, 1979, 13 people were released by Khomeini's order, while the others, some 50 of whom had diplomatic or consular status, continued to be detained. The invaders conditioned the release of the hostages on the Shah's extradition and a confession by the United States to spying activities inside Iran. At the same time, the Iranian authorities refused any contact or negotiations with US representatives. On November

[128] E. Denza, Diplomatic Law, op.cit. p. 166. The rules regarding the inviolability of diplomatic mission premises came back to the force with the case of Julian Assange, author, publisher, and founder of the nongovernmental organization WikiLeaks, who in 2012 sought asylum at the Ecuadorian Embassy in London. The question was raised as to whether the UK government would waive its recognition of the premises as diplomatic and therefore inviolable, or whether it would have to sever diplomatic relations with Ecuador to arrest Assange. In 2019, Ecuadorian authorities finally waived his immunity and Julian Assange was arrested by the British authorities.

[129] S. E. Nahlik, Development of Diplomatic Law, op. cit., p. 311–312.

9, 1979, the United States assembled the Security Council and, on November 29, 1979, appealed to the International Court of Justice, demanding the release of the hostages and the payment of compensation. Simultaneously, they requested provisional measures.

With regard to the International Court of Justice's hearing of the case, it should be noted that Iran did not participate in the proceedings and only sent two letters—on December 9, 1979 and March 16, 1980, respectively. The Court, taking into consideration high tension between the parties,[130] unanimously ordered interim measures—return of the embassy to the US diplomatic and consular staff, measures for full protection of the staff, immediate release of the hostages, allowing them to leave Iranian territory—and in its final judgment[131] condemned Iran in the strongest possible terms for violating the Convention on Diplomatic Relations and Consular Relations,[132] stressing that Iran, as a host state, should have taken appropriate measures to protect the US embassy and consulates, their staff, records, and the free movement of employees.[133]

The ICJ ruling did not resolve the case, as the hostages were not released until after tortuous negotiations on January 20, 1981, having been illegally detained for 444 days.[134]

4.10.4 Immunity from Jurisdiction

The customary procedural rule of immunity from jurisdiction (Exterritoriality/ Immunité de jurisdiction or Exterriorialité/Exterritorialität) provides for the exclusion of a foreign natural or legal person from the jurisdiction of national courts. In particular, it is "the limitation introduced by international law on the jurisdiction of the courts of a state, leading to a greater or lesser degree of evasion of that jurisdiction by foreign states and their heads of state, members of diplomatic missions…".[135]

[130] K. Antonopoulos, The resolution of disputes by the International Court of the United Nations, Jurisprudence and Practice, Second Edition, Publications. Ant. N. Sakkoula, Athens-Komotini, 2007 (in Greek).

[131] Case concerning United States Diplomatic and Consular Staff in Tehran (USA v. Iran), Judgment of 24 May 1980, ICJ Reports (1980), p. 3ff.

[132] Ch. Dipla – E. Doussi, The International Court of Justice of the United Nations, op. cit., pp. 8 et cit. and the bibliography therein.

[133] ICJ Reports (1980) par. 337–338, par. 340.

[134] S. E. Nahlik, Development of Diplomatic Law, op. cit., p.316 et seq.

[135] Dictionnaire de la terminologie du droit international, ibid., p. 322. According to Black's Law Dictionary, St. Dal, Minn.: West Publishing Co., 1968, p. 695, immunity is the "privilege of those persons (such as the Ministers of Foreign Affairs) who, though temporarily residing within a State, are not subject to the functioning of its laws."

Depending on the subject of the immunity, the question of the immunity from jurisdiction of states,[136] the immunity from jurisdiction of officials of international organizations,[137] and, of course, the immunity from jurisdiction of diplomatic and consular agents is raised.

The Convention on Diplomatic Relations establishes the general immunity of diplomatic agents as follows:

"A diplomatic agent shall enjoy immunity from the criminal jurisdiction of the receiving state. He shall also enjoy immunity from its civil and administrative jurisdiction…".[138]

Immunity from jurisdiction is procedural in nature and implies that the national court is not competent to review the legality of the acts of diplomatic agents for lack of jurisdiction.[139]

Immunity from criminal jurisdiction was established in international law because of the fact that diplomatic agents are persons against whom unsubstantiated charges could potentially be brought. Immunity from criminal jurisdiction is absolute, cannot be waived under any circumstances, and is not open to any exception.[140] In other words, the courts of the receiving state are not competent to hear cases relating to offences committed by diplomatic agents. This principle applies irrespective of the nature or severity of the offence committed and irrespective of whether it was committed while the diplomatic agent was on or off duty.

The invocation of immunity shall be governed by the domestic law of each state. As far as Greece is concerned, in accordance with the current Code of Penal Procedure (Article 2, "Exceptions to immunity from criminal jurisdiction"):

"The jurisdiction of the Greek criminal courts shall not include:

(a) The heads of foreign states,
(b) The diplomatic agents accredited in Greece,
(c) The staff of the diplomatic mission of a foreign state accredited in Greece,

---

[136] See K. Koufa, The operation of the phenomenon of government acts in international relations, vol. I, ibid., p. 132, E. Roukounas, International Law, fourth ed., Nomiki Bibliothiki, Athens, 2021, pp. 78ff., Chr. Rozakis in K. Ioannou—K. Economides—Ch. Rozakis—A. Fatouros, Public International Law—Competencies in International Law, Ant. N. Sakkoulas, Athens-Komotini, 1991, pp. 104 et seq., and B. Markezinis, The sovereign immunity of states in private and public international law", Court Case 5 (1974), p. 603, regarding the extent of this subject, it is not worthy that even at that time it included "the material collected by the writer so far … about 100 articles, monographs and commentaries on decisions as well as almost 500 decisions … occupying more than 5000 pages and having a purpose of several tens of millions of dollars" (references in Greek).

[137] See K. Koufa, The legal organization of international society, Sakkoulas, Thessaloniki, 1988, pp. 118–119, S. Varouxakis, International organizations, vol. 2, Legal theory of international organizations, Papazisis, Athens, 1987, pp. 161–165.

[138] Article 31 § 1, subpar. a' of the Convention on Diplomatic Relations.

[139] See A.-V. Papakostas, The Immunity of Diplomatic Agents, op. cit., p. 5.

[140] See A.-V. Papakostas, The Immunity of Diplomatic Agents, ibid., p. 59 et seq., K. Economides, Inviolability and immunity of diplomatic officials, op. cit., p. 174 et seq., and, on applicable customarily, Seferiades, International Public Law, op. cit., pp. 493–496.

(d) Members of the family of the persons referred to in points (a) and (b) who reside with them,
(e) the service staff of the persons referred to in points (a) and (b) where they are of the same nationality; and
(f) all other persons enjoying the privilege of being subject to the jurisdiction of the courts by virtue of conventions concluded with other states or international customs accepted by all states."

Consequently, the immunity of diplomatic agents, their family members, staff of the mission, and service staff is absolute in the context of criminal proceedings.

As Iakovos Iakovidis has noted, the authorities and judicial bodies of accrediting states around the world ultimately comply, albeit sometimes reluctantly, with the Convention's provisions on immunity from criminal jurisdiction. According to relevant case law, diplomatic agents who have been accused of even extremely serious offenses, such as bombings and torture, have been released after a short period of detention, but these cases are of course rare.[141] It has been argued, however, that immunity from criminal jurisdiction should be waived in cases where war crimes or crimes against humanity are being investigated.[142]

It should be noted that the privileges and immunities of diplomatic agents also apply intransitu, i.e., when passing through third states.[143] However, it must again be stressed that criminal immunity does not negate the obligation of diplomats to respect the legal order of the state where they serve.[144]

Immunity from civil jurisdiction. Prior to the adoption of the 1961 Convention, there was controversy over whether diplomatic representatives were excluded from the jurisdiction of civil courts.[145] However, as Stylianos Seferiades mentioned in a lecture, as early as the 1920s, "the privilege of acquittal from criminal and civil jurisdiction has always been regarded as a necessary guarantee for the seriousness of their duties."[146]

According to the Convention on Diplomatic Relations, civil and administrative immunity cover "official acts" or "acts performed in the course of their duties" of diplomatic agents.[147]

Regarding immunity in civil proceedings, Article 3 of the current Code of Civil Procedure reads:

"1. Greek and foreign nationals fall within the jurisdiction of the civil courts, provided that there is jurisdiction of a Greek court.

[141] I. Iakovidis, Judicial Immunities and Human Rights, op. cit., p. 142–143, 269 et seq.

[142] J. Salmon, Manuel de Droit Diplomatique, op. cit., p. 302 et seq.

[143] Article 40 of the Convention on Diplomatic Relations.

[144] Article 41 § 1 of the Convention on Diplomatic Relations.

[145] A.-V. Papakostas, The Immunity of Diplomatic Agents, op. cit., p. 65 et seq. K. Economides, Inviolability and immunity of diplomatic officials, op. cit., p. 211.

[146] S. Seferiades, International Public Law, op. cit., p. 495.

[147] J. Salmon, Manuel de Droit Diplomatique, op. cit., p. 436.

2. Foreign nationals involved in judicial proceedings shall be excluded from the jurisdiction of the Greek courts, except in the case of disputes covered by the provisions of Article 29."[148]

In accordance with Article 313 of the Code of Civil Procedure:

"1. Recognition of the absence of a judgment may be sought by means of an action or objection only in the following cases: [...] (e) if it was executed against a person who has the privilege of immunity."

As Konstantinos Kerameas observes, "exemption presupposes that its institutions have foreign nationality. It is never awarded to persons with Greek nationality or even permanent residence—regardless of their service—in Greece."[149]

Submission to the jurisdiction of the Greek courts is a procedural requirement of the case, the lack of which entails the nullity of the relevant procedural acts.[150] The examination of whether a person is a party to a dispute is carried out ex officio and leads to the dismissal of the claim as inadmissible.[151] Regarding diplomatic agents, "immunity from jurisdiction is understood as the exclusion and non-submission of a person to the jurisdiction of the domestic courts, and foreign diplomatic agents of all ranks in the Greek state enjoy this privilege, among others, in accordance with the rules of international law."[152] According to Greek case-law, judgments relating to persons who are not parties to the proceedings are declared null[153] or invalid[154] and do not produce res judicata and, therefore, enforceability.[155]

[148] Article 29 of the Code of Civil Procedure exempts from immunity from jurisdiction disputes for property. See below.

[149] See K. Kerameas, Civil Procedural Law, General Section, Sakkoulas, Athens—Thessaloniki, 1986, p.14., K. Pappa, The Legal Position of Foreigners in International Law, Athens, 1971, p.41., L. Plionis, International jurisdiction of the Greek courts according to the Code of Civil Procedure, Athens, 1971, pp. 106–114, G. Mitsopoulos, Civil Procedure, vol. A, Athens, 1972, pp. 163–164, G. Rammos, Handbook of Civil Procedure Law, vol. 1, Athens, 1972, p. 22 and S. Delikostopoulos—L. Sinaniotis, Interpretation of the Code of Civil Procedure, vol. A, Athens, 1968, p. 42.

[150] S. Delikostopoulos and L. Sinaniotis, Interpretation of the Code of Civil Procedure, op. cit., p. 44.

[151] K. Kerameas, Civil Procedural Law, op. cit., p.14.

[152] No. 1481/1972 Athens' Court of First Instance, Legal Step, vol. 20, p. 1222–1223 (in Greek).

[153] S. Delikostopoulos and L. Sinaniotis, Interpretation of the Code of Civil Procedure, op. cit.

[154] Mitsopoulos, Civil Procedure, op. cit., p.171.

[155] See K. Bei, Civil Procedure, vol. IA', (Articles 1–105), 1973, p. 152.

4.10.5 Specific Exceptions to Diplomatic Immunity in Civil Proceedings: Greek Practice

In the case of diplomatic immunity in civil proceedings, the protected status of the diplomatic agent is waived in certain cases defined by international law.[156]

The first exception arises in actions in rem concerning possession of residence in private immovable property situated in the territory of the receiving state unless the diplomatic agent holds that property on behalf of the state and for the purposes of the mission.[157] Specifically, in cases of actions in rem regarding immovable property[158]—rather than actions related to property—held by the diplomatic agent as an individual and not within the context of diplomatic competence, the lex reisitae (the law of the state where the immovable property is situated) shall apply.

In accordance with international law, Articles 3 §2 and 29 §1 of the Code of Penal Procedure (CPP) exempt "disputes "concerning rights in rem over immovable property, the possession or occupation thereof, the division of common property, the establishment of limits, claims against any person in possession, compensation for expropriation, as well as disputes arising out of a lease of immovable property or a right connected with the use thereof or from a land lease, shall be subject to the exclusive jurisdiction of the court within the district in which the property is situated."[159]

As G. Mitsopoulos pointed out, "the considerations of public international law that dictate immunity from legal proceedings recede against the desire to control the domestic territory."

Second, immunity in civil proceedings is waived in cases related to inheritance, where the diplomatic agent acts as an executor of a will, administrator, heir, or legatee in an individual capacity, and not as a representative of the accrediting state.[160] This rule was incorporated into the Convention based on the imperative unity of inheritance requiring a sole court to address the related problems.

The third exception is introduced in cases where the lawsuit concerns professional or commercial activity carried out by the diplomatic representative in the accredited state, apart from official duties.[161] This reasonable exception reinforces

---

[156] Article 31 § 1 a′–c′ of the Convention on Diplomatic Relations. For commentary, inter alia, Economides, Inviolability and immunity of diplomatic officials, op. cit., p. 213ff.

[157] Article 31 § 1 a′–c′ of the Convention on Diplomatic Relations. See Seferiades, International Public Law, op. cit., p. 495: "whatever the nature of the civil law obligation of the defendant… the courts… must in principle willingly accept the plea of incompetence," referring to civil jurisdiction of diplomatic agents, even in relation to movable objects (citation in Greek).

[158] Athens Court of Appeal, No. 4610/1982, Armenopoulos (1986), p. 1089. Conversely, the Athens Court of Appeals No. 4848/72, Law Journal Archives ΚΔ′ (1972), p. 73 (in Greek).

[159] Mitsopoulos, Civil Procedure, op. cit., p. 166. For the issues arising from the regulation of the Code of Civil Procedure in relation to the provisions of Greek law, see Economides, Inviolability and immunity of diplomatic officials, ibid., p. 221 et seq. (in Greek).

[160] Article 31 § 1b′ of the Convention on Diplomatic Relations.

[161] Article 31 § 1c′ of the Convention on Diplomatic Relations.

the prohibition on exercising private professional or commercial activity by diplomatic agents, which is introduced elsewhere in the Convention.[162]

Finally, the Convention states that if a diplomat or a person enjoying immunity in civil proceedings initiates legal proceedings before a court, then the invocation of jurisdiction is not allowed regarding any counterclaim directly related to the main claim.[163] This exception is justified from the moment the diplomat seeks legal protection and, therefore, accepts the jurisdiction of the receiving state.[164] In this case, filing a lawsuit is equivalent to waiving jurisdiction.

Counterclaim, characterized in jurisprudence as "pleas" and an "act of distraction,"[165] is admissible against the diplomatic agent only as a means of defense,[166] i.e., a means of defending against the main lawsuit and countering its claim, without having a broader basis than that. Consequently, jurisdiction is also waived when legal remedies are brought against the decision issued at first instance.

4.11 Waiver of Immunity

It is argued that the framework of the Convention on Diplomatic Relations' rules on the immunity of diplomatic agents is unreasonably broad.[167] Although the comital of wrongful acts by diplomatic agents is not a frequent occurrence, nevertheless, malicious conduct of a diplomatic agent acting in bad faith could nevertheless leave those dealing with or affected by him or her unprotected in the event of his or her bad faith conduct—as, for example, in the case of a claim for damages for a car accident caused by negligence on his or her part.

In such cases, an appeal may be brought before the courts of the state represented by the diplomatic agent—if there are competent courts to hear such cases and the injured party is able to meet the financial requirements involved in such proceedings.

Sovereign immunity, however, does not necessarily imply impunity. In that sense, the state may expressly waive in writing the civil and criminal immunity of the diplomatic agent ("waiver of immunity").[168] The waiver of immunity is not exercised by the diplomatic agent, but by the state he or she represents. In fact, the

[162] Article 42 of the Convention on Diplomatic Relations.

[163] Article 32 § 3 of the Convention on Diplomatic Relations.

[164] S. Delikostopoulos – L. Sinaniotis, Interpretation of the Code of Civil Procedure, op. cit., p. 44 (in Greek).

[165] See P. Gessiou-Faltsi – Ath. Kaises, Civil Procedure in Motion, vol. I, Sakkoulas, Thessaloniki, 1985, p. 113, who also observe that counterclaim "[essentially] is primarily a counterattack, because it constitutes, in its legal nature, a new, separate lawsuit… in exception, the counterclaim may also be a means of defense." (in Greek).

[166] K. P. Economides, Inviolability and immunity of diplomatic officials with reference to consular officers, op. cit., p.219.

[167] See the critical remarks of Professor K. P. Economides, Inviolability and immunity of diplomatic officials, op. cit., pp. 250–251.

[168] Article 32 of the Convention on Diplomatic Relations.

diplomatic agent's consent is not necessary for the waiver of immunity. That being said, in 1970, the Dutch government waived the immunity of its military attaché in London at his own request in order to bring him to court for causing a fatal accident.[169] In a separate case, an employee of the US embassy in London was put on trial on charges of document theft and espionage after the US government lifted his diplomatic immunity. In another case, the Antigua and Barbuda ambassador borrowed US$ 250,000 from Fidelity Bank and lost it at the casino. The bank filed a lawsuit against the ambassador and the latter agreed to have his immunity waived and to be tried in the United States. In the case of Deputy Commissioner McMahon v. Kevin McDonald, an administrative staff member of the Irish Embassy in London issued illegal passports and was therefore dismissed by the Irish government and had his immunity waived. He secretly fled to his own country, which then extradited him to the English authorities so that he could be brought to trial in Britain.[170]

Article 32(1) provides the operational aspect of the Convention, already set out in the Preamble, and states that the purpose of privileges and immunities is not for the benefit of the individual, but rather to ensure the effective fulfilment of diplomatic missions as states' representatives.

Article 32(3) states that in the event that a diplomatic agent initiates legal proceeding he/she does not enjoy diplomatic immunity, while the same applies in the case of a counterclaim. However, this does not mean that there is an explicit statement of waiver of immunity, nor that there is an obligation to approve a similar action by the sending state. A prominent example is the case of a US diplomat in the Netherlands (Hart v. Helsinki) who filed a lawsuit against a landlord of a house because of high rent. When the landlord subsequently filed a lawsuit against the diplomat, the latter claimed diplomatic immunity, a claim which the court did not accept as it considered that the diplomat's filing of a lawsuit constituted an implicit waiver of immunity. In the case of ReR.F.N. involving an official of an international organization (Atomic Energy—IAEA), the official brought a case before an Austrian court seeking custody of his child and, when his ex-wife filed a claim against him, he invoked diplomatic immunity, which the court rejected.[171]

In another case, the Thai government in 1992 waived the immunity of the Second Secretary at its London embassy facing charges of illegally importing heroin into Britain. The diplomat was eventually tried and sentenced to 20 years in prison. A similar thing occurred in 1996 when the French government requested that Zaire's government waive the immunity of the French ambassador, who drove his car into two young children in the south of France and killed them; the diplomat was convicted by the French courts. Another similar case is that of a senior diplomat at the Georgian embassy in Washington DC when, in 1997, Georgia waived his

[169] See C. P. Economides, Inviolability and immunity of diplomatic officials, op. cit., p. 225 et seq. (in Greek).

[170] E. Denza, Diplomatic Law, op. cit., p.273 et seq. There are a number of similar cases.

[171] Ibid., p. 341.

immunity to prosecute him for his involvement in a multiple car crash in which a teenage girl had died.

It is worth noting that the waiver of diplomatic immunity may also apply to diplomatic mission buildings, archives, correspondence, or property of the person whose immunity is waived.

4.12 Other Privileges

The Convention provides for the exemption of diplomatic agents from the obligation of testifying as a witness[172]—this exemption is also applied to members of the diplomatic agent's family. This provision of the Article 31(2) codifies a customary law, which has been in force since the early twentieth century with several notable examples such as the case of the Dutch Ambassador to the United States before whom a murder was committed and who, when called as a witness, refused to testify in court, causing the United States to react by requesting the intervention of the Netherlands. The United States disputed that there was a general customary law allowing the Ambassador to abstain from such a duty. The Netherlands, on the other hand, did not permit him to appear in court and testify, but instead suggested that he give sworn evidence to the Ministry of Foreign Affairs, which was not accepted by the United States, which demanded the immediate revocation of the Ambassador.[173]

Moreover, the diplomatic agent is exempt from all personal benefits, public service of any kind, and military duties,[174] as well as from the payment of national, local, and community taxes and fees.[175] It is also provided that diplomatic agents shall not be subject to any enforcement measures, except in cases under Article 31(1) and, in any event, this shall not affect the integrity of the person and residence of the diplomatic agent.[176]

A series of provisions have also been introduced regarding the exemption of diplomatic agents from the provisions relating to social security,[177] taxes and fees[178] (subject to conditions), and customs expenses.[179]

[172] Article 31 (2) of the Convention on Diplomatic Relations.

[173] E. Denza, Diplomatic Law, op.cit., p. 261 et seq.

[174] Article 35 of the Convention on Diplomatic Relations. The justification is that diplomats as foreigners cannot be subject to the obligations of the citizens of the state.

[175] Article 23 (1) of the Convention on Diplomatic Relations.

[176] Article 31 (3) of the Convention on Diplomatic Relations.

[177] Article 33 (1) and (3) of the Convention on Diplomatic Relations.

[178] Article 34 of the Convention on Diplomatic Relations.

[179] Article 36 of the Convention on Diplomatic Relations.

4.13 Extension of Diplomatic Privileges and Immunities to Further Categories of Persons

Some of the privileges and immunities of diplomatic agents are extended to other categories of persons. In particular, the integrity of the diplomatic agent also covers:

1. the diplomatic courier,[180]
2. members of the diplomatic agent's family residing with him/her, provided that they are not nationals of the state where the accreditation is granted, and
3. members of the administrative and technical staff, provided that they are not nationals of, or permanently resident in, the state in which accreditation is granted.[181] In the case of family members and members of the administrative and technical staff who are nationals of the state where the accreditation was granted, the integrity of the accreditation shall be granted to the extent acknowledged by the state.[182]

The immunity of the diplomatic agent shall also cover:

1. Members of the diplomatic agent's family living with him/her, provided that they are not nationals of the state where the accreditation is granted.
2. Members of the administrative and technical staff and members of their families who are not nationals of the state in which accreditation is granted and who do not reside permanently in that state. Immunity from civil jurisdiction shall cover only acts carried out in the conduct of their duties.
3. Members of the administrative and technical staff who are not nationals of the state where the accreditation is granted and do not permanently reside there. Their immunity from criminal and civil jurisdiction shall extend exclusively to acts connected to the conduct of their duties.[183]

Private servants working on behalf of the members of the diplomatic mission shall not enjoy immunity.[184]

In particular, members of the family of the diplomatic agent shall be subject to:

1. the integrity of the person,[185]
2. the inviolability of residence, documents, and correspondence,[186]

[180] Article 27 (5) of the Convention on Diplomatic Relations.

[181] Article 37 of the Convention on Diplomatic Relations.

[182] Article 38 (2) of the Convention on Diplomatic Relations.

[183] Article 37 of the Convention on Diplomatic Relations.

[184] K. Efstathiadis, International Law, I, op.cit., p. 294.

[185] Article 29 of the Convention on Diplomatic Relations.

[186] Article 30 of the Convention on Diplomatic Relations.

3. the immunity from legal process and immunity from execution,[187] and.
4. exemption from social security,[188] taxes, duties, fees, and benefits,[189] and customs duties.[190]

Finally, the following are exempted from the payment of social security contributions:

1. the diplomatic agent,[191]
2. members of his/her family,[192]
3. members of the administrative and technical staff if they are not nationals of, or permanently resident in, the state of accreditation,[193]
4. domestic staff provided that they are not nationals of the state of accreditation and are not subject to the relevant legislation of another state,[194] and
5. service staff provided that they are not nationals of, or permanently resident in, the state where the accreditation was granted.[195]

4.14 Persona Non Grata

There are certain cases in which a diplomatic agent who has been admitted to a State becomes a persona non grata ("unwelcome person") at a later point in time.[196]

The designation of a diplomatic agent as persona non grata is an incriminating punitive measure of a personal nature.[197] By being declared as persona non grata, the diplomatic agent is rendered incapable of carrying out the duties entrusted to him/her, and his/her diplomatic status is terminated—at least as far as the relations between the state he/she represents and the state where he/she serves are concerned.[198]

In this case, the diplomatic agent is not subject to an expulsion order, but to a request for his/her revocation by the state he/she represents, and the diplomatic agent

[187] Articles 31 and 32 of the Convention on Diplomatic Relations.

[188] Article 33 of the Convention on Diplomatic Relations.

[189] Articles 34 and 35 of the Convention on Diplomatic Relations.

[190] Article 36 of the Convention on Diplomatic Relations.

[191] 107 Article 33 (1) of the Convention on Diplomatic Relations.

[192] Article 37 (1) of the Convention on Diplomatic Relations.

[193] Article 37 (2) of the Convention on Diplomatic Relations.

[194] Article 33 (2) of the Convention on Diplomatic Relations.

[195] Article 37 (4) of the Convention on Diplomatic Relations.

[196] Article 9 of the Convention on Diplomatic Relations and Denza, op. cit., p. 61 et seq.

[197] K. P. Economides, Inviolability and immunity of diplomatic officials, op.cit., p. 64 (in Greek).

[198] 114 See also Article 43(b) of the Convention on Diplomatic Relations.

is obliged to leave the state where he/she is serving.[199] States comply when their representatives are declared non-gratae, occasionally by lodging some form of protest.[200] Naturally, the diplomatic agent becomes accountable to his/her service, while such cases attract a great deal of publicity.

The declaration of a diplomatic agent as persona non grata does not require formal justification.[201] The grounds for taking such a measure may be the improper conduct of the diplomatic agent, which may include the violation of the law, as, for example, in the case of illicit trafficking of archaeological artifacts.[202]

Other reasons that may lead to a diplomatic agent being declared persona non grata include interference in the internal affairs of the state where the accreditation was granted and social behavior, which, although not illegal, is considered socially unacceptable. For example, in 1951, the Turkish Ambassador in Bonn invited Von Papen, Hitler's former ambassador to Ankara, to lunch, leading Chancellor Adenauer to call for his removal.[203]

On some occasions, diplomats abuse their sovereign diplomatic privileges. Such a phenomenon has been attributed to the rapid increase of diplomatic agents around the world, to inadequate training, and to the poor wages of diplomatic staff in certain states.[204]

According to a UK Foreign Office report, 40% of the offenses involving diplomatic agents revolve around traffic violations—indeed, in 1984 alone,[205] 104,690 tickets were issued to diplomats for traffic offenses in British territory, of which 80% went unpaid. The first place in terms of tickets issued was held by the mission of Nigeria (6618), with Egypt (6294) following in second place.[206]

In certain cases of road violations, the outcome is disastrous. For example, the car driven by the United States' Dr. Hallie Brown collided with a car driven by Panama's cultural attaché. Brown was paralyzed as a result of the negligent driving of the diplomatic agent, receiving no financial compensation because the person at fault was not insured and the Panamanian Embassy refused to pay any kind of compensation.[207] According to another Foreign Office publication (1986), in the year 1985, 25 diplomats were declared non-gratae, half of which due to drunk driving or traffic violations, 6 for theft, 3 for disorderly conduct, 2 for vehicular accidents, 1 for

---

[199] See, among others, B. Sen, A Diplomats handbook on International Law and Practice, op. cit., pp. 54–55.

[200] See, to that effect, J. Salmon, Manuel de Droit Diplomatique, op.cit., p. 491.

[201] See, to that effect, J. Salmon, Manuel de Droit Diplomatique, ibid., p.482et seq.

[202] Seevarious cases in Salmon, Manuel de Droit Diplomatique, ibid., p. 484.

[203] J. Salmon, Manuel de Droit Diplomatique, ibid., p. 488.

[204] S.E. Nahlik, Development of Diplomatic Law, op. cit., p. 332 et seq.

[205] See, for example, H. Faupin, Les problèmes juridiques posés par la circulation automobile des diplomates, AFDI Vol. 44, 1998, pp. 167–186.

[206] S.E. Nahlik, Development of Diplomatic Law, op.cit., p. 335.

[207] S.E. Nahlik, Development of Diplomatic Law, op.cit., p. 336.

weapons possession, 1 for drug trafficking, and 1 for refusing to comply with a court order.[208]

Of course, it should be noted that the declaration of a diplomatic agent as persona non grata is an exceptional and rare adverse event, given the number of diplomatic agents around the world and the work they carry out daily. It is worth pointing out that in the 1980s, in the United States alone, the number of persons with diplomatic status was 50,000.[209]

Moreover, diplomatic agents themselves are frequently victims of legal infringements, which is why international protection has become imperative.

4.15 The Language and Documents of Diplomacy

The "language" of diplomacy was originally Latin. Then, the French language was imposed to such an extent that international diplomacy is considered to be traditionally associated with the French language. At the Paris Peace Conference of 1919, the English language emerged as an equal to French and, over the years, it eventually prevailed.[210] Today, each state is entitled to draft its diplomatic documents in its official language. Subject to this proviso, the most widespread official languages in international diplomatic practice are English and French.[211]

Within the multilateral framework of the United Nations, the official languages are English, French, Russian, Chinese, Arabic, and Spanish. Nevertheless, the official languages of the International Court of Justice remain English and French.[212]

Each diplomatic mission shall have various written and oral means at its disposal for the conduct of its official contacts. Diplomatic documents are, in principle, drawn up in a decorous style with the usual courtesy of diplomatic etiquette.

The most common are:

The Note through which the state announces significant decisions, such as the stance it is going to take on an international treaty, a request, or a demand for clarification on an issue.

A Note verbale is one of the most common documents in diplomatic practice, sometimes unsigned, concerning a request or a remark or any matter that may concern the mutual relations between two states. The memorandum or promemoria is the most detailed form of a note, which it usually supplements,

[208] J. Salmon, Manuel de Droit Diplomatique, op.cit., pp. 486, référence in Revue Générale de Droit International Public, 1986, p. 671.

[209] S.E. Nahlik, Development of Diplomatic Law, op.cit., p. 332.

[210] K. I. Skaltza, Diplomatic representatives in the context of international relations and international law, op.cit., p. 16 et seq.

[211] G. K. Tenekidis, Public International Law, T. A, Section One – General Theory of Public International Law/Sources of International Law, fourth edition, Papazisis, Athens, 1975, pp. 420–421 (in Greek).

[212] See the United Nations website http://ww.un.org

and is neither signed nor dated. It provides a detailed account of events or the elaboration of legal arguments.

4.16 Termination of Diplomatic Relations

There is no clear definition of the right to terminate diplomatic relations in the Convention. As expressly stated in Article 2, diplomatic relations between two states are "established by mutual consent"; therefore, the lack of such consent leads to the termination of diplomatic relations.[213] However, termination of diplomatic relations may also occur for a variety of other reasons. One of these is the decision to sever diplomatic relations. The severance of diplomatic relations is a unilateral act that leads to the termination of diplomatic relations between two states and brings forth specific legal effects. The severance of diplomatic relations implies the termination of permanent diplomatic representations but does not mean that all diplomatic contacts are excluded. The reasons leading to a severance are generally based on the deterioration of political relations as a result of dispute.[214] For example, in 1954, relations between India and Portugal were severed over the disputed territory of Goa. Similarly, in 1982, Great Britain and Argentina severed relations over the Malvinas/Falkland Islands. In October 1956, Egypt's relations with France and Great Britain were severed because of the Franco-British military operation to occupy the Suez Canal Zone, following the nationalization declared by the then President of Egypt, Gamal Abdel Nasser. France was represented diplomatically in Egypt by the Embassy of Switzerland.[215]

It should be noted that the severance of diplomatic relations may be decided as a collective sanction against a state, as was the case with UN Council Resolution 757 (1992) concerning (former) Yugoslavia.[216]

Whereas armed conflict constitutes another reason for the termination of diplomatic relations.[217] It is argued that "the termination of diplomatic relations on account of war may precede, coincide with or follow it."[218] On the other hand, the establishment of diplomatic relations ends warfare between two states. For example, it is argued that the armed conflict between Greece and Albania as a result of the

[213] Article 45 of the Convention on Diplomatic Relations.

[214] See G. K. Tenekidis, Public International Law, op. cit., pp. 419–420 and, in more detail, A. V. Papakostas, The Law of Diplomatic and Consular Relations, op. cit., p. 102 et seq. (in Greek).

[215] S.E. Nahlik, Development of Diplomatic Law, op.cit., pp.309–310.

[216] J. Salmon, Manuel de Droit Diplomatique, op.cit., p. 496 et seq.

[217] For an analysis of the diplomatic relations between Greece and Germany after the outbreak of the Second World War, see D. S. Konstantopoulos, The explosion of the war between Germany and Greece (1941) and the protection of their interests by their respective protectors, Greece and the war in the Balkans (1940–41)B, Institute for BalKan Studies Thessaloniki, (v. 245), 1992, pp. 119–161.

[218] K. Efstathiadis, International Law, I, op.cit., p. 286.

Second World War was formally brought to an end in 1971, when the two states established diplomatic relations.[219]

Changes in the state's "identity" may lead to the termination of diplomatic relations. In this respect, emphasis is placed on the case of so-called capitis diminutio, i.e., the cessation of the existence of a state as an independent political entity. Such cases include the incorporation of a state into another state, the split of a state into two or more (e.g., Czechoslovakia, Yugoslavia, Soviet Union) or the union of two or more states into a new state (e.g., Tanganyika and Zanzibar forming the state of Tanzania).

Nonrecognition of an entity as a state or nonrecognition of a government are also grounds for termination of diplomatic relations.

Termination of diplomatic relations may occur due to the abolition of the diplomatic mission, e.g., due to lack of practical interest in maintaining the mission or due to financial considerations.

It is also argued that, in accordance with customary law, constitutional reform and change of Head of State are also factors for terminating diplomatic relations. In such cases, the renewal of credentials and their delivery to the new Head of State are required.[220]

This issue emerged on the occasion of the presence of the diplomatic agents of the United States in Iraq following the fall of the Saddam Hussein regime. State Department spokesman Richard Boucher stated in May 2003 that "There are diplomats who were previously accredited to the Saddam regime, who have been residing in former mission residences, who are still there. We do not regard those as diplomatic missions. They're accredited to a regime that is no longer existent, and, therefore, their accreditation would have lapsed." and added that there are no diplomatic privileges in Iraq "because there's no government in Iraq to grant those privileges," but that the embassy building is protected by the inviolable. This stance differs from that taken after the collapse of the Shah's regime in Iran in 1979; at the time, US diplomatic agents were not reaccredited to the regime of Ayatollah Khomeini, which bore responsibility for the flagrant violation of diplomatic law leading to Iran's conviction by the International Court of Justice.[221]

Finally, the termination of diplomatic relations may be due to reasons relating to the person of the diplomatic agent, such as the notification that the function of the diplomatic agent has come to an end,[222] revocation for diplomatic difficulties or in

---

[219] K. P. Economides, Bringing an end the hostilities with Albania, International Law and International Policy 16 (1988), p. 49 et seq., on an analysis of all views on when the conflicts with the neighboring state ended.

[220] K. I. Skaltsas, Diplomatic representatives in the context of international relations and international law, op.cit., p. 48 (in Greek).

[221] F. Kirgis, Diplomatic Immunities in Iraq, The American Society of International Law—ASIL Insights (June 2003) (in Greek).

[222] Article 43 (a) of the Convention on Diplomatic Relations.

"retaliation," change of service,[223] change of rank, dismissal, retirement, death, or resignation for personal or medical reasons, or declaration of persona non grata.[224]

The diplomatic agent is recalled by means of letters de rappel (letters of recall), which the agent presents in order to obtain a letter of recall from the Head of State or the Minister for Foreign Affairs, depending on his or her rank.[225]

It should be noted that in the event of temporary or definitive recall of the mission or of a break in diplomatic relations, or even in the event of armed conflict, states must respect and protect the premises, records, and property of diplomatic missions. Custody may be entrusted to a third state, which may be entrusted with the protection of the interests of the accrediting state and its nationals.[226]

Dr. Dr.h.c Paraskevi (Paroula) Naskou-Perraki, ret. Professor of International Law and International Organizations, Department of International and European Studies, University of Macedonia, Thessaloniki (1994–2014). She has served for 20 years at the Law Faculty of Democritus University of Thrace, in Komotini (1974–1993). She has been teaching International Law, International Organizations, Diplomatic Law and Human Rights in different universities in Greece, Europe, and the USA, recently at the Masters Programme "On Human Rights and Migration Studies," University of Macedonia (2019–2025). Founder and Director of the UNESCO Chair on Intercultural Policy for an Active Citizenship and Solidarity (2004–2014), she was a representative of the Greek Ministry of Foreign Affairs at the Conference held in Brussels (2003) and then Tehran (2004) between Iran and the EU on Human Rights and in 2003 at the conference held in Beijing between China and the EU on Human Rights. She was awarded as Dr. Honoris Causa from the Faculty of Law and History of Neofit Rilski University in Blagoevgrad, Bulgaria, in 2003. She was member of the Scientific Committee of International Law at the Ministry of Foreign Affairs (2016–2019), President of the board of the Institute of Balkan Studies (2019–2021), Director of the Hellenic Institute for UN Affairs (2017-), Vice-President of the Board of the UNESCO Center for the Women and Peace in the Balkans (2012–2020), Secretary General of the board of CIEEL, Secretary General of the Kalliopi Koufa Foundation for the promotion of International Law and the protection of Human Rights, (2015–2019). Ad Hoc Judge of the European Court of Human Rights (ECtHR) (2011–2013), Awarded with the title F.U.N.—Friend of the United Nations for her contribution in the dissemination of the work of the Organization through the UN Models (2007). Since 2016 she has been responsible for the "Students as Diplomats," an annual Model UN addressed to Greek high school students, on issues concerning the work of UN Human Rights Committees. Editor in Chief of Evrigenis Yearbook of International and European Law, published by Ant. N. Sakkoulas, Athens (issues 2019–2023) she has published in Greek, English, and French.

[223] K. Efstathiadis, International Law, I, op.cit., p. 286.

[224] See, inter alia, Do Nascimento e Silva, Diplomatic Law, op.cit., p.172 et seq.

[225] See, extensively, C. I. Skaltsas, Diplomatic Representatives in the context of international relations and international law, op.cit., p. 44 et seq. (in Greek).

[226] Article 45 (c) of the Convention on Diplomatic Relations and K. Efstathiadis, International Law, I, op. cit., p. 286.

The Law of Consular Relations

5

Paraskevi Naskou-Perraki

Abstract

The Vienna Convention on Consular Relations was adopted in 1963. Based on the consensus of states, being subject to an agreement between the sending and the receiving state, the consular relations are dealing with the appointment of consular posts, the duties of consuls in the consular district, facilities and obligations, privileges and immunities, and the termination of consular functions. Emphasis is given to the obligations of the state of residence to provide facilities for the consular posts. A number of cases concerning this Convention were dealt before the International Court of Justice, the Hague.

5.1 General Remarks on Consular Relations

The institution of "proxenies" or "proxenia," in the sense of protecting citizens of a foreign city, was first evidenced in ancient Greece. Its long history appears also in the Preamble of the Vienna Convention on Consular Relations where ".... consular relations have been established between peoples since ancient times."[1] In fact, Pindar, Thucydides, Alciviades, Kimon, and Demosthenes were proxenoi

[1]The Vienna Convention on Consular Relations was adopted at Vienna on April 24, 1963, and entered into force on May 19, 1967. UN Treaty Series, vol. 596, p. 261, Preamble para. 1.

P. Naskou-Perraki (✉)
Department of International Studies, University of Macedonia, Thessaloniki, Greece
e-mail: perraki@uom.edu.gr

P. Naskou-Perraki (ed.), *Contemporary Diplomatic and Consular Relations*,
https://doi.org/10.1007/978-3-031-99243-8_5

(consuls).[2] In its modern form, the institution of consul began shaping in the second half of the Middle Ages,[3] as a result of the flourishing of international trade.[4]

Today, diplomatic and consular relations are distinct forms of relations between states; hence, they share certain characteristics. Like diplomatic relations, consular relations are based on the consensus of states, being subject to an agreement between the sending and the receiving state. Although the existence of one is independent of the existence of the other, consent to the establishment of diplomatic relations generally implies consent to the establishment of consular relations.[5] In this context, it should be noted that the establishment of consular relations does not entail the recognition of a state[6]; consular relations can also be established implicitly, provided that diplomatic relations between two states have been established prior to them. This would imply that there is consent to the establishment of consular relations, should there be an objection, in which case a separate agreement can be expected. The states' practice suggests that the existence of diplomatic relations entails the existence of consular relations. However, consular relations with a state do not necessarily indicate the existence of diplomatic relations, but rather may suggest the receiving state's desire to establish diplomatic relations in the future.

5.2 The Modern International Legal Framework of Consular Relations: The Convention on Consular Relations

Contemporary transnational consular relations are governed by a network of numerous bilateral agreements.[7] Within the framework of the United Nations, the Convention on Consular Relations has been adopted, which has universal scope and a dual purpose, as it codifies existing customary law on the one hand, and on the other hand, it supplements and further develops consular law by adding new rules of purely

[2]See C. Tissot, Des proxenies grecques et de leur analogie avec les institutions consulaires modernes, Dijon, 1863, also K. Efstathiadis, International Law, Athens, 1977, p. 299 (in Greek).

[3]See G. Salles. L institution des consulats, son origine, son développement au Moyen Age chez les differentspeulpes, Paris 1898, also L. Oppeheim, International Law, vol. I., eighth ed., Longmans, 1967, p.829 et seq. For the status of capitulations, see K. Efstathiadis, International Law, op. cit., p. 314 et seq. (in Greek).

[4]For more details of the institution in its historical route, see K.P. Economides, Introduction to Diplomatic and Consular Law. The institutions of the State in international relations, Ant. N. Sakkoulas, Athens – Komotini 1991, p. 100 et seq (in Greek).

[5]Article 3 (2) of the Convention on Diplomatic Relations and Article 2 (2) of the Convention on Consular Relations.

[6]See, among others, J. Salmon, Manuel de Droit Diplomatique, Bruylant, Bruxelles, 1994, p. 522.

[7]K. P. Economides, Inviolability and immunity of diplomatic officials, Athens, 1975, p. 30, with a list of the first bilateral consular conventions signed by Greece (in Greek).

contractual nature.[8] In this sense, the Convention becomes mandatory for all states and non-signatories, holding declarative significance.

During the preparatory work of the Convention, the need for the implementation of uniform rules for consular matters at the international level was emphasized, as well as the uniform regulation of consular matters on an equal basis. Like the Convention on Diplomatic Relations, the Convention on Consular Relations is considered particularly successful, as it gathers one hundred and eighty-two (182) contracting parties.[9] Along with the Convention, an Optional Protocol on the Acquisition of Nationality and an Optional Protocol on the Compulsory Settlement of Disputes were adopted.[10] Both Protocols entered into force on March 19, 1967, and count fifty-one (51) ratifications for the first and fifty-two (52) for the second. According to the second Protocol, any dispute arising regarding the interpretation or application of the Convention shall be compulsorily referred to the jurisdiction of the International Court of Justice. The Convention consists of 79 articles and is divided into five chapters. Its provisions do not affect other international agreements in force, nor do they prevent states from concluding international agreements that confirm, supplement, or develop its provisions.[11]

5.3 The Appointment of Consular Posts

The procedure for the appointment of consular posts has similarities with the procedure of appointing heads of diplomatic missions. Consent from both states involved is requisite,[12] whether expressed in writing or orally, representing a fundamental principle of consular law.[13]

The individual designated as the head of the consular mission receives a Consular Diploma (Patente/Lettre de Provision) or a similar document outlining their full name, consular rank, consular district, and official residence, among other details. The sending state designates the location of the consular office, as well as the district and jurisdiction within which the mission's functions are to be carried out, with the

[8]As noted by K. P. Economides, Introduction to Diplomatic and Consular Law, Ant. N. Sakkoulas, Athens-Komotini, 1991, p. 106 (in Greek), who underlines that the Convention is also considered the most important text for consular relations. See also E. Roukounas, Public International Law, fourth ed. Nomiki Bibliothiki, Athens 2021, p. 405 et seq.

[9]United Nations Treaty Collection, https://treaties.un.org/pages/ViewDetails.aspx?src=TREATY&mtdsg_no=III-6&chapter=3&clang=_en (Retrieved: February 26, 2024).

[10]Ibid, pp. 70 and 72, see The Work of the International Law Commission, op. cit., pp. 333–334 and 334–336.

[11]In accordance with Article 73 of the Convention on Consular Relations.

[12]Articles 10 and 19 of the Convention on Consular Relations, K. P. Economides, Inviolability and immunity of diplomatic officials, Athens, 1975, p. 65 (in Greek).

[13]Article 2(1) of the Convention on Consular Relations.

consent of the receiving state.[14] Additionally, the sending state determines the legal status of consular personnel, including their appointment, date of arrival in the receiving state, status, and conditions governing the arrival, departure, or alteration of personal staff associated with the consular mission.

For the head of the consular mission to undertake their duties, they must be formally recognized by the receiving state.[15] Upon acceptance, the receiving state issues what is known as an "exequatur" document (derived from the Latin "exsequor" meaning "to enforce"[16]), granting authorization for the posting of the head of the consular mission and the execution of their duties within their consular district.[17] The receiving state retains the discretion to refuse to grand an exequatur document without providing reasons for refusal.[18]

The rules governing the acceptance of diplomatic agents and their notification as persona non grata apply mutatis mutandis to consular agents.[19] Consequently, if the sending state does not recall a nominated consul upon request, the receiving state may either withdraw the exequatur document or cease to consider him as member of the consular staff.[20]

5.4 Consular Post

The consular post may take the form of a consulate-general, consulate, vice-consulate, or consular agency.[21] Consular personnel encompass consular officers (Fonctionnaires Consulaires), who are affiliated with the head of the consular post and its serving members.

Consuls are categorized into regular or paid consuls (consules electi) and honorary or unpaid consuls (consules missi).[22] Their similarities and distinctions are outlined as follows[23]:

[14] Article 4 of the Convention on Consular Relations. Some countries, such as Greece, shall set up consular authorities in cities abroad where there are significant Greek communities, shipping, tourism, or other interests (in accordance with Article 297 of Law 4781/2021).

[15] Article 4 (1) of the Convention on Consular Relations. See also K. P. Economides, Inviolability and immunity of diplomatic officials, op. cit., pp. 65–66.

[16] Article 12 (1) of the Convention on Consular Relations. See L. Oppenheim, International Law, op. cit., p. 835, p. 1.

[17] Articles 10–15 of the Convention on Consular Relations and K. Efstathiadis, International Law, op. cit., p. 302 (in Greek).

[18] Article 12 (2) of the Convention on Consular Relations.

[19] Articles 12 and 23 of the Convention on Consular Relations. See also L.T. Lee, Vienna Convention on Consular Relations, A. W. Sijthoff, Leyden, 1966, p. 32 et seq.

[20] Article 23(2) of the Convention on Consular Relations.

[21] Article 9 of the Convention on Consular Relations. See also J. Zourek, Le statut et les fonctions des consuls, RCADI, 1962, vol. 106.

[22] K. Efstathiadis, International Law, op. cit., p. 301 et seq.

[23] J. Salmon, Manuel de Droit Diplomatique, op.cit., p. 519.

HonoraryConsuls	RegularConsuls
1. Are unpaid (except the Netherlands)	1. Are paid
2. Are bound by a service contract	2. Are likewise bound by a service contract
3. Do not hold the nationality of the state they represent but the nationality of the state where they reside	3. Hold the nationality of the state they represent, as well as the nationality of the state where they reside
4. Typically lack specialized training	4. Have specialized training
5. May engage in other primary professions (e.g., trader, lawyer, banker)	5. Are prohibited from engaging in other professions
6. Have limited privileges and immunities, primarily pertaining to their consular duties	6. Enjoy broader privileges and immunities

The hierarchy among consular officers is determined by their classification and the date of the grant of the exequatur. Precedence is given to those having provisional admission, in order to paid consuls over unpaid ones within the same category.[24]

The staff of the consular post includes consular officers without the status of head of the consular post, consular officials (Employés Consulaires), and service staff. These personnel are appointed by the sending state through notification, without requiring express acceptance from the receiving state (unless the consular officer is a national of the receiving state), following a process similar to issuing an exequatur document.[25] The number of personnel serving at the consulate, in the absence of explicit agreement, is proportionate to the consular district's size and the requirements of the consular authority.[26]

Regarding diplomatic relations, the state reserves the right to designate a consular officer as unwelcome (persona non grata) at any time, as well as to deem a member of the consular post staff as unacceptable (non-acceptable).[27] A person may also be declared inadmissible before arriving in or commencing duties in the host country.[28]

Furthermore, in accordance with the provisions of the Convention on Diplomatic Relations, two additional categories exist outside the consular post's staff: members of consular officers' families and private staff of the consular authority. In all instances, the Ministry of Foreign Affairs of the receiving State or the authority designated by the Ministry shall be notified of the arrival and departure of consular authority members, changes in their official status, the arrival and departure of consuls' family members, private staff, and any other individuals residing with them.[29]

[24] For more details, see Article 16 of the Convention on Consular Relations.

[25] Article 19 (1) and (2) and Article 24 (1)(a) of the Convention on Consular Relations.

[26] Article 20 of the Convention on Consular Relations.

[27] Article 23 (1) of the Convention on Consular Relations.

[28] Article 23(3) of the Convention on Consular Relations.

[29] Article 24 of the Convention on Consular Relations.

5.5 Honorary Consuls

The institution of Honorary Consuls is solely within the purview of each state, as states assess and determine whether to appoint or accept consuls.[30] Honorary Consuls, designated by the sending state, are nationals of the receiving state endowed with consular status.[31] They must hold the nationality of the receiving state. Their responsibilities resembling those of consuls, with the provisions of articles 28, 29, 30, 34, 35, 36, 37, 38 and 39, as well articles 54(3) and 55(2) and (3) also applicable to honorary consuls. Similarly, the privileges and immunities afforded to consuls apply to honorary consuls as well (refer to articles 59, 60, 61, and 62).[32] Honorary Consuls are protected by reason of their official position.[33]

It is important to note that the privileges and immunities granted to Honorary Consuls[34] shall not be accorded to their families, consular staff, or other employees under his Directorate.[35] As for the exchange of consular bags between consular authorities situated in different countries, it requires the consent of the receiving state.[36] Additionally, Honorary Consuls enjoy tax exemptions for consular premises[37] and are exempt from customs duties, fees, or related obligations.[38]

5.6 Diplomatic and Consular Posts: Similarities and Differences

Despite a trend in modern international law to equate the legal status of consuls with that of diplomats, distinctions persist between these two categories.[39] Consuls are not regarded as "representatives" of states, although this interpretation may vary depending on the understanding of the term "representation."[40] Nonetheless, the sending state retains responsibility for the actions of its consular officers.[41]

---

[30] Article 58 underlines its optional character.

[31] See Chap. 3 Regime related to Honorary Consular Officers and Consular posts, Article 58 of the Convention on Consular Relations.

[32] In accordance with Article 58(1) of the Convention on Consular Relations.

[33] Article 64 of the Convention on Consular Relations.

[34] In accordance with Article 58(2) of the Convention on Consular Relations.

[35] Article 58 (3) of the Convention on Consular Relations.

[36] Article 58 (4) of the Convention on Consular Relations.

[37] Article 60 of the Convention on Consular Relations.

[38] Article 62 of the Convention on Consular Relations.

[39] S. E. Nahlik, 'Development of Diplomatic Law', RCADI, vol.222, 1990, pp. 209.

[40] Ch. Rousseau, Droit International Public, v. IV, p. 218.

[41] See L.G. Marcantonatos, Les Relations consulaires aux termes de la Convention de Vienne du 24 Avril 1963, Institute of International Public Law and International Relations (Scientific Publications7/Directorate: D.S. Konstantopoulos), Thessaloniki, 1974, p. 59.

As mentioned, consuls do not undergo accreditation before the authorities of the receiving state but assume their duties following the issuance of an exequatur document. Consuls are not concerned with political issues. They primarily engage with local authorities on matters concerning finance or administration and the safeguarding and assistance of nationals of the consular state within the territory where they operate. Moreover, while diplomatic agents have territorial jurisdiction over the entirety of the state where accreditation occurs, consular authorities' jurisdiction is limited to their consular district (circonscription consulaire), which constitutes only a portion of the receiving state's territory.[42]

However, it should be noted that in contemporary international practice, consular duties are often fulfilled by ambassadors or other diplomatic agents.[43] Consequently, consular relations between two states may exist without dedicated consular missions.[44] Furthermore, in some instances, consular offices are integrated into embassies as a consular component of the diplomatic mission, a practice adopted for reasons of efficiency and economy.[45] Finally, it is pertinent to recognize that consular officials occasionally perform diplomatic functions, albeit without entitlement to diplomatic privileges and immunities.[46]

5.7 International Mission and Consular Functions

Consuls' functions encompass a broad spectrum. As per article 5(a) of the Convention on Consular Relations, the consul's primary responsibility is to safeguard the interests of the sending state and its nationals, within the limits prescribed by international law. Additionally, the consul serves as a channel for fostering commercial, economic, cultural, and scientific relations between the sending and receiving states, promoting friendly relations between them.[47]

Furthermore, the consular duties cycle includes, inter alia: issuance and renewal of passports or travel documents, issuance and renewal of entry permits,[48] provision of assistance to individuals and bodies corporate,[49] execution of notarial and civil status functions (e.g., record-keeping of contracts, marriages, births, and

[42] See, for example, B. Sen, A diplomat's handbook on International Law and practice, third ed., Martinus Nijhoff, 1., Dordrecht, 1988, pp.268, et seq., J. Salmon, Manuel de Droit Diplomatique, Bruylant, Bruxelles, 1994, p.515 et seq., A. B. Papakostas, Jurisdictional and Consular Relations, Ant., N., Sakkoulas, Athens-Komotini, 1989, p.251, et seq. (in Greek).

[43] Article 3 of the Convention on Consular Relations.

[44] L.T. Lee, Vienna Convention on Consular Relations, A. W. Sijthoff, Leyden. 1966, op. cit., p. 25 et seq.

[45] E. Denza, Diplomatic Law, op. cit., pp.33–34.

[46] Article 17 of the Convention on Consular Relations.

[47] Article 5 (b)and (c) of the Convention on Consular Relations.

[48] Article 5 (d) of the Convention on Consular Relations.

[49] Article5 (e) of the Convention on Consular Relations.

acknowledgment of children),[50] protection of inheritance rights of nationals of the sending state,[51] and the rights of individuals who are physically incapacitated or minors.[52] The consul also represents nationals of the sending state before the authorities of the receiving state,[53] transmitting judicial and extrajudicial documents,[54] conducts control, supervision, and aids ships and aircraft of the sending state and their crew, and carries out any other tasks defined by the dispatching state,[55] provided they are not prohibited by the laws of the receiving state.[56]

5.8 Obligations of the State of Residence

The state of residence is obliged to provide consular services with adequate space to execute their mission and provide all essential facilities. Consular services are entitled to display their national flag and coat-of-arms,[57] and both the consulate premises and the residence of the head of the consular service are exempt from taxes and fees.[58] Furthermore, there is a right to communication between the consular service and the sending state as well as freedom of movement and travel to all members of the consular post.[59]

The Convention on Consular Relations confers inviolability upon consular premises to the extent that the authorities of the receiving state may not enter there on without the consent of the consul. Also, they have a special duty to protect the premises.[60] Established regulations include the inviolability of consular archives and documents, official correspondence,[61] and consular posts, as well as the prohibition on opening or detaining consular bags containing exclusively official correspondence or items for official use. In case state authorities suspect illegal contents in the bag, they may request its opening. If denied, the bag is returned to the place of

50 Article5 (f) of the Convention on Consular Relations.

51 Article 5 (f) of the Convention on Consular Relations.

52 Article5 (h) of the Convention on Consular Relations.

53 Article 5 (i) of the Convention on Consular Relations.

54 Article 5 (j) of the Convention on Consular Relations.

55 Article 5 (k) (l) of the Convention on Consular Relations.

56 Article 5 (m) and (m) of the Convention on Consular Relations.

57 Article 29(1) of the Convention on Consular Relations.

58 Article 32 of the Convention on Consular Relations.

59 Article 34 of the Convention on Consular Relations.

60 D.P.O Connel, International Law, second ed. vol. 2, London, Stevens and Sons, 1970, p. 920 et seq.

61 Article 33 of the Convention on Consular Relations.

origin.[62] The consul, protected by the state due to their official position,[63] is exempt from entry in foreigners' registers or residence permits[64] and enjoys allowances or remuneration exemptions[65] for personal benefits.[66]

5.9 Facilities for the Consular Posts

The general obligation of the receiving state is to provide every possible facility for the functioning of consular posts.[67] Within these provisions, the sending state is entitled to:

(a) Utilize its national flag, coat-of-arms, and emblems[68] within the consular building, the consul's residence and his means of transport used for business service-related purposes.[69]
(b) Assist in securing suitable accommodation for the consular authority and the consul's residence.[70]
(c) Exempt consular premises and the consul's residence from taxes and fees of any nature.[71]
(d) Allow freedom of movement within the territory, subject to the laws and regulations of the host country.[72]
(e) Collect any dues and fees to which it is entitled according to the regulations of the sending state.
(f) Permit and safeguard the freedom of communication of the consular post for official purposes, such as communication with governments and other consular posts.[73] However, unauthorized installation and use of a radio transmitter without the consent of the receiving state are prohibited.[74]

[62] Article 35(3) of the Convention on Consular Relations. See K. Efstathiadis, International Law, op. cit., p. 308 et seq. (in Greek).
[63] Article 64 of the Convention on Consular Relations.
[64] Article 65 of the Convention on Consular Relations.
[65] Article 66 of the Convention on Consular Relations.
[66] Article 67 of the Convention on Consular Relations.
[67] Article 28 of the Convention on Consular Relations.
[68] Article 29 (1) of the Convention on Consular Relations.
[69] Article 29 (2) of the Convention on Consular Relations.
[70] Article 30 of the Convention on Consular Relations.
[71] Article 32 of the Convention on Consular Relations.
[72] Article 34 of the Convention on Consular Relations.
[73] Article 35 of the Convention on Consular Relations.
[74] Article 35 (1) of the Convention on Consular Relations.

Paraguay's appeal was based on alleged violations of Articles 5 and 36(1, b) of the Vienna Convention on Consular Relations by the United States. They also contested the application of procedural rules conflicting with the United States' international obligations, as Breard was not informed of the Paraguayan prisoner's existence, lacked access to information regarding his rights, including translation assistance, and faced challenges understanding differences in the penal systems of both countries.

Following the court's ruling, US Secretary of State Madeleine Albright urged Virginia's Governor to postpone Breard's execution pending the Court's decision. Albright's letter acknowledged the gravity of Breard's crime while emphasizing her responsibility to safeguard American citizens abroad. Despite interpreting the Court's interim measures as nonbinding advice, the United States expressed its commitment to comply with the Vienna Convention on Consular Relations[85] in the future in an official apology issued after the Supreme Federal Court rejected Breard's habeas corpus petition on April 14, leading to his execution that afternoon.

Consequently, although initially expressing a desire to pursue the case even after Breard's execution, Paraguay withdrew its appeal and requested the case's removal from the docket, which the International Court of Justice granted on November 10, 1998.

5.9.1.2 Case LaGrand (Germany v. USA)

Facts

The facts in the case of LaGrand were similar. In 1982, Arizona state authorities arrested two German citizens, Karl and Walter LaGrand, for armed robbery resulting in the death of one individual and severe injury to another. Despite their German citizenship, and their respective ages of 4 and 5 years upon arrival in America, neither brother had undergone naturalization. Both were subsequently tried and sentenced to capital punishment without being informed by US authorities of their entitlement to contact their consular representatives pursuant to the Vienna Convention on Consular Relations. By 1992, all available legal remedies had been exhausted to no avail, and after federal courts, as seen in the Breard case, cited procedural default as grounds for not addressing their plea regarding the breach of their consular protection rights, political negotiations ensued in a bid to forestall execution, albeit unsuccessfully.[86] Despite extensive diplomatic efforts by the German government, Karl LaGrand was executed via lethal injection on February 24, 1999, while his brother was slated for execution on March 3, 1999.

[85] Letter of Madeleine K. Albright, US Secretary of State, to James Gilmore III, Governor of Virginia, April 13, 1998.

[86] Both President R. Herzog and Chancellor G. Schroeder of the Federal Republic of Germany addressed the President of the United States. The Secretary of State and the Minister of Justice also had a say in their counterparts, while Germany's diplomatic mission appeared before the Charité Commission and the Governor of Arizona himself.

The Judgment of the International Court of Justice

On March 2, Germany exercised diplomatic protection on behalf of its citizen by filing a suit against the United States before the International Court of Justice. Germany contended that the United States had violated the Vienna Convention on Consular Relations and sought reparations for the execution of Karl LaGrand, which was carried out in contravention of the nation's international obligations. Germany also sought restoration of the status quo ante in Walter LaGrand's case.[87]

Given the imminent execution of LaGrand, Germany, on the day following the filing of its application, petitioned the Court to recommend interim measures proprio motu, citing insufficient time for a thorough examination of its petition. The US trial attorney countered, arguing that such a suggestion would constitute unwarranted interference with the US judicial system, particularly at the eleventh hour, as there was a possibility that Germany's demands lacked substantive merit owing to the absence of a hearing.

In its interim judgment of March 3, 1999 (Interim Measures), the Court, acting proprio motu[88] and unanimously, directed the United States to take all necessary steps to halt Walter LaGrand's execution pending the Court's final ruling. The Court further clarified that the grant of interim measures does not hinge on a conclusive and unequivocal determination of its jurisdiction to adjudicate on the merits but is contingent upon the provisions cited by the parties providing prima facie jurisdiction to the Court. In this instance, both states were signatories to the Optional Protocol on the Compulsory Settlement of Disputes, which confers mandatory jurisdiction upon the International Court of Justice in matters concerning the interpretation and application of the Vienna Convention on Consular Relations. The Court also, in an obiter dictum in the Order for Interim Measures, stipulated that "the international responsibility of a State is engaged by the action of the competent organs and authorities acting in that State, whatever they may be."[89]

The Court unanimously decreed the following interim measures:

(a) The United States must take all available measures to prevent the execution of Mr. LaGrand in the present case and inform the Court of the actions taken to comply with the judgment.
(b) The US government must transmit this decision to the Governor of Arizona.

Regrettably, Mr. LaGrand was executed later that same day via gas chamber.

In contrast to the Paraguayan government, the German government expressed a desire for the case to proceed unhindered despite the demise of its citizen. In its final

[87] Reestablishment of the previous situation.

[88] "On the Court's own volition." On its own initiative the Court may, in exceptional and particularly urgent cases, order interim measures without hearing each other's submissions.

[89] Madeleine Albright sent a letter to the Court in which she claimed that due to the federal system the Washington government was unable to intervene in proceedings that, under the US constitution, belong to the jurisdiction of the individual States. See E. Roukounas, Public International Law, fourth ed., Nomiki Bibliothiki, Athens, 2021, p. 36.

judgment, the Court ruled that the United States had breached its obligations under Articles 36(1)(b) and 36(2) of the Vienna Convention on Consular Relations. Furthermore, the International Court of Justice clarified, for the first time in its judgment, that provisional measures are legally binding and not merely recommendations to states, interpreting Article 41 of the Statute of the International Court of Justice in harmony with the Vienna Convention on the Law of Treaties[90] in order to seek an interpretation aligned with the aims and objectives of the Statute. Additionally, it underscored that the parties' obligation to comply, as articulated in Article 94(1) of the UN Charter, extends beyond final judgments to interim measures.[91]

Transitioning to the crux of the dispute, the Court affirmed that, pursuant to Article 36(1) of the Vienna Convention on Consular Relations, consular officers must be afforded the liberty to communicate with nationals of the accrediting state. Furthermore, authorities of the host state are obliged to promptly notify the consular authorities of the detainee's nationality upon arrest, if desired. Consular officials are then entitled to visit the detainee and facilitate their access to legal representation. The Court determined that this provision confers an individual right, which, if violated, may be invoked by the detaining state's nationality before the Court, as in this instance, by Germany. The Court further opined that procedural default, in itself, does not constitute a violation of Article 36. However, issues arise when this procedural rule precludes a detained individual from contesting their conviction based on Article 36(1) due to the failure of competent authorities to promptly notify them of their rights, thereby hindering their acceptance of consular protection. Consequently, the Court concluded that, in the LaGrand brothers' cases, it is evident that the United States breached the Vienna Convention on Consular Relations and the Interim Measures Decision.

It is apparent that the issues discussed in the aforementioned cases have been of profound sensitivity and significance, sparking intense scholarly interest and numerous publications around the world.[92]

[90] Articles 31(1) and 33(4) of the Vienna Convention on the Law of Treaties (1969).

[91] K. Antonopoulos, The resolution of disputes by the International Court of Justice of the United Nations, Case-law & Practice, second edition, Ant. N. Sakkoulas, Athens – Komotini, 2007, pp. 143–146 (in Greek).

[92] See, in addition to bibliographical indications X. Dipla—E. Doussis, The International Cour of Justice of the United Nations, Volume II, Summary of the Court of Justice 1980–2000, op. cit. (in Greek), C. Schultze, Jurisprudence of the International Court of Justice: Order issued in the Case concerning the Vienna Convention on Consular Relations (Paraguay v. United States of America), http://www.ejil.org/journal/vol9/No4/sr.2.html. Downloaded on 2.8.2003 (EJI Vol. 9, No. 4 (1998)), M.F. Tinta, Due process and the right to life in the context of the Vienna Convention on Consular Relations: Arguing the LaGrand case, http://www.ejil.org/journal/vol2/No2/index.html (published in EJIL Vol. 12, No. 2 (2001)), C.J. Tams, Consular assistance and rights and remedies: Comments on the ICJ's Judgment in the LaGrand case, http://www.ejil.org/journal/vol3/No5/sr.pdf (published in EJIL Vol. 13, No. 5 (2002)), M. K. Addo, Vienna Convention on Consular Relations (Paraguay v. United States of America) ("Breard") and Lagrand (Germany v. United States of America), applications for provisional measures, ICLQ Vol. 48, No. 3 (1999),

5.9.1.3 Avena and Other Mexican Nationals (Mexico v. USA)

Mexico initiated an appeal against the United States at the International Court of Justice on January 9, 2003, in the case of Avena and Other Mexican Nationals. This appeal was prompted by the disputed provision of the Convention on Consular Relations pertaining to 51 Mexican citizens facing the death penalty in the United States. With the imminent execution of three of the convicted Mexicans (César Roberto Fierro, Reyna Roberto Moreno Ramos, Osvaldo Torres Aguilera), and following the request for interim measures, the International Court of Justice issued an order calling on the United States to suspend the execution of the sentences until the final judgment of the Court. As in previous cases, the International Court of Justice emphasized that the issues at hand did not concern the competence of federal states to impose the death penalty for serious crimes, nor did it function as a secondary criminal court. Furthermore, it noted that appropriate interim measures did not infringe upon the sovereign right of the United States to define and operate its criminal justice system.[93]

Subsequently, based on the final judgment in Avena v. USA, the government of President George H.W. Bush notified the UN Secretary-General in 2005 of its decision to withdraw from the Optional Protocol.[94] The United States ratified the

---

pp.673–681, W. J. Aceves, The Vienna Convention on Consular Relations: a study of rights, wrongs, and remedies, V.J.T.L. Vol. 31, No. 2 (1998), pp.257–324, J.J. Paust, Breard and treaty-based rights under the Consular Convention, AJIL Vol.92, No. 4 (1998), pp.691–697, M. Pinto, De la protection diplomatique à la protection des droits de l' homme, RGDIP Vol.106, No. 3 (2002), pp.513–548, Z. Deen-Raczmány, Diplomatic protection and the LaGrand case, LJIL Vol.15, No. 1 (2002), pp.87–103, S. Babcock, The role of international law in United States death penalty cases, LJIL Vol.15, No. 1 (2002), pp.367–387, J.L. Weinman, The clash between U.S. criminal procedure and the Vienna Convention on Consular Relations: an analysis of the International Court of Justice decision in the LaGrand case, American University International Law Review Vol. 17, No. 4 (2002), pp.857–904, M. Mennecke, Towards the humanization of the Vienna Convention of Consular Rights: The LaGrand case before the International Court of Justice, GYIL Vol. 44 (2001), pp.430–468, J. Fitzpatrick, The unreality of international law in the United States and the LaGrand case, YJIL Vol.27, No. 2 (2002), pp.427–433, J. Quigley, LaGrand: a challenge to the U.S. judiciary, YJIL Vol. 27, No. 2 (2002), pp. 435–440, W.A. Schabas, The ICJ ruling against the United States: is it really about the death penalty?, YJIL Vol. 27, No. 2 (2002), pp.445–452, C. Tams, Recognizing guarantees and assurances of non-repetition: LaGrand and the law of state responsibility, YJIL Vol. 27, No. 2 (2002), pp.441–444.

[93] See P.H.F. Bekker, Consular notification and the death penalty: The World Court's Provisional Measures, in Avena and Other Mexican Nationals (Mexico v. United States), The American Society of International Law – ASIL Insights (April 2003), http://www.asil.org/insights/insigh104.htm

[94] The communication read as follows:

"Dear Mr. Secretary-General:

I have the honor on behalf of the government of the United States of America to refer to the Optional Protocol to the Vienna Convention on Consular Relations Concerning the Compulsory Settlement of Disputes, done at Vienna April 24, 1963.

This letter constitutes notification by the United States of America that it currently withdraws from the aforesaid Protocol. As a consequence of this withdrawal, the United States will no longer recognize the jurisdiction of the International Court of Justice reflected in that Protocol.

Sincerely,

Condoleezza Rice"

Optional Protocol in 1969 as a commitment to protect American citizens worldwide, exercising this right in the case of 52 American diplomats held hostage in Tehran against Iran. The Protocol enables the International Court of Justice to adjudicate disputes between states concerning the interpretation of the Vienna Convention on Consular Relations, including Article 36 on consular assistance. However, in cases where the United States was found to violate this provision and faced subsequent convictions, the government formally withdrew, citing that the ICJ rulings were detrimental to the proper functioning of the national criminal justice system.[95]

5.9.1.4 Case Jadhav (India v. Pakistan)

Facts

On July 17, 2019, the International Court of Justice rendered its judgment in the Jadhav case. In essence, this case involves an Indian citizen named Kulbhushan Sudhir Jadhav, who had been detained by Pakistani authorities since March 3, 2016.[96] On March 25, 2016, Pakistan released a video featuring Mr. Jadhav confessing to espionage and acts of terrorism, subsequently informing the UN Security Council. Mr. Jadhav's trial commenced on September 21, 2016, in the General Military Court of Pakistan, and he was granted an additional 3 weeks to prepare his defense. Despite repeated requests from the Indian government to ensure Mr. Jadhav's right to pre-start protection, all requests were denied by Pakistani authorities.[97]

The Judgment of the International Court of Justice

India appealed to the International Court of Justice against Pakistan,[98] simultaneously requesting interim measures under the Vienna Convention on Consular Relations, asserting that Pakistan had deprived its citizen of the protection mandated by the Convention. The Court determined that it had jurisdiction under the Optional Protocol on the Compulsory Settlement of Disputes to the Vienna Treaty. It found

[95] In any case, it is worth noting that the United States withdrew the recognition of the jurisdiction of the International Court of Justice as early as 1986 in connection with US military and paramilitary activities on the territory of Nicaragua (Nicaragua v. USA). See St. Perrakis, The International Court of Justice of the United Nations, Detections of a Judicial Route in the Peaceful Settlement of International Disputes, Ant. N. Sakkoulas, Athens-Komotini, 2001.

[96] According to India, Mr. Jadhav was abducted from Iran where he was staying for work purposes after he retired from the Indian Navy. On the other hand, the Pakistani government accused Mr. Jadhav of espionage and terrorism and therefore arrested him at the time of illegal entry into the territory of the present Pakistan. At the time of his arrest, the Pakistani authorities found that he was in possession of a false passport.

[97] Pakistan testified that it had asked India for help in the investigation without any response.

[98] ICJ, Application Instituting Proceedings, Jadhav Case (India v. Pakistan), 8 May 2017. See for the analysis of the case, M. Vagias and M. Dib, If he so requests? The Jadhav Judgement and Article 36(1)b of the Vienna Convention on Consular Relations', EvrYIEL vol.3, 2021, pp. 38–108.

India's appeal admissible[99] and proceeded to examine its merits. Pakistan argued that the bilateral agreement concluded with India in 2008 constituted a lex specialis, precluding the application of the Vienna Convention. However, the Court deemed it a supplementary subsequent agreement that did not negate obligations arising from the Vienna Treaty. Moreover, the Court held that by failing to inform Jadhav without delay of his rights under Article 36(1)(b) of the Treaty, Pakistan breached its international obligations and bore international responsibility. The Court further ruled that Pakistan was obligated to promptly inform Indian consular authorities of its citizen's situation and had deprived India of its right to contact, visit, and arrange legal representation for Mr. Jadhav. Consequently, the Court ordered that Mr. Jadhav be immediately informed to enable Indian authorities to contact him, demanded Pakistan reconsider his conviction and sentence (which Pakistan may choose to comply with), and suspended the sentence.[100]

5.10 Privileges and Immunities of Consular Officers

Consular officers, akin to diplomatic agents, enjoy immunities and privileges[101] within the receiving state to facilitate the smooth and effective discharge of their duties. These prerogatives serve the interests of both the consular post and the sending state, albeit at the expense of curtailing the sovereign rights of the receiving state. Concurrently, consular officers are bound to abide by the laws and regulations of the host state and refrain from interfering in its internal affairs.[102]

The nature and extent of the privileges and immunities granted to consuls are contingent upon the functional role they fulfil in interstate relations—a role typically more circumscribed than that of diplomats, characterized by a special and localized scope.[103] Specifically, consular officers are recognized to possess inviolability,[104] immunity from legal proceedings concerning acts performed in the course of their consular mission, and exemption from taxes[105] and customs duties.[106] They are also relieved from obligations such as registration in official aliens registries or the

[99] Rejected Pakistan's complaints concerning the abuse of procedure and the abuse of rights by Jadhav.

[100] F. Baetens, The International Court of Justice renders its judgement in the Jadhav case (India v. Pakistan), EJIL: Talk! 18 July 2019? R. Buchan, I. Navarrete, The Jadhav Judgement: Espionage, Carve-Outs and Customary Exceptions, EJIL: Talk! August 8, 2019.

[101] Article 53 of the Convention on Consular Relations.

[102] Article 55 of the Convention on Consular Relations.

[103] Articles 28 and 43 (1) of the Convention on Consular Relations.

[104] An exception to the rule on staff inviolability of consular officers is where they commit a serious crime and are convicted by a competent judicial authority. See Article 41 of the Convention on Consular Relations.

[105] Article 49 of the Convention on Consular Relations.

[106] Article 50 of the Convention on Consular Relations.

procurement of residence permits[107] under the social security scheme. Furthermore, they are not required to obtain work permits[108] and are exempt from testifying in court as witnesses.[109]

5.11 Termination of Consular Functions

Consular functions shall be terminated for a number of reasons, starting with the notification by the sending state that his functions were terminated, the withdrawal of the exequatur document by the receiving state, notification by the receiving state that has ceased to consider him as a member of the consular staff.[110] Further, termination occurs by decision to terminate consular relations by one of the two states, or because of war.[111] In this case, the sending state shall entrust the custody of the premises, the archives, and the protection of its nationals to another state, provided that the receiving state also consents.[112] The local authorities should not touch the consular archives, until peace is concluded. According to the Convention, the termination of diplomatic relations does not automatically entail the termination of consular relations.[113]

Dr. Dr.h.c Paraskevi (Paroula) Naskou-Perraki, ret. Professor of International Law and International Organizations, Department of International and European Studies, University of Macedonia, Thessaloniki (1994–2014). She has served for 20 years at the Law Faculty of Democritus University of Thrace, in Komotini (1974–1993). She has been teaching International Law, International Organizations, Diplomatic Law and Human Rights in different universities in Greece, Europe, and the USA, recently at the Masters Programme "On Human Rights and Migration Studies," University of Macedonia (2019–2025). Founder and Director of the UNESCO Chair on Intercultural Policy for an Active Citizenship and Solidarity (2004–2014), she was a representative of the Greek Ministry of Foreign Affairs at the Conference held in Brussels (2003) and then Tehran (2004) between Iran and the EU on Human Rights and in 2003 at the conference held in Beijing between China and the EU on Human Rights. She was awarded as Dr. Honoris Causa from the Faculty of Law and History of Neofit Rilski University in Blagoevgrad, Bulgaria, in 2003. She was member of the Scientific Committee of International Law at the Ministry of Foreign Affairs (2016–2019), President of the board of the Institute of Balkan Studies (2019–2021), Director of the Hellenic Institute for UN Affairs (2017–), Vice-President of the Board of the UNESCO Center for the Women and Peace in the Balkans (2012–2020), Secretary General of the board of CIEEL, Secretary General of the Kalliopi Koufa Foundation for the promotion of International Law and the protection of Human Rights, (2015–2019). Ad Hoc Judge of the European Court of Human Rights (ECtHR) (2011–2013), Awarded with the title F.U.N.—Friend of the United Nations for her contribution in the dissemination of the work of the Organization

[107] Article 46 of the Convention on Consular Relations.

[108] Article 48 of the Convention on Consular Relations.

[109] Article 44 of the Convention on Consular Relations.

[110] Article 25 of the Convention on Consular Relations.

[111] See K. Efstathiadis, International Law, op. cit., p. 303.

[112] Article 45 of the Convention on Consular Relations.

[113] Article 2(3) of the Convention on Consular Relations.

through the UN Models (2007). Since 2016 she has been responsible for the "Students as Diplomats," an annual Model UN addressed to Greek high school students, on issues concerning the work of UN Human Rights Committees. Editor in Chief of Evrigenis Yearbook of International and European Law, published by Ant. N. Sakkoulas, Athens (issues 2019–2023) she has published in Greek, English, and French.

Special Aspects of the Law of Diplomatic Relations

6

Paraskevi Naskou-Perraki

Abstract

The Convention on Special Missions and its accompanying Optional Protocol are presented in this chapter. Special missions involve diplomatic agents and experts negotiating matters such as military or border demarcations. Also, the Convention on the Representation of States in their Relations with International Organizations of a Universal Character, where international organizations enjoy a number of privileges and immunities in the territory of the member states on the basis of the operating principle as well as the protection of diplomatic agents. Also, the diplomatic bag not accompanied by a diplomatic courier.

6.1 Special Missions

In contemporary international relations, states regularly dispatch groups of officials or diplomats abroad for specific matters and within a limited time frame, known as "special missions." This phenomenon constitutes ad hoc diplomacy, referring to missions of two or more states convening within the framework of international conferences or meetings, typically addressing issues of high political significance or specialization.[1]

[1] Ph. Cahier, Bilan et perspectives de la codification—Rapport général, Société Française pour le Droit International, La codification du droit international, Colloque d'Aix-en-Provence (Actes du XXXIIe colloque de la Société Française pour le Droit International qui s'est tenu à l'Université d'Aix-Marseille les 1er, 2 et 3 Octobre 1998), Pedone, Paris, 1999, pp. 266–267.

P. Naskou-Perraki (✉)
Department of International Studies, University of Macedonia, Thessaloniki, Greece
e-mail: perraki@uom.edu.gr

P. Naskou-Perraki (ed.), *Contemporary Diplomatic and Consular Relations*,
https://doi.org/10.1007/978-3-031-99243-8_6

be drawn up worldwide since the early 1960s.[18] Similar international conventions have since been established at a regional level.[19]

The Convention garnered the required 22 ratifications for entry into force, albeit at a concerning slow pace, on February 20, 1977, almost 3 years after it was signed. Despite its initial lukewarm reception, in the years that followed the Convention eventually gathered a rare international consensus. Within a decade, the number of states ratifying it surged from 106 (2003) to 176 (2013), and today, it stands at 180 states (2022)[20]—thus, the Convention approaches universality and is particularly successful from this perspective.

The Convention is a relatively short text, consisting of a Preamble and 20 Articles. It introduces a new legal term, "internationally protected persons," which includes state officials in international relations—heads of state, prime ministers, ministers of foreign affairs, and their family members when in a foreign state (Art. 1§1a of the Convention)—as well as representatives or officials of states or intergovernmental organizations and their family members (Art. 1§1b).

According to the Convention, criminal offenses shall include:

- A murder, kidnapping, or other attack upon the person or liberty of an internationally protected person (Art. 2§1a)
- A violent attack upon the official premises, the private accommodation, or the means of transport (Art. 2§1b)
- A threat (Art. 2§1c), an attempt (Art. 2§1d), or the participation in the aforementioned criminal acts, which should be formalized as crimes under the state party's internal law (Art. 2§1e) shall make these crimes punishable by appropriate penalties that take into account their grave nature (Art. 2§2)

The Convention reiterates the relevant provisions of earlier international conventions for the suppression of terrorism, such as the Hague Convention for the Suppression of Unlawful Seizure of Aircraft (1970) and the Montreal Convention for the Suppression of Unlawful Acts against the Safety of Civil Aviation (1971), aiming to eliminate impunity.[21]

The criminal jurisdiction of the state is based on three criteria:

[18] The Tokyo Convention of 1963 on Offenses and Certain Other Acts Committed on Board Aircraft, the Hague Convention of 1970 for the Suppression of Unlawful Seizure of Aircraft, and the Montreal Convention of 1971 for the Suppression of Unlawful Acts against the Safety of Civil Aviation had preceded.

[19] Indicatively: Convention for the Prevention and Punishment of Acts of Terrorism Taking the Form of Crimes against Persons and Related Punishment that are of International Significance within the framework of the Organization of American States (February 2, 1971) and European Convention for the Suppression of Terrorism within the framework of the Council of Europe (November 10, 1976).

[20] United Nations Treaty Collection, https://treaties.un.org/pages/ViewDetails.aspx?src=TREATY&mtdsg_no=XVIII-7&chapter=18&clang=_en (Retrieved: June 28, 2024).

[21] H. F. Shamwell, Jr., Implementing the Convention on the Prevention and Punishment of Crimes against Internationally Protected Persons, Including Diplomatic Agents, Terrorism 6/4 (1983), p. 535.

(a) Location of the crime—i.e., the territory of the state where the crime was committed or the ship or aircraft registered in the state (Art. 3§1a),
(b) Nationality of the offender (Art. 3§1b), and
(c) Nationality of the victim (Art. 3§1c).

It should be noted that the above provisions have led to a change in national criminal law in states such as the United States of America, where extraterritorial criminal jurisdiction had previously been applied to a limited extent.[22]

The Convention provides that state parties are to cooperate both for the prevention (Art. 4) and the prosecution of crimes (Art. 5). It is governed by the general principle autdedere, autjudicare—i.e., suspects will either be tried before national courts or extradited for trial in another state (Art. 3§2 and Art. 6 et seq.).[23] These procedures are accompanied by safeguards to ensure a fair trial (Art. 8 et seq.).

The demand for effective protection of diplomats and their families is a constant concern of the international community, as the successive relevant UN General Assembly[24] resolutions show. It should be borne in mind that in the early 1980s the International Court of Justice was seized of the case of the American diplomats (Case of the United States Diplomatic and Consular Staff in Tehran/USA v. Iran)—one of the most severe cases of violation of diplomatic immunity in the entirety of the twentieth century.[25]

It should also be noted that the Convention on the Safety of United Nations and Associated Personnel (which had 95 state parties as of 2022)[26] and the most recent Optional Protocol of 2005 (with 33 state parties)[27] introduced new protective provisions for personnel of the global organization in military, police, political, and humanitarian operations.

During armed conflicts in Syria,[28] Libya,[29] and Pakistan,[30] serious attacks targeting embassies and diplomatic personnel were observed. These cases demonstrate that while international law does introduce protective regulations, procedures,

---

[22] H. F. Shamwell, ibid, p. 536.

[23] For commentary, S. E. Nahlik, Development of Diplomatic Law, op. cit., p. 328ff.

[24] See GA Res. 36/33, GA Res. 37/108, GA Res. 38/136, GA Res. 39/83, GA Res. 40/73, GA Res. 41/78, GA Res. 42/154, GA Res. 43/167, GA Res. 45/39, GA Res. 47/31, GA Res. 49/49.

[25] Ch. Dipla–E. Doussi, op. cit., pp. 7–8.

[26] Convention on the Safety of United Nations and Associated Personnel (New York, December 9, 1994), UNTS 2051, p. 363. Adopted by General Assembly resolution 49/59 (December 9, 1994). Entered into force on January 15, 1995. Text: UNTS 2051, p. 363ff. Greece ratified the Convention through Law No. 2584/1998, Greek Government Gazette A′ 45.

[27] Optional Protocol to the Convention on the Safety of United Nations and Associated Personnel (New York, December 8, 2005) A/RES/60/42. Enforced on August 19, 2010. Has not been ratified by Greece.

[28] N. Bakri, Crowds in Syria Attack U.S. and French Embassies, New York Times (July 11, 2011).

[29] S. Denyer, Foreign embassies attacked in Tripoli after NATO airstrike that kills Gaddafi son, grandchildren, Washington Post (May 1, 2011).

[30] See E. Bumiller & J. Perlez, Pakistan's Spy Agency Is Tied to Attack on U.S. Embassy, New York Times (September 22, 2011). The above cases are cited in P. Sean Morris, 'iSpy:

and measures to address violence,[31] there are deeper international sociopolitical factors that ultimately make the world dangerous for diplomats. The resilience of legal safeguards is tested by new forms of pervasive violence and blatant violations, necessitating adherence to the legal framework for the exercise of diplomatic functions.

6.3 Diplomacy and International Organizations

In the -mid-nineteenth century, the states of the time set up the first permanent international intergovernmental organizations (in simpler terms: IOs). This technical term in international law denotes permanent institutions established by interstate agreement, having their own institutions, and coordinating the actions of states in areas where it is expected that there will be common benefits. The first international organizations were developed in the fields of river navigation, telecommunications, and intellectual property. Since the beginning of the twentieth century, technological advances have resulted in the establishment of more and more new IOs in ever new subject areas, such as, for example, aviation, economics, trade, meteorology, and health.[32]

The two World Wars caused appalling human losses and damaged the institutional structure of international relations. After the end of World War I, the League of Nations, the International Labor Organization, and other IOs were established, but the widespread hostilities of World War II resulted in their discontinuation. After 1945, states reorganized the international institutional environment with the main objective of avoiding another major military conflict and promoting peaceful cooperation. In 1945, the United Nations Organization (UN, 1945) was established, the main purpose of which is to maintain international peace and security, as well as other international organizations with a global reach that operate successfully to this day. At the same time, international organizations were established operating at the continental level (e.g., the Council of Europe, 1949, and the IOs that evolved into today's European Union/EU, 1951) or at the regional level (e.g., today there are hundreds of international organizations, each of which is active in the specific field defined in its own statute, e.g., economy, telecommunications, trade, atomic energy, military defense, culture, immigration, agriculture, human rights, etc.).

The member states of intergovernmental organizations normally send permanent delegations to the headquarters of each organization whose work is of importance to

International Silent Conflicts, Cyber Warfare and Developments in International Diplomatic Law', http://ssrn.com/abstract=2168741 (Social Science Research Network).

[31] N. Zaikos, Considerations on the international legal regulation of war in the post-Cold War world, in K. Kentrotis (ed.), Twenty Years After the Fall of the Berlin Wall: Assessments and Prospects, I. Sideris, Athens, 2012, pp. 165 et seq.

[32] T. Gutner, International organizations in world politics. Sage, Los Angeles, 2017. J. Katz Cogan, I., Hurd & I. Johnstone, The Oxford Handbook of International Organizations. Oxford: University Press, Oxford, 2017.

Prerogatives of Consular Function 7

Stelio Campanale

Abstract

Traditionally, first the Legations and then the Embassies were the real hub and driving force behind international relations and relationships. However, the major economic and social upheavals that took place in the twentieth century profoundly affected international relations and the role of diplomacy.

The end of Soviet-style communism, and the dissolution of many governments and systems of satellite countries of the Soviet Union, has given rise, among many other phenomena, to growing mobility resulting from globalization. These events led to major phenomena of immigration, tourism, and trade.

This increasing mobility of people-citizens necessitates the presence of subjects-bodies of the State of which they are nationals, who can protect the interests of nationals of the State of nationality as well as of the State itself, within the limits allowed by international law; provide the citizens with assistance and rescue; perform administrative functions to the extent not prohibited by the rules of the country where such services are required; and promote the development of commercial, economic, cultural, and scientific relations. The existence of a more "citizen/tax-payer oriented" spirit of the international relations seems to appear from the differences in the list of functions of Diplomats and Consuls, made by the States Parties of the two Vienna Conventions, that give evidence of duties and services, which in terms of quantity and quality are particularly demanding for Consuls, in the interest and benefit of the citizens rather than of the sending State itself.

S. Campanale (✉)
Libera Università Mediterranea-LUM Giuseppe Degennaro, Casamassima - Bari, Italy

Universiteti Katolik "Zoja e KëshillittëMirë", Tirana, Albania
e-mail: scampanale@campanalelawfirm.com

P. Naskou-Perraki (ed.), *Contemporary Diplomatic and Consular Relations*,
https://doi.org/10.1007/978-3-031-99243-8_7

7.1 Birth and Evolution of the Consular Function

Traditionally, international relations, especially in times of peace, have been characterized primarily by the stationing of agents sent from one nation to another in order to safeguard the interests of their compatriots and national trade. These agents or delegates were persons whom the "Sovereign" of a nation kept, mainly in the ports and trading posts of a foreign country, to oversee the observance of the rights and privileges that the local Sovereign of that particular city or territory had granted to the subjects of the sending Sovereign and to exercise certain administrative and judicial functions (to judge disputes between foreign merchants of nationality of the agent/delegate appointing country) under the agreement concluded, to this extent, with that local Sovereign.

These subjects were called "Consules" but also, more rarely, named: telonari, bajuli, prepositi, seneschalli, priores mercatorum, seniores.

With the passing of the centuries and the increase in trade, merchants began to distrust the judges appointed by the various local rulers, who were often ignorant of both the language and the trade customs of those they had to judge, thus merchants obtaining from the rulers of certain towns and ports the privilege of electing their "own" judges.

This phenomenon was much more pronounced in the Middle East and the Southern Mediterranean, which, during and after the Crusades, would became the theatre of development of trades between West and East; later widespread to all, around Mediterranean, Muslim countries, which found their own benefit in fostering trade with the Western World, which, in turn, would have been reluctant to develop it without adequate guarantees.

The treaties or privileges by virtue of which many cities developed trade, organized fairs, and appointed consuls in Barbary coast countries (Morocco, Algeria, Tunisia) such as in Egypt, Syria, or Constantinople were, in the beginning, the result of negotiations undertaken and concluded by the single cities Authorities, directly and autonomously. But soon the relevant Monarchs ceased to be indifferent to the progress of trade and the financial flow it brought about and, consequently, decided to intervene in the appointment of Consuls; until Sovereigns became, more and more, the only ones who had the right to admit Consuls or to revoke and replace them.

As long as Consuls were appointed by the merchants of a city or by an ethnic community, they were nothing more than arbitrators whose public character resulted exclusively from the consent given to the exercise of their service by the local Sovereign. But, when the appointments of Consuls/arbitrators started to be made by the Sovereigns of subjects, who lived abroad and outside from their national kingdom, to solve disputes between those nationals but in a foreign territory ruled by a local King, it changed their nature to true judges.

This system of appointing Consuls spread rapidly, starting in the Middle Ages, among the various European Courts that elected Consuls in various cities, mostly port cities, in the Mediterranean and Baltic, and was justified by the need to guarantee a certain level of security for traders operating in foreign lands, who were exposed to frequent harassment just because they were strangers to a certain territory and its inhabitants, and the relevant rules and customs. The figure of the Consulates of the Sea, ad hoc bodies whose consuls-judges had the task of settling maritime law disputes, became widespread, particularly in Mediterranean ports. Among the best known are those of Barcelona and Venice, which in 1494 and 1599, respectively, collected in codifications the maritime customs of the time.

The establishment of Consuls was easy as it did not require the prior sending of a legate or other permanently operating diplomat, with all the costs it would have entailed.

The growth of trade and the opening of new maritime routes, a consequence of the discovery of America and other lands and continents, increased the prestige and consular functions, hand in hand with the assertion of the role of diplomacy.

During the nineteenth century, a debate arose in doctrine as to the legal status of the consular official and whether the Consul should be equated with the public minister, a term by which the diplomatic agent was also called in the nineteenth century. Some publicists of the time, including Bynckershoeck, Wicquefort and Rèal, denied this equation; contrary to others who starting from the consideration that consuls are public in character, the functions they perform must also be considered public.[1] Another aspect of the debate concerned the privileges and immunities that should be granted to them. In this regard, it can be said that the dominant thesis favored the full subjection of Consuls to the special protection of the customary law such as diplomatic agents; it recognized the privileges necessary to perform their duties and the right to exemption from local taxes; but, at the same time, it sanctioned the obligation to submit to local jurisdiction, especially when the Consuls were nationals of the receiving State.[2]

[1] Doctrinal positions were variously articulated. Bouchaud, in his Théorie des Traités, while not recognizing the consuls as public ministers, nevertheless places them under the protection and tutelage of the Law of Peoples. Moser, in his Essai sur le Droit des gens de l'Europe, recognizes the public character of consuls and considers them as public ministries, albeit of a lower order than the others. Both Martens, in his work Précis du Droit de gens moderne, and Kluber, in his Droit des gens moderne de l'Europe, share the inclination toward the thesis of the public nature of the consuls.

[2] On this point, see De Garden in his Complete Treatise on Diplomacy and Massé for whom: "Les Consules jouissent dans les pays où ils résident, des certains privilèges ou immunitès analogues à cuex des Ministres ou Ambassadeurs, quoique moins étendus. Comme les agents diplomatiques, ils sont sous tous les rapports politiques, placés sous la garantie du Droit des Gens, en ce qui touché la liberté et la sureté de leur personne, l'inviolabilité de leur chancelleries, l'exemption des taxes locales; mais sous tous les rapports purement civils, ils ne peuvent prétendre aux memes immunités. Comme ils ne sont pas envoyés représenter le souverain et la nation qui les délèguent, mais seulement pour protéger le commerce, et juger les commerçants, il n'y a pas de motif pour leur accorder le privilège de l'exterritorialité qui prend sa source relativement aux Ministres publics, précisément dans leur caractère de représentants de la Nation et de souverain...Les Consules, inviolables, politiquement parlant, en ce sens que le gouvernement près duquel ils résident , ne peut jamais les traiter comme ennemis, manquer aux égards dus à leur caractère, les arrêter pour des raisons politiques, restant soumis aux règles du Droit commun dans tous les autres cas et quand leur qualité de Consul n'est pas en cause."

Without prejudice to specific and different agreements contained in individual Treaties between States, Consuls were subject to the civil and criminal jurisdiction of the State in which they resided for the obligations they had contracted and any crimes they had committed. However, in the latter case, it was the practice, resulting from the rules of *comitas gentium*, to request the authorization of the sending State before commencing proceedings against the Consul.

Furthermore, the jurisdiction of the foreign Court was excluded if the actions at issue related to the performance of the Consul's functions and for which, therefore, there was a presumption that he had carried out an order or instructions from his government. In that case, the wrongs or offences of which the Consul was guilty would have to be remedied through diplomatic channels, as the Courts do not have jurisdiction over facts that concern relations between nations or judge the acts of Sovereigns or their agents.[3]

The application of jurisdictional immunity was more circumscribed in the case of the Consul being a citizen of the receiving State, since the acceptance of an appointment by a foreign government does not result in the loss of the nationality of a person and, therefore, of the rights but also of the duties that compliance with one's own national rules entails.

There is, therefore, no justification for any kind of asylum in the case of their violation, provided that it is committed not in the exercise of Consul specific functions.

More sensitive in this respect was the issue in the case of Legates and Ambassadors of the nationality of the country where the diplomatic mission was based. The doctrine was divided on whether accepting to be an agent of a foreign state automatically entailed the loss of person's original nationality.[4]

In the international practice of the time, an exception was the role of the Consul of the Western powers in the Ottoman Empire and within which, particularly, in the costal localities, the figure of the Consul had originally developed.

In fact, thanks to treaties concluded by the emperors and rulers of the Christian kingdoms with the various Sultans who had succeeded on the throne of the Sublime Porte, the Consuls were, almost in all respects, equated with the Legates, and therefore with the Ambassadors.

In this case, therefore, conventional diplomatic law, far from limiting itself to formally transposing what the custom of the time had consolidated concerning

[3]In this sense, the decision of the Court of Bordeaux of May 20, 1826, in which the Court declared that the French courts lacked jurisdiction to decide a dispute between Consul and Vice-Consul concerning the criterion for distributing consular income between them, since such disputes, even if one of the parties were of French nationality, relate to the exercise of consular functions in a foreign country, on behalf of a foreign government.

[4]For the two leading experts and scholars of diplomatic law of the nineteenth century who supported the thesis that an individual, by accepting the appointment of a public minister by a sovereign, fulfils the public functions delegated to him by the sovereign but does not abdicate his nationality, Bynckershoeck and Hubero: "he who appoints one of our subjects as ambassador, abandons his activity but not his person from our jurisdiction."

Consul jurisdictional function, placed Consuls on the same footing as Ambassadors both in terms of the accreditation procedure and in terms of identical prerogatives and treatment.

But only after the second half of the twentieth century, the States developed a new vision and advanced concept of the role and functions of Diplomats and Consuls, embodied and transfused over the 1961 and 1963 Conventions, regarding, respectively, Diplomatic and Consular relations, bringing very close togheter the significance of those relations, even if clarifying the distinction of roles and tasks.

In fact, the Preambles of the above-mentioned Conventions, to this regard, state:

- Vienna Convention on Diplomatic Relations (18/4/1961).

The States Parties to the present Convention;

Recalling that peoples of all nations from ancient times have recognized the status of diplomatic agents;

Having in mind the purposes and principles of the Charter of the United Nations concerning the sovereign equality of States, the maintenance of international peace and security, and the promotion of friendly relations among nations;

Believing that an international convention on diplomatic intercourse, privileges, and immunities would contribute to the development of friendly relations among nations, irrespective of their differing constitutional and social systems;

Realizing that the purpose of such privileges and immunities is not to benefit individuals but to ensure the efficient performance of the functions of diplomatic missions as representing States;

Affirming that the rules of customary international law should continue to govern questions not expressly regulated by the provisions of the present Convention.

- Vienna Convention on Consular Relations (24/4/1963).

The States Parties to the present Convention;

Recalling that consular relations have been established between peoples since ancient times;

Having in mind the purposes and principles of the Charter of the United Nations concerning the sovereign equality of States, the maintenance of international peace and security, and the promotion of friendly relations among nations;

Considering that the United Nations Conference on Diplomatic Intercourse and Immunities adopted the Vienna Convention on Diplomatic Relations, which was opened for signature on April 18, 1961;

Believing that an international convention on consular relations, privileges, and immunities would also contribute to the development of friendly relations among nations, irrespective of their differing constitutional and social systems;

Realizing that the purpose of such privileges and immunities is not to benefit individuals but to ensure the efficient performance of functions by consular posts on behalf of their respective States;

Affirming that the rules of customary international law continue to govern matters not expressly regulated by the provisions of the present Convention.

(l) extending assistance to vessels and aircraft mentioned in subparagraph (k) of this article, and to their crews, taking statements regarding the voyage of a vessel, examining and stamping the ship's papers, and, without prejudice to the powers of the authorities of the receiving State, conducting investigations into any incidents that occurred during the voyage, and settling disputes of any kind between the master, the officers, and the seamen insofar as this may be authorized by the laws and regulations of the sending State;
(m) performing any other functions entrusted to a consular post by the sending State, which are not prohibited by the laws and regulations of the receiving State or to which no objection is taken by the receiving State or which are referred to in the international agreements in force between the sending State and the receiving State.

A further argument in support of the view of a particular importance and relevance of the role of Consuls recognized by the contracting States is symbolized by the fact that the content of consular functions mentioned under point (a), (b), and (c) are almost identical to those of the diplomatic mission referred to points (b), (d), (e) of the 1961 Convention.

The increasing international mobility and expectations of citizen-voters/taxpayers toward the administrative organization of their country and the services that their government must provide for them leads States to open new consular posts, the costs of which, however, cannot easily be borne by all the countries, especially in times of economic crisis.

This is why there is either a gradual replacement of consular posts that are headed by Consules *missi* (in Latin, Career Consuls) with a Consules *electi* (in Latin, Honorary Consuls) headed ones or the direct opening of new consular posts headed by the latter, who, unlike the former, are not career officials but honorary officials without the right to remuneration, travel, or mission allowances.

Furthermore, the fact that Honorary Consuls are, usually, nationals of the receiving State and residents in the territorial context in which their consular district falls, means that the actions of local scope that consular duties require them to carry out are often performed much more effectively and efficiently than they could be by Consules missi. The Honorary Consuls introduction in the economic and social, local environment and the experience and knowledge of laws, regulations, administrative and bureaucratic apparatus and procedures, consequence of their being nationals of the receiving State and carrying on commercial or professional activities in that country, is beneficial to the sending State and its nationals.

The legal status of consular officials is governed:

By the Vienna Convention of April 24, 1963, on Consular Relations
By the rules that individual national legal systems have decided to adopt to list their functions and tasks and
By rules of customary international law[5]

[5]With regard to their functions, mention should be made of the existence of the European Convention on Consular Functions adopted by the Council of Europe in Paris on December 11, 1967, and entered into force on June 9, 2011. This Convention, in addition to being restricted

In particular, the Convention codified the status of consular officials and the treatment of them in Chapter II "Facilities, privileges and immunities relating to consular posts, career officers and other members of a consular post" and in Chapter III "Regime relating to Honorary Consul officers and the Consular post headed by such officers."

The listing of the privileges and immunities granted to consular officers largely recalls that one made in the Vienna Convention on Diplomatic Relations of 1961, further proving the rationale of these prerogatives as a means of ensuring the effective fulfilment of their functions through consular offices on behalf of their respective States, as the preamble to the 1963 Vienna Convention on Consular Relations states: "Realizing that the purpose of such privileges and immunities is not to benefit individuals but to ensure the efficient performance of functions by consular posts on behalf of their respective States."

Relevant custom and international practice have distinguished the privileges and other facilities between those reserved for Consules missi and those attributed to Consules electi.

This distinction is also reflected in the Vienna Convention of 1963, which in Chapter II, Section I entitled "Facilities, privileges and immunities relating to consular post" and Section II "Facilities, privileges and immunities relating to career consular officers and other members of a consular post" lists those granted to career consular officers and the consular post they head; while the subsequent chapter entitled "Regime relating to honorary consular officers and the consular post headed by such officers" make reference only to some of these facilities, privileges, and immunities (Art. 58 et seq. of the 1963 Vienna Convention on Consular Relations).

7.3 The Facilities Granted to the Exercise of Consular Office

The study of the articles of the 1963 Convention on Consular Relations and an analysis of the points in its preamble reveals the will of its signatory States to consider consular relations as an instrument for the development of friendly relations between nations, complementary to the diplomatic relations Convention expressly referred to in the preamble to the 1963 Convention. The latter, together with the one regulating diplomatic relations signed in Vienna in 1961, shares all the points of the respective preambles, with the exception of the reference to the diplomatic mission's status as a foreign state representation, which the consular post is not.

---

to the countries that are members of the Council of Europe, has only been ratified by a small number of States. Therefore, at present, it is not possible to detect its full operativeness and consequences. The Convention identifies certain rules concerning consular relations between states that have adopted it. It defines the general functions of consuls, which are to protect the rights and interests of the state to which they belong and its citizens. This Convention also sets out the rules concerning the establishment and delivery of documents, the administration of property, and the assistance of ships of the state's nationality.

Having said this, it follows logically from the above that the facilities, privileges, and immunities concerning consular officials, the consular office, and the members of its staff are, to a certain extent, common to those granted to diplomatic agents and the other persons referred to in Article 37 of the 1961 Vienna Convention on Diplomatic Relations, as well as sharing the justifications and purposes of their raison d'être. Like diplomats, consuls also benefit from a special treatment that has evolved and been consolidated over time, so as to become international practice. On the other hand, given that the role of officials and members of the consular post is different from that of the diplomatic agent and the staff of the diplomatic mission, since it is largely of a technical–administrative nature and requires them to interface with the local authorities, they benefit from more limited facilities, privileges, and immunities than those provided for by the Vienna Convention 1961 on diplomatic relations.

However, the listing of the privileges and immunities granted to consular officers largely recalls the main of them provided for by the Vienna Convention on Diplomatic Relations of 1961, further proving the rationale of these prerogatives as a means for enabling and facilitating the achievement of the Consul's tasks: "Realizing that the purpose of such privileges and immunities is not to benefit individuals but to ensure the efficient performance of functions by consular posts on behalf of their respective States," point "e," preambles to the 1963 Vienna Convention on Consular Relations.

The 1963 Convention distinguishes privileges and immunities between those granted Career Consuls and those conferred on Honorary Consuls : "Chapter III. Regime relating to honorary consular officers and consular posts headed by such officers" (Art. 58 et seq. of the 1963 Vienna Convention on Consular Relations).

By virtue of the principle *ne impediatur legatio*, the consular post and its head are granted by the receiving State those prerogatives necessary to assist the nationals of its sending State and to carry out, in the name of the Consul appointing State, its functions as provided for by Article 5 of the 1963 Vienna Convention on Consular Relations, customary law, international practice, and regulations resulting from bilateral agreements.[6]

The main privileges, facilities, and immunities are:

Consular officers and consular employees, as defined by the 1963 Convention, enjoy the same immunities as diplomatic agents, but exclusively for acts performed and facts committed in the exercise of their functions. Insofar as for a foreign State acting independently of its sovereign power, putting itself in the same way as a private citizen, the receiving State's jurisdiction over foreign State cannot be excluded since the latter carries out in the receiving State its acts iure privatorum, the Consul and consular employees do not enjoy immunity from prosecution and are required to answer as witnesses in the course of judicial or administrative proceedings for acts and facts extraneous to their functions. It should therefore be

[6] See, for example, art. 5, letter (m), art. 10, art. 11 n.3, art. 20 of the Vienna Convention on Consular Relation of 1963.

noted, with reference to the provisions of Article 43 of the Vienna Convention of April 24, 1963, on Consular Relations, that various national Court have affirmed the immunity in civil litigations is not applicable not only in the cases regarding workers with merely auxiliary duties but also in the case of employees with consular duties, where the claim is only for salary increases or wages or in any case of judicial complaint concerning exclusively pecuniary matters.

Unlike the diplomatic agent, whose criminal immunity is absolute, the career Consular officer enjoys, as an organ of a state abroad, personal inviolability when the criminal acts with which he is charged do not amount to "grave crimes"; except what above, the arrest or other form of restriction of personal freedom is enforceable in execution of a judicial decision of final effect. The career consular officer and the member of the consular post, headed by a career Consul, and members of their families forming part of their households are except from personal services and contributions, taxation, custom duties, baggage inspection save if there is a serious reason of concerns about the content, requisitions for military purposes.

Unlike what is stated for the residence of the diplomatic agent, the Consul's residence is not protected by inviolability and the same applies to his personal property. However, in international practice, the house of residence in the receiving State of Consules missi also benefits from protection by the local authorities, according to obligations stated by Art. 40 of the 1963 Convention.

The career consular officer and the member of the consular post, headed by a career Consul, and members of their families forming part of their households are except from tax and customs duties. This exemption is not unlimited, since have to be paid receiving State's taxes and duties on real estate owned personally by consular officers and employees and their families, inheritance taxes, taxes on income whose source is in the receiving State and on income for services and activities carried out in the receiving State, indirect taxes incorporated in the price of goods, and so on. By virtue of Article 50 of the 1963 Convention, the career Consul benefits from the duty-free allowance for the duration of his mission.

Not unlike diplomatic agents, consular officers and other members of the consular office are excluded from the personal sphere of application of the rules of the receiving State with regard to immigration of foreigners and with regard to social security obligations; with certain exceptions provided for in Articles 46, 47, and 48 of the 1963 Convention, and in particular for employees and consular officers who are nationals of the receiving State.

As for the facilities and privileges reserved for the premises of the consular office, the treatment is largely similar to that provided for the premises of the diplomatic mission, and in particular:

- Inviolability: prevents local authorities from accessing them without the prior approval of the head of the consular post or if access has been expressly requested by the latter;
- Protection against invasion and damage: measures to be adopted by the receiving State to ensure peaceful working and that the dignity of the consular post is not diminished;

- Tax immunity of consular posts headed by Consules missi, or by Consules electi but only if the premises are owned by the sending State;
- Inviolability of archives and documents;
- Right to display the flag of the sending State and national emblems such as the coat-of-arms, but having regard, however, to the applicable local laws, regulations, and usages;
- Guarantees and facilities with regard to communications from the consular office, to exchange of correspondence relating to consular posts and its functions, to use of consular bag. To this regard, however, there is a difference with respect to the diplomatic bag, which may not be opened or detained under any circumstances. If there are serious reasons to doubt the bag's compliance with the consular office's functions, the consular bag may be subject to a request for opening by the local authorities. If the request is not granted, the consular bag shall be returned to its place of origin.

Like diplomatic bodies, consular officers are subject to rules that not only grant favorable treatment but also lay down specific duties.

In particular:

- Consular seat may not be used in a manner incompatible with the performance of consular duties;
- If other offices are located in the same building as the consular post, they must be clearly separated from the premises intended for the consular post;
- Consular officers and any person receiving special treatment related to consular status have a duty to comply with the laws and regulations of the receiving State;
- Staff employed in the technical and administrative services of a consular office (so-called consular employees) and members of the service staff as well as their family members are not entitled to the privileges and immunities if they are engaged in a private gainful activity during their stay at the consular post;
- Consular officers and any person receiving special treatment related to consular status are prohibited from interfering with the internal affairs of the receiving State. This specific duty, however, is not interpreted uniformly across the different national legal systems. The event that an honorary Consul, who is a national of the receiving State, may run for and be elected to a political party, so as to hold a position in government bodies or in the opposition, at national or local level, is a matter of debate. Although the right to stand as a candidate is constitutionally guaranteed to all the nationals of the receiving State including, therefore, the honorary Consul citizen of the receiving State, the fact that consul officers are an international relations body, occasionally expressing their appointing State policy advice, could be a source of misunderstanding or concerns as to the capacity in which the Consul is expressing a possible reservation or is voicing criticism concerning conducts of receiving State govern, detrimental to the interests of nationals of sending State or of the sending State itself, as for Art. 5, letters (a), (e), (i), where elected to a political role.

Regarding the treatment of Consules electi, as already mentioned, it partly differs from that granted to career Consuls (Consules missi), due to the fact that the latter are fully-fledged officials of the sending State structure and bureaucratic apparatus, being employees of the sending State; unlike honorary Consuls, who are honorary public officials, carry out professions or private activities from which they derive their livelihood and, in most cases, are nationals and residents of the receiving State.

With regard to status of Public Official of the honorary consul officer should be emphasized and pointed out that, depending on the functions exercised, especially those referred to in letters (d), (f), (j), (k), (l) of Article 5 of the Convention on Consular Relations, Consuls have the status of Public Official, since they exercise an administrative task; or even judicial public function in the case referred to in letter (l) of Article 5: "... and settling disputes of any kind between the master, the officers and the seamen insofar as this may be authorized by the laws and regulations of the sending State."

Indeed, when an honorary consular officer:

- Issues passports and travel documents to nationals of the sending State, and visas or appropriate documents to persons wishing to travel to the sending State (Art. 5, lett. d);
- Acts as notary and civil registrar and in capacities of a similar kind, and performing certain functions of an administrative nature, provided that there is nothing contrary thereto in the laws and regulations of the receiving State (Art. 5, lett. f);
- Transmits judicial and extrajudicial documents or executing letters rogatory or commissions to take evidence for the courts of the sending State in accordance with international agreements in force or, in the absence of such international agreements, in any other manner compatible with the laws and regulations of the receiving State (Art. 5, lett. j);
- Exercises rights of supervision and inspection provided for in the laws and regulations of the sending State in respect of vessels having the nationality of the sending State, and of aircraft registered in that State, and in respect of their crews (Art. 5, lett. k);
- Extends assistance to vessels and aircraft mentioned in subparagraph (k) of this article, and to their crews, taking statements regarding the voyage of a vessel, examining and stamping the ship's papers, and, without prejudice to the powers of the authorities of the receiving State, conducting investigations into any incidents that occurred during the voyage, and settling ... (Art. 5, lett. l);
- Performs an administrative function governed by provisions of public law and authoritative acts, pursuant to which they form and express the will of the Public Administration or contribute to its performance through authoritative or certifying powers[7]

[7]To be considered, to this extent, activities such as (1) the issuing of Nulla Osta, needed for celebrating marriages and (2) the issuing of a permanent residence certificate in the receiving State, needed for the permanent discharge from military service by the military Authorities of the sending State.

7.4 Beginning and End of Consular Immunities

As with diplomatic status, the starting point for the acquisition of consular status, for the purposes of granting the above-mentioned prerogatives, is identified with the moment at which the consular officer crosses the border of the receiving State, provided that the necessary formalities to establish that the consular officer is a "persona grata" of the State have been fulfilled beforehand.

As provided for by the Vienna Convention of 1961 on Diplomatic Relations and by international practice, also for the Vienna Convention of 1963 on Consular Relations, the final term of the facilities, privileges, and immunities of the consular post member is his departure from the territory of the receiving State and, if this does not coincide with the end of his duties, a reasonable period of time for him to prepare his departure, which in that case will be granted to him.

Also in consular law, as in diplomatic law, there is no *ius legationis* provided for by international law, so it is the agreement between the States that constitutes the legal basis of the obligation for the receiving State to accept the consular officer, as well as the subjective right of the other State to do the same (Art. 2, Vienna Convention of 1961 on Diplomatic Relations and Art. 2, Vienna Convention of 1963 on Consular Relations).

The special benefits enjoyed by consular officials as well as diplomatic agents, whether working in missions abroad or in international organizations, are considered to be ad personam treatments, as the consular official and the diplomatic agent are qualified as organs of the sending State; accordingly, these prerogatives cease with: the end of the period of employment, or the completion of mandate in the function with the sending State, or the withdrawal of the *exequatur*, or the notification by the receiving State to the sending State that the receiving State has ceased to consider him as member of consular staff or has refused to renew the *exequatur* after its term.

Since Diplomats or Consuls are no longer organs of the sending State, they will not enjoy their respective status and, consequently, will revert to being mere foreigners in the territory of the receiving State, if they decide to stay in the receiving State, subject to the laws relating to the treatment of foreigners.

Furthermore, there can be several causes for the termination of the privileges of a diplomatic agent and consular official. Some pertain to the person holding the function, others to the State itself.

As far as the State is concerned, the main causes are the loss of State sovereignty and the extinction of the State itself.

---

sending State in respect of the exercise of consular functions. Article 67—Exemption from personal services and contributions. The receiving State shall exempt honorary consular officers from all personal services and from all public services of any kind whatsoever and from military obligations such as those connected with requisitioning, military contributions, and billeting.

In the consular sphere, the most common are the closure of the consular office due to the decision in this regard of the sending State, the outbreak of a state of war, the consequences of the reorganization of the sending State consular network, the breakdown of consular relations between sending and receiving States; it should be emphasized in this regard that, according to Article 2, para. 3, the breakdown of diplomatic relations does not automatically entail the breakdown of consular relations.

In the subjective perspective of the individual organ, the status of diplomatic or consul ceases due to death, revocation, resignation, retirement, and assignment to another task of the person holding the seat.

With regard to consuls and consular officers, it may be noted that the rules of general international law grant all special treatment from the moment they are invested with the mission and throughout the course of their mandate until its end, whatever the cause.

Unlike Consules missi, whose stay in a given seat or performance of a specific tasks is only a part of their career path, Consules electi are appointed to the office, by established practice, for life. In recent years, however, the practice of limiting the appointment to a specific period of time has become widespread, at the end of which the sending State will submit a request to the Ministry of Foreign Affairs of the receiving State to renew the exequatur for a further 5 years and so on. This implies that both consular immunities and all treatment legally commence at the end of the accreditation procedure carried out by the receiving State, with the granting of the exequatur to the official of the sending State or to the person who is a national of the receiving State if he is an honorary Consul.

There may, however, be special conditions that transcend the rule of granting privileges and immunities.

This is the case if the Consul is present in the territory of the receiving State:

- Pending the delivery of the exequatur but from the moment when he enters on his duties with the consular post;
- Or at a later date, following the expiry of the period of validity of the exequatur issued to the honorary Consul and pending the issuance of a new exequatur upon request made by the Embassy of the sending State to the Ministry of Foreign Affairs, or other competent Authority, of the receiving State;
- Or after the end of its term, for the time necessary for leaving;
- Or, in the event that the consular officer has to cross the territory of a third State to reach his consular post, where it will take up its functions, or to return to the sending State.

The granting of immunities to other persons, specifically member of his family part of his household or member of consul private staff, inevitably presupposes their substantial connection with the carrier consul or consular officer. As in the case of the carrier Consul, the moment from which such persons begin to enjoy immunities, or cease to enjoy them, relates to the beginning and end of the mission.

Like the *perpetuatio* provided for the diplomatic agent and for the mission staff listed in Article 37 of the 1961 Vienna Convention, Article 53 of the 1963 Vienna Convention also provides in paragraphs 4 and 5: "Nevertheless, in respect of acts performed by a consular officer or consular employee in the exercise of his functions, immunity from jurisdiction exists without limitation as to duration."

Similarly to diplomatic law, the benefits, privileges, and immunities have been codified by conventional law in order to clearly regulate the scope and the duration of these prerogatives, so that they cannot be attenuated, circumscribed, modified, supplemented, or extinguished *ad nutum* by receiving States.

It should be noted, in this regard, that the immunity regime is enshrined in international rules that clearly have States as beneficiaries; specifically, the sending State and the receiving State. Diplomatic agents and consular agents, who are the "material beneficiaries" of the special treatment, even though they are organs of the State, cannot dispose of the management of such matters, as only States have the right to request and the obligation to grant the treatment due to them and the individual immunities.

Therefore, where it is necessary to deprive of the protections that immunities provide for the diplomatic agent or consular officer, it is essential that the State concerned with their offices, in the exercise of its sovereignty and in compliance with international law, formalizes the waiver of the treatment and immunities of its agents and officers.

Both the Vienna Conventions on Diplomatic Relations and Consular Relations codify international practice, assigning to the governing bodies of the sending State the power to declare the waiver, which, precisely because of the exceptional nature of the act, must be express and unequivocal. Article 45, paragraph 1, states: "The sending State may waive, with regard to a member of the consular post, any of the privileges and immunities provided for in article 41, 43 and 44."

The doctrine has posed the problem of the possible revocability of the waiver, debating the existence of a right of the State that has expressed its decision to renounce certain privileges to revise it, revoking the waiver in whole or in part, so as to "reappropriate" what it had renounced.

Both customary diplomatic law and conventional law are silent on the matter and, therefore, the prevailing doctrine has been that immunities and other privileges cannot be invoked when waiver has taken place.

7.5 The State-of-the-Art of the Vienna Convention on Consular Relations After 60 Years of Life

It could be interesting to assess the uniformity of application in the contracting Parties of the Convention, both from the side of the receiving State and the sending State.

A survey carried out by Ficac—World Federation of Consuls on 2022, by submission of quantitative questionnaires to Deans of various Consular Corps and Consular Associations and to honorary Consuls representing a total of 60 sending

States showed a different application of the Vienna Convention on Consular Relations of April 24, 1963.

1. The research has shown that according to 67% of the sample of sending States, honorary Consuls are requested to perform the functions referred to in Article 5, points letters:
   (a) Protecting in the receiving State the interests of the sending State and of its nationals, both individuals and bodies corporate, within the limits permitted by international law;
   (b) Furthering the development of commercial, economic, cultural, and scientific relations between the sending State and the receiving State and otherwise promoting friendly relations between them in accordance with the provisions of the present Convention;
   (c) Ascertaining by all lawful means conditions and developments in the commercial, economic, cultural, and scientific life of the receiving State, reporting thereon to the Government of the sending State and giving information to persons interested;
   (e) Helping and assisting nationals, both individuals and bodies corporate, of the sending State.

The research has shown that according to 74.5% of the sample of the receiving States, honorary Consuls are allowed to perform the same functions referred to in points a, b, c, and e.

2. The research has shown that according to 32% of the sample of sending States, honorary Consuls are requested to perform the functions referred to in Article 5, point d: issuing passports and travel documents to nationals of the sending State, and visas or appropriate documents to persons wishing to travel to the sending State.
   The research has shown that according to 55% of the sample of the receiving States, honorary Consuls are allowed to perform the same function referred in point d.
3. The research has shown that according to 28.3% of the sample of sending States, honorary Consuls are requested to perform the functions referred to in Article 5, points:
   (f) Acting as notary and civil registrar and in capacities of a similar kind, and performing certain functions of an administrative nature, provided that there is nothing contrary thereto in the laws and regulations of the receiving State
   (g) Safeguarding the interests of nationals, both individuals and bodies corporate, of the sending States in cases of succession *mortis causa* in the territory of the receiving State, in accordance with the laws and regulations of the receiving State
   (j) Transmitting judicial and extrajudicial documents or executing letters rogatory or commissions to take evidence for the courts of the sending

State in accordance with international agreements in force or, in the absence of such international agreements, in any other manner compatible with the laws and regulations of the receiving State

(m) Performing any other functions entrusted to a consular post by the sending State which are not prohibited by the laws and regulations of the receiving State or to which no objection is taken by the receiving State or which are referred to in the international agreements in force between the sending State and the receiving State

The research has shown that according to 74.5% of the sample of the receiving States, honorary Consuls are allowed to perform the same functions referred to in points f, g, j, and m.

In conclusion, although the Vienna Convention on Consular Relations of 1963 gives honorary Consuls a large set of powers, when it comes to the laws of individual States, these powers are often relatively limited, specifically with regard to the public official functions. The survey has shown that it happens in different countries, on different continents, and with different types of governments (parliamentary democracy, monarchy, totalitarianism, one-party State), factors not influencing the field of implementation.

Within the fierce debate among the members of the international community seeking an update of the Vienna Convention on Consul Relations, given the increasing globalization that has characterized the last decades and the ever-increasing number of movements of people, goods and services, it is advisable that the States should, first of all, fully implement the contents of the "existing" Vienna Convention, and ensure its uniform application in all national legal systems.

Prof. Avv. Stelio Campanale Professor of International Law, Diplomatic and Consular Law and of International Trade Law (Libera Università Mediterranea-LUM Giuseppe Degennaro—Bari, IT). Visiting professor of International Markets Law (Universiteti Katolik "Zoja e KëshillittëMirë," Tirana). Lawyer and Auditor. Teacher of company management, corporate and compliance issues, international business contracts in many masters, PHD courses, business and management schools, in Italy and foreign countries. Visiting Professor UE Erasmus + at Universidad Publica de Navarra (ES) and Ecole Supérieure des Technologies et des Affaires (ESTA), Belfort (FR). For more than 30 years and in force, member of various Board of Directors and Compliance Supervisory Boards of Italian and foreign companies, including ones listed at New York Stock Exchange and Italian Stock Exchange. Author of books, chapters, and articles in academic or professional journals on diplomatic and consular relations, international business and trade law, international law. Honorary Consul of Hellenic Republic in Bari, Italy. Member of the Board of Directors of the World Federation of Consular Corps and Associations (F.I.C.A.C.), NGO-UN ECOSOC, Brussel (Be). From 2016 to 2023, Co-Chairman of the Legal Committee and Co-Chairman of Security and Privileges Committee of F.I.C.A.C. From 2004 to 2020, President of Greek-Italian Business Chamber of Rome. From 2013 to 2016, Senior Advisor to the Secretary General of the Parliamentary Assembly of the Mediterranean (PAM), Malta/San Marino. Member of the Official Delegation of the Greek Government at the: signature of the Pact of Twinning between the Province of Rome and Nomarchia Attikis. Athens, (Gr) 27/5/2005; Meeting of Minister of Transportation of the European Corridor VIII countries. Bari, (It) 18/9/2003; Adriatic & Ionian Initiative. Bari, (It) 13/5/2003; Working table on economic reconstruction, development, and cooperation of the stability pact for the Balkans. Bari, (It) 7–8/10/1999.

Diplomacy and International Organizations: Interactions and Incongruities

8

Konstantinos D. Magliveras

Abstract

The chapter seeks to discuss how diplomacy operates inside international organizations and how the latter use diplomacy to carry out their aims and goals not only to fulfil their duties but also to become active within the global community engaging with other organizations and non-Member States. Considering that international organizations are made up of sovereign states, the chapter notes the apparent paradox that, while states might not recognize each other other's independence or even existence, they co-exist and transact together in the context of organizations. It follows that such transactions could very well be different from other kinds of diplomatic engagements. Moreover, the chapter describes how organizations are engaged in multilateral treaty-making (and, in the case of the United Nations, universal norms making) and how they 'export' their principles and values, especially as regards human rights, the rule of law, democracy and good governance. The chapter also shows how global (United Nations) and regional organizations (e.g. European Union, African Union, Organization of American States) exhibit a great deal of proficiency in a different kind of diplomacy, namely the peaceful resolution of disputes. Finally, the chapter argues that, while states transfer authority and powers to international organizations by simultaneously limiting their own rights, they still control them; therefore, the role and outcomes of diplomacy exercised by international organizations is often limited by members, who prefer to pursue national diplomacy and foreign policy at the expense of the organization's welfare.

K. D. Magliveras (✉)
Department of Mediterranean Studies, University of the Aegean, Rhodes, Greece
e-mail: kmagliveras@aegean.gr

P. Naskou-Perraki (ed.), *Contemporary Diplomatic and Consular Relations*,
https://doi.org/10.1007/978-3-031-99243-8_8

8.1 Introduction

There is no standard definition of 'diplomacy'. From the perspective of international relations and international politics, diplomacy has the following five broad functions: (1) communication and exchange of information between the leaders of states and the heads of international institutions; (2) the negotiation of international legal instruments (agreements, treaties, etc.) and the representation of states in international transactions; (3) information/intelligence gathering as regards third countries; (4) the management of the image of a state; and (5) resolving disputes on the international plane and diminishing their consequences. The above functions are the content of what is generally referred to as 'public diplomacy' and constitute the principal duties of diplomats. Equally, there is no standard definition of 'international organization'. From the perspective of international law, it could be described as a transnational legal entity/institution that has been set up by (at least three) states, has predetermined objectives and goals, comprises one or more organs, is invariably created by a multilateral treaty and its decisions oblige, even if only ethically, its members to do something or to abstain from doing something. The aim of this chapter is to show how diplomacy and international organizations interact and how they may differ by concentrating on two of the above functions, namely negotiation of international legal instruments and resolving disputes.

8.2 States Co-exist in International Organizations Even Though They Might Not Recognize Each Other Diplomatically

There can be no doubt that many things connect diplomacy with international organizations and vice versa.[1] One could even speak of a strong interrelation: after all, international organizations are born out of the diplomatic efforts of a group of states that has resolved to establish a new multilateral institution, a new actor in the international community.[2] Not only are international organizations created by means of diplomatic efforts but what is fascinating is that the states engaged in these efforts are not actually required to have recognized each other. Thus, a state that has reserved the recognition of the sovereignty of a third country or has vehemently rejected its existence could participate with the unrecognized state in the same negotiations and partake in the conclusion of the new institution's constitutive instrument. Thereafter, they will be fellow members with the same rights and obligations and must work together to attain its goals. And while these states will

[1] Generally, see M. P. Karns and K. A. Mingst, 'International Organizations and Diplomacy' in A. Cooper et al (eds), The Oxford Handbook of Modern Diplomacy, Oxford University Press, Oxford, 2013, 142–159.

[2] On the relationship between states and international organizations, see J. S. Barkin, International Organization: Theories and Institutions, 2nd ed., Palgrave Macmillan, New York, 2023, 1 et seq.

continue to have no official diplomatic relations, their representatives will meet and transact in its organs. Thus, the diplomatic status of the relations among the various Member States is of no concern for the operation of an international organization: states having no diplomatic relations could practice the art of diplomacy in it, an opportunity that would not have existed otherwise.[3]

A relevant example is the creation of the Eastern Mediterranean Gas Forum (EMGM) in 2020, an international organization whose aim is to develop a regional gas market. In particular, from the beginning the State of Israel and the State of Palestine were parties to the deliberations for the EMGM Statute. And while one might have thought that this fact would have resulted in delays, as is noted in the EMGM's website, 'agreement on a final document for the EMGF Statute [was reached] in a worldwide record of 12 Months'.[4] Presently, they co-exist as fellow Members even though, as is well known, they have never recognized each other.[5] Risking being accused of repetition, one should emphasize that it is not a necessary condition that all Member States recognize each other and/or maintain diplomatic relations. Thus, the State of Palestine participates as a full Member State in several other international organizations and institutions,[6] while the Republic of Kosovo joined in 2009 the International Monetary Fund (IMF)[7] and in 2012 the European Bank for Reconstruction and Development (EBRD).[8]

8.3 Interstate Relations and Transactions Within International Organizations: A Different Kind of Diplomatic Engagement

When the representatives of states come together and, by exercising the tools of diplomacy, negotiate the text of the constitutive instrument of an international organization (effectively a multilateral founding treaty), they will no doubt attempt

---

[3]It has been argued, A. James, 'Diplomatic Relations between States' in C. M. Constantinou, P. Kerr and P. Shaer (eds), The SAGE Handbook of Diplomacy, SAGE Publications, London, 2016, 257–267, that 'diplomacy' is not identical with 'diplomatic relations' in the sense that the latter is a conditio sine qua non for the former. However, for purposes of simplicity, the two terms will here be regarded as synonymous.

[4]See EMGF Overview at https://emgf.org/about-us/overview/.

[5]Generally, see G. Naldi & K. Magliveras, 'The East Mediterranean Gas Forum: A Regional Institution Struggling in the Mire of Energy Insecurities' [2023] 20 International Organizations Law Review 194–227.

[6]Generally, see K. Magliveras & G. Naldi, 'The State of Palestine as a Sovereign Actor in the International Community: Implications for its Legal Status' in S. Abidde (ed.), Palestine, Taiwan, and Western Sahara: Statehood, Sovereignty, and the International System, Rowman & Littlefield/Lexington Books, Lanham, MD, 2023, 93–118. Presently, Palestine enjoys (bilateral) recognition from 139 states, for details see the website of the Mission of the State of Palestine to the United Nations at http://palestineun.org/about-palestine/diplomatic-relations/.

[7]For details, see https://www.imf.org/en/Countries/KOS.

[8]For details, see https://www.ebrd.com/kosovo.html.

to secure the best negotiation position for their country.[9] There is no guarantee that the negotiations will be successful and that a treaty will finally be signed and, more importantly, ratified by the required number of signatories to enter into force.[10] Diplomatic endeavours have always had an inherent element of failure. It follows that the birth (or not) of a new international organization will depend, inter alia, on the outcome of certain diplomatic initiatives and political activities.[11] In most cases, the negotiations achieve the desired goal, and the founding treaty is clinched. The large success rate of such negotiations might have a rather simple explanation: states participate in the deliberations not because their aim is to antagonize other states but because they are convinced that, through cooperation and collaboration, they will achieve many goals. To offer some examples, they will be able to tackle pressing problems that they cannot address by themselves; acquire significant (political, economic, commercial, military, technological, etc.) gains and benefits; upgrade their position and status (whether real or perceived) regionally, internationally or even globally (as a result of the previous goal); consolidate and increase their power and authority; and so on. In this process, which could very well last for several years, one should not underestimate the role and significance of the human factor, namely the vital position of diplomats/plenipotentiaries. They are the ones who must find the pertinent solutions and overcome the challenges that invariably arise. But then diplomats are, overall, intelligent as well as shrewd people and coming up with answers to complex matters is part of their job description.

In the period after World War II, the advent of international organizations and their ever-increasing importance on the world stage have diminished the traditional methods of states' diplomatic engagement through embassies and ambassadors. Interstate diplomatic relations have been recalibrated and, to a larger or smaller degree, the centuries old art of diplomacy with its etiquette and protocol has been replaced by dealings and transactions that take place in the corridors of international organizations. The bilateral nature of diplomatic relations has given way to multilateralism, the level of which might not have been possible had international organizations not become the vehicle of choice for organizing the global community

[9] On how states use international organizations to further their interests, see A. Wivel and T. V. Paul (eds), International Institutions and Power Politics, Georgetown University Press, Washington, DC, 2019.

[10] While not directly relevant, one could mention the two treaties of accession of the Kingdom of Norway to the European Union, neither of which was approved by the population.

[11] The use of the term 'diplomatic' here is used to describe both 'the process of international political argument and its eventual success or failure in reaching agreement' and 'the administrative mechanism of diplomacy itself', as aptly put by R. Longhorne, 'The Regulation of Diplomatic Practice: The Beginnings to the Vienna Convention on Diplomatic Relations 1961' [1992] 18 Review of International Studies 3–17.

of nations.[12] The degree at which international organizations have the capacity to multiply diplomatic transactions is simply awesome.

Suffice to mention the regular sessions of the UN General Assembly (UNGA) that commence every year 'on the Tuesday of the third week in September, counting from the first week that contains at least one working day'.[13] The general debate at the UNGA, which is held without interruption over a period of 9 working days immediately following the opening of each regular session,[14] brings together a score of heads of state and prime ministers. These dignitaries, over and above presenting at plenary sessions their views and opinions on matters of global interest, have the opportunity to meet with their counterparts from all parts of the world, whether friends or foes. And, without having to observe the strict diplomatic protocol that is required, for example, of state visits, the opportunity arises to discuss issues of mutual concern or attempt to resolve outstanding disputes (we will return to this). Especially, if state visits are not possible, owing, as explained above, to non-recognition or for whatever other reason, the fringes of UNGA general debates have proven to be the perfect occasion for putting diplomacy to work.

It is diplomacy being exercised at the highest possible level. In a more or less similar manner, these high-powered but informal diplomatic dealings take place in other international organizations as well, whether it is the European Union, the African Union, the Association of South East Nations (ASEAN), the League of Arab States, the Organization of American States (OAS) or the Organisation of Islamic Cooperation (OIC). The basic tenets of diplomacy are there. What differs is that international organizations, being as it were built upon an array of organs that are mandated to bring about their goals and to materialize their aims, offer different arrangements for pursuing diplomacy, if compared to, what might be called, traditional diplomatic exchanges. This probably needs some explication. In most international organizations, there is a certain hierarchy, a certain ranking, among the various organs, which is expressly stipulated or derives from the constitutive instrument. Even though this ranking may not necessarily be a reflection on their importance vis-à-vis their operation, whether they are higher or lower in the hierarchy is of significance regarding the seniority of the Member States' representatives. Succinctly and as a rule of the thumb, heads of state and prime ministers participate in General Assemblies/Assemblies of Member States; (usually foreign) ministers—or ambassadors as their replacement—participate in Councils/Executive Councils; senior state officials participate in the various Commissions/Committees; lower-level (state) officials or nationally appointed experts participate in working groups.

It follows that all these persons, invariably acting as representatives and/or agents of their respective countries/governments, have the opportunity, in line with the

---

[12] Generally, see K. Magliveras, "'Organization' and 'International Organizations': A Discourse on Synthesis" in L. Boisson de Chazournes et al. (eds), Liber Amicorum en l'honneur de H. Dipla—Enjeux et Perspectives, Editions A. Pedone, Paris, 2020, 513–531.

[13] See paragraph 1 of UNGA Resolution 57/301 of 17 March 2003.

[14] See Rules of Procedure of the General Assembly, UN Doc. A/520/Rev.18 (2017).

prevailing rules and norms in each international organization,[15] to promote foreign policy goals at a level and intensity different from traditional diplomatic exchanges. This is the case irrespective of whether national diplomatic endeavours are pursued at the level of head of state or of lower-level official. In this context, one should view them all as diplomatic agents, who take advantage of the meetings and deliberations in an international organization to put forward their states' views or to oppose the opinions expressed by another state or to lend support to a third Member State that is in a difficult situation, expecting of course that the latter will come to its aid if the situation arises, and so on.

It has argued that international organizations are like social clubs, allowing states to favour friends while excluding rivals.[16] That Member States assist friendly nations or transfer their rivalries inside an international organization is neither novel nor extraordinary but follows from the manner that states conduct their diplomatic relations. Indeed, in larger international organizations, such as the UN, Member States act and behave as groups of states, in other words as clusters of states that share common characteristics. From a diplomatic point of view, they do so because they have decided to promote specific policies and positions or to support certain causes, always in unison. To take the example of the EU: very often during debates at other international organizations (e.g. the UN and its Specialized Agencies), one of its Member States speaks on behalf of all '27', often on behalf of EU candidate states as well. The statements and declarations by the Member State in question are construed to be the EU's official point of view. Another example of a regional organization that strives but with rather limited success to speak with 'one voice' is the African Union (AU). For several years now, putting forward 'common African positions' on the international plane has been a priority for the AU's diplomatic efforts to consolidate the continent's position globally.[17] The recent acceptance of AU as a permanent member of the G20 should promote this goal.[18] In conclusion, the Member State speaking with 'one voice' could be regarded as the 'ambassador' of an international organization in the 'court'

[15] For example, there exists the principle of sincere cooperation: as contained in Article 4(3) of the Treaty on European Union (Consolidated version of the Treaty on European Union as in force on 1 March 2020, at https://eur-lex.europa.eu/eli/treaty/teu_2016/2020-03-01), it means that the EU and the Member States are obliged, in full mutual respect, to assist each other in carrying out the tasks flowing from this Treaty and the Treaty for the Functioning of the European Union (TFEU). The general obligation of states to cooperate (i.e. irrespective of whether they participate in the same international organization) was laid down in the so-called 'Friendly Relations Declaration', which was adopted by the UNGA as Resolution 2625 (XXV) of 24 October 1970, this being the year that the UN celebrated its 25th anniversary.

[16] See C. Davis, Discriminatory Clubs: The Geopolitics of International Organizations, Princeton University Press, Princeton, NJ, 2023.

[17] See African Union Commission, *Agenda 2063—The Africa we Want*, Popular Version, September 2015, para. 61: 'Africa [should] continue to speak with one voice and act collectively to promote our common interests and positions in the international arena'.

[18] See G20 New Delhi Leaders' Declaration, 9–10 September 2023, para. 76.

of another organization carrying 'messages' to use the terminology of traditional diplomacy.

8.4 Diplomacy, International Organizations and Multilateral Treaty Making

The operation of international organizations could also be associated by what, for the purposes of this chapter, would be called 'massive scale diplomacy', in other words the contemporaneous holding of diplomatic transactions by a very large number of states. This type of diplomacy is mostly associated with the UN. The fact that for a long period of time now almost all states participate in it, leading to the UN having finally achieved universality,[19] means that when a new area or a new sector must be regulated or when a particular challenge needs to be addressed, the negotiations that initiated by the UN are at a gigantic scale. Effectively, this has replaced the need to have recourse to the traditional diplomatic methods and downgrading even more bilateral diplomatic transactions. As regards the negotiation of new treaties, usually one or more states take the initiative and convene a diplomatic conference of plenipotentiaries for that purpose. Over the years, the UN, acting through resolutions adopted by the UNGA, has organized what it itself calls 'diplomatic conferences'. These have led to successful treaty-making in areas ranging from diplomatic relations[20] to the law of the sea[21] to the law of treaties[22] to international criminal justice.[23]

It might be hyperbole to argue that, had these conferences been held in the traditional manner, they would not have resulted in the adoption of multilateral

[19] Arguably the text of the UN Charter (1945) did not envisage universality in the sense that Article 4 thereof, the clause on membership, divided applicant states between 'peace-loving' and 'not peace-loving', the latter being by inference the Tripartite Axis and collaborating states. When the Federal Republic of Germany and the German Democratic Republic were admitted to UN membership in September 1973, this distinction no longer applied.

[20] See the United Nations Conference on Diplomatic Intercourse and Immunities, which was held from March to April 1961. It culminated to the Vienna Convention on Diplomatic Relations (1961), 500 *United Nations Treaty Series* (UNTS) 95, the Optional Protocol concerning Acquisition of Nationality (1961), 500 *UNTS* 223, and the Optional Protocol concerning the Compulsory Settlement of Disputes (1961), 500 *UNTS* 241.

[21] See the United Nations Conference on the Law of the Sea, which was held from February to April 1958; the Second United Nations Conference on the Law of the Sea was held from March to April 1960; and the Third United Nations Conference on the Law of the Sea lasted from 1973 until 1982.

[22] See the United Nations Conference on the Law of Treaties, which was held from March to May 1968 and from April to May 1969.

[23] See the United Nations Diplomatic Conference of Plenipotentiaries on the Establishment of an International Criminal Court, which was held from June to July 1998. For the full list of these conferences, see https://legal.un.org/diplomaticconferences/.

treaties as these 'diplomatic conferences' have had.[24] The difference lies in what the latter have to offer in terms of advantages, benefits and added value. Suffice to mention that UN-led discussions bring with them a wealth of experience, structured deliberations, cost-effective negotiations and the opportunity to entrust the preparation of draft treaties to the International Law Commission (ILC), a subsidiary organ of the UNGA, part of its Sixth (Legal) Committee.[25] The tasks of the ILC are the progressive development and the codification of international law.[26] To put it rather plainly, the ILC, in accordance with the parameters set by the UNGA, prepares draft treaties on behalf of the entire UN membership. When the draft instruments have been finalized, UN Member States, acting through the UNGA, are free to adopt them as they stand, to amend/revise them or to completely ignore and abandon them. In the latter case, there is nothing preventing them to rejuvenate the negotiations and follow the method of the traditional diplomatic conference.

8.4.1 Regional International Organizations and Treaty-Making

Of course, the contemporary practice of treaty-making through negotiations conducted within the organs of international organizations is not something that happens only in the context of the UN. Indeed, one should mention the experience of the AU and the predecessor Organisation of African Unity. Under their auspices, more than 40 multilateral treaties have been concluded since the mid-1960s regulating such diverse matters as the promotion of human rights and fundamental freedoms, the protection of the environment, the prohibition of nuclear weapons, the refugee problem, the scourges of mercenarism, of terrorism and of corruption, the promotion of culture, and so on.[27] Taken as a whole, it has been argued that this corpus of treaties has contributed to the emergence and development of an AU legal system, an African Union law.[28] Other international organizations that have engaged

[24] Over and above the Vienna Convention on Diplomatic Relations, suffice to mention the Vienna Convention on the Law of Treaties (1969), 1155 *UNTS* 331; the UN Convention on the Law of the Sea (1982), 1833 *UNTS* 3; and the Rome Statute of the International Criminal Court (1998), 2187 *UNTS* 3.

[25] Note that there is a similar organ of advisory capacity operating in the AU, the African Union Commission of International Law, whose Statute was adopted in February 2009 by the Assembly of the Heads of States and Government (Decision Assembly/AU/Dec.209 (XII)). See K. Magliveras and G. Naldi, The African Union (AU), Third revised edition, Wolters Kluwer, Alphen aan den Rijn, 2023, 262–265.

[26] See Articles 16 et seq. of the Statute of the International Law Commission (1947).

[27] For the complete list, see https://au.int/treaties. See Magliveras and Naldi, *The African Union (AU)*, supra.

[28] See K. Magliveras, 'The Implications of African Union Law: Conceptual Analysis with Emphasis on the Institutional Consequences' in F. Amao, M. Olivier and K. Magliveras (eds), The Emergent African Union Law: Conceptualization, Delimitation, and Application, Oxford University Press, Oxford, 2021, 30–44.

in treaty-making include (in chronological order) are the Organization of American States (OAS)[29] and the Council of Europe (CoE).

As regards the CoE, its Statute adopted in 1949 expressly refers to the conclusion of agreements in economic, social, cultural, scientific, legal and administrative matters and 'in the maintenance and further realization of human rights and fundamental freedoms'.[30] Very impressively, so far more than 224 multilateral instruments have been concluded under the CoE auspices (including amendments and revisions), although as of late there has not been much activity (the last treaty, the Council of Europe Convention on Offences relating to Cultural Property, was adopted in May 2017).[31] However, not all of these instruments have entered into force, a fact that no doubt shows the apparent limitations in treaty-making as a form of multilateral diplomacy exercised through a regional international organization. The case of the Convention on the Protection of the Environment through Criminal Law, opened for signature in November 1998, deserves to be mentioned. Even though it deals with a burning issue[32] and requires only three ratifications to enter into force, until today it has only been ratified by Estonia.[33] And if this were not noteworthy, reference should be made to the Convention on Civil Liability for Damage resulting from Activities Dangerous to the Environment, which was adopted in June 1993 and has never been ratified![34]

8.4.2 International Organizations 'Exporting' Values and Norms: A Different Kind of Diplomacy

But CoE treaties should also be mentioned because they promote a rather different kind of diplomacy. More specifically, many a CoE treaty stipulate that non-Member States as well as the EU may become contracting parties, if they had participated in the negotiations.[35] No doubt, opening treaties to non-members and to the EU allows for a dialogue to take place, the essence of diplomacy. Through this dialogue one can

[29] For the complete list, see https://www.oas.org/en/sla/dil/inter_american_treaties_text.asp.

[30] See Article 1(b) of the Statute of the Council of Europe, 87 UNTS 103.

[31] For the full list, see https://www.coe.int/en/web/conventions/full-list.

[32] Reference should also be made to a quite pioneering but long forgotten treaty, the Convention on Nature Protection and Wild Life Preservation in the Western Hemisphere, adopted in October 1940 under the auspices of the Pan American Union, the predecessor to OAS, entered into force April 1942, 161 UNTS 193.

[33] For details on signatures and ratification, see https://www.coe.int/en/web/conventions/full-list?module=signatures-by-treaty&treatynum=172.

[34] For details on signatures, see https://www.coe.int/en/web/conventions/full-list?module=signatures-by-treaty&treatynum=150.

[35] Note that joining these treaties has financial implications for the third states and/or the EU; see Council of Europe, Committee of Ministers, Resolution CM/Res(2022)6 concerning financial arrangements for the participation of the European Union and non-Member States in Council of Europe conventions, adopted on 6 April 2022.

expect that experiences will be exchanged, knowledge shared, best practices discussed, and so on. Notwithstanding these aspects of treaty-making, what is of importance is that the CoE is given the opportunity to 'export' its values, its norms and its standards to other parts of the world.[36] The example of the Convention on Cybercrime is more than telling. It opened for signature in November 2001 and presently it has been ratified by some 36 non-Member States, which include not only G20 countries (USA, Brazil, Japan and Australia) but also small countries (Cabo Verde, Costa Rica, Sri Lanka, etc.).[37] It follows that, on account of the large number of non-CoE members that subscribe to its treaties and implement their stipulations in domestic legal orders, the CoE has become an international setter of standards.

Even though his kind of diplomacy often goes unnoticed, it is interesting to note that the EU is eager to advertise its role as a global standard setter, as it did, for example, before the US Supreme Court in 2012 in context of *Kiobel v Royal Dutch Petroleum.*[38] However, the Organisation for Economic Co-operation and Development (OECD), whose membership comes from all continents, could be regarded as a transnational setter. In particular, the Convention on Combating Bribery of Foreign Public Officials in International Business Transactions, adopted in 1997 (it came into force in 1999), establishes legally binding standards to criminalize the bribery of foreign public officials during international business transactions. By containing a list of measures to ensure that it remains an effective multilateral instrument, the Convention is the oldest international yardstick in fighting corruption. Presently, it has been ratified by eight non-OECD members, including Costa Rica, Peru, Colombia, the Russian Federation and Brazil.[39] What is also of interest is that the Convention has been supplemented by soft-law instruments (lastly by the 2021 Recommendation for Further Combating Bribery of Foreign Public Officials in International Business Transactions)[40] and that it sets up a mechanism monitoring whether contracting parties have implemented the international obligations assumed under it. The 'Working Group on Bribery' is the competent OECD body that monitors and evaluates the compliance of contracting parties' legislation with the

[36] Generally, see K. Magliveras, 'The Role of International Organisations as Promoters, Enforcers and Exporters of Democratic Ideals and the Rule of Law' in European Center for Research and Training of Human Rights and Humanitarian Action, Safeguarding Democratic Institutions within a Europe in Crisis: Challenges and Responses, Proceedings of the International Conference, Nafplion, 11–12 May 2018, I. Sideris Publishers, Athens, 2021, 85–106.

[37] For details on signatures and ratifications, see https://www.coe.int/en/web/conventions/full-list?module=signatures-by-treaty&treatynum=185.

[38] See Brief of the European Commission on behalf of the European Union as amicus curiae in support of neither party in Kiobel v Royal Dutch Petroleum, Supreme Court of the United States, No. 10-1491, 13 June 2012; Decision of the Supreme Court of the United States, *Kiobel v Royal Dutch Petroleum*, 17 April 2013, 569 U.S. 108.

[39] For international organizations as actors engaged in international policymaking, see B. Verbeek, 'Leadership of International Organizations' in J. Kane et al (eds), Dispersed Democratic Leadership: Origins, Dynamics, and Implications, Oxford University Press, Oxford, 2009, 235–254.

[40] Available at https://legalinstruments.oecd.org/en/instruments/OECD-LEGAL-0378.

Convention and issues 'country reports'.[41] This continuous process of monitoring and evaluation could also be regarded as a kind of diplomatic exchange.[42]

8.5 Diplomacy, International Organizations and the Peaceful Resolution of Disputes

Reference has been made above to diplomacy and the peaceful resolution of disputes. Today, the international community has moved away from the pre-World War II state of affairs, aptly described by Georg Schwarzenberger as follows: '[w]ar is … the last resort of power politics when diplomacy fails to achieve its objects by the threat of force'.[43] If one reads the Preamble as well as Articles 1 and 2 of the UN Charter, setting out, respectively, its purposes and principles and reflecting the timing of its creation in the midst of the worst armed conflict in history, it transpires that its goal is the 'adjustment or settlement of international disputes or situations which might lead to a breach of the peace'.[44] For, if international disputes are not settled by peaceful means (and resorting to war is the exact opposite), international peace and security and justice will be endangered.[45] Since ancient times, the diplomatic efforts to resolve interstate disputes have been undertaken by or entrusted to emperors, kings, princes, religious figure heads and, generally, whoever possessed status, power and prestige.

In the end of the nineteenth and the beginning of the twentieth century, the 'civilized nations' from Asia, the Americas and Europe participated in two conferences to lay down the methods, tools and procedures for peacefully resolving disputes when the 'diplomatic channels' had failed. Respectively, they culminated in the Convention for the Pacific Settlement of International Disputes of 1899 and 1907, the latter being a more progressed version of the former. The understanding that, if a dispute cannot be settled by diplomacy, it will be submitted to arbitration or to judicial settlement was included in Article 13 of the Covenant of the League of Nations (LoN, 1919), a most pioneering instrument. As the founding treaty of the first modern international political organization, the Covenant advanced the requirement for interstate open diplomacy by requiring that all treaties be registered with, and published by, the LoN Secretariat.[46]

---

[41] These reports are available at https://www.oecd.org/daf/anti-bribery/countryreportsontheimplementationoftheoecdanti-briberyconvention.htm.

[42] For the case of Australia, one of the first contracting parties, see https://www.aph.gov.au/About_Parliament/Parliamentary_Departments/Parliamentary_Library/pubs/rp/rp1920/Anti-BriberyConvention.

[43] G. Schwarzenberger, Power Politics—An Introduction to the Study of International Relations and Post-War Planning, Jonathan Cape, London, 1941, 132.

[44] See Article 1(1) of the UN Charter.

[45] Cf. ibid, Article 2(3).

[46] See Article 18 of the Covenant. The League of Nations Treaty Series (succeeded by the UNTS) was the place where the whole text of the treaties appeared in the official language/s.

Organization for Security and Co-operation in Europe (OSCE), whose membership comprises 57 states from Europe, Central Asia and North America. The Court was set up by the Convention on Conciliation and Arbitration within the Conference on Security and Co-operation in Europe (1992). Despite its name, the Court does not adjudicate disputes, it only establishes conciliation commissions having obligatory jurisdiction and arbitral tribunals on an ad hoc basis, which may resolve conflicts of any nature, for example territorial issues, questions of maritime delimitation, environmental issues, and so on. But for a conciliation commission to be established, one of the contracting parties must first submit, pursuant to the procedure laid down in the Convention, its 'dispute with another State party which has not been settled within a reasonable period of time through negotiation'.[58] It follows that the Convention deals with instances when using the most basic form of diplomacy (negotiation) has not produced the desired results. Thus, the Court has at the same time a diplomatic and a juridical character.[59]

Presently, the Convention does not enjoy universal acceptance by OSCE members as it has only 34 contracting parties, while three powerful members (the United Kingdom, the United States of America, and the Russian Federation) continue to shun it. But this is perhaps not its most significant problem: almost 30 years after its entry into force, not a single dispute has been submitted to it! Given that Ukraine is a party to the Convention, were the Russian Federation also a party, one can easily understand how different the question of Russo-Ukrainian relations after 2014, and in particularly after February 2022, could have been from a legal point of view. Bearing in mind that the Court was established at the time of the Soviet Union's collapse, the disintegration of the Federal Socialist Republic of Yugoslavia, and the termination of 'the Cold War', arguably its raison d'être was to play a role in such conflicts as Russia v Ukraine.

It might sound too harsh to call the Court a failure, but one can reasonably feel tempted. In May 2022, its President, during a seminar on 'Conflict Resolution within the OSCE: The Role of the Court of Conciliation and Arbitration', had this to say: 'To go further would require the … Convention to be reopened, which does not seem appropriate in a period as uncertain as the one we are going through'.[60] One should disagree with the attitude of 'let things slide'. For if the power and abilities of diplomacy are trusted, things can lead to change. And certainly, there is a need for seismic shifts in international justice. Not to give diplomacy a change as regards this specific OSCE organ is deplorable and irresponsible and only perpetuates a deficient state of affairs.

[58] See Article 18(1) of the Convention on Conciliation and Arbitration.

[59] See L. Caflisch and L. Cuny, 'The OSCE Court of Conciliation and Arbitration: Current Problems', Institut für Friedensforschung und Sicherheitspolitik (ed.),OSCE Yearbook 1997, 1998, 347–355, 353.

[60] See Court of Conciliation and Arbitration within the OSCE, Annual Report 2022, March 2023, 20.

8.7 Conclusions

There exists a very close relationship between diplomacy and international organizations. The latter are not only born out of diplomatic efforts, but they also practice the art of diplomacy. The present charter concentrated on two areas of the activities of international organizations that are intently connected to diplomacy, treaty-making and the peaceful resolution of disputes. In these two areas, both at a global level (UN) and at a regional level (EU, CoE, AU, OAS, etc.), they have shown a great deal of proficiency. Many of the multilateral instruments concluded under their auspices can be described as bold achievements. The global community of nations would have been very different if international organizations had not promoted the adoption of treaties to regulate such matters as the conduct of diplomatic relations, the seas and oceans, the protection and promotion of human rights and fundamental rights, the safeguarding of the environment and natural resources, and so on. But also, in the resolution of disputes through diplomatic means and methods, a lot can be said about the positive role played by international organizations, a role that certainly can become more active and effective.[61] That states often do not follow the advice and guidance they are given preferring to place national interests above everything else and jeopardizing at the same time peace and security is most unfortunate. But one should not underestimate the fact that, despite states transferring en masse powers to international organizations and limiting their sovereign rights, the 'sovereign state' remains the prevailing norm in international law. It follows that, in such instances, the role and outcomes of diplomacy, as exercised in and by international organizations, cannot but be limited.

Dr. Konstantinos D. Magliveras, Professor of the Law of International Organizations and Public International Law, Department of Mediterranean Studies, University of the Aegean, Greece; he is also an Attorney-at-Law. Previously, he had taught at the University of Aberdeen, Sussex University, and the University of East Anglia. He holds a D.Phil. from Oxford University in the field of international institutional law. He is a member of the International Law Association—Hellenic Branch, the African Studies Centre Leiden Community, and the Hansischer Geschichtsverein. He has written extensively on the operation and functioning of intergovernmental organizations. He is presently working on an edited volume on regional human rights courts of justice, an edited volume on the legal system of the African Union, and a monograph on infidelity and international law.

[61] See C. A. Crocker, F. Osler Hampson and P. Aall (eds), Diplomacy and the Future of World Order, Georgetown University Press, Washington DC, 2021.

Consular Protection of Unrepresented European Citizens in Third Countries by the Diplomatic and Consular Authorities

9

Despoina Anagnostopoulou

Abstract

This chapter examines the duty of the Member States' diplomatic and consular authorities as well as EU delegations in third countries to assist "unrepresented" EU citizens, nationals of another Member State, under the same conditions as for their own nationals. It analyzes primary and secondary EU law on consular protection and focuses on the coordination and cooperation measures to facilitate consular protection for unrepresented Union citizens in third countries according to Directive 2015/637/EU; and the simplified cooperation and coordination procedure for the issuance of emergency travel documents (EU ETDs) provided by Directive 2019/997/EU.

9.1 Consular Protection as a Right of the European Citizen Before 2015

The Maastricht Treaty (1993) established the European citizenship for all nationals of the EU Member States and set out a list of rights conferred upon them.[1] Among these was the right of European citizens to "enjoy, in the territory of a third country in which the Member State of which they are nationals is not represented, the

[1] See, inter alia, D. Anagnostopoulou, The Enhancement of the Rights of the European Citizen, in T. Skouteris and M. Vagias (eds), International Organisations and the Protection of Human Rights, Essays in honour of Professor Paroula Naskou-Perraki, Themis Publications, N. A. Sakkoulas and Co., Athens 2014, pp. 153–172.

D. Anagnostopoulou (✉)
Department of International and European Studies, University of Macedonia, Thessaloniki, Greece
e-mail: danag@uom.edu.gr

P. Naskou-Perraki (ed.), *Contemporary Diplomatic and Consular Relations*,
https://doi.org/10.1007/978-3-031-99243-8_9

protection of the diplomatic and consular authorities of another Member State on the same conditions as the nationals of that State."[2]

Member States' diplomatic and consular authorities and EU delegations in third countries, as well as their delegations to international organizations "should contribute to the implementation and protection of the right of citizens of the Union in the territory of a third country."[3] Indeed, Member State citizens traveling and residing in a third country[4] need consular protection in situations such as arrest or detention, serious accident, serious illness or death, natural disaster or civil unrest, and loss of passport or travel documents. As not all EU Member States have an embassy or consulate in every country outside the EU,[5] Member States have the duty to assist "unrepresented" EU citizens under the same conditions as for their own nationals. The right to consular protection is an expression of EU solidarity and one of the practical benefits of EU citizenship.[6]

In 1995, the Decision of the Representatives of the Member States No 95/553/EC[7] laid down the conditions regarding the rights of European citizens in third countries and the obligations of the diplomatic and consular authorities of the Member States in third countries. According to that Decision, every citizen of the European Union was entitled to consular protection by any diplomatic or consular authority of a Member State provided that, in the territory in which he or she was present, there was:

- No accessible permanent representation
- No accessible Honorary Consul, competent for such matters and
- No other Member State representing it in a permanent manner[8]

---

[2] See article 8C of the Maastricht Treaty, which is now article 20(2) point (c) of the Treaty on the Functioning of the European Union (TFEU).

[3] See article 35 Treaty Establishing the European Union (TEU).

[4] Almost 7 million EU citizens travel or live outside the EU in countries where their Member State of nationality does not have an embassy or consulate. See European Parliament, Resolution of February 12, 2019, on the application of the Treaty provisions on EU citizenship, P8_TA(2019) 0076, (2018/2111(INI)) (2020/C 449/02), OJ C 449/6, 23.12.2020, para. 19.

[5] For example, in 2020, it was found that 13 EU Member States did not have an embassy in the Philippines. See European External Action Service, Consular Protection for EU/Schengen citizens in the Philippines, 20.1.2020, available at https://www.eeas.europa.eu/delegations/philippines/consular-protection-eu-schengen-citizens-philippines_en.

[6] European Commission, Proposal for a Council Directive establishing an EU emergency travel document and repealing Decision 96/409/CFSP, COM(2018) 358 final, 2018/0186(CNS), Brussels, 31.5.2018.

[7] Decision 95/553/EC of the Representatives of the Governments of the Member States, meeting within the Council, of December 19, 1995, regarding protection for citizens of the European Union by diplomatic and consular representations, OJ L 314, 28.12.1995, p. 73.

[8] Decision 95/553, article 1. Under article 8 of the Vienna Convention on Consular Relations, Member States may provide consular protection on behalf of another Member State upon appropriate notification and unless the third country concerned objects.

The diplomatic and consular authorities to which the person concerned applied would need to follow up his/her application for protection if it was proven that he/she was a national of a EU Member State by means of a passport or identity card. In case of lost or stolen documents, any other proof of nationality could be accepted after verification through the central authorities of the Member State of which the person concerned claimed to be a national or the nearest diplomatic mission or consular post of that State.[9] In fact, it was established in 1996 that consular and diplomatic authorities of Member States in third countries may issue Emergency Travel Documents (ETDs) to EU citizens (but not for family members with third country nationality) whose country of nationality is not represented and whose passport or travel document has been lost, stolen, destroyed, or is temporarily unavailable.[10]

Diplomatic and consular authorities of EU Member States accredited in a third country could:

(a) Agree on practical arrangements to allow for the effective management of protection applications[11] and
(b) Offer assistance to a Union citizen submitting a request in cases other than those expressly provided for by the 1995 Decision.[12]

The protection of the European citizen included:

(a) Assistance in cases of death
(b) Assistance in cases of serious accident or serious illness
(c) Assistance in cases of arrest or detention
(d) Assistance to victims of violent crime and
(e) Relief and repatriation of Union citizens in need of assistance[13]

The procedure for the advance payment, financial assistance, or expenditure to a national of a Member State by a diplomatic or consular authority of a Member State in a third country, except in cases of extreme urgency, was the following:

1. The permission of the competent authorities of the Member State of which the citizen is a national was required, which was given either by the Ministry of Foreign Affairs or by the nearest diplomatic mission.[14]

[9] Decision 95/553, article 2.

[10] Decision 96/409/CSFP of the Representatives of the Governments of the Member States, meeting within the Council of June 25, 1996, on the establishment of an emergency travel document, OJ L 168, 6.7.1996, pp. 4–11.

[11] Decision 95/553, article 4.

[12] Decision 95/553, article 5 para. 3.

[13] Decision 95/553, article 5 para. 1.

[14] Decision 95/553, article 6 para. 1.

The Directive provides that the competent diplomatic or consular authorities of a Member State may represent the diplomatic or consular authorities of another EU Member State on a permanent basis and may, whenever necessary, enter into practical arrangements with other Member States for the sharing of responsibilities regarding the provision of consular protection to unrepresented citizens. The competent authorities shall notify the arrangements to the European Commission and the European External Action Service (EEAS).[28] The Directive allows the Member State, which is not represented in a third country, to provide consular protection to one of its nationals—for example, by offering online consular services—or to request the transfer of the application submitted by its national in order to deliver consular protection itself. [29]

European Union delegations to third countries closely cooperate and coordinate with Member States' embassies and consulates to contribute to local and crisis cooperation and coordination (e.g., by providing available logistical support, including office accommodation and organizational facilities, such as temporary accommodation for consular staff and for intervention teams).[30]

Consular protection includes assistance in the same cases mentioned in Decision 95/553/EC. The protection included (1) assistance in cases of death; (2) assistance in cases of serious accident or serious illness; (3) assistance in cases of arrest or detention; (4) assistance to victims of violent crime; and (5) relief and repatriation of Union citizens in need of assistance. The Directive 2015/637 broadened the consular assistance to a victim of any crime (instead of a violent crime mentioned in Decision 95/553/EC), and added the issuance of Emergency Travel Documents (ETDs).[31]

The Directive provides for the reimbursement of expenses. In principle, unrepresented citizens undertake to repay to their Member State of nationality the cost of consular protection, on the same conditions as the nationals of the assisting Member State, using the standard form set out in Annex I of the Directive 2015/637 before receiving assistance.[32] Detailed rules are provided for reimbursement of expenses by the Member State of nationality, particularly in the event of a crisis, and by a third party.[33]

[28] Directive 2015/637, article 7 para. 2.

[29] Directive 2015/637, preamble, para. 11.

[30] Directive 2015/637, article 11.

[31] Directive 2015/637/EU, Article 9, point (f).

[32] Directive 2015/637, article 14 para. 1. See document in the Annex 1.

[33] Directive 2015/637, articles 14 and 15.

9.3 Consular Protection in the Event of a Crisis in a Third Country

The EU and its Member States can make joint consular representations when EU citizens face persistent violations of their rights or difficult circumstances in a third country. Following the consular enquiry, both the EU and its Member States can decide to launch a consular cooperation to improve the situation of EU citizens.[34]

The consular network of Member States holds meetings in third countries to discuss issues of common interest to EU citizens in that country. In addition, consular staff of Member States represented in the country concerned may meet with the EU delegation to prepare for crisis situations, developing a joint contingency plan. Member States' consular services and crisis units, as well as EU Delegations, may also use an online platform for information exchange and contingency planning.[35]

In the event of a crisis, the Directive 2015/637 provides for cooperation between all diplomatic authorities of the Member States in the third country and the Delegation of the European Commission through local meetings, exchange of information and practical arrangements between them.[36]

In this context, a State may be designated to lead the assistance or coordinate assistance with other Member States (Lead State) and ensure coordination of emergency plans and coordination of assistance. Support may also be sought from intervention teams at Union level and consular experts, in particular from Member States not represented, other Member States, the Delegations, the crisis management structures of the EEAS (ISP4 Consular Affairs Section)[37] and the Union Civil Protection Mechanism.[38]

The contribution of the Consular Affairs Working Party (COCON), a preparatory body of the Council of the EU, responsible for discussing consular cooperation issues, is also important. It focuses on coordinating consular cooperation with EU Member States and the European External Action Service (EEAS) in third countries,[39] exchanging views on consular crises and related consular cooperation issues, monitoring draft consular cooperation initiatives and holding discussions on

---

[34] Council of the EU, Consular protection, available at https://www.consilium.europa.eu/el/policies/consular-protection/.

[35] Council of the EU, Consular protection, available at https://www.consilium.europa.eu/el/policies/consular-protection/.

[36] Directive 2015/637, preamble paras. 10 and 19 and Articles 11- 12.

[37] See European Union External Action Service, https://www.eeas.europa.eu/sites/default/files/documents/2022_-_03_-_16_-_eeas_orgchart.pdf.

[38] Directive 2015/637, article 13.

[39] European Council, Council of the EU, Consular protection, available at https://www.consilium.europa.eu/el/policies/consular-protection/.

coordination and cooperation measures to facilitate consular protection of EU citizens in third countries.[40]

9.4 Emergency Travel Document

The most common form of consular assistance provided under Directive 2015/637 to unrepresented non-EU citizens is the issuance of Emergency Travel Documents ("ETDs") by Member States' embassies and consulates in a third country. An Emergency Travel Document is valid for 15 days, and is intented for a single journey.[41]It allows its holder to return to his/her country or, in exceptional cases, to travel to another destination. ETDs are documents issued to European citizens or the members of their family who are in a third country where their home country does not have an embassy or consulate in situations where:

(a) Their passports or travel documents have been lost, stolen, or destroyed or
(b) Their travel documents can otherwise not be obtained within a reasonable time[42]

The latter situation may apply in the case of newborns born during the journey or persons whose documents have expired and cannot be easily replaced by the Member State of nationality.[43]

In addition, Directive 2019/997/EU sets out a simplified cooperation and coordination procedure between the "assisting Member State" in the third country and the "Member State of nationality" of the unrepresented citizen. It also provides that in situations of extreme urgency the assisting Member State may issue an EU ETD without prior consultation with the Member State of nationality of the unrepresented citizen, if the available means of communication are exhausted.[44]

---

[40] Council of the EU, Preparatory bodies: Consular Affairs Group, available at https://www.consilium.europa.eu/el/council-eu/preparatory-bodies/working-party-consular-affairs/.

[41] Directive 2019/997, article 6.

[42] Directive 2019/997, preamble, para. 4 and article 2.

[43] Directive 2019/997, preamble, para. 4 and article 3.

[44] Directive 2019/997, preamble, para. 5 and article 4(4) para. 8.

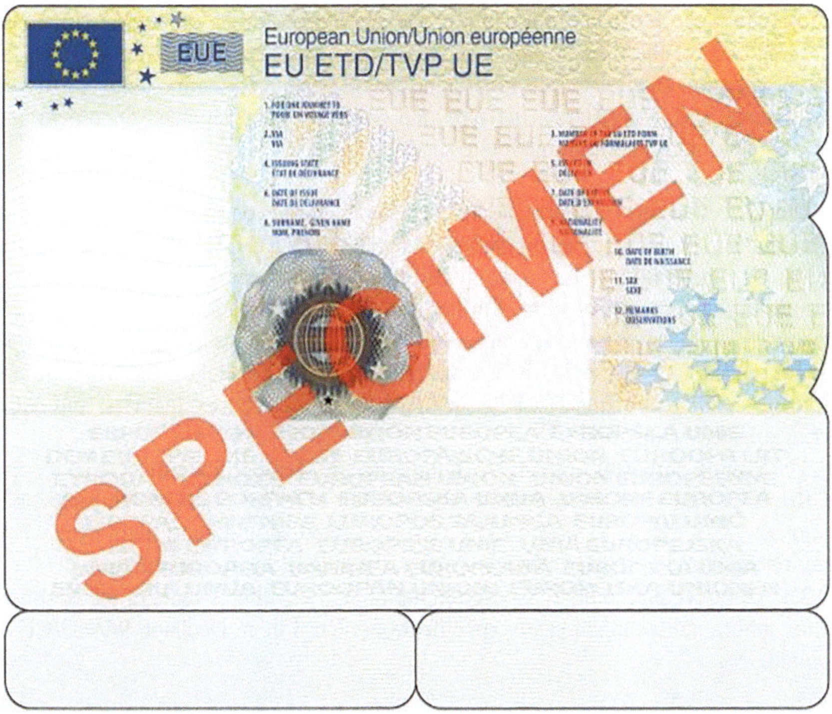

Source: European Commission at https://commission.europa.eu/strategy-and-policy/policies/justice-and-fundamental-rights/eu-citizenship-and-democracy/consular-protection_en

When a Member State receives an application for an EU ETD, it will consult the Member State of nationality as soon as possible and no later than 2 working days after receipt of the application, in order to verify the nationality and identity of the applicant.[45] Importantly, the citizen's Member State of nationality may object to the granting of an EU ETD by another Member State and have that Member State assume responsibility for providing consular protection.[46]

The assisting Member State shall provide the Member State of nationality with all relevant information, including:

(a) The surname, name(s), nationality, date of birth, and sex of the applicant
(b) An image of the applicant's face taken by the authorities of the assisting Member State at the time of application or, only where this is not possible, a

[45] Directive 2019/997, article 4 para. 1.

[46] Article 4 para. 4.

scanned or digital photograph of the applicant, based on the international standards of the International Civil Aviation Organization (ICAO)[47]

(c) A copy of any means of identification, such as an identity card or driving license, and, if available, the type and number of the replaced document and the national registration or social security number[48]

The Directive sets out the standard format to be used for an EU ETD, consisting of a standard form and an accompanying sticker.[49] The EU ETD must contain all the necessary information and meet high technical standards, to protect against counterfeiting and falsification. Further technical specifications for the EU ETD was provided for by European Commission implementing acts as regards the design, format, and colors of the EU PTE standard form and the sticker, the material and printing techniques of the EU PTE standard form, the security features, and additional rules to be respected.[50]

The issuing authority of the ETD in the relevant Member State must store a copy of the ETD and send an additional copy to the Member State of the recipient's nationality.[51] Citizens to whom EU ETDs are issued should hand them over when they return home to border officials or passport authorities for destruction.[52]

The Directive had to be transposed in national law within 2 years of the adoption of the additional technical safety specifications. Until then, Decision 96/409/CFSP applied.

9.5 Conclusion

It follows from the above provisions of primary and secondary EU law that they confer on the diplomatic and consular authorities of another Member State some of the functions of a diplomatic mission and a consulate of the Member State of which the citizen is a national, for the protection, within the limits permitted by international law, of the interests of, but only in specific cases of exceptional necessity. In this way, the right to diplomatic and consular protection of European citizens, as

---

[47] Directive 2019/997, International Civil Aviation Organization (ICAO) Document No. 9303, Part 3, on machine-readable travel documents (seventh edition, 2015) ("ICAO Document 9303").

[48] Directive 2019/997, article 4 para. 2.

[49] Directive 2019/997, article 8.

[50] Directive 2019/997, article 9. See Commission Implementing Decision (EU) 2022/2452 of December 8, 2022, laying down additional technical specifications for the EU Emergency Travel Document established by Council Directive (EU) 2019/997 (SECRET UE/EU SECRET non classifiéeenl'absence de la partie II de l'annexe/when detached from Part II of the Annex—non-classified) (notified under document C(2022) 8938) C/2022/8938, OJ L 320, 14.12.2022, pp. 47–53.

[51] Directive 2019/997, article 4 para. 7.

[52] Directive 2019/997, preamble, para. 6 and article 8.

described above, aims to strengthen the image of the Union's identity in third countries and the principle of European solidarity.

In recent years, several events have posed challenges relevant to consular protection, in particular the COVID-19 pandemic, the crisis in Afghanistan, and Russia's war of aggression against Ukraine. These crises demonstrated the benefits of consular protection to EU citizens, as part of the rights flowing from EU citizenship.[53]

Dr. Despoina Anagnostopoulou is a Professor in EU Law and Policies at the University of Macedonia, Greece, and Director of the UNESCO Chair of Intercultural Policy for an Active Citizenship and Solidarity. She has been the Jean Monnet Chairholder on New Dimensions on EU Legal Studies (2012–2015), the Academic Coordinator of the Jean Monnet Centre of Excellence on "Research on Crucial Issues of European Integration" and the Academic Coordinator of the Jean Monnet Project on Intercultural Dialogue, EU Values and Diversity (University of Macedonia). Since

2021, she has been an elected member of the Council at the European Law Institute, in Vienna, Austria. She studied law (Aristotle University of Thessaloniki). She obtained a Master's Degree at the *Libre Universite de Bruxelles* (ULB) and a PhD in EU law at the Democritus Universigyo of Thrace.

She was awarded undergraduate and postgraduate state scholarships, a Jean Monnet 3-month scholarship (European University Institute, Florence), a distinction for her contribution in national matters (Democritus University of Thrace) and a distinction for excellent teaching at the Open University Cyprus (2021). She has been stagiaire at the EU Commission Legal Service (also traveled to Japan) and a researcher at the Centre of International and European Economic Law (Thessaloniki), for more than 10 years. She taught EU Law: (a) at the Law School of Capital University, Ohio, US (one course), (b) in summer courses that had been organized by the same US University in Greece, (c) at the National School of Judges (1999–2002), and (d) at the Open University of Cyprus since 2016. She also taught Racism and Xenophobia at the National School of Judges, Greece (2016–2021).

[53] European Commission, Report from the Commission to the European Parliament and the Council, on the implementation and application of Council Directive (EU) 2015/637 of April 20, 2015, on the coordination and cooperation measures to facilitate consular protection for unrepresented citizens of the Union in third countries and repealing Decision 95/553/EC, COM (2022) 437 final, Brussels, 2.9.2022.

Climate Diplomacy Under the UNFCCC: Past, Present, and Future

10

Emmanuella Doussis and George Dikaios

Abstract

This chapter pinpoints the special characteristics that can be attributed to the functioning of international climate diplomacy and, more specifically, the relations within the structure/regime of the United Nations Framework Convention on Climate Change (UNFCCC). The chapter follows the timeline of the adoption of the seminal climate conventions (UNFCCC, Kyoto Protocol, Paris Agreement) by the international community; it discusses the developments that took place in the 27th Conference of the Parties and the challenging future of climate action. The chapter highlights the complex nature of climate diplomacy.

10.1 Introduction

Although climate change has been at the forefront of the international community's agenda for over 30 years, progress toward a successful problem-solving solution has not been achieved. Global greenhouse gas emissions, and as a consequence the global temperature, continue to rise, leading to a series of climate, environmental, and other disasters that humanity cannot tackle. A group of scholars recently published an article claiming that planet Earth has entered "uncharted territory" in terms of its climate situation, as several of its components, such as forests, oceans, and ice, are under extreme conditions expected to contribute to the worsening of the

E. Doussis (✉) · G. Dikaios
Department of Political Science and Public Administration, National and Kapodistrian University of Athens, Athens, Greece
e-mail: edoussis@pspa.uoa.gr; gdikaios@uoa.gr

P. Naskou-Perraki (ed.), *Contemporary Diplomatic and Consular Relations*,
https://doi.org/10.1007/978-3-031-99243-8_10

global climate state.[1] Despite this brooding image of today, the international community has been trying to tackle climate change since 1992 and the Earth Summit, where the United Nations Convention on Climate Change (UNFCCC) was adopted. This point in time can be perceived as the formal starting point of the history of climate diplomacy.

This chapter will present the timeline of the most important milestones of climate diplomacy. As all the milestones take place within the UNFCCC institutional framework, i.e., its Conference of the Parties (COPs), it is evident that climate diplomacy is highly interconnected with international law-making.[2] The COPs produce international documents with commitments that the UNFCCC Member States are expected to implement. As the scope of this book is to draw a picture of the "new modes" of diplomacy, the chapter goes through the milestones of climate diplomacy while exploring the special characteristics that one can attribute to its function. Concluding remarks will follow.

10.2 United Nations Convention on Climate Change (UNFCCC)

On June 5, 1992, the UNFCCC was adopted, during the Earth Summit in Rio de Janeiro. The adoption came after scientific observations of imbalances in the planet's climate. As the evidence was significant, in 1988, the international community established the Intergovernmental Panel on Climate Change (IPCC), which gathers scientists from all around the world and canvasses the situation of the planet's climate. Thus, a first characteristic of climate diplomacy is that it is significantly based on the state of the current scientific knowledge.

The problem was recognized as another environmental and, as such, technical, global problem that needed coordinated international efforts to be tackled.[3] Therefore, a second characteristic of climate diplomacy is that it began as a low politics issue—or even not at all political. The reason that climate change as a subject was raised in the global political agenda was that the environmental movement put pressure on several governments of the so-called West, not allowing the latter to avoid putting it on the international agenda.[4] One could argue that it was also a window of opportunity for the United Nations (UN) to gain an essential role in dealing with a global problem. As such, within the new globalization era starting at the time, by adopting the UNFCCC, the UN would stay relevant and have a role in a period where international peace seemed closer than ever.

The UNFCCC recognized the existence of the problem of climate change, the role of human activities in its acceleration, and gathered almost all the countries

[1] W. J, Ripple., C. Wolf, J. W. Gregg, J. Rockström, T. M. Newsome, B. E. Law, L. Marques, T. M. Lenton, C. Xu, S. Hug, L. Simons and Sir D. A. King, "The 2023 state of the climate report: Entering uncharted territory", BioScience, ahead of print, doi: 10.1093/biosci/biad080, 2023.

[2] E. Doussis, International Law and Diplomacy of Climate Change, Nomiki Bibliothiki, Athens, 2020 [in Greek].

[3] In essence, following the example of the Montreal Protocol on the Ozone Depletion.

[4] H. Gary & P. Alistair, Environmentalism since 1945, Routledge, London and New York, 2012.

worldwide under a conventional structure.[5] It set the basic framework by putting forward general obligations of conduct and the principles based on which the parties to the Convention would work in order to combat climate change. The main objective that was adopted was that the greenhouse gas emissions concentrations in the atmosphere needed to be stabilized at a safe level so as to avoid a significant rise in the temperature (Article 2). For this to be achieved, the developed countries would and should carry the majority of the burden, based on the principle of common but differentiated responsibility (CBDR), which would also allow the rest of the world to develop to a certain degree.

The UNFCCC is a progressive legal text that entrenches the fact that the acceleration of climate change is due to contemporary anthropogenic activity. Nevertheless, it was also the first international text on the issue, which did not entail specific measures or a timeline. As put by Daniel Bodansky, UNFCCC was "not an end point, but rather a punctuation mark in an ongoing process of negotiation,"[6] a process that continues to this day. This open negotiation process would take place—and still does—within the framework of the annual COPs. The functions of the COPs are "explicitly defined or implied by silence in the treaty that they are provided for, include—inter alia—the monitoring of the implementation of the treaty from the contracting parties, the decision-making for specific issues concerning the implementation of the treaty, the adoption of guidelines or codes of practice,"[7] and many more, in order to keep the treaty up-to-date according to the constantly evolving needs. Thus, a third characteristic of climate diplomacy is that it is highly institutionalized, with the UNFCCC COPs being the capstone of international climate diplomacy.

10.3 Kyoto Protocol

The UNFCCC was indeed the first significant step toward combatting climate change. This was made evident in the first and second COPs, where actual solutions that would lead to the reduction of greenhouse gas emissions were negotiated. During the third COP in Kyoto, a second significant output was produced: the Kyoto Protocol to the UNFCCC. The Protocol entails specific obligations that attempt to implement what had been agreed in the UNFCCC, i.e., the stabilization of the emissions. For this to be successful, the so-called developed world was supposed to mitigate its emissions. In contrast, the so-called developing world was allowed to continue emitting in the name of economic growth.

More specifically, during the negotiations of the Protocol (in all three COPs), two distinct, competing approaches were observed. The first, represented by the United

[5]Currently, there are 198 parties (197 states and the EU) to the UNFCCC.

[6]D. Bodansky, "The United Nations Framework Convention on Climate Change: A Commentary", Yale Journal of International Law, vol. 18, 1993, p. 451.

[7]E. Doussis, Environmental Governance in Crisis: Rio+20: Promises with Doubtful Implementation, Papazisis, Athens, 2014, pp. 158–159 [in Greek].

limiting temperature rise to no more than 2 °C; it established a process for recording the mitigation targets and actions to be implemented by developed and developing countries alike; it put significant new money on the table for climate change mitigation and adaptation by developing countries; it provided for international consultation and analysis of developing country mitigation actions, plus a more complete measurement, reporting, and verification of developed country targets and financing. Based on this rationale, the following COPs tried to build consensus and overcome the inward-looking period looming above the international climate negotiations.

10.5 Paris Agreement

COP 21 took place in Paris in 2015. Although the international environment was again more in favor of agreeing on new climate rules, the decisiveness of France (as the host country to the COP) played an essential role in concluding the COP with flying colors.[12] The signing of the Paris Agreement marks a turning point in climate governance as the top-down approach used in the Kyoto Protocol was reversed, and a bottom-up rationale was adopted. This bottom-up rationale puts forward the capabilities of each country to contribute to tackling the problem of climate change by, first, mitigating as much as possible its greenhouse gas emissions and, second, by implementing adaptation policies to climate change in order to avoid climate disasters as much as possible. Again, the CBDR principle is central to the implementation of this bottom-up approach by foreseeing financial and technology transfer from the developing to the developed countries. The goal of the precepts of the Paris Agreement, which do not have an expiry date but an innovative system of reviewing the progress made every 5 years, is to halt the rising of the Earth's temperature to 1.5 °C.[13]

Thus, an additional characteristic of climate diplomacy is the high adaptivity. It took less than 20 years to reverse the logic behind the obligations countries had to follow, as the initial model failed to deal with the problem. Moreover, through diplomacy, all countries were included in the legal framework and are expected to implement climate policies.

Two additional features show the adaptivity of climate diplomacy: First, it is the decision to name the final output "Agreement." This was a request from the then USA President, Barak Obama, which would allow him to ratify the Agreement without the permission of the USA Congress. This builds up to the Byrd-Hagel Resolution, which prohibits the USA from adopting any international convention or protocol that pose obligations only to some countries rather than all. Consequently, climate diplomacy is also adaptive to the internal political reality of (some)

[12] S. Lütz, T. Leeg, D. Otto, and V. Woyames Dreher, The European Union as a Global Actor: Trade, Finance and Climate Policy: Springer, Cham, 2021.

[13] For a detailed analysis on the Paris Agreement, see E. Doussis (2020) op. cit.

countries. Second, it is the depleted power of the successive body of the Kyoto Protocol's Compliance Committee. The Committee to Facilitate Implementation and Promote Compliance cannot impose sanctions on states that are not compliant with the Paris Agreement, but—as evident by the body's name—it facilitates them through consultations to implement better what has been agreed. One can argue that this was decided, so all states could sign the Agreement without having the concern that they could be brought up in front of an independent body that could defame them. Adaptivity, here, reflects the need to strike a proper balance between all the different state interests and—unfortunately—the least common denominator.

Nevertheless, the Paris Agreement is one of the best legal texts that could be produced through climate diplomacy, which has shown an extremely forward-looking character from the beginning, as during the negotiations, only obligations arise for states paired with the need to alter their business-as-usual plans, which would easily end up to failure every time. However, climate diplomacy still attracts great attention, and states continue to discuss and negotiate on climate change and its tackling in a systematic manner, sometimes by breakthroughs and others by going slower.

10.6 From Paris and Beyond

Where do we stand today, several years after the adoption of this landmark agreement?[14] The national climate mitigation plans (national determined contributions—NDCs) that the contracting parties to the Paris Agreement have announced so far are not enough to avoid crossing over dangerous temperature thresholds, even though 2021 marked the creation of a window of opportunity to better deal with the climate crisis and make progress toward the implementation of the Paris Agreement. After the Covid-19 pandemic, hope lied in a "green" recovery and in making climate action an integral part of national relief plans. State authorities had never been in a stronger position to boost a sustainable agenda as industry, business, and individuals clamor for state aid. New relationships could be forged with the private sector, introducing conditions that encourage businesses to decarbonize.

In fact, climate change became an issue of major public concern and since then governments, including the big emitters, seem to be more committed. The USA, after an unfortunate break of 4 years during the Trump Administration, has rejoined the Paris Agreement and promised to achieve carbon neutrality within the next three decades. In December 2022, the Biden Administration passed an important legislative package, the US Inflation Reduction Act, which is expected to close two-thirds of the greenhouse gas emissions gap between current policy and 2030 targets.

China has committed to net-zero emissions before 2060. In November 2021, China submitted its updated NDC to the UN confirming this target of becoming carbon neutral by 2060. To ensure the implementation of its climate pledges, China set up the "1+N" climate policy framework and its government has created a

[14]This chapter was finalized and submitted in October 2023.

taskforce to provide high-level coordination between different departments and local governments on climate strategies, policies, and plans.

The EU has launched the most ambitious plan so far, the European Green Deal, which is the road map for decarbonizing the European economy by 2050 with a parallel commitment for a just transition where no one will be left behind.

Since China, the United States, and the EU—combined and in this order—are responsible today for more than half of global carbon emissions, these commitments send a clear message to investors, producers, and consumers that the global transition to clean energy is an ongoing process and that resources must shift away from fossil fuels. The recognition of this endeavor in the Glasgow Climate Pact, during the COP 26, was an important step. The Pact called for a phase down of coal and a phase out of inefficient fossil fuel subsidies, two key issues that have never been explicitly mentioned at climate COP decisions before. Therefore, COP 26 signaled a shift away from fossil fuels and toward renewable/clean energy, albeit not in bold language.

In COP 27, convened in Sharm-El-Sheikh, funds for loss and damage were at the center of discussions. Loss and damage had already been on the agenda in previous negotiations rounds. Financial support, however, was explicitly put on the agenda for the first time in COP 27. This kind of support is not about adapting to climate change, but about providing finance in response to the destruction brought by climate change. Developed countries have for long opposed the idea due to concerns about the legal implications that any formal recognition of responsibility could have. In line with this logic, compensation and liability were excluded from the discussions. Instead, the core demand of the developing countries was to create a dedicated Fund for Loss and Damage from which eligible states could receive payments. Finally, there was an agreement on this critical issue to establish a new fund and this is an important achievement even though many key aspects remain to be fleshed out (e.g., which countries are eligible, who is going to contribute, issues of governance).

However, COP 27 was also marked by multiple crises and the shaken confidence of developing countries in the multilateral process. It seems that the credibility gap that exists, in particular regarding emission reductions, threatens to worsen. Many states have not updated their NDCs to align with the Glasgow Pact commitment (and update their 2030 target) and there is still a global emissions gap to a level compatible with the 1.5 degree trajectory. This could be partially attributed to the shift of political priorities after the attack of Russia on Ukraine in 2022. The importance of climate action has somehow diminished; it has lost its momentum, at least temporarily, in view of the enormous energy security challenges and the emergence of conflicting goals between energy security and climate change mitigation. However, delaying coal phase-out or even investing in new fossil fuel extracting activities and infrastructures are measures that might send confusing messages to third countries, and could justify delays in their own climate transition.

Therefore, one of the biggest challenges for the COP 28 in Dubai (November–December 2023) is to restore trust and strengthen the credibility to multilateral cooperation and the implementation of the Paris Agreement. The question though is how this can be achieved in a world of increasing polarization and competition, now aggravated by the ongoing Israel–Hamas war, which began in early October 2023.

The conflict in Gaza comes to further complicate an already fragile multilateral process, as it threatens to fracture an already divided world. Moreover, it can impact the raise of oil and gas prices, tempting countries to secure their supplies of fossil fuels instead of transitioning away from them. Can the COP 28 deliberations focus only on technical issues of climate policy, namely implementing existing commitments and pledges, updating the 2030 targets and backing them up with real action, delivering promised financial resources to the most vulnerable; leaving aside exchanges on the ongoing war? If the conflict expands across the Middle East, it would be very difficult to have any progress on climate diplomacy to prevent further global warming.

10.7 Concluding Remarks

This chapter was structured around the primary achievements of climate diplomacy—or even its hard core—i.e., the international agreements that the international community has managed to adopt so far, namely the UNFCCC, the Kyoto Protocol, and the Paris Agreement. It also highlighted the special characteristics that climate diplomacy displays, which make it unique among other strands of diplomacy. Compiling these characteristics, we can observe that they could be categorized into two streams. The first describes the nature of climate diplomacy: it is scientifically- and expert-based; highly institutionalized, technical and adaptive; innovative both in theory and practice. The second describes the externalities that give climate diplomacy those characteristics: it is subject to the broader international environment, usually divided into two groups (especially regarding climate change) and is often considered (on purpose) as a low politics issue.

Nevertheless, diplomacy is a tool that offers (necessary) venues between states to negotiate and agree on positions on which they find commonplaces. Within this context, climate diplomacy is a targeted policy that frames climate change as an element of external action policy and pinpoints the need to integrate climate objectives and address climate risks at the highest diplomatic level, and across all policy areas. It aims, through continuous (mostly soft) law-making, to mainstream climate action, shape foreign policy agendas, share experiences, and build partnerships that tackle both climate and other policy objectives (such as just transition, human rights, etc.) that are affected by climate change. Above all, climate diplomacy is a preventive diplomacy that strives to adjust all policy fields in the contemporary climate needs.

Apart from the short history and the special characteristics that have been discussed in this chapter, it is worth to say that today, climate diplomacy covers a broad array of relations that go very much beyond the traditional state-to-state diplomacy or span over different policy fields and international fora of negotiations. For instance, climate diplomacy involves other actors, such as nongovernmental organizations, the private sector and business, unions, cities, regions, the local level, youth and women, and science. Moreover, climate diplomacy also takes place outside the UNFCCC, as different policy areas must adopt climate measures. For example, heated negotiations occur at the International Civil Aviation Organization and the International Maritime Organization, and even the North Atlantic Treaty Organization (NATO) has added climate diplomacy to its agenda. Finally, the EU is the most active international actor performing climate diplomacy, in an attempt to convince others to do something about climate change.[15] This fragmented picture of climate diplomacy is complemented by the totality of human activity influenced by climate change: How can diplomacy help alleviate the consequences of climate migration? How will climate diplomacy influence global trade and investments? After all, how can climate diplomacy ensure its effectiveness in a world full of growing turbulence, where national priorities diverge from long-term planning and sustainability, and focus on short-term and ephemeral goals?

In conclusion, climate diplomacy is a necessary part of diplomatic practice, ultimately aiming at the improvement of living standards and a sustainable future for all.

Dr. Emmanuella Doussis is a Professor of International Institutions at the National and Kapodistrian University of Athens, and UNESCO Chairholder on Climate Diplomacy. She lectures on international law, international organization, environmental policies, and climate diplomacy. She has been a visiting professor at several universities in France and a Fulbright visiting scholar at the University of California, Berkeley, USA (2022). She has served as advisor to the rapporteur of the European Economic and Social Committee for the preparation of the opinion on EU Climate Diplomacy. She is currently the director of the master's programme on Southeast European Studies: politics, history, and economics and she coordinates a Jean Monnet module (2024–2027) on climate policies and diplomacy in Southeast Europe. She is also the head of the climate and sustainability programme at the Hellenic Foundation for European and Foreign Policy (ELIAMEP). Her most recent book explores the role of international law in addressing climate change (International Law and Climate Change Diplomacy, Nomiki Vivliothiki, Athens, 2020).

Dr. George Dikaios is an adjunct lecturer and a postdoctoral researcher at the National and Kapodistrian University of Athens (NKUA). He is affiliated with the Department of Ports Management and Shipping and the Department of Political Science and Public Administration. He is a

[15]For the issues raised in this paragraph, see, for example: A. Causevic, Facing an unpredictable threat: Is NATO ideally placed to manage climate change as a non-traditional threat multiplier?, Connections: The Quarterly Journal, vol. 16, no. 2, 2017, pp. 59–80; G. Dikaios (2024) EU Climate Diplomacy towards the IMO and ICAO (Cham: Palgrave Macmillan); E. Doussis (2020) *op. cit.*; J. Earsom and T. Delreux, Evaluating EU responsiveness to the evolution of the international regime complex on climate change, International Environmental Agreements: Politics, Law and Economics, vol. 21, no. 4, 2021, pp. 711–728; H. Han and S. W. Ahn, Youth mobilization to stop global climate change, Sustainability, vol. 12, no. 41272020; J. L. Manfredi Sánchez and F. Seoane Pérez, Climate change begins at home: City diplomacy in the age of the Anthropocene, in Surowiec, P. and I. Manor (eds.) Public Diplomacy and the Politics of Uncertainty (Cham: Palgrave Macmillan), 2020, pp. 57–81.

Senior Research Fellow of the UNESCO Chair on Climate Diplomacy and the Hellenic Foundation for European and Foreign Policy (ELIAMEP), a SYLFF fellow and a Research Fellow of the Institute of European Integration and Policy (NKUA). His first book is EU Climate Diplomacy Towards the IMO and ICAO (Palgrave Macmillan, 2024). From September 2025, he will be a Marie Curie Postdoctoral Fellow at Leiden University.

hegemony, power, influence, collaboration, financial strength, international organization, diplomacy, and others[1] thus most ruling people tend to exploit them.[2]

Sports have been used for diplomatic purposes since ancient times. Significant examples are the Olympic, Pythian, Isthmian, and Nemean games organized in ancient Greece, where only Greeks could participate, fostering a sense of common identity, heritage, language, and religion among citizens of Greek cities spread around the then-known world.[3] Especially in the Olympic Games, a month-long peace (Truce) was agreed upon between the city-states to cease fighting, so that hostilities would not interfere with the event, essentially establishing an institution of sports diplomacy.[4]

In modern times sports started to get organized at the end of the 19th and the beginning of the 20th century. In 1894, the International Olympic Committee (IOC) was established, making it the only human institution that was organized at the international level first.[5] Later, International Sports Federations (ISFs) were established to govern each sport at a global level and created specific rules. In a world where there is a strong interdependence between sectors of societies at the domestic level, as well as internationally between states,[6] sport: (a) functions as a cohesive element of this interdependence,[7] (b) develops in many different political, cultural, and societal environments, and (c) exhibits competitive and noncompetitive activities (seminars, conferences, committees, etc.).[8] Confirming the above,[9] IOC President, stated that: "… sport is one of the most powerful social forces of our times."

At the noncompetitive level, it has been widely acknowledged by prominent psychologists, anthropologists, sociologists, and many other scientists that sport presents a diplomatic ability to pacify, or provide an outlet for aggression, or mimic war, conflict, and battle short of violence; sport also sublimates, absorbs, and mitigates conflicts within and between groups of disparate peoples, nations, and

[1]Happel, D., & Kramer, R. The objectives of sport and international understanding. In the Proceedings of the Congress Sport and International Understanding, 108-110, Helsinki, 1984, 7-10.7.82, Ilmirinen, M. (editor). Springer-Verlag, Berlin.

[2]Murray, S. Sports diplomacy: origins, theory, and practice, Routledge, 2018.

[3]Pomeroy, S. B., Burstein, S. M., Donlan, W., & Tolber-Roberts, J. Ancient Greece: a political, social, and cultural history. 3rd edition. Oxford University Press, Abington, 2014.

[4]Freeman, W. Physical education, exercise, and sport science in a changing society. 7th edition. Sudbury, MA: Jones & Bartlett (2012).

[5]MacAloon, J. The turn of two centuries: sport and the politics of international relations. In Sport… The Third Millennium, International Symposium, Quebec City, Canada, (1991). 21-25.05.1990, Landry, F., Landry, M., Yerles, M., (editors). Saint-Foy: Les Presses De L' Université Laval.

[6]Theodoropoulos, V. Foreign policy – Diplomacy – Diplomats, O Typos, Athens, 1990.

[7]Gargalianos, D., The new European Sports Charter, Pandektis, 2, Athens, 1992.

[8]Erbach, G. On the character and contents of sport and of international sporting activities at present and in the future. In the Proceedings of the Congress "Sport and International Understanding" (31-37), Helsinki, 07-10.07.1982, Ilmirinen, M. (editor). Springer-Verlag, Berlin, 1984.

[9]Samaranch, J. A. Olympic Review, March (1984), 156.

states.[10] According to Lorenz,[11] "... sporting contests between nations are beneficial not only because they provide an outlet for the collective militant enthusiasm of nations, but also because they have two other effects that counter the danger of war: they promote personal acquaintance between people of different nations or parties and they unite, in enthusiasm for a common people who otherwise would have little in common." Along the same line, in the 2000 Laureus World Sports Awards, Nelson Mandela underlined that: "... sport has the power to change the world. It has the power to inspire. It has the power to unite people in a way that little else does. It speaks to youth in a language they understand. Sport can create hope, where once there was only despair. It is more powerful than governments in breaking down racial barriers" (https://www.un.org).

11.2 The Concept of Sport Diplomacy

Sports diplomacy is a new term that describes an old practice: the unique power of sport to bring people, nations, and communities closer together via a shared love of physical pursuits. According to Murray and Price (2020), a diplomatic perspective focuses on the processes, actors involved, and networks created by state and non-state actors and international sports. Consequently, sports diplomacy can be defined as the conscious, strategic use of sports people and sporting events by state and non-state actors to: (a) engage, inform, and create a favorable image among foreign publics and organizations, (b) shape their perceptions in a way that is (more) conducive to the sending group's goals, and (c) build relationships and amplify profile, policy and attractiveness to invest or study in, trade with, or visit.[12] The term encapsulates a more inclusive method of policy formulation: state and non-state actors, along with sports organizations work together for win-win outcomes.

11.3 Why Are Governments Attracted to Sport as a Tool for Diplomacy?

Murray and Price (2020) claimed that governments are attracted to sport as a tool for diplomacy for several reasons, which can be summarized as follows:

Sport instigates informal ephemeral relationships, which can lead to formal, long-term ones.
Sport is an attractive and popular vessel, through which diplomacy is conducted.
Sports diplomacy is a "low-risk, low-cost and—often—high profile" activity.

[10] Allport, G. W. The nature of prejudice. MA: Addison-Wesley, Cambridge, 1954.

[11] Lorenz, K. On aggression. MJF Books, New York, 1966.

[12] Murray, S., & Pigman, P. A., Mapping the relationship between international sport and diplomacy. Sport in Society, 2014, 17(9), 1098-1118.

11.5 The Role of the International Olympic Committee (IOC)

Based on Fundamental Principle 5 (Olympic Charter, 2023), which states: "Recognizing that sport occurs within the framework of society, sports organizations within the Olympic Movement shall apply political neutrality. They have the rights and obligations of autonomy, which include freely establishing and controlling the rules of sport, determining the structure and governance of their organizations, enjoying the right of elections free from any outside influence, and the responsibility for ensuring that principles of good governance be applied," the IOC plays a central role in sports diplomacy.

The principles not limited to the recognition of the obligation to respect the neutrality that should be enjoyed by sports institutions in general, but also indirectly extends to the possibility that enables them to emerge as a diplomatic force that can intervene in specific cases in a political scene.[18] This becomes evident in Article 3 (Recognition by the IOC) of the Olympic Charter (2023), which states that the IOC holds the right to recognize National Olympic Committees (NOCs) and other sports organizations. More specifically:

The IOC may grant formal recognition to the constituents of the Olympic Movement.

The IOC may recognize NOCs as national sports organizations, the activities of which are linked to its mission and role.

The IOC may also recognize associations of NOCs formed at the continental or world level. All NOCs and associations of NOCs shall have, where possible, the status of legal persons. They must comply with the Olympic Charter. Their statutes are subject to the approval of the IOC.

The IOC may recognize International Federations (IFs) and associations of IFs.

The recognition of associations of NOCs or IFs does not in any way affect the right of each NOC and IF to deal directly with the IOC, and vice-versa.

The IOC may recognize nongovernmental organizations connected with sport, operating on an international level, the statutes, and activities of which conform with the Olympic Charter. In each case, the consequences of recognition are determined by the IOC Executive Board.

Recognition by the IOC may be provisional or full. Provisional recognition, or its withdrawal, is decided by the IOC Executive Board for a specific or indefinite period. The IOC Executive Board may determine the conditions according to which provisional recognition may lapse. Full recognition, or its withdrawal, is decided by the Session. All details of recognition procedures are determined by the IOC Executive Board.

[18]Gangas, D. Olympic Movement and international politics: a confrontational coexistence over time, International Olympic Academy. Athens, 2021.

Generally, the Olympic Games and the Olympic system reflect the world's political structure. Nation-states participate in the Games, the NOCs are organized within nation-state boundaries, the athlete is a representative of a nation-state, the IFs are composed of National Federations that are also organized within nation-state boundaries, the IOC is the umbrella organization for the other sports organizations within the context of the Olympic Games and other Olympic-sanctioned events, and IOC members themselves are considered to be ambassadors to nation-state areas.[19]

11.6 Significant Geopolitical Situations Within the Olympic Movement

According to Gangas (2021), Post World War II, the IOC faced a series of significant geopolitical situations, the most important of which are presented below.

The "two Germanies". One of the most important interventions in shaping a new political situation was East Germany's recognition as an independent state through sporting excellence. In the 1950s, the anti-German sentiment had noticeably subsided in Europe and the IOC accepted the German NOC within the Olympic Movement. After a while, East German people approached the IOC asking for the recognition of their own, separate NOC. However, according to the Olympic Charter, only one NOC per country could be recognized and most IOC members considered that, at least in sports, the two parts of Germany were essentially one country. East Germany invested a lot of time, energy, and resources in developing sports and the extraordinary performances of the East German athletes at the events in which they participated significantly contributed to the country's acceptance into the Olympic family (1968) and a little later (1973) in the UN.

The "two Chinas". Immediately following the war in China between nationalists and communists, in 1951, most of the Chinese NOC people fled to Taiwan and, as far as the IOC was concerned, continued to theoretically represent China. The new political regime in mainland China continued sports activities domestically through the All-China Athletic Committee, without participating in international events. Shortly after, in 1952, operating as a NOC, the ACAC submitted a request to the IOC for separate recognition of China. A bitter conflict arose between China and Taiwan over the names, anthems, and flags their NOCs would use, which was settled by the following IOC's decision: "The Olympic Committee of the PRC to be recognized as the 'Chinese Olympic Committee' with its distinctive anthem and flag and the Olympic Committee of Taiwan as 'Chinese Taipei Olympic Committee' with a different anthem and a different flag." The agreement was officially announced in April 1981, putting an end to the struggle between politics and sport that lasted 30 whole years.

The "two Koreas". The division of Korea into North and South created a similar problem for the IOC as those of the "two Germanies" and the "two Chinas". The IOC

[19] Espy, R. The politics of the Olympic Games. University of California Press, 1979.

recognized the South Korean Olympic Committee in 1947 and the North Korean Olympic Committee in 1963 and since then many attempts have been made to reconcile the two countries with limited success.

The South Africa Case (Apartheid). Because colored South African citizens were not allowed to practice sports and compete alongside whites, the IOC decided to exclude the country from seven Olympic Games (1964, 1968, 1972, 1976, 1980, 1984, and 1988). It was readmitted at the 1992 Barcelona Games after apartheid was no longer practiced in the country.

11.7 Diplomacy in the Context of the Summer Olympic Games

According to Gangas (2021), there have been many instances in the history of the modern Olympic Movement that the Games were used as grounds for diplomacy:

Antwerp 1920. Even though it was against the Olympic Charter for political reasons the IOC did not invite Germany and its allies (Austria, Bulgaria, Turkey, Hungary).

Paris 1924. Austria, Bulgaria, Turkey, Hungary were invited to the Games but not Germany.

Amsterdam 1928. Uruguay tried to impress the world with the performance of the country's football team. However, the successes of the team also drew the attention of people to the political situations in the nondemocratic countries in South America.[20]

Los Angeles 1932. The Americans used the Olympic Games to strengthen their prestige over the rest of the world, which was shaken by the great economic crisis of 1929.

Berlin 1936. Nazi Germany was the first nation to organize the Olympic Games with the purpose to show its power to the whole world. Hitler viewed the Games as a showcase event, and he authorized extensive funding for "monumental construction and political theatre."

London 1948. As it happened in 1920, Germany and its allies were not invited. Arab countries threatened to boycott the Games if the newly established state of Israel participated. Egypt stated that: "…acceptance of the Israeli team would mean partial recognition of the state."[21] The IOC decided that Israel could not participate because it was recognized as Palestine.

Helsinki 1952. Humanity began to overcome the devastation of war and was entering a period of peace. The climate of optimism was favored by the participation of the Soviet Union, West Germany, and Israel. Due to the IOC's refusal to

[20] Giatsis, S. Contemporary Olympic Games. University lectures. Department of Physical Education & Sport Science, Aristotle University of Thessaloniki, 1991.

[21] Espy, R., The politics of the Olympic Games. University of California Press, 1979, p. 159.

recognize their state, the East Germans stayed away from the Games. Negative was also the fact that Nationalist China and Red China withdrew.[22]

Melbourne 1956. The Games came close to being postponed because of two global events that occurred.[23] The first was the invasion of the Soviet army into Hungary. Netherlands, Spain, and Switzerland withdrew in protest, while Hungary, loyal to the Olympic ideals, remained. The second was the Suez Canal situation, during which England, France, and Israel waged war against Egypt. In protest, Egypt, Iraq, and Lebanon withdrew from the Games. Moreover, the People's Republic of China did not participate because Taiwan was invited.[24]

Rome 1960. With the intense pursuit of medals and points the countries of the East and the West transformed the Games into a field of confrontation, within the general context of their competition. Extraordinary events were the IOC's coercion of Taiwan to participate under the name of Formosa,[25] and the blessing of the Games by Pope John third, who thus signified that the church agreed with the purposes of the Olympic Games.

Tokyo 1964. This Games: (a) proved that Japan was fully reintegrated into the international community,[26] (b) showed that the demilitarized country was not a threat to the rest of the world,[27] (c) consisted of a clear indication of the country's economic progress,[28] and (d) contributed to the improvement of the legislation regarding the Trade Unions.[29] South Africa and Rhodesia (today Zimbabwe) were excluded from the Games because of racist policies enforcement. Moreover, after the IOC's decision not to invite the countries that participated in the 1963 Games of New Emerging Forces (GANEFO), Indonesia and North Korea withdrew their teams.[30]

Mexico City 1968. The IOC's decision to invite South Africa led 32 African countries to threaten that they would boycott the Games. The IOC canceled the decision, and the boycott did not happen (Edwards, 1984). East Germany was allowed to field a separate team. During the Games, the Americans Karlos and Smith (first and third place respectively at the 200 m race in track & field), as well as James, Evans, Freeman, and Matthews (first place at the 4 X 400 m relay in track & field), during the recoil of the national anthem of their country had one gloved fist

[22]Espy, R. The politics of the Olympic Games. University of California Press, 1979.

[23]Arnold, P. Οι Ο.Α.: Αθήνα 1896 - Σεούλ 1988, Αθηναϊκές Εκδόσεις, Αθήνα, 1983.

[24]Pound, R. Five rings over Korea: the secret negotiations behind the 1988 Olympic Games in Seoul, Little, Brown & Company, London, 1994.

[25]Pound, R. Five rings over Korea: the secret negotiations behind the 1988 Olympic Games in Seou,. Little, Brown & Company, London, 1994.

[26]Taylor, T. Politics and the Seoul Olympics. The Pacific Review, 1988, 1(2), 190-195.

[27]Giatsis, S. Contemporary Olympic Games. University lectures. Department of Physical Education & Sport Science, Aristotle University of Thessaloniki, 1991.

[28]Pound, R. Five rings over Korea: the secret negotiations behind the 1988 Olympic Games in Seoul, Little, Brown & Company, London, 1994.

[29]Nafziger, J. International Sports Law, Hatzikonstantinou (translation), Paratiritis, Thessaloninki.

[30]Edwards, H. Sport politics - Los Angeles 1984: the Olympic tradition continues. Journal of Sociology of Sports, (1984). 1991, 1, 172-183.

raised, thus protesting against racial discrimination occurred in the USA and the unequal opportunities black people had in education.

Munich 1972. Political tension was heightened before the Games because the IOC decided to invite Rhodesia, a country with racist policies. Once more many African countries threatened to boycott, resulting in the withdrawal of the decision. During the competitions, the most tragic event in the history of the Olympic Games happened. On 5 September, Palestinian members of the "Black September" group captured Israeli athletes in their quarters in the Olympic Village and to set them free they demanded the release of 200 compatriots of theirs who were imprisoned in Israel and an airplane to escape. The German authorities ordered an attack during their boarding, but things went sideways resulting in the death of 11 Israeli athletes, four Palestinians, and one German policeman.[31]

Montreal 1976. Canadians used the Games to (1) attract the interest of tourists both domestically and internationally,[32] and (2) to differentiate their policy on Far East issues from the Americans. They did that for two main reasons: (a) they had different views on Vietnam, and (b) their sales of wheat to the People's Republic of China (PRC) were continuously increasing. To that extent, a few weeks before the Opening Ceremony the leadership of the country decided to terminate Taiwan's recognition; hence, Taiwan did not participate.[33] Another significant decision they made was to invite New Zealand, which before the Games permitted a rugby team of the country to compete against a team from racist South Africa. The result of this decision was that 16 African states were dissatisfied and in protest, they boycotted the Games.[34] In this Games, East German athletes dominated most sports, making it clear that the country considered sport as a high national priority and successes in sports events strengthened its political ideology.

Moscow 1980. A few months earlier (27.12.1979), the Soviet army had invaded Afghanistan and in protest, the USA, Canada, West Germany, Japan, Kenya, Israel, and Turkey did not participate.[35] Coghlan (1990), observed that all three Soviet invasions (the other two were in Hungary [1956] and Czechoslovakia [1968]), happened at a time when all countries were in their final preparations to participate in the Olympic Games, and wondered whether it was just a coincidence or was a parameter that was taken into consideration for their decisions.

Los Angeles 1984. Under the pretext of the safety of their athletes, the Soviets, and their allies (except for Romania) did not participate in the Games. The People's

[31] Segrave, J., & Chu, D. (eds). The Olympic Games in transition. Champaign, Human Kinetics, Illinois, 1988.

[32] Giatsis, S. Contemporary Olympic Games. University lectures. Department of Physical Education & Sport Science, Aristotle University of Thessaloniki, 1991.

[33] Olafson, G., & Brown-John, C. Canadian international sport policy: a public policy analysis. In "The 1984 Olympic Scientific Congress Proceedings", Redmond, G., Editor, Human Kinetics Publishers, 1986, 7, 69-76.

[34] Lapchick, R. E. The politics of race and international sport, Greenwood Press, Westport, 1975.

[35] Giatsis, S. Contemporary Olympic Games. University lectures. Department of Physical Education & Sport Science, Aristotle University of Thessaloniki, 1991.

Republic of China and Yugoslavia did not participate as well because of different political reasons.[36] The Games were characterized as "Capitalist Games" because the organizers aimed to exhibit the superiority of private initiative and its contribution to national development (Edwards, 1984).

Seoul 1988. According to the President of the Organizing Committee, Park Seh-Jik (1991), the Games greatly promoted the national interests of the country because: (a) the image of South Korea was enhanced internationally, (b) the power of the country and its economic achievements were exhibited, (c) friendly relations with foreign countries were developed, (d) favorable conditions for the establishment of diplomatic relations with communist states and states that did not belong to either of the two great alliances (nonaligned) were created, and (e) national unity was forged.

Barcelona 1992. The Games created a significant opportunity for Catalan nationalists to make their views known to a wider audience. The appointment of the Catalan language, which was banned by Franko, as the fourth official of the event made it acknowledged.[37]

Sydney 2000. Various aboriginal leaders organized a few small-scale protests attempting to utilize the Games to highlight their plight to the world, and to convince the State to recognize for them equal rights with other Australian citizens. Significant was the fact that even though North and South Korea competed as separate nations, at the Opening Ceremony they marched together under the name "Korea", giving rise to hopes that someday in the future they might be reunited.

Athens 2004. Amid the preparations, the 9/11 terrorist attack in New York changed the security specifications used internationally up to that time. The international political environment with Sudan and Somalia being ravaged by civil wars and the further worsening of the situation in the Middle East increased the fears of experts about a possible terrorist attack during the Games, a view that ended up costing a great deal, because: (a) a lot more people (approx. 45,000) than initially calculated had to be employed in the Games Security sector,[38] (b) the arrival of spectators from abroad was not in line with expectations, as many of those who had bought a large number of tickets decided not to come, resulting in a sizable cut in the budgeted revenue for the Committee, and (c) the expenses budgeted by the government, albeit unrelated to the Organizing Committee, increased significantly, greatly changing the action plan and the means to be deployed. Moreover, many terrorist groups had operated in Greek territory over many years, the most important being "17 November". In June 2002, a mistake of a member of this organization resulted in the arrest of almost all its leaders and operatives, something that was welcomed with great relief both domestically in Greece and internationally.

[36] Toohey, K. The politics of the 1984 Los Angeles Olympics, In The 1984 Olympic Scientific Congress Proceedings, Redmond, G., Editor, Human Kinetics Publishers, 1986, 7, 161-170.

[37] Lucas, J. Future of the Olympic Games, Human Kinetics, Champaign, Ill, 1992.

[38] Kennelly, M., & Toohey, K. Terrorism and the Olympics: the Games have gone on. Sporting Traditions, 2007, 24(1-2), 1-22.

gender, age, physical ability, and ethnic background). The aim was to assess the value of sport in EU external policies, identify how sport can help the EU reach its external political ambitions (e.g., fostering relations with partner countries), and be an element of dialogue with third countries and regions as part of EU public diplomacy (European Commission, 2018). In June 2016, the High-Level Group on Sport Diplomacy delivered a Report with several recommendations. Following this work, in November 2016, Council Conclusions on Sport Diplomacy were adopted by all the EU Ministers responsible for sport. Then sports diplomacy became a key priority of the EU Work Plan for Sport (2017–2020), which: (a) recognized that sport can improve national and European foreign policy and international relations, reach out to external stakeholders, and improve the image and influence of the EU and its Member States across the world, and (b) acknowledged the need of EU and its Member States to strengthen diplomatic, social, and political relations with countries outside of the EU and to cooperate with third countries, in particular candidate countries and potential candidates to the EU, to promote European values through sports diplomacy.

11.9 The Dark Side of Sports Diplomacy

Sports have an association with violence, terrorism, jingoism, ideology, cheating, doping, gambling, and corruption, and to that extent sports diplomacy has a dark side as well. Some indicative recent examples are the following:

In 2012, the cyclist Lance Armstrong was banned from the sport for life, stripped of his record seven Tour de France titles, and publicly lambasted. Speaking of the "biggest crisis" the sport had ever faced, International Cycling Union (UCI) President, Pat McQuaid, stated that "Lance Armstrong has no place in cycling … he deserves to be forgotten" (ABC News, 2013).

In 2016, a World Anti-Doping Agency (WADA) report asserted that more than 1.000 Russian athletes, across more than 30 sports, were involved in or benefited from state-sponsored doping between 2011 and 2015. In December 2019, WADA banned Russia from major international sporting events for 4 years on charges of tampering with doping-related reports.[41]

In 2018, three Australian cricket players, including the captain Steve Smith, were caught ball-tampering during a tour in South Africa, charged with bringing the game into disrepute and banned from all international and domestic cricket for 12 months.[42]

[41] McLaren, R. H. The Independent Person. 2nd Report. Montréal: World Anti-Doping Agency, 2016. Available at: https://www.wada-ama.org/sites/default/files/resources/files/mclaren_report_part_ii_2.pdf

[42] Ferris, S. Trio suspended by Cricket Australia, 2018. Available at: https://www.cricket.com.au/news/3294494

These examples provide a reminder that in international sports things can and often do go wrong. Fortunately, however, these dark episodes are the exception rather than the rule. It seems that sport is far more beneficial to international relations than detrimental.

11.10 Closing Remarks

In contemporary society, sports: (a) convince the participants that its fundamental values (e.g., pursuit of the best possible performance) coincide with the values of society as a whole, (b) is one of a few activities that people can participate in without needing to communicate with other people, (c) is governed by rules, which are universally recognized and accepted, (d) is a democratic domain, and allows people from every walk of life to participate both as athletes, as well as in other capacities (e.g. administrators), and (e) functions as an interface between private and public life.[43] These attributes establish political ability, which can be used to the benefit of society. Unfortunately, to this day sports have minimal influence on political priorities at all levels (local, national, and international); on the contrary, in many cases, it has been acknowledged that politics influence sport.[44]

It would be beneficial to recognize that society is left with few opportunities for peace to prevail, and certainly sport is one of them.[45] The collapse of the Soviet Union and the consequent end of the Cold War significantly contributed to the creation of a proper international environment for a general reconsideration of the role of sports,[46] during which political leaders might be enlightened on the power of this popular, easy to understand, and irrefutable means of domestic and foreign policy. With the cooperation of the state authority for sport with the administrators of sports organizations and the Ministry of Foreign Affairs in each country, a policy could be created, which would encourage the inclusion of sport in the set of "tools" that are available to its international relations processes.

Dimitris Gargalianos, Professor at the Department of Physical Education & Sport Science, Democritus University of Thrace, Greece. Born in Thessaloniki, Greece, in 1959. International level track and field athlete (110 m hurdles). Holder of: (a) a Bachelor's degree in Physical Education (1980), (b) a Master's degree in Sport Management (1983), (c) a Bachelor's degree in International Relations (1992), (d) a Doctoral degree in International Relations of Sport (1996), and

[43] Heinemann, K. Sports as an instrument of political integration and conflict solution. In The Seoul Olympiad Anniversary Conference Toward One World Beyond All Barriers, Poong Nam Publishing Co., Seoul, 1990.

[44] Coakley, J. Sport in society: issues and controversies. 3rd ed., Mosby, St. Louis, 1986.

[45] Taylor, T. Politics and the Seoul Olympics. The Pacific Review, 1988. 1(2), 190-195.

[46] Peppard, V., & Riordan, J. Playing politics: Soviet sports diplomacy to 1992. Russian & East European Studies, Vol., 3, Batalden, S., & Nooman, T., Editors, London,1993 Jai Press Inc.

Seppanen, P., The Olympics: A sociological perspective. International Review for the Sociology of Sport, 1984, 19(2), 113-127.

(e) a Diploma in Communication Management (2000). Worked for the Hellenic Federation of Track & Field as a technical advisor responsible for the education of coaches (1985–1990), and the Hellenic Ministry of Sport as an international relations consultant (1990–1992). Initiated the Hellenic Association of Sport Management (1993) (president until 1999, vice-president until 2003, and general secretary until 2013). Attended the preparations for the Sydney 2000 Olympic Games as an official observer of the 2004 OCOG (July 1998–November 2000). Worked as a communication consultant in the Athens 2004 OCOG (May 2001–May 2002) and as Athens Headquarters Coordinator for the United States Olympic Committee (January 2003–December 2004). Presently, he is a teaching sport management, event management, and international relations of sport. Authored/co-authored books on these subjects. Published many articles in Greek and international journals. Attended, taught, and presented at many Greek and international seminars/conferences.

Cultural Diplomacy 12

Antonia Zervaki

Abstract

This chapter explores the concept, evolution, and role of cultural diplomacy in contemporary international relations. Drawing on the plurality of perceptions and objectives of cultural diplomacy that have emerged across different historical periods, the author aims to depict its current features as a dimension of public diplomacy and as a soft power tool, applied in different national contexts as well as within the framework of international organizations. The latter function as fora for the conduct of state-driven cultural diplomacy; however, international organizations also use the transformative power of culture to promote ideational, political, and operational objectives that transcend the confines of states' foreign policy objectives and advance a new type of cultural diplomacy linked to the discourse and practice of contemporary global governance in the domains of security, development, and human rights.

12.1 Historical Overview

Cultural diplomacy, whether perceived as a special dimension of public diplomacy or as the empirical manifestation of the use of "soft power" by a polity,[1] does not constitute a recent practice in the history of international relations. It traces its roots back to classical antiquity. In Pericles' Funeral Oration, Thucydides pays tribute to the

[1] See J.S. Nye, Soft Power: The Means to Success in World Politics, Public Affairs Books, New York, 2004, p. 8 and J. Melissen (ed.), The New Public Diplomacy. Soft Power in International Relations, Palgrave Macmillan, Basingstoke, 2005.

A. Zervaki (✉)
Department of Political Science and Public Administration, National and Kapodistrian University of Athens, Athens, Greece
e-mail: azervaki@pspa.uoa.gr

P. Naskou-Perraki (ed.), *Contemporary Diplomatic and Consular Relations*,
https://doi.org/10.1007/978-3-031-99243-8_12

moral, cultural, and civic legacy of Athens, relating these features with the empowerment and greatness of the city (*polis*).[2] In the Hellenistic and Roman world, culture is used as "a means of exerting soft power"[3] contributing to the maintenance of the empire's "status quo and dominion with peaceful means."[4] During the Byzantine era cultural exports such as the Christianization and the introduction of the Cyrillic alphabet in the neighboring Slav States represented a similar approach.[5]

Moving on to our more recent past, cultural diplomacy was once again identified with the promotion of the cultural achievements and superiority of the great powers, often revealing the dark side of the transformative power of culture in international relations. Colonial practices aiming at cultural domination through the means of imposing European values on the populations in colonial territories constituted an illustrative example of this tactic.[6]

In the interwar period, cultural diplomacy, conducted mainly through cultural agencies, manifests the inherent antagonism between the two dominant imperialist models of the time: on the one hand, the institutionalized efforts of cultural domination by the colonial powers, illustrated in the cases of the British Council and Alliance française; on the other hand, a similar practice seems to be adopted by states following the national socialist and fascist paths, as in the cases of the Verein für das Deutschtum im Ausland and the Dante Alighieri Society.[7]

During the Cold War, antagonism between the Western and Eastern blocs also spread to the cultural domain. Cultural diplomacy became part of the broader foreign policy agenda of the two great powers and their coalitions. Cultural diplomacy was linked to national security broadly conceived as "freedom from foreign dictation."[8] The latter was not solely interpreted in relation to states' territorial integrity; it also implied "the absence of threats to acquired values."[9] Reference to "acquired values" had a cultural and ideological connotation since it was related to principles, standards, and ways of life as crystallized in states' sociocultural fabric and the different prevailing governance systems following the liberal and the socialist paradigms.

Cultural diplomacy reflected the sense of pride nations felt about their cultural achievements, and the pursuit of cultural leadership that went in hand with ideological supremacy. Its transformative potential was highly appreciated by foreign policy

[2] Thucydides, Pericles' Funeral Oration, Thucydidis historiae, vol. II, § 35-46.

[3] N. Vasileiadis, Cultural Diplomacy. Historical retrospection. Definitions. In N. Vasileiadis, S. Mpoutsiouki, Cultural Diplomacy. Greek and International Dimensions, SEAB, Zografou, 2015, p. 7 (in Greek).

[4] Ibid.

[5] A.-E. N. Tachiaos, Byzantine Legacy to the Slav World: Approach and Dialectic Process, Cyrillomethodianum, Vol. XIX (2015), p. 5.

[6] N. Vasileiadis, op. cit., p. 17.

[7] T. van Kessel, Foreign Cultural Policy in the Interbellum. The Italian Dante Alighieri Society and the British Council Contesting the Mediterranean, Amsterdam University Press, Amsterdam, 2016.

[8] H.D. Lasswell, National security and individual freedom, McGraw-Hill, New York, 1950, p. 79.

[9] A. Wolfers, 'National Security' as an Ambiguous Symbol, Political Science Quarterly 67 (4) (1952), p. 485.

makers at the time in relation to both official relations and public opinion impact; thus, cultural diplomacy was soon instrumentalized to serve the goal of extending the two blocs' spheres of influence in the world, often by the means of cultural propaganda aimed at influencing intellectual elites and the broader public.[10]

At the same time, the process of decolonization, along with the confrontation between the West, representing the colonial powers, and the East and South, led to the emergence of the concept of cultural resistance. It should be mentioned that Western cultural leadership at the time was perceived in different places of the world as a form of hegemony in line with the Gramscian approach.[11] In these cases, along with armed resistance, a process of "cultural resistance to imperialism"[12] emerged; the movement of cultural resistance has contributed to the formation of national identities serving the goal of self-determination and national independence. This process had a great impact on the orientations of the cultural diplomacy of the new independent states that were added to the international community after decolonization. For these states, cultural diplomacy encapsulated their ideological aspirations regarding self-determination,[13] through the linkage of culture in its diversity with the rights deriving from the sovereign equality of states. The claims of these states for the restitution of cultural objects, looted or exported during the colonial era, epitomizes the ideological orientations of their cultural diplomacy, mainly conducted in multilateral institutions in order to legitimize and reinforce their institutional standing.[14]

---

[10]Characteristic examples include the Voice of America radio broadcasts and the CIA's direct funding of publications such as Encounter and Perseus, see H.K. Finn, The Case for Cultural Diplomacy. Engaging Foreign Audiences, Foreign Affairs, 82 (6) (2003), p. 16; Jean-François Fayet, VOKS, The Third Dimension of Soviet Foreign Policy. In J.C.E. Gienow-Hecht, M.C. Donfried (eds.), Searching for a Cultural Diplomacy, Berghahn Books, New York-Oxford, 2013, pp. 33-49; Rósa Magnúsdóttir, Mission Impossible: Selling Soviet Socialism to Americans, 1955–1958, ibid., pp. 50-72; and N. Prevots, Dance for Export: Cultural Diplomacy and the Cold War, Wesleyan University Press, Middletown,1998.

[11]A. Gramsci, Selections from the Prison. Notebooks of Antonio Gramsci, International Publishers, New York, 1971.

[12]E.W. Said, Culture and Imperialism, Vintage Books, New York, 1994, p. 275.

[13]E. Stamatoudi, Cultural Property Law and Restitution. A Commentary to International Conventions and European Union Law, Edward Elgar, Cheltenham, UK/Northampton, MA, USA, 2011, p. 238.

[14]UN General Assembly's Resolutions 3148 and 3187 illustrate this effort. According to Resolution 3148, the UN General Assembly "Recognizes that contacts and exchanges among various cultures, conducted on the basis of equality and with due regard to the principle of sovereignty of States, may positively contribute to the enrichment and development of national cultures and regional cultural values". UN GA Resolution 3148 (XXVIII) Preservation and further development of cultural values, 14 December 1973. Resolution 3187 deplores "the wholesale removal, virtually without payment, of *objets d'art* from one country to another, frequently as a result of colonial or foreign occupation" and "[a]ffirms that the prompt restitution to a country of its *objets d'art*, monuments, museum pieces, manuscripts and documents by another country … constitutes just reparation for damage done", "[r]ecognizes the special obligations in this connection of those countries which had access to such valuable objects only as a result of colonial or foreign occupation;" and "[c]alls upon all the States concerned to prohibit the expropriation of works of art from Territories still under colonial or alien domination". UN GA Resolution 3187 (XXVIII). Restitution of works of art to countries victims of expropriation, 18 December 1973.

In both senses, cultural diplomacy aims at using different cultural manifestations "to exert positive influence"[28] on the public opinion in third states[29] in the service the following ends[30]:

(a) Promoting and/or restoring a country's profile abroad, by means of projecting cultural expressions and norms usually bearing universal values[31] or interpretations. This is achieved (i) by promoting the uniqueness of cultural heritage as the legacy of a polity's glorious past and projecting its image through diachrony, as the current stage of a long cultural continuum (as in the case of Greece or Italy); or (ii) by identifying a country's image with contemporary cultural creativity and expressions (such as fashion, music, cinema production) in its synchrony.
(b) Implementing more specialized or foreign policy goals,[32] such as the conclusion of educational or cultural trade agreements, diaspora policies, the resolution of cultural heritage disputes, and so on.

In both cases, cultural diplomacy, as a dimension of a state's public diplomacy as well as a soft power tool, aspires to establish a "climate of trust, aiming in the long term at mutual understanding and avoiding political crises and conflicts."[33]

[28] N. Vasileiadis, op. cit., p.15.

[29] G. Malone, Political advocacy and cultural communication: organizing the nation's public diplomacy, University Press of America/Miller Center University of Virginia, Lanham Md, 1988; B.H. Signitzer, Public Relations and Public Diplomacy. In A. Zerfass, B. van Ruler, Sriramesh (eds.), Public Relations Research, VS Verlag fürSozialwissenschaften, Wiesbaden, 2008, pp. 205-218.

[30] According to the distinction made in S. Mark, A Greater Role for Cultural Diplomacy, Discussion Papers in Diplomacy, Netherlands Institute of International Relations Clingendael, April 2009, p. 9.

[31] Ch. Giannaras, op. cit., p. 33.

[32] It is appropriate to refer to the inclusion of such functional objectives in the context of a broader international cultural strategy of a state, since only in this case we can refer to cultural diplomacy and not simply to the conduct of cultural relations, which may also be promoted by private bodies without necessarily being framed by an official state policy, according to Mitchell's classic distinction between cultural diplomacy and international cultural relations. See J.M. Mitchell, International Cultural Relations, Allenand Unwin, London 1986, p. 5.

[33] N. Vasileiadis, op. cit., p. 15.

12.3 Cultural Diplomacy Institutions[34]

12.3.1 States

Traditionally, cultural diplomacy, as a supporting tool of foreign policy, is developed and implemented by competent state authorities depending on the constitutional and administrative organization of each polity. In states with a centralized administrative structure, cultural diplomacy is mainly conducted by central government, as in the case of France[35] or Greece.[36] In federal states there is a wide range of institutional arrangements regarding the conduct of cultural diplomacy. In the US administration model, for example, cultural diplomacy constitutes a policy domain falling under the competence of the Ministry of Foreign Affairs.[37] Canada on the other hand, opts for a more decentralized cultural diplomacy model. Although the Global Affairs Canada along with the Ministry of Canadian Heritage constitute the main governmental departments in charge of Canadian cultural diplomacy, Quebec, also pursues its own cultural diplomacy, through its delegations in different states and organizations.[38]

In this context, cultural diplomacy is conducted abroad by state agents, mainly diplomats and cultural attachés, implementing national (or subnational) strategies and instructions issued by the respective competent governmental bodies.

Leaving aside the conventional conduct of cultural diplomacy, one should not neglect the role of cultural diplomacy institutions. Apart from cultural diplomacy being practiced by the officials of the competent ministries, the role of various specialized cultural institutions active abroad in promoting culture in its different manifestations, such as language, education, literary tradition, cultural industry productions, and so on, is also significant.

[34]This section is limited to the presentation of state and intergovernmental bodies related to cultural diplomacy. The contribution of civil society and the business sector is not analyzed since it is beyond the scope of this paper.

[35]<http://www.diplomatie.gouv.fr/fr/politique-etrangere-de-la-france/diplomatie-culturelle/>.

[36]In Greece, cultural diplomacy is practiced by the Ministry of Foreign Affairs and the Ministry of Culture and Sports <http://www.mfa.gr/igesia/genikoi-grammateis/eidikos-grammateas-threskeutikes-kai-politistikes-diplomatias.html>

[37]<https://eca.state.gov/programs-initiatives/cultural-diplomacy>.

[38]Quebec has established 14 delegations in 9 countries and 15 bureaus around the globe. See <http://www.mrif.gouv.qc.ca/fr/ministere/representation-etranger#> and S.L. Mark, Rethinking cultural diplomacy: The cultural diplomacy of New Zealand, the Canadian Federation and Quebec, Political Science, 62, 1 (2010), pp. 62-83; Ch. Kirkey, S. Paquin, S. Roussel, Charting Quebec's Engagement with the International Community, American Review of Canadian Studies, 46 (2016), pp. 135-148.

These are cultural organizations or services that are supervised by the state, as in the case of the Hellenic Foundation for Culture,[39] the French Institute,[40] or the British Council.[41] In the case of these organizations, there is a different regime that governs their employees, depending on their institutional profile and the relevant national legislation. A typical example is Canada's institutional framework regarding the establishment of foreign educational institutions or the creation of cultural centers. The first case concerns cultural activities, whether for-profit or not-for-profit, conducted in rented or privately owned facilities of third states on the territory of Canada or organizations established under bilateral agreements and are not eligible for privileges and immunities. The second case concerns cultural centers that are part of the diplomatic mission of the said states in Canada and are eligible for privileges and immunities.[42] Another example is the British Council, whose staff are distinguished into those based in the United Kingdom; those who work for a certain period in one of the branches abroad and enjoy the immunities and privileges provided for accredited diplomatic missions; and field personnel for whom no such provision exists.[43]

12.3.2 International Organizations

12.3.2.1 Cultural Diplomacy and UNESCO

The establishment of UNESCO in 1946 created the conditions for the development of contemporary international cultural relations. The purpose of the organization, according to its statutory text, is to "maintain, and diffuse knowledge: by assuring the conservation and protection of the world's inheritance of books, works of art and

[39] A private law entity which was initially supervised by the Ministry of Foreign Affairs (Article 19 of Law 2026/1992 Government Gazette 43 A') and was subsequently renamed as 'Hellenic Foundation for Culture', placed under the supervision of the Ministry of Culture (Law 3057/2002 Government Gazette 239 A').

[40] It is a public institution responsible for France's cultural diplomacy. Supervised by the French Ministry of Foreign Affairs, it has been operating with an expanded madate since 2010 in accordance with the French Foreign Cultural Act of 27 July 2010 and the corresponding implementing decree of 30 December 2010. See <http://www.institutfrancais.com/en/about-us>.

[41] It is a public organization that is not supervised by any specific Ministry, but is financed through state resources and remains accountable for its financial management to the Foreign Affairs Committee of the British Parliament. See <https://www.britishcouncil.gr/>. For the role of the British Council in the international cultural relations of the United Kingdom, see T. Rivera, Distinguishing Cultural Relations from Cultural Diplomacy: The British Council's Relationship with Her Majesty's Government, Figueroa Press, Los Angeles, 2015.

[42] See Government of Canada, Guidelines for establishing cultural sections of Diplomatic Missions and Consular Posts <http://www.international.gc.ca/protocol-protocole/policies-politiques/cultural-sections_sections-culturelles.aspx?lang=eng>.

[43] See the response given to a relevant question to the Foreign Affairs Committee of the House of Commons, Foreign Affairs Committee, House of Commons, Public Diplomacy: Third Report of Session 2005-06; Report, Together with Formal Minutes, Oral and Written Evidence. The Stationary Office, 7 April 2006.

monuments of history and science" and to encourage international cooperation in all the fields of intellectual activity through cultural exchanges (Article 1 §2c).[44]

Cultural diplomacy within UNESCO has a dual nature.[45] States leverage their participation in this institution to engage in traditional cultural diplomacy, and to exert "soft power" by promoting their public image, highlighting their cultural achievements. However, in the institutional environment of the organization, culture is not used solely as a tool of public diplomacy to advance the broader foreign policy goals of states. Diplomacy at UNESCO serves culture itself in all its dimensions by promoting universal ideals and the concept of the universal public interest, while contributing to the creation and reinforcement of specific standards of conduct and their consolidation in the collective consciousness of the international community.

This dual approach of cultural diplomacy is discerned in all the activities of the organization:

(a) In the process of adopting principles and regulations for the protection of cultural heritage and the promotion of cultural diversity and creativity,[46] perhaps the organization's most important contribution lies in how it has changed the way protected cultural monuments are perceived by the international community.[47] From the perception of cultural "property" (propriété) prevailing in national legislations, often associated with the right or power to use and abuse (*utendi et abutendi*), or "good" (*bien*), which reflects public and private aspects of protection, UNESCO's main normative achievement was the shift to the concept of "heritage" connected with humanity as a whole.[48]
(b) In the monitoring process regarding the implementation of the international obligations undertaken by states, carried out by the UNESCO Conventions' monitoring bodies as well as the organization's institutions. In this process, the

[44]Constitution of the United Nations Educational, Scientific and Cultural Organisation, 16th November 1945. 4 UNTS 275, <http://www.icomos.org/unesco/unesco_constitution.html>.

[45]I. Kozymka, The Diplomacy of Culture: The Role of UNESCO in Sustaining Cultural Diversity Palgrave, Macmillan, New York, 2014, pp. 9-10.

[46]See P. Naskou-Perraki, D. Bachtsevanidou (ed.), UNESCO. Conventions, Ant. N. Sakkoula, Athens-Komotini, 2008; A. Zervaki, Culture and International Organization: UNESCO's contribution to contemporary international cultural relations and governance in M. Kontochristou (ed.), International making and Culture. Challenges and Policies, I. Sideris, Athens, 2018, pp. 79-99 (in Greek) and <http://en.unesco.org/themes/protecting-our-heritage-and-fostering-creativity>.

[47]See A. Zervaki, The concept of the cultural and natural heritage of humanity: the contribution of UNESCO, Ant. N. Sakkoula, Athens-Komotini, 2010 (in Greek).

[48]See F. Francioni, Des biens culturels au patrimoine culturel: l'évolution dynamique d'un concept et de son extension. In A.A. Yusuf (dir.), Elaboration de règles internationales sur l'éducation, la science et la culture, Vol. I Editions UNESCO/Martinus Nijhoff Publishers, Paris, 2007, pp. 239-241; and T. Scovazzi, Le patrimoine culturel de l'humanité, Académie de Droit International de la Haye, Centre d'Etude et de Recherche de Droit International et des Relations Internationales 2005, Martinus Nijhoff Publishers, Leiden/Boston, 2007, pp. 31-32.

role of the relevant Operational Guidelines of the various Conventions' Committees is significant. While these are formally non-legally binding texts, they actually perform a quasi-legislative function,[49] since, in practice, the contracting parties cannot deviate from their application. These Guidelines interpret the conventions in light of new challenges (such as climate change, use of new technologies in the illegal trafficking of cultural goods, and so on), while incorporating good practices and the latest developments in the management and protection of different monuments and goods.

(c) In managing issues that extend beyond the individual cultural heritage and creativity protection regimes, UNESCO has played a pivotal role. In the first decades following its establishment, the salvage of monuments threatened from natural disasters or large-scale technical projects offered timely opportunities to launch major international campaigns. Notable examples were the restoration project implemented after the catastrophic floods in Venice and Florence in the 1960s and the salvage operation of the Nubian temples of Abu Simbel endangered by the construction of the Aswan High Dam in Egypt during Nasser's presidency. In recent decades, international mobilization has focused mainly on the impact of extremism, terrorism, and armed conflict on culture.

A typical case is the organization's response to the Taliban regime's destruction of the Buddha statues in Afghanistan's Bamiyan Valley. Its General Conference adopted the Declaration concerning the Intentional Destruction of Cultural Heritage.[50] This text, although not legally binding, includes strong wording, which stresses the common concern for the shared interest of humanity in the protection of cultural heritage[51] by the organization's member states.

More recent experience includes UNESCO's contribution to the restoration of mausoleums and other cultural heritage sites in Mali,[52] as well as the response to the destruction of cultural heritage by ISIS in Syria and Iraq. The public discourse, recalling the statements of the Director General of the Organization, with the use of

[49] See D. Zacharias, The UNESCO Regime for the Protection of World Heritage as Prototype of an Autonomy Gaining Institution, German Law Review, Vol. 9, No 11 (2008), pp. 1833-1864.

[50] See UNESCO General Conference, 32nd Session, 32 C/25, 17th July 2003, Annex II, p. 7.

[51] See UNESCO Declaration concerning the Intentional Destruction of Cultural Heritage, Article II§1.

[52] UNESCO has been mobilized since the beginning of the crisis in Mali due to the widespread destruction of religious monuments caused by extremist Islamist organizations, in cooperation with the peacekeeping force MINUSMA <https://whc.unesco.org/en/intassistance/2477>. Recent actions also concerned, in addition to the reconstruction of the mausoleums, the restoration of the cultural landscape of Bandiagara, a mixed site of the World Heritage List, whose tangible and intangible attributes were significantly affected by civil unrest and intercommunal conflicts. <https://whc.unesco.org/en/soc/4125>.

characterizations such as "cultural cleansing"[53] and "war crimes"[54] attempted to underline the cultural loss suffered by humanity as a whole. Moreover, the use of such wording aimed at mobilizing the international community towards taking measures to save or restore the monuments. Last but not least, it linked such acts with accountability and the conviction that perpetrators of such crimes should be held accountable before national or international justice. In the same spirit, the meetings of the UNESCO Director General with the Secretary General of the United Nations as well as with the President of the Security Council were initiatives bearing a strong political symbolism. They underscored the firm position of the UN system as a whole against such acts, as reflected in the subsequent adoption of Security Council Resolution 2347 in 2017.[55]

At the programmatic level, in November 2015 the organization's General Conference adopted the Strategy for the Reinforcement of UNESCO's Action for the Protection of Culture and the Promotion of Cultural Pluralism in the Event of Armed Conflict,[56] in an effort to formulate a framework of principles adapted to contemporary protection challenges. In the same year, the Unite4Heritage initiative was adopted, aiming at raising awareness and mobilizing the public, particularly young people, for the protection of cultural heritage in areas threatened by extremism.[57]

The protection of cultural heritage during armed conflict has once again become topical in response to the Russian Federation's invasion of Ukraine in early 2022. UNESCO has repeatedly emphasized the obligation of parties in conflict to respect international humanitarian law. The organization proposed to the Ukrainian authorities to mark important monuments with the Blue Shield emblem of the 1954 Hague Convention to prevent the destruction of cultural heritage, and conducted damage assessment of monuments either by making use of satellite imagery systems or by communicating with those responsible for their management.[58]

---

[53] <http://whc.unesco.org/en/news/1244> and <http://www.independent.co.uk/news/world/middle-east/unesco-chief-irina-bokova-accuses-islamist-groups-of-cultural-cleansing-isis-a6679761.html>.

[54] <http://whc.unesco.org/en/news/1244>.

[55] <http://www.un.org/apps/news/story.asp?NewsID=50256#.V1lR7bXLnJa>.

[56] UNESCO, Strategy for Reinforcing UNESCO's Action for the Protection of Culture and the Promotion of Cultural Pluralism in the Event of Armed Conflict, <https://en.unesco.org/system/files/unesco_clt_strategy_en.pdf>.

[57] «#Unite4Heritage», <https://www.unite4heritage.org/>.

[58] <https://www.unesco.org/en/articles/endangered-heritage-ukraine-unesco-reinforces-protective-measures>.

Finally, UNESCO's contribution to the formulation,[59] implementation,[60] and assessment[61] of the Sustainable Development Goals of the United Nations[62] in the field of culture is yet another important dimension of the cooperation between the two organizations, which aims to establish and promote a human-centered and comprehensive approach to development.[63]

12.3.2.2 Cultural Diplomacy and the Council of Europe

The Council of Europe constitutes a pan-European organization of democratic states.[64] Its establishment expressed the expectations for a peaceful and democratic European space, after the devastating wars of the first half of the twentieth century. As stated by its Statute, the aim of the organization is the achievement of greater unity between states, based on the fundamental and interdependent values of democracy, human rights, and the rule of law. According to Article 1 §b:

> This aim shall be pursued through the organs of the Council by discussion of questions of common concern and by agreements and common action in economic, social, cultural, scientific, legal and administrative matters and in the maintenance and further realization of human rights and fundamental freedoms.

In the field of culture, the Council of Europe has contributed to the adoption of rules governing intergovernmental cooperation for the protection of European cultural heritage and cultural rights. A typical example is article 5 of the European Cultural Convention,[65] which refers to the obligation of the contracting parties to:

> regard the objects of European cultural value placed under their control as integral parts of the common cultural heritage of Europe, and to take appropriate measures to safeguard them and ensure reasonable access thereto.

After the adoption of the European Cultural Convention in 1954, which set the general framework for cultural cooperation in the European continent, a series of

[59] UNESCO participation in the preparations for a post-2015 development agenda, General Resolution 64. In UNESCO, Records of the General Conference, 37th Session, Paris 5-20 December 2013, Resolutions Vol. I, Paris, UNESCO, 2014.

[60] UNESCO Task Force on the 2030 Agenda for Sustainable Development, UNESCO moving forward the 2030 Sustainable Development Agenda, Paris, UNESCO 2017, <https://en.unesco.org/creativity/sites/creativity/files/247785en.pdf>.

[61] By adopting specific thematic indicators to assess the contribution of culture to sustainable development <https://unesdoc.unesco.org/ark:/48223/pf0000371562>.

[62] A/RES/70/L.1 op. cit.

[63] A. Zervaki, Culture and Sustainability, 2018, op. cit.

[64] The end of the Cold War rendered the Council of Europe an institution of pan-European membership. Today, it has 46 members, after Russian Federation exclusion in 2022 <www.coe.int/en/>. For the organization's institutional profile and activities, see P. Naskou-Perraki, K. Antonopoulos, M. Sarigiannidis, International Organizations, 3rd ed., Sakkoulas Publications, Athens-Thessaloniki, 2024, pp. 341-344 (in Greek).

[65] European Cultural Convention, Paris, 19.12.1054, ETS No 18.

thematic conventions followed concerning: architectural heritage,[66] archaeological heritage,[67] landscape protection[68] as well as offenses related to the destruction and illegal trafficking of cultural goods.[69]

The role of culture as a strategic priority of the organization was decisive in fostering the goal of social cohesion and understanding, initially among the peoples of Western Europe,[70] and later, during the post-Cold War era, at the pan-European level.

After the end of the Cold War, four summits of Heads of State and Governments of the Council of Europe were held. The four Declarations adopted at these summits represent major strategic milestones in the organization's evolution and adaptation to a European and global reality marked by multiple challenges and threats. All these Declarations included provisions for culture as well. More specifically:

(a) The Vienna Summit (1993): The relevant Declaration[71] highlights the important role of cultural cooperation in promoting cultural diversity as a means of ensuring democracy and stability. It called on states to undertake legally binding obligations regarding the protection of cultural rights, among other commitments. A first step towards this goal was the adoption of the European Framework Convention for the Protection of National Minorities of 1995.[72]
(b) The Strasbourg Summit (1997): It resulted in the adoption of a new Declaration which highlighted the importance of education and culture in fostering mutual understanding among Europe's peoples, with particular focus on the protection of cultural and natural heritage. Following this line, the European Landscape Convention was adopted in 2000.[73]
(c) The Warsaw Summit (2005): In the Declaration[74] and the Action Plan[75] adopted, it is evident that the threat of terrorism and the rise of religious

[66] Convention for the Protection of the Architectural Heritage of Europe, Granada, 3.10.1985, CETS No 121.

[67] European Convention on the Protection of the Archaeological Heritage, London, 6.5.1969, CETS No 066. This Convention was revised in 1992. Convention for the Protection of the Archaeological Heritage of Europe (revised), Valletta, 16.1.1992.

[68] European Landscape Convention, Florence, 20.10.2000, ETS No 176.

[69] Council of Europe Convention on Offences relating to Cultural Property, Nicosia, 19.5.2017, CETS No 221.

[70] Despite the fact that the preservation and further development of the common heritage and the expansion of cultural relations was presented as a common interest of all European states by the Committee of Ministers in 1985. See Committee of Ministers, Resolution (85) 6 on European Cultural Identity, 25.4.1985.

[71] Declaration of the Council of Europe's First Summit, Vienna, 9.10.1993, <https://rm.coe.int/1680536c83>.

[72] Framework Convention for the Protection of National Minorities, Strasbourg, 1.2.1995, ETS No. 157.

[73] Strasbourg Final Declaration and Action Plan, 11.10.1997 <https://rm.coe.int/168063dced> and Council of Europe Landscape Convention, Florence, 20.10.2000, ETS No. 176.

[74] Warsaw Declaration, 17.5.2005 <https://www.coe.int/t/dcr/summit/20050517_decl_varsovie_en.asp>.

[75] Action Plan, CM (2005) 80 final, 17.5.2005.

extremism do not leave cultural heritage unscathed. Indeed, the destruction of the Buddha statues in Afghanistan's Bamiyan Valley (mentioned above) has been the catalyst for upgrading intercultural and interreligious dialogue in the organization's priorities.

(d) The Reykjavík summit (2023): European leaders reaffirmed their commitment to the core values underpinning Council of Europe membership in light of Russian Federation's aggression against Ukraine. They also agreed to adopt an Enlarged Partial Agreement on the Register of Damage caused by the Aggression of the Russian Federation against Ukraine. The latter includes documentation of harm inflicted on Ukraine's cultural and religious heritage.[76]

12.3.2.3 Cultural Diplomacy and the EU

For the greatest part of the evolution of the European edifice, culture remained connected to the functioning of the EC market and the unhindered implementation of its four freedoms.[77] The inclusion of culture as a separate title in its statutory agreements was realized only in 1992, with the incorporation of Article 128 in the Maastricht Treaty.[78]

The timing and the content of the said article are by no means a random choice: the emphasis on the political dimension of the European integration with the Maastricht Treaty required a coherent cultural background, a common cultural identity, which would provide social legitimacy to the project of political integration, thereby contributing to its acceptance by European citizens. For this reason, the concept of the common European heritage was particularly highlighted in the early 1990s. In the 2000s, especially following the adoption of the Charter of Fundamental

[76] Reykjavík Declaration, 17.5.2023 <https://edoc.coe.int/en/the-council-of-europe-in-brief/11619-united-around-our-values-reykjavik-declaration.html>.

[77] A typical example is provided by article 36 of the Treaty TEC which was the first article in a statutory text of the Community that referred to the field of culture: "the provisions of Articles 34 and 35 [on the prohibition of quantitative restrictions between Member States] shall not preclude prohibitions or restrictions on imports, exports or goods in transit justified on grounds, protection of national treasures possessing artistic, historic or archaeological value ... Such prohibitions or restrictions shall not, however, constitute a means of arbitrary discrimination or a disguised restriction on trade between Member States". This provision is complemented by secondary Community law adopted to address the challenges arising from completing the internal market, the smooth implementation of the four freedoms and the lack of border controls. See Council Regulation (EEC) 3911/92 on the export of cultural goods, OJ L 395, 31.12.1992 and Council Directive 93/7/EEC of 15 March 1993 on the return of illegally removed cultural goods from the territory of a Member State, OJ L 074, 27.3.1993. The acts in question have been replaced by Council Regulation (EU) 116/2009 of 18 December 2008 on the export of cultural goods, OJ L 39, 10.2.2009 and Directive 2014/60/EU of the European Parliament and of the Council of 15 May 2014 on the return of cultural property illegally removed from the territory of a Member State and the amendment of Regulation (EU) No. 1024/2012 (recast), OJ L 159, 28.5.2014.

[78] For a presentation of the evolution of the integration of culture in the European construction, see M. Kontochristou, Building Europe. Cultural policies in the European Union. In M. Kontochristou (ed.), Culture in the International. Challenges and Policies, I. Sideris, Athens, 2018, pp. 37-58 (in Greek).

Rights[79] and the failure of the Constitutional Treaty to enter into force, interest shifted towards the idea of cultural pluralism within the context of the European integration process.

Article 3 of the Treaty on the European Union adopted in Lisbon (hereinafter TEU) includes in the organization's general objectives the respect for the richness of "cultural and linguistic diversity" and the provision to "ensure that Europe's[80] cultural heritage is safeguarded and enhanced." This provision is specified in Article 167 of the Treaty on the Functioning of the European Union (hereinafter TFEU),[81] according to which "the Union shall contribute to the flowering of the cultures of the Member States, while respecting their national and regional diversity and at the same time bringing the common cultural heritage to the fore." The same article includes the so-called cultural mainstreaming clause on the basis of which the Union takes "cultural aspects into account in its action under other provisions of the Treaties, in particular in order to respect and to promote the diversity of its cultures."[82] In this context, the Union's cultural action, including its practice of cultural diplomacy, is structured across two levels: among member states (Article 167 par. 2) and within the framework of the Union's external relations with third countries and international organizations (Article 167 par. 3).

In terms of strategic planning, the European Commission published the European Agenda for Culture in 2007. The Agenda was adopted by the Council in November of the same year.[83] The priorities set out in this text concerned:

(a) The promotion of cultural diversity and intercultural dialogue. In 2008, the European Union officially designated the year as the European Year of Intercultural Dialogue. Member States have drawn up national programs and implemented a series of actions in order to promote the idea of a "European citizenship, which is open to the world, respects cultural diversity and is based on common values in the European Union," as defined in Article 6 of the TEU and the Charter of Fundamental Rights of the European Union.[84]
(b) The promotion of culture as a driving force of creativity in the context of the Lisbon Strategy for growth, employment, and the environment. This objective

[79] According to Article 22 of the Charter, "the Union shall respect cultural, religious and linguistic diversity".

[80] Reference is made to "Europe's cultural heritage" and not to "European cultural heritage".

[81] Which replaced Articles 151 of the Treaty of Nice and Amsterdam and 128 of the Maastricht Treaty. See V. Christianos (ed.), EU Treaty & TFEU. Article interpretation, Nomiki Bibliothiki, Athens, 2012, pp. 829-832.

[82] See E. Psychogiopoulou, European Cultural Policy: The cultural mainstreaming clause of article 167 par. 4 of the Treaty on the Functioning of the European Union and its implementation. In M. Kontochristou, op. cit., pp. 59-78.

[83] Resolution of the Council of 16 November 2007 on a European Agenda for Culture, OJ C 287, 29/11/2007.

[84] Decision No 1983/2006/EC of the European Parliament and of the Council of 18 December 2006 concerning the European Year of Intercultural Dialogue (2008), OJ L 412, 30.12.2006.

was primarily advanced through the implementation of the UNESCO Convention on the Protection and Promotion of the Diversity of Cultural Expressions,[85] alongside targeted funding through the Union's relevant mechanisms, such as the Culture Program 2007–2013[86] and the Creative Europe 2014–2020 Program.[87]

(c) The inclusion of culture in the agenda of the Union's external relations.[88] It is important to note that between 2012 and 2014 the preparatory action entitled "Culture in the External Relations of the European Union" has been implemented. It consisted of a survey that covered 54 countries, the 28 Member States at the time, the countries participating in the European Neighborhood Policy,[89] and the countries that have entered into a Strategic Partnership with the organization.[90] The final report contained proposals concerning the basic principles that should govern the action of the Union; the establishment of a coherent strategy for the international cultural relations of the Union; and the adaptation of cultural governance model in the EU in order to enhance synergies among EU institutions, Member States, creators, professionals and civil society in the field of culture and the arts.[91]

In 2015, the Council of Ministers redefined the cultural action of the Union, in light of the challenges in the field of internal security as well as the impact of the economic and refugee crises, adopting two texts on:

---

[85] The Convention is based on the dual understanding of cultural activities and goods: the strictly cultural one and the economic one. In particular, it connects human creativity to the sustainable development of communities, peoples and nations; it treats diversity as both an intangible and a tangible resource that contributes to the preservation of cultural-spiritual as well as material wealth. Finally, it links cultural diversity with human rights and their international protection status. <https://www.unesco.org/en/legal-affairs/convention-protection-and-promotion-diversity-cultural-expressions>.

[86] Decision No 1855/2006/EC of the European Parliament and of the Council of 12 December 2006 establishing the Culture Programme (2007 to 2013)OJ L 372, 27.12.2006.

[87] Regulation (EU) No 1295/2013 of the European Parliament and of the Council of 11 December 2013 establishing the Creative Europe Programme (2014 to 2020) and repealing Decisions No 1718/2006/EC, No 1855/2006/EC and No 1041/2009/EC, OJ L 347, 20.12.2013.

[88] See Y.R. Isar, Culture in EE external relations: an idea whose time has come?, International Journal of Cultural Policy, 21, 4 (2015), pp. 494-508.

[89] These were Egypt, Algeria, Azerbaijan, Armenia, Georgia, Jordan, Israel, Belarus, Lebanon, Libya, Morocco, Moldova, Palestine, Ukraine, Tunisia and Syria. For the current state of EU bilateral relations in the context of the Neighborhood Policy see <https://ec.europa.eu/neighbourhood-enlargement/european-neighbourhood-policy_en>.

[90] These were Brazil, Canada, China, India, Japan, Mexico, Russia, South Africa, South Korea and the USA.

[91] See Y.R. Isar, *Engaging the World: Towards Global Cultural Citizenship, Final Report, European Union, 2014* <http://cultureinexternalrelations.eu/wp-content/uploads/2013/05/Engaging-The-World-Towards-Global-Cultural-Citizenship-eBook-1.5_13.06.2014.pdf>.

(a) "Internal" cultural diplomacy, prioritizing intercultural dialogue with an emphasis on the role of arts and culture in mutual understanding and the smooth integration of refugees and immigrants in the European society.[92]
(b) Cultural diplomacy beyond the European Union, introducing a concrete cultural dimension in the organization's external relations. More specifically, the Council decided to integrate culture into the Union's international development cooperation actions (in line with the United Nations Agenda 2030). It also called on the High Representative for the Union's Foreign Affairs and the Commission to prepare and present to the Council a strategic approach to the integration of culture in the Union's external relations.[93]

In June 2016, the publication of the EU Strategy for International Cultural Relations followed. The principles on which it was founded are respect for human rights as well as the promotion of cultural diversity and intercultural dialogue. The Strategy attempts to further integrate the cultural dimension in various domains of the organization's external relations.[94]

Subsequently, the 2018 New European Agenda for Culture[95] underlined as a key objective the improvement of the "attractiveness of the Union"[96] through culture after the end of the financial crisis. Once again, the political capital of the common European heritage is mobilized, in an effort to strengthen the sense of a common European identity, which came out wounded by the shocks of the crisis in question. Its main strategic axes included:

(a) The reinforcement of social cohesion and well-being, based on the development of the "cultural and creative capacities", echoing Amartya Sen's[97] theory on

[92] It is the revision of the Council's work-plan for culture for the period 2015-2018 <http://ec.europa.eu/culture/news/2014/2711-work-plan-culture_en.htm>.

[93] Council Conclusions on culture in the EU's external relations with a focus on culture in development cooperation, Brussels, 24 November 2015, 14443/15.

[94] JOIN (2016) 29, Brussels 8.6.2016. Joint Communication to the European Parliament and the Council. Towards an EU Strategy for international cultural relations.

[95] COM (2018) 267, Brussels 22.5.2018. Communication from the Commission to the European Parliament, the Council, the European Economic and Social Committee and the Committee of the Regions, New European Agenda for Culture.

[96] As mentioned in the 2016 Bratislava Declaration <https://www.consilium.europa.eu/en/press/press-releases/2016/09/16/bratislava-declaration-and-roadmap/>.

[97] Amartya Sen is a Nobel prize laureate for his work on welfare economics, through which he raised the question of the role of human potential as a development parameter in the context of the theory of social choice. This approach that was incorporated into policy with the concept of human development as it emerged in the 1990s, and laid the foundations for the expanded understanding of human security in the context of the United Nations. See Amartya Sen, Equality of what?. The Tanner Lecture on Human Values, Delivered at Stanford University, May 22 1979, M.C. Nussbaum, *Creating Capabilities, The Human Development Approach* (The Belknap Press, *Harvard*, 2011) and M. Wählisch, "Human Security", Max Planck Encyclopedia of International Law (2016).

human capabilities, and fostering participation in cultural activities. In other words, the strategy attempts to reintroduce a more human-centered development model, with culture serving as a vehicle for sustainable and inclusive growth.
(b) The promotion of cultural creativity, attempting to improve the conditions to boost creative economy in the field of culture.
(c) Strengthening the cultural dimension in the external relations of the European Union, with a renewed emphasis on intercultural dialogue as a tool for promoting peaceful relations with third countries and improving synergies to leverage the added value of culture at both the economic and political levels. Reference is also made to the Union's contribution to initiatives to restore cultural monuments in areas that have experienced conflicts.

Finally, protecting and further harnessing cultural heritage, along with extending the use of digital technology in the field of culture, remain priorities.

From an operational standpoint, in 2016 it was decided to set up an EU Cultural Diplomacy Platform[98] with the mission to engage with the public and stakeholders from third countries as well as to facilitate their participation in European cultural diplomacy activities. In addition, participating bodies in the project consortium offer support and expertise to the Union's services, in particular to the EU delegations in third countries.[99]

The issue of the destruction of cultural heritage and the illegal trafficking of cultural goods in times of armed conflict is a cross-cutting issue of the Union's cultural diplomacy. In addition to the relevant legislation (Council Regulation 1210/2003[100] on the implementation of the Security Council resolution 1483/2003 on Iraq and Council Regulation 1332/2013[101] on Syria), in a public debate[102] on this issue, the Council recognized the need to take further initiatives to inform the public and the entities involved in the trade of cultural goods, as well as to promote the effective implementation of relevant international law and the cooperation with UNESCO. Finally, the Council pointed out the need to investigate the adoption of legislation on the import of cultural goods, where there was a loophole in EU legislation. Indeed,

---

[98] This was a funded project in accordance with the relevant framework for the financial programs of the Union's external action and cooperation with third countries. See Regulation (EU) no. 236/2014 of the European Parliament and of the Council of 11 March 2014 laying down common rules and procedures for the implementation of the Union's external action financing mechanisms, OJ L 77 15.3.2014 and Regulation (EU) no. 234/2014 of the European Parliament and of the Council of 11 March 2014 establishing a Partnership Instrument for cooperation with third countries, OJ L 77 15.3.2014.

[99] See <http://ec.europa.eu/dgs/fpi/announcements/news/20160401_1_en.htm>.

[100] *Council Regulation (EC) No 1210/2003 of 7 July 2003 concerning certain specific restrictions on economic and financial relations with Iraq and repealing Regulation (EC) No 2465/96, OJ L 169, 8.7.2003.*

[101] Council Regulation (EU) No 1332/2013 of 13 December 2013 amending Regulation (EU) No 36/2012 concerning restrictive measures in view of the situation in Syria, OJ L 335, 14.12.2013.

[102] <http://www.eu2015lu.eu/en/actualites/articles-actualite/2015/11/24-conseil-eycs-culture/index.html>.

the Commission proceeded with a new legislative initiative to tackle this lacuna and to combat the financing of terrorism through the illegal trafficking and trade of cultural goods,[103] which led to the adoption of a relevant Regulation in 2019, fully operationalized in 2025.[104]

Last but not least, the 2021 Council Conclusions on the EU approach in the context of conflicts and crises[105] envisage the integration of the dimension of culture in the organization's toolbox in this area, in the context of the Common Security and Defense Policy (including the missions of the Union that contribute to peace building actions) but also in the existing financial instruments for third countries.

Antonia Zervaki, Assistant Professor of International Relations at the National and Kapodistrian University of Athens (NKUA). A graduate of the Athens School of Philosophy, she holds an MA in European Studies (University of Exeter/Institut d'Etudes Politiques de Rennes) and an MA in European Organization and Diplomacy (School of Law, Economics and Political Science—NKUA). In 2006 she was awarded a PhD in international relations (Athens School of Law, Economics and Political Science—NKUA). She has been a EUSSRIF research fellow at the European University Institute and a researcher at the Hellenic Centre for European Studies. She has served as Special Advisor at the Ministries of Foreign Affairs and Employment. She was member of the working group of the Ministry of Culture on the revision of the legislative framework for safeguarding intangible heritage (2022–2023). She has taught in several academic institutions in Greece, including the Diplomatic Academy of the Ministry of Foreign Affairs and the National Security School of the Greek Police Academy and she has been involved in numerous EU-funded research projects in the field of cultural, environmental, and maritime governance. She is a member of the Hellenic Society of International Law and International Relations, the Academic Council on the United Nations System and member of the Board of the Hellenic Committee of the Blue Shield. Her current research interests lie in the international relations—international law dual agenda, international peace and security with a special focus on the United Nations, maritime and cultural governance. Her more recent publications include «The cultural dimension of sustaining peace: What role for UN peace operations? », Global Governance, Vol. 31(2) May 2025 and «International law and international relations 'dual agenda': Is it still working? » in L. Boisson De Chazournes, E. Doussis, G. Andreone, A. Zervaki (dir.), Droit International: Enjeux et Perspectives. Mélanges en l'honneur de la Professeure Haritini Dipla, Paris, Pedone, 2020.

[103] COM(2016) 50 final, Strasbourg 2.2.2016, Communication from the Commission to the European Parliament and the Council on an Action Plan for strengthening the fight against terrorist financing, pp. 12-13.

[104] Regulation (EU) 2019/880 of the European Parliament and of the Council of 17 April 2019 on the introduction and the import of cultural goods OJ L 151/1 of 7.6.2019.

[105] Council Conclusions on EU Approach to Cultural Heritage in conflicts and crises, Brussels, 21 June 2021, 9837/21.

Energy Diplomacy in an Era of Transition 13

Styliani Gerani and Komninos Komnios

Abstract

Energy diplomacy is a complex and pivotal aspect of international relations, yet remains rather underexplored in academic discourse. This study aims to address this gap by examining how states utilise energy diplomacy to bolster their power in a global landscape marked by significant transitions. It begins by exploring the strategic engagements of states in energy diplomacy, particularly in light of heightened concerns over energy security amid persistent geopolitical conflicts. Furthermore, this study analyses the evolving role of energy diplomacy in the context of the global shift from fossil fuels to renewable energy sources. By examining these dynamics, this research aims to contribute to a deeper understanding of energy diplomacy's role in contemporary international politics and its implications for sustainable energy transitions.

13.1 Introduction

Energy is not merely another commodity. It is of paramount importance for human survival and, as a consequence, a crucial factor in the economic and industrial development of modern societies. Access to natural resources is inextricably linked with national security, which in turn affects all aspects of a state's survival. Energy is a fundamental factor in the economy, defence, infrastructure, and social systems of a state. In this context, energy policy is a central concern for decision-makers in both domestic and external affairs. Given the impact of energy supplies on social and

S. Gerani (✉)
Department of International and European Studies University of Macedonia, Thessaloniki, Greece

K. Komnios
International Hellenic University, Thessaloniki, Greece
e-mail: k.komnios@ihu.edu.gr

P. Naskou-Perraki (ed.), *Contemporary Diplomatic and Consular Relations*,
https://doi.org/10.1007/978-3-031-99243-8_13

economic activity, it is prudent for leaders to secure access to energy supplies, particularly at affordable prices, in advance to ensure energy security.[1]

In this context, energy diplomacy assumes a pivotal role. From bilateral to multilateral schemes with other actors of the international system, the conclusion of arrangements on energy remains a fundamental aspect of a state's governance. From the perspective of either the state as an energy provider or the state as an energy consumer, energy diplomacy plays a crucial role in the complex arena of international relations, where energy will continue to be a significant global concern.

In the present era, the discourse on the transition from fossil fuels to renewable energy has become a prominent topic, not merely as an imperative of the climate crisis but also as a result of the ongoing conflicts in key regions, such as the Middle East and Eurasia. The implications of the climate crisis in conjunction with conflicts demonstrate that the interruption of energy flow from resourceful regions should not affect modern societies. Nevertheless, despite the existence of multilateral diplomacy on energy and agreements in international organisations and institutions, the recent energy crisis resulting from terrorist attacks in the Red Sea, perpetrated by the Houthis, serves to illustrate that the goal of energy security has not yet been achieved. Energy diplomacy offers a promising avenue for achieving this goal. In this frame, it is necessary to distinguish energy diplomacy from other disciplines.

In academic research, energy diplomacy has been extensively examined from an interdisciplinary perspective, encompassing policymaking, national energy policies, international relations, and foreign policy. Despite the significance and pervasiveness of energy diplomacy in all aspects of domestic and international politics, its multifaceted nature has resulted in a paucity of systematic work on energy diplomacy. This is where this work comes in.

13.1.1 Objective

This research investigates how states engage in energy diplomacy in an era where energy security plays a central role, especially given the persistence of conflicts and the significant impact of energy security on interstate relations. Then, it continues with the examination of energy diplomacy's importance in the context of the transition from fossil fuels to clean and renewable energy sources.

[1] International Energy Agency defines energy security as the uninterrupted availability of energy sources at an affordable price. IEA, "Energy security in energy transitions", available at: https://www.iea.org/reports/world-energy-outlook-2022/energy-security-in-energy-transitions

13.1.2 Methodology

In order to achieve this objective, this study commences with the conceptualisation of energy diplomacy. As it will be demonstrated, there is no clear definition of what is meant by the term "energy diplomacy". A number of scholars and international organisations or institutions with an interest in energy have attempted to define energy diplomacy by incorporating its characteristics and functions. As is the case with any conundrum concerning definition, it is for the authors of a study to choose or define one that, in their view, best explains the predicament.

Following the conceptualisation and definition of energy diplomacy, this study examines the role of energy in the hands of three categories of states: consumers, producers, and transit states. The aim of presenting a holistic approach is to understand how these states exercise energy diplomacy in an era of transition. This leads to the question of whether there are other avenues for deepening a state's diplomatic engagement, beyond the formal channels of embassies, forums, and international organisations. Is it part of a state's foreign policy to secure energy security?

The second issue addressed in this study is the relevance of energy diplomacy in the context of the ongoing energy transition. The term "transition" is used in this study to refer to two distinct phenomena: the transition resulting from systemic changes and the transition towards greater reliance on renewable energy sources. However, these two concepts are inextricably linked. As the international community moves towards a low-carbon energy transition, international relations are fundamentally changing. The consequences of this energy transition, occurring alongside the current global context of protracted armed conflicts and minimal tensions in regions with significant energy resources, have a profound impact on the relationship between energy producers and consumers. At the same time, this is exacerbating the antagonism between transit states seeking to play a more prominent role in the global energy sector. Consequently, both issues addressed in this study can be seen as examples of energy diplomacy, a tool used by states to enhance their power and achieve energy security. To this end, it also highlights the potential of state-centred diplomacy, which should seek to mobilise international and regional organisations, the private sector and inter-state relations to secure a state's national interest.

13.2 Defining and Conceptualising Energy Diplomacy

13.2.1 Origins of Energy Diplomacy

Diplomacy is one of the most important tools in a state's arsenal. The "talk to anyone" principle shapes collaborations, forms coalitions, enhances a state's power, and maintains open channels of communication which can prove invaluable in times of crisis. For powerful states with significant influence, diplomacy is translated into power projection. For less powerful states, diplomacy represents a critical tool for the pursuit of their interests through a variety of strategies. As diplomatic activity encompasses a vast array of modern societal aspects, including economic, military, cultural, environmental, scientific, sporting, and health diplomacy, energy diplomacy occupies a particularly prominent position due to its multifaceted nature.

"Energy diplomacy" is the aftereffect of the United States' intense diplomatic endeavours to address the consequences of the oil embargo imposed by the Organisation of Petroleum Exporting Countries (OPEC) during the 1973 crisis. The disruption of energy generated by the 1973 Arab-Israeli placed the United States in a position of diplomatic weakness with regard to energy matters. The resourceful Arab states employed the oil weapon against the United States of America and other supporters of Israel. And indeed, oil disruption and the subsequent increase in prices were efficient to produce undesired effects on the US economy, including domestic instability due to the energy restrictions that followed. In order to prevent a recurrence of such an aggressive act, the United States implemented a series of preventive measures aimed at enhancing energy security.

These measures included a significant increase in diplomatic efforts, particularly with key allies such as Saudi Arabia, Kuwait, and the European Economic Community (EEC). The objective of these diplomatic initiatives was to stabilise energy flows, break the monopoly of the OPEC and eventually establish détente with the Soviet Union. This approach, which involved the use of diplomatic tools to influence energy markets, is commonly referred to as "energy diplomacy".

Henry Kissinger during this period explicitly related the oil crisis to political crisis.[2] For the producing countries that automatically assumed that oil is linked to any economic activity, the relationship between access to raw materials and the re-ordering of the international economic system was their oil weapon and that was their opportunity to reset the consumer-producer dialogue. During the 1973 oil crisis, a phenomenal number of visits to Washington by Yamani and other high-level Saudi officials and an equally impressive number of high-level Aramco conferences in Saudi Arabia took place.[3] The lesson learned from the 1973 crisis led to the creation of the US Department of Energy and subsequent production legislation.[4]

In addition to the 1973 crisis, the subsequent events prompted the United States to pursue a systematic approach to what is known as "energy diplomacy". The balance of power as it was shaped during the Cold War between the USSR and the USA showed the formation of relations between the USSR and its satellite states with a special focus on gas and oil exports. In this frame, energy diplomacy placed a strong emphasis on energy security, both in a state, and regional context thus shaping the foreign policy of the involved states.

---

[2] A.-M. Walton, Atlantic Bargaining Over Energy. International Affairs (Royal Institute of International Affairs 1944-) 52, no. 2, 1976, pp.180–96.

[3] J. Stork, Middle East Oil and the Energy Crisis: Part Two, MERIP Reports, no. 21, 1973, pp. 3–26. JSTOR, p. 19.

[4] P. Dabbar, US Energy Superpower Status and a New US Energy Diplomacy, February 13, 2024, Hoover Institution Press, available at: https://www.hoover.org/research/us-energy-superpower-status-and-new-us-energy-diplomacy

The United States, in light of the 1973 OPEC-generated crisis, took further preventive actions in order to ensure energy security, particularly in the context of the Cold War developments in power politics and energy security. Confronted with these circumstances, the United States' energy diplomacy sought to establish partnerships with producers outside of OPEC countries, with the objective of expanding the scope of long-term supply agreements and facilitating the construction of new domestic refineries, such as those in Texas, which were specifically designed to process oil from Venezuela, the newly established US energy partner.[5]

The aftermath of the oil crisis led to significant institutional developments, including the creation of the International Energy Agency (IEA) in 1974. The IEA was established to coordinate energy policies among member countries and to promote energy security through collective action.

In conclusion, the United States serves as a salient example of the pivotal role of energy diplomacy. The United States has transformed its energy vulnerability into a powerful instrument, propelling it to become one of the most influential global energy powers. Hence, from coining energy diplomacy and once being the world's largest importer of energy, during the last decade the USA has managed to become a net energy exporter thus showing the importance of conducting efficient energy diplomacy.[6]

13.2.2 Literature Review

From Kissinger to Zhiznin, we can discern the build-up of a systematic approach to energy diplomacy.[7] Energy diplomacy has been studied thoroughly but interdisciplinary. This fact justifies the paucity of in-depth analysis of energy security per se. Undoubtedly, a plethora of case studies have yielded significant research conclusions for academic consideration. Nevertheless, these conclusions have been reached primarily within the context of foreign policy, but also in relation to energy policies, international relations, and political economy.

In this context, academic research has focused on the international energy relations, particularly in the wake of the 1973 oil crisis and the subsequent shift towards energy security, with a particular emphasis on the contributions of scholars and practitioners based in the USA.[8] Literature has extensively explored the

[5]A. Cheatham and D. Roy, Venezuela: The Rise and Fall of a Petrostate, Council on Foreign Relations, December 22, 2023, available at: https://www.cfr.org/backgrounder/venezuela-crisis

[6]P. Dabbar, US Energy Superpower Status and a New US Energy Diplomacy, February 13, 2024, Hoover Institution Press, available at: https://www.hoover.org/research/us-energy-superpower-status-and-new-us-energy-diplomacy

[7]**St. Zhiznin, Energy Diplomacy: Russia and the World** Wang, East Brook Publishing Company, Moscow, 2007, Haiyun and Qinhua Xu, An introduction to energy diplomacy: China's Perspective, Springer Nature, 2022.

[8]M. Conant and F. R. Gold, Geopolitics of energy, No. 95, US Government Printing Office, 1977., H. Kissinger, Years of upheaval, Simon and Schuster, 2011., D. A., Deese and J. S. Nye, Energy

multifaceted aspects of energy politics, encompassing a wide range of topics such as international politics and economics, energy cooperation, the oil industry and state power, economic interests, industrial technology, geopolitics and energy, and world energy politics and energy diplomacy from global, regional, and national perspectives. The nexus between energy security and the potential of energy diplomacy is revealed in numerous case studies that demonstrate the strategies employed by states such as Russia, China, and the Gulf states.

In the contemporary context, where energy transition is a key objective, research in the field of energy security and strategic oil reserves, diversification of energy structures and alternative energy sources, energy and environmental protection, international cooperation and international law on energy, and energy conservation and improvement of energy efficiency is also a thriving area of scholarship within the broader discipline of energy diplomacy. Despite the extensive research conducted to date, a notable research gap remains in the field of energy diplomacy with a lack of consensus on the definition and conceptualisation of this emerging discipline. Although the terms "energy diplomacy" or "energy strategy" are frequently encountered in academic and state documents, including those of the U.-S. Department of Energy and the European Union, there is no universally accepted definition.[9]

13.2.3 Defining Energy Diplomacy

Energy diplomacy is concerned with the achievement of domestic and external policy goals related to the uninterrupted flow of energy, with the objective of ensuring that the economy, social cohesion, and the environment are not adversely affected. However, the recent energy crisis resulted from the 2022 war in Ukraine shows that conflicting interests within supranational institutions as the European Union, an energy diplomacy producer, accentuate the importance of states as primary units of analysis.[10] In this regard, an accepted definition with respect to states as unitary actors and energy diplomacy is the following:

> the way countries give their energy companies a competitive edge in biding of resources by using the state's power: consumer countries strengthen their supply situation by

---

and security, [Book: report of Harvard's Energy and Security Research Project], 1981, D. Yergin, The prize: The epic quest for oil, money & power. Simon and Schuster, 2011.

[9] S. Lobanov, and Y. Surkhayeva, International Legal Approach to Understanding Energy Diplomacy, *Moscow Journal of International Law,* 2024., St. Zhiznin, International Energy Politics and Diplomacy, 2005.

[10] N. Chaban and M. Knodt, Energy Diplomacy in the Context of Multistakeholder Diplomacy: The EU and BICS., Cooperation and Conflict, vol. 50, no. 4, 2015, pp. 457–74.

> diplomatically flanking energy contracts, whereas producer countries use diplomacy to enhance access to markets or reserves.[11]

Although Goldthau's definition provides an adequate description of the energy diplomacy of consumers and producers, to serve the purpose of this study, we also add the conceptualisation that energy diplomacy aims at ensuring energy security, a cornerstone of national security:

National interest lies at the core of energy diplomacy, which is influenced by both tangible and intangible components of power[12]—such as location, geography, neighbourliness, and geopolitical dynamics—all of which have significant implications for a state's foreign policy objectives. As a matter of national security it affects national economy, defence, and in times of crisis, it can challenge domestic cohesion. Finally, energy diplomacy has been concerned with the transition from fossil fuels to renewable clean energy thus evolving the energy diplomacy to include also technology, energy infrastructure, and transportation in its agenda.

13.3 Perspectives on Energy Diplomacy: Producers-Consumers-Transit States

> No one disputes that the resources, including the energy resources, are there for the future if they are used wisely and well. Who is to control them, and who is to profit from that control, will be the focus of struggle in all countries and regions in the coming decades.[13]

There is a scope of energy diplomacy contingent on the status of the state. Resourceful states, especially those with large energy reserves, have built their domestic and foreign policies around the "energy weapon". Their aim is to expand their customer base and extend their network. These states also exercise greater control over resources. Conversely, consumer states, a strategy of diversification is most likely to be adopted in order to reduce interdependence and ensure energy security.

The complexity of practicing energy diplomacy emanates from the engagement of many actors, both domestic and international. At the domestic level, one must also analyse a state's energy strategy and grand strategy. The latter is based on political and economic relations within the international system. In addition, states, regional and international organisations and institutions associated with energy regulation,

[11] And. Goldthau, Energy diplomacy in Trade and Investment of Oil and Gas. In: Andreas Goldthau and Jan Martin Witte (eds), Global Energy Governance: The New Rules of the Game, DC: Brookings Institute Press, Washington, 2010, pp. 25–48.

[12] On components of power see, Th. A. Couloumbis and J. Hastings Wolfe, Introduction to international relations: power and justice, Prentice Hall, Englewood Cliffs, N.J.,1990, pp. 65–78.

[13] J. Stork, Middle East Oil and the Energy Crisis: Part Two, MERIP Reports, no. 21, 1973, pp. 3–26. JSTOR, p. 22.

such as OPEC, the European Union and the International Energy Agency, all play a key role in energy diplomacy.

This work brings energy diplomacy back to its state-centred diplomacy, where the primary goal is to mobilise all means such as international and regional organisations, private sector and inter-state relations to secure a state's national interest. Thus, to explore the predicament of this study, states are classified into three categories: producers, consumers, and transits. The aim is to show that energy strategy, and consequently energy security, is designed according to the specific needs of a given state. These three categories are not exclusive. The boundaries are blurred when a country fits into more than one category. It can be a consumer but also a transit state, a producer and a transit state at the same time. In this respect, it is essential to understand both the potential and the limitations of a state's energy diplomacy in order to describe its endeavours.

The following analysis delves into how states engage in energy diplomacy in an era where energy security plays a central role, given the persistence of conflicts and the significant impact of energy security on interstate relations. To this end, past and contemporary examples are necessary to illustrate perspectives on energy diplomacy.

Energy resources can enhance a state's power and influence. This may involve a transition to green energy, too. A state adjusts its international energy relations and accordingly its diplomatic activities subject to its national interests. From the perspective of a producer state, it directs its energy policies towards solidifying its international status and strengthening its collaborative efforts. The 1973 OPEC oil crisis provides a clear illustration that economic factors are not the predominant cause of supply and demand chain disruptions. Nevertheless, in the case of producers and especially of those in gas market, they likely aim at serving exclusively consumers and buying more gas fields. As gas prices are linked to and dictated by oil prices, the ultimate goal for producer countries is to benefit from their stable consumers and secure stable revenues.

Russia is an excellent example of exercising energy diplomacy. As a producer and transit country, Russia strategically exploits its location, its neighbourhood and the dependence of other states on Russian oil and gas. The aforementioned assets benefit Russia's energy diplomacy since most of the times it does not even need to negotiate with other actors. The Commonwealth of Independent States (CIS) is 80–100% dependent on foreign oil and gas. At the same time, most CIS countries are gas pipeline transit countries. Dependence on Russian gas has led to disputes and conflicts over resources, as in Georgia, Ukraine, and Belarus. Nevertheless, Russia does not wish to deteriorate its bilateral relations with the CIS countries, nor do the CIS countries themselves. Therefore, the CIS transit states have agreed with Russia on a win-win situation, whereby they collect transit fees and use them to reduce the cost of energy purchases. Such arrangements are common in international energy relations.[14]

Coercion and influence are at the core of Russia's energy policy and an important part of its energy diplomacy. The 2022 war in Ukraine and its impact on the European energy system shows that a resourceful state can benefit not only financially from the exploitation of its resources, but above all politically, which inevitably leads to an increase in its power and status in the international system.

National energy capabilities can even transform a less powerful actor into a powerful one. Should domestic political conditions be met, a resourceful but small state can increase both its power and influence by weaponising its resources. The Emirate of Qatar is a perfect example of the ability of a small state to exert significant influence over powerful actors in the international system. Since the decade of the 1990s, Qatar has replaced oil revenues with gas revenues as its main source of income and its international activities. Today, Qatar is an exquisite paradigm of a producer state with a phenomenal network that touches upon engagement with international organisations and institutions such as the EU, and third countries. It is one of the largest investors in European state industries such as aerospace, pharmaceuticals and biotechnology in Germany, France, Spain, and the UK. It is also involved in European state-owned oil companies, such as France's TOTAL, and even in exploration efforts in Cyprus, giving it a strong voice in energy policy in Europe, Asia, and Africa. All in all, Qatar's efforts to develop a sustainable energy sector, combined with a proactive foreign policy and determined leadership, have resulted in the creation of one of the most influential actors in contemporary politics in Europe, America, and Asia. This small state's energy sector became the incubator of its energy diplomacy thus allowing it to implement its ideological and expansionist goals.[15]

Resources can be used by powerful or less powerful actors in ways that can significantly increase their power. From resource swaps to aid, political and diplomatic support or even overseas infrastructure, energy resources have proven to be a valuable asset. Weak, usually non-democratic states that don't meet Western criteria for aid because of a lack of good governance barter resources for aid. China, a major investor in Africa, tends to provide financial assistance to Sudan and Zimbabwe, where the West is unwilling to provide economic aid because of their political situation. More broadly, China is engaged in a diplomatic marathon in Africa aiming at exchanging oil for infrastructure. From building hospitals to preventing the spread of disease, China is helping African states in a variety of ways to secure their valuable energy sources.[16]

[14]P. Mathieu and Clinton R. Shiells, The Commonwealth of Independent States' Troubled Energy Sectors, International Monetary Fund, September 2002, Vol. 39, No. 3, available at: https://www.imf.org/external/pubs/ft/fandd/2002/09/mathieu.htm

[15]R. Miller, Qatar, Energy Security, and Strategic Vision in a Small State, Journal of Arabian Studies, 2020, 10:1, pp. 122–138.

[16]L. Barber, China's Response to Sudan's Political Transition. US Institute of Peace, 2020. JSTOR, http://www.jstor.org/stable/resrep24904

A weak state can trade oil for diplomatic support, especially in international organisations. Setting the agenda in international organisations and gaining political support is important for less powerful states seeking to extract influence from the powerful. The United Nations is a perfect example of this trade-off. China, one of the "big five" on the United Nations Security Council, has benefited from Sudan to prevent international action on Sudan.[17]

In the case of resourceful but weak actors in the international system, domestic politics play critical role. Fragile but resourceful states with signs of corruption and prone to violence are particularly interested in negotiations with powerful states. Nigeria belongs to this category of fragile states. Resourceful but incapable of dealing with domestic energy problems, it makes deals with powerful actors such as India, trading oil for financial stability, investment, infrastructure, and renewable energy technology.[18]

There is a plethora of factors that define the relationships between the energy-producing and energy-consuming states. Geography, location, distance from the producer are all crucial. This is where the prominent role of transit states comes in. For transit states, location can be both a blessing and a curse. If a transit state has resources, it can negotiate from an advantageous position, especially with a powerful state. Russia's goal of expanding its network is aimed at greater interdependence. Cooperation with the CIS states, their dependence on Russian gas and their importance as transit routes for Russia force the latter to systematically tailor its bilateral relations to the needs of the states involved.

A transit country can be a landlocked country like Azerbaijan, a maritime transport corridor to Europe like Egypt, or a gas producer and exporter like Turkmenistan. Coastal states with oil transport corridors have an advantage in geopolitics and international negotiations. Looking back at history, the Suez crisis or today's developments in the Strait of Hormuz, the presence of military deployments around these areas for security reasons to protect the flow of energy and free trade is an acknowledgement of their importance. From another perspective, we have the paradigm of the Caspian Sea and its surrounding states. Privileged as they are with energy transport routes, they are also cursed by great power antagonism. In this case, energy diplomacy plays a crucial role between the United States and the EU, which are jointly promoting the construction of oil and gas pipelines in the Caspian Sea in order to minimise energy dependence on Russia.

In some cases, neither location nor resources are sufficient to advance a state's negotiating position. The case of Turkmenistan is an interesting one. The 2003 Turkmenistan-Russia deal demonstrates the dominance of Realpolitik for states that are perceived to be in an advantageous position. Russia's expansionist gas policy, supported by the state-owned gas monopoly Gazprom, leverages Russia to provide a solution for Turkmenistan to export its gas due to the lack of alternative

[17] A. Goldthau, Energy diplomacy in trade and investment of oil and gas. Global energy governance: The new rules of the game, 2010, pp. 25–48, p. 34.

[18] Dash Sandipani, India-Nigeria Oil Partnership, Indian Journal of African Studies, 2023, 84.

routes.[19] Meanwhile, Azerbaijan, Georgia, Turkey, and Ukraine, which are key geostrategic locations for Europe and the United States, are trying to make the most of this great power competition, driven by domestic factors and concerns about the impact of their preferences in international politics. Finally, Iran, a rogue state based in the Strait of Hormuz, rich in oil and gas reserves, but also in its potential to exploit the Caspian Sea, is playing its trump card and testing its ability to evade sanctions.

The subregional system of the Eastern Mediterranean offers intriguing cases of transit, consumer or producer states. Since the beginning of 2000, the prospect of gas exploration in the Levant Basin has dominated international affairs. What is different in this area is the role that energy diplomacy plays between states such as Turkey-Cyprus, Israel-Lebanon, Greece-Turkey, where enmity is the state of their bilateral affairs.

The Republic of Cyprus is an interesting case, both as a transit country and as a possible producer. As the south-eastern part of the EU, close to the Suez Canal and bordering large oil and gas fields, Cyprus is well placed to be a hub. As new collaborations emerged in the Eastern Mediterranean in the first decade of the 2000s, Cyprus saw an opportunity to strengthen itself internally, but more importantly, externally. It shifted its foreign policy towards energy, which is not unusual for a small state. Intensive diplomatic efforts led to the delimitation of Cyprus' exclusive economic zone, while the formation of bilateral and trilateral partnerships with neighbouring states led to the attraction of colossal energy companies such as ENI and EXXON, which translates into influence.

The paradigm of the Republic of Cyprus (RoC) is important for the following reasons: a small state shows that it is possible to exploit its assets, such as its strategic location and external environment, i.e. European efforts to reduce dependence on Russia. By presenting itself as a reliable partner, it has not only managed to attract major energy companies that enjoy the support of their countries, but it has also projected a plan to become part of a solution to a common energy security conundrum of the European Union. Cyprus' energy diplomacy not only shows how resources can enhance sovereignty, given that 37% of its territory has been under illegal Turkish occupation for 50 years. More importantly, the RoC case demonstrates that energy diplomacy affects other important components of power, such as military and political power. The importance of involving the private sector in the complex framework of energy relations is evident in Cyprus' energy diplomacy. Its role as a reliable partner in the region, combined with the creation of a friendly environment for international companies, as well as Cyprus' efforts to build political and defence relations based on its energy cooperation, make the island of Aphrodite an important partner for the EU, the US and the Eastern Mediterranean

[19]M. Elder, Putin lands a deal for Turkmen gas, The Moscow Times, May 14, 2007, available at: https://www.themoscowtimes.com/archive/putin-lands-a-deal-for-turkmen-gas

region.[20] Finally, the EuroAsia Interconnector, now named the Great Sea Interconnector, a 1208 km cross-border electricity link between Crete, Cyprus, and Israel funded by various sources, is an illustrative paradigm of what energy diplomacy can also achieve in the non-fossil fuel sector.[21]

From the perspective of the producer states energy diplomacy is key to capitalise on their resources. Depending on various factors as location, abundance of resources, domestic politics, network to transfer energy, and proximity of the consumer states, producers deploy various strategies to achieve more than energy security. Meanwhile, for consumer states, it is more advantageous to conclude bilateral agreements based on individual needs. A militarily and economically strong producer state can expand its network by penetrating energy markets. Usually, the target is also a producer state, but a weak one. The provision of financial, technological, and military assistance and the development of infrastructure are effective weapons. If the domestic politics of a weak state are marred by corruption and a lack of democratic institutions, bilateral agreements can be concluded with a powerful producer under the pretext of informal energy negotiations.

China is one of the most prominent paradigms of a consumer but powerful state that systematically links development aid to access to resources. By providing financial and development aid in the form of concessional loans and converting them into grants and debt relief, China has infiltrated resourceful African states using the aid weapon.[22] Military aid is another common practice. Oil for arms is a common trade, especially in African states, and is usually accompanied by political support. The Nigeria-China relationship has been established within this framework.

On the African continent, where there are resourceful but weak states, most of the strategies are based on bilateral cooperation between producers and consumers and on resource trade-offs. India is an interesting case of a consumer state. India is one of the main consumers of Nigerian oil. This relationship dates back to the middle of the twentieth century. India is a developing economy that lacks the resources to support its industry. Nigeria is Africa's largest oil producer and has a significant energy relationship with India. The latter trades oil with European countries, the USA and India, among others. When Nigeria was looking for international partners to develop its energy sector, India and its companies came along. Indian oil companies have made substantial investments in Nigeria's upstream oil sector and have signed bilateral agreements to strengthen their cooperation. The India-Nigeria relationship is based on the exchange of resources for trade, Indian investment, technological cooperation, and policy alignment. It perfectly illustrates the dynamics of energy diplomacy in forging strong ties in many areas of interest, where resources can be

[20] St. Gerani, Small States in regional conflicts: the cases of Kuwait and Cyprus, Thesis, University of Macedonia, 2019, pp. 193–205.

[21] European Commission, Ending energy isolation - Project of Common Interest EuroAsia Interconnector, available at: https://commission.europa.eu/projects/ending-energy-isolation-project-common-interest-euroasia-interconnector_en

[22] A. Goldthau, Energy diplomacy in trade and investment of oil and gas. Global energy governance: The new rules of the game, 2010, pp. 25–48, p. 34.

exchanged for capacity building and training programmes for the Nigerian oil and gas industry as it moves towards renewable energy. Today, India is offering expertise and technology to support Nigeria's efforts to diversify its energy portfolio from oil to renewables, making this collaboration sustainable and stronger in an era of transition.[23]

Finally, US energy diplomacy provides the most explanatory paradigm to summarise this very timely issue of energy diplomacy. The USA is both a producer and a consumer of energy. However, the prospect of a change in the 1974 petrodollar deal with the Saudis will be the issue that the international energy community will be watching.

The USA's dependence on oil has long influenced its foreign policy. Energy diplomacy as a function of diplomacy has been shaped by the USA itself. Exemplary is the paradigm of the negotiations between the US President Roosevelt and King Abdulaziz of Saudi Arabia in 1945. Despite the fact that the USA had domestic production, concerns about growing demand and the taxation of US domestic production after the Second World War led to the declaration that "Saudi oil is vital to U.S. security" and thus the USA provided financial support.[24]

The US oil development spans three major periods: the rise of oil as a commodity in the early 1850s, the post-World War II era of geopolitical competition, and the post-Cold War era of deregulation and diversification. Today, US oil production is booming, along with its renewed energy transition efforts to phase out fossil fuels globally.[25] Nevertheless, Saudi oil will be in demand not only in Asian and Gulf markets, but also in the USA for at least 20 years.

The oil-for-security deal between the USA and Saudi Arabia is the quintessence of energy diplomacy. It embodies all the fundamentals of energy diplomacy as it emerged in the twentieth century and continues to function today. However, almost eight decades after the Saudi-US oil-for-security pact, the kingdom is adopting a more pragmatic foreign policy. The bilateral relationship between the USA and Saudi Arabia has been shattered not only by the rise of China and Russia, but above all by trust issues between the USA and the Saudis. The latter is putting security concerns on the negotiating table as the US military power continues to withdraw from the region, while the former is facing a real danger: the surge in oil prices, escalating global inflationary pressures and China's growing demand for Saudi oil.[26]

[23] Yaruingam Awungshi and PamreihorKhashimwo, Mapping India-Nigeria Relations: Bringing energy sector into focus, Journal of Advance Research in Social Science & Humanities ISSN 2208: 2387, Volume-9, Issue-9, Sep, 2023.

[24] Council on Foreign Relations, 1850–2023. Oil Dependence and U.S. Foreign Policy, Council on Foreign Relations, available at: https://www.cfr.org/timeline/oil-dependence-and-us-foreign-policy

[25] Ibid.

[26] J. Spalding, The Deal That Keeps the Oil Flowing, June 1, 2023, Epicenter, Weatherhead Center for International Affairs, Harvard University, available at: https://epicenter.wcfia.harvard.edu/blog/deal-keeps-oil-flowing

The Kingdom of Saudi Arabia, a major oil producer with sufficient refining capacity for decades to come, is seeking to reform its relationship with Washington to take account of the convergence of Saudi interests with its non-Western neighbours, notably China and Russia. At stake, however, is the 1974 US-Saudi agreement that established the US dollar as the currency in which Saudi Arabia agreed to sell oil exclusively in exchange for US military, security, and economic development aid.[27] Today's frictions in this bilateral relationship, coupled with a transition to a multipolar international system and green energy, require pragmatic decisions in US foreign policy, as was the case in 1943 when President Franklin Roosevelt declared Saudi oil vital to US security and provided financial support.[28]

In contemporary politics, a variety of factors, including conflict and international relations, terrorism and environmental catastrophes, dominate energy policy and are a linchpin for building cooperative relationships, particularly between consumers and producers. Global demands for human economic and social development have outstripped traditional reliance on fossil fuels. While oil and gas continue to play an important role in energy diplomacy, growing environmental concerns and the increasing share of clean energy sources are forcing the international community to direct investment towards renewable energy sources, including solar, wind, geothermal, hydro, and other forms of energy. This energy transition will inevitably lead to the need to broaden the scope of energy diplomacy and to include more parameters in the negotiation process. Given the timeframe set by Western industrialised countries for the energy transition, it is possible that factors such as technological innovation and technical cooperation will lead to a reduction in the competitive advantages of fossil fuel producing countries. This could lead to a change in the landscape of international energy relations due to the shifting dynamics of the energy transition.

13.4 The Significance of Energy Diplomacy in the Context of the Ongoing Energy Transition

The global energy landscape is undergoing profound change, driven by the urgent need to address climate change, secure sustainable energy and promote economic resilience. The transition from fossil fuels to renewable energy sources marks one of the most significant shifts in contemporary history, with far-reaching implications for international relations. The urgency of climate action necessitates a more comprehensive and multifaceted approach to energy diplomacy. Energy diplomacy is no

[27] B. Gwertzman, Milestone' pact is signed by U.S. and Saudi Arabia, The New York Times, June 9, 1974, available at: https://www.nytimes.com/1974/06/09/archives/milestone-pact-is-signed-by-us-and-saudi-arabia-acclaimed-by.html

[28] Council on Foreign Relations, 1850–2023. Oil Dependence and U.S. Foreign Policy, Council on Foreign Relations, available at: https://www.cfr.org/timeline/oil-dependence-and-us-foreign-policy

longer just oil and gas diplomacy. It has emerged as a critical tool for managing the multiple challenges and opportunities associated with this transition and requires a focus on fostering international cooperation. This section discusses the role of energy diplomacy in enhancing international cooperation, ensuring energy security and addressing geopolitical dynamics during this transformative period.

13.4.1 Enhancing International Cooperation

The energy transition is an inherently global endeavour that requires an unprecedented level of international cooperation. The creation and strengthening of global partnerships that enable countries to work together to develop and deploy renewable energy technologies is a necessity. Through diplomatic channels, countries can share best practices, technological advancements and research findings, accelerating the global adoption of clean energy.

The Paris Agreement, for example, epitomises the collaborative spirit, committing countries to collectively reduce carbon emissions and build resilience to climate impacts.[29] This landmark agreement, signed by 195 countries, sets legally binding greenhouse gas reduction targets and establishes a framework for transparency and accountability in climate action. By building a sense of shared responsibility, the Paris Agreement has catalysed global efforts towards a low-carbon future. However, while international agreements such as the Paris Agreement represent a step forward, translating these agreements into concrete action remains a hurdle. National interests often clash with broader goals, hindering progress. Moreover, domestic political resistance, bureaucratic inertia, and a lack of financial resources can stall implementation. This is particularly true in developing countries with limited governance capacity.

Bilateral and multilateral diplomatic engagement plays a critical role in harmonising regulatory standards and policies across borders, creating an enabling environment for international investment in renewable energy. For example, initiatives such as the Clean Energy Ministerial (CEM) provide a high-level forum to promote policies and programmes that advance clean energy technologies. In addition, the International Renewable Energy Agency (IRENA) has been instrumental in stimulating such cooperation and assisting countries in their transition efforts through technical assistance and policy guidance.[30] By aligning energy policies, countries can attract foreign direct investment, mobilise financial resources and facilitate technology transfer, which is essential for scaling up renewable energy projects. Yet, the success of these efforts depends on the willingness of countries to

[29] United Nations Framework Convention on Climate Change (UNFCCC), 'Paris Agreement' (2015).

[30] International Renewable Energy Agency (IRENA), 'Geopolitics of the Energy Transition' (2024), availableat:https://www.irena.org/Publications/2024/Apr/Geopolitics-of-the-energy-transition-Energy-security

prioritise long-term cooperation over short-term national gains, which is not always guaranteed. In the European Union, the implementation of unified energy policies has been occasionally impeded by divergent national priorities. For instance, Poland has been reluctant to implement EU-wide climate policies that necessitate a swift reduction in coal usage, given its substantial reliance on coal for energy and employment. This resistance serves to illustrate the inherent conflict between national economic interests and collective goals, thereby underscoring the difficulties encountered in the pursuit of unified energy diplomacy.

In addition, energy diplomacy can help address potential conflicts arising from the competitive nature of resource allocation and technological advances, and promote a cooperative approach to global energy governance.[31] The role of energy diplomacy today extends to the establishment of regional cooperation frameworks, such as the European Union's Green Deal, which aims to ensure secure, sustainable and affordable energy for its member states.[32]

13.4.2 Ensuring Energy Security

The transition from fossil fuels to renewable energy sources presents both opportunities and challenges for energy security. While renewable energy can reduce dependence on imported fossil fuels and increase energy autonomy, it also introduces new vulnerabilities, such as the intermittency of solar and wind power and the criticality of supply chains for renewable technologies. Energy diplomacy has an important role to play in mitigating these risks by promoting diversified and resilient energy partnerships.

As previously stated, the Russian invasion of Ukraine in 2022 has fundamentally reshaped European energy policy, exposing vulnerabilities in energy security, and prompting a significant realignment of strategies. Disruptions to natural gas supplies from Russia, historically a primary source of energy for Europe, have led to an urgent search for alternative suppliers through increased imports of liquefied natural gas (LNG) from the United States and Qatar, necessitating infrastructure improvements for LNG terminals. The crisis has also accelerated the transition to renewable energy, with the European Union's REPowerEU plan[33] aiming to increase the share of renewables in the energy mix alongside energy efficiency measures. To further enhance security, European countries are forging strategic

[31] Global Commission on the Geopolitics of Energy Transformation, 'A New World: The Geopolitics of the Energy Transformation' (2019), available at:https://www.irena.org/publications/2019/Jan/A-New-World-The-Geopolitics-of-the-Energy-Transformation

[32] European Union, 'The European Green Deal' (2020), available at: https://eur-lex.europa.eu/legal-content/EN/TXT/?uri=CELEX%3A52019DC0640

[33] European Union, 'REPowerEU Plan' (2022), available at: https://commission.europa.eu/strategy-and-policy/priorities-2019-2024/european-green-deal/repowereu-affordable-secure-and-sustainable-energy-europe_en

alliances with energy-rich regions such as the Eastern Mediterranean and North Africa.

Diplomatic initiatives have facilitated the development of regional energy markets and interconnection projects, such as cross-border electricity grids and gas pipelines that support the integration of renewables. The North Sea Wind Power Hub project is an example of how diplomatic cooperation can enable the construction of interconnected offshore wind farms, enhancing energy security for several countries.[34] This ambitious project aims to create a modular hub-and-spoke network of offshore wind farms in the North Sea, providing clean energy to millions of European homes and businesses.

The clean energy revolution hinges on access to critical minerals like lithium, cobalt, and rare earth elements. These elements are geographically concentrated, with a significant proportion in politically volatile regions. This concentration creates a potential geopolitical choke point where countries controlling these resources can exert undue influence. The recent race between the United States and China to secure lithium resources in South America and Africa underscores this challenge. This scramble for resources can lead to unsustainable mining practices and destabilise already fragile regions.

Strategic partnerships and trade agreements, such as the EU-Morocco Green Partnership[35] and the European Raw Materials Alliance,[36] help ensure a stable supply of these materials, reducing the risk of supply chain disruptions. Additionally, initiatives like the Extractive Industries Transparency Initiative (EITI) promote transparent and accountable management of mineral resources. To this end, the Minerals Security Partnership (MSP) was established to enhance collaboration among nations such as Australia, Canada, and a coalition including Estonia, Finland, France, Germany, India, Italy, Japan, Norway, the Republic of Korea, Sweden, the United Kingdom, the United States, and the European Union (represented by the European Commission). MSP aims to accelerate the development of diverse and sustainable supply chains for critical energy minerals.[37]

Moreover, the increasing digitalisation and interconnection of energy systems introduces a new layer of vulnerability, namely the risk of cyberattacks. To address this growing threat, international cooperation on cybersecurity measures is critical. Diplomatic efforts can facilitate international cooperation on cybersecurity measures, ensuring that countries are equipped to protect their energy infrastructure

[34] North Sea Wind Power Hub, 'Programme Overview' (2021), available at: https://northseawindpowerhub.eu/knowledge/towards-the-first-hub-and-spoke-project

[35] See, e.g. European Commission, 'EU-Morocco Green Partnership' (2021), available at:https://climate.ec.europa.eu/news-your-voice/news/eu-and-morocco-form-green-partnership-energy-climate-and-environment-ahead-cop-26-2021-06-28_en

[36] https://erma.eu/

[37] https://www.state.gov/minerals-security-partnership/. Recently, in a significant development for securing critical resources, the European Union, the United States, and other members of the Minerals Security Partnership (MSP) have joined forces with Kazakhstan, Namibia, Ukraine, and Uzbekistan to establish the Minerals Security Partnership Forum (MSP Forum).

from potential threats. The International Energy Agency has highlighted the importance of cybersecurity in the energy sector and advocated for increased international cooperation to protect critical energy assets.[38]

13.4.3 Addressing Geopolitical Dynamics

The energy transition is reshaping global geopolitical dynamics, with significant implications for international relations. Traditional energy geopolitics, centred on oil and gas, is gradually being replaced by new forms of geopolitical influence linked to renewable energy resources and technologies. Managing this evolving dynamic and ensuring that the transition does not exacerbate geopolitical tensions is not an easy task. For example, renewable energy resources are more evenly distributed around the world than fossil fuels, potentially reducing the likelihood of energy-related conflicts. In addition, renewable energy technologies often require different infrastructure, such as grids and storage systems, which can encourage new forms of international cooperation. However, the benefits of the transition are not evenly distributed. Developed countries with advanced technological capabilities and financial resources are better positioned to capitalise on the new energy landscape. This may create new power imbalances and exacerbate existing geopolitical tensions.

Countries rich in renewable energy resources such as solar, wind, and hydropower are emerging as new centres of geopolitical influence. The production of hydrogen from renewable sources, commonly referred to as green hydrogen, is emerging as a pivotal component of future energy systems. Countries such as Australia and Saudi Arabia are investing heavily in green hydrogen projects, thereby positioning themselves as future energy leaders. For example, Morocco has become a key player in renewable energy diplomacy through its ambitious solar projects and partnerships with the European Union. The Noor Ouarzazate Solar Complex, one of the largest solar power plants in the world, exemplifies Morocco's commitment to renewable energy and its strategic use of energy diplomacy to strengthen ties with Europe.

Conversely, countries heavily dependent on fossil fuel exports face economic and geopolitical challenges as global demand for oil and gas declines. Africa is a continent with vast renewable energy potential (solar, wind, hydro) but limited access to modern energy infrastructure.[39] Despite its minimal contribution to global carbon emissions, African countries face the brunt of the impacts of climate change. International pressure to reduce greenhouse gas emissions is driving a rapid transition away from fossil fuels, including Africa's abundant natural gas reserves. Diplomatic efforts are needed to assist these countries in diversifying their

[38] International Energy Agency (IEA), 'Power Systems in Transition' (2020), available at: https://www.iea.org/reports/power-systems-in-transition

[39] International Renewable Energy Agency (IRENA), 'Geopolitics of the Energy Transition' (2024), p. 55.

economies and transitioning to sustainable energy systems in order to avoid potential destabilisation. The Gulf Cooperation Council (GCC) countries, for example, are exploring renewable energy projects and economic diversification strategies to reduce their dependence on oil revenues.[40] There is scepticism, however, about whether such projects can really change the geopolitical dynamics, or whether they merely shift the centres of influence without addressing the underlying power imbalances.

Energy diplomacy can also facilitate the resolution of conflicts arising from competition for renewable energy resources and infrastructure. The management of shared water resources for hydropower in transboundary river basins requires diplomatic negotiation and cooperation to ensure equitable and sustainable use. The Nile Basin Initiative, involving countries along the Nile River, is an example of how diplomatic efforts can manage and resolve disputes over shared water resources.[41] This cooperative framework aims to promote sustainable development and equitable use of the Nile's resources, thereby fostering peace and stability in the region.

By promoting dialogue and cooperation, energy diplomacy can turn potential conflicts into opportunities for joint development and regional integration. For example, the Renewable Energy and Energy Efficiency Partnership (REEEP) promotes international cooperation on renewable energy projects and facilitates knowledge exchange and capacity building among member countries.[42] Such initiatives highlight the role of energy diplomacy in promoting mutual benefits and reducing geopolitical tensions. Nonetheless, the effectiveness of such initiatives is often questioned due to persistent political tensions and differing national interests among the involved countries.

13.5 Concluding Remarks

The ongoing global energy transition is a messy and uneven process, driven by a mix of environmental concerns, geopolitical competition, and economic realities. The exploration of energy diplomacy in the context of the global energy transition has led to several important conclusions and strategic proposals.

History offers valuable lessons, but the past doesn't always apply to the present. The 1973 oil crisis highlighted the vulnerability of over-reliance on fossil fuels, but international cooperation in response has been uneven. The IEA, for example, has struggled to balance the interests of member states with different energy needs and priorities. Today's threats, such as climate change and cyberattacks, require

[40]Fahad Radhi Alharbi and Denes Csala, 'Gulf Cooperation Council Countries' Climate Change Mitigation Challenges and Exploration of Solar and Wind Energy Resource Potential' (2021) 11 Applied Sciences 2648.

[41]See also the Agreement on the Nile River Basin Cooperative Framework, available at:https://nilebasin.org/sites/default/files/attachments/CFA%20%20English%20FrenchVersion.pdf

[42]Renewable Energy and Energy Efficiency Partnership (REEEP), 'Annual Report' (2020), available at: https://reeep.org/wp-content/uploads/2023/10/REEEP-Annual-Report-2020.pdf

international cooperation, but reaching consensus can be a slow and difficult process. Competing national interests and entrenched historical grievances often complicate the path to effective cooperation.

The shift to renewable energy is reshaping the geopolitical landscape, but the benefits are not evenly distributed. Resource-rich countries are gaining leverage, while traditional fossil fuel exporters are facing difficult economic transitions. The GCC's diversification efforts offer a glimmer of hope, but their success depends on complex factors. Energy diplomacy can play a role in mitigating conflicts over shared resources, but this requires strong leadership and commitment from all stakeholders. Regional rivalries can easily derail progress, and ensuring equitable access to resources remains a challenge.

The uneven distribution of renewable resources is a significant barrier for developing countries. Diplomatic efforts can promote technology transfer and capacity building, but these initiatives are often resource-intensive and require long-term commitment. Bridging the gap between developed and developing countries will be a critical but likely slow process.

Navigating the complexities of the global energy transition will require a multifaceted approach: Strengthening international bodies such as the IEA and ISA can facilitate cooperation, but member states with conflicting interests can make progress difficult. Incremental steps and a focus on areas of common ground may be more realistic than sweeping reforms. Technology transfer is crucial, but concerns about intellectual property rights and national security can create obstacles. Finding a balance between sharing knowledge and protecting sensitive technologies will be essential. The transition away from fossil fuels is a complex economic undertaking. Diplomatic strategies should prioritise practical measures such as skills training and infrastructure development to support a smooth economic transition. Regional initiatives can foster dialogue, but managing expectations is key. Success is likely to come in small wins and will require ongoing commitment from all parties. Policies that address energy poverty and ensure just transitions for workers displaced by the shift away from fossil fuels will also be crucial.

The road ahead for energy diplomacy is far from smooth. Geopolitical competition, economic interests, and the sheer complexity of the transition itself will all pose challenges. But by acknowledging these realities and focusing on pragmatic solutions, energy diplomacy can play a vital role in steering the global energy transition towards a more secure and sustainable future, even if that future arrives only gradually.

Acknowledgement The authors would like to express their gratitude to Christos Liperis, Ministry of Foreign Affairs, Republic of Cyprus, for his invaluable insights during the drafting of this work.

Styliani Gerani, graduated in Classics from Aristotle University of Thessaloniki. In 2019 she was awarded a PhD from the Department of International and European Studies of the University of Macedonia. During her doctoral studies she was member of the Research team at "Thucydides Chair," of University of Macedonia and The Hellenic National Defence General Staff Chair in Strategic Studies (2016–2018). Her research focused on the Hellenic Republic, the Republic of Cyprus and the State of Israel, the dynamics of the region on the issues of Defense, Energy and Security. In 2016, she was granted a Research Scholarship from the Ministry of Foreign Affairs of the State of Israel to conduct Research at the "Begin-Sadat Center for Strategic Studies," at Bar-Ilan University, in Tel Aviv. She teaches Energy Politics and Security for the Postgraduate Program "MSc in Energy Law, Business, Regulation and Policy" at the International Hellenic University. She has also a teaching experience in International Relations, Turkish Politics and War Theory at the University of Macedonia in ante graduate and postgraduate studies. Her research has been published in academic journals and has been presented in international and European conferences.

Komninos Komnios, Associate Professor of Energy Law at the International Hellenic University (IHU) and a Fellow for the academic year 2023-24 at the Cattolica Global School of Law. He also serves as a member of the Board of the Hellenic Regulatory Authority for Energy, Waste and Water and as the Hellenic Energy Ombudsman. Prof. Komnios holds a Ph.D. (Doctor Iuris) from the Saarland University and completed a postdoctoral thesis on evidence in domestic and international commercial arbitration. In addition to his academic and regulatory roles, Dr Komnios is the Scientific Director of the MSc in Energy Law, Business, Regulation & Policy, the LLM in Transnational and European Commercial Law, Banking Law, Arbitration/Mediation and the MA in Art Law & Arts Management at IHU. He is a highly qualified lawyer and accredited mediator with extensive experience in legal advice and dispute resolution, having provided legal advice to various organizations. His research interests focus on energy law, ADR, and the intersection of procedural law and digital technologies. Prof. Komnios has published more than 70 books and articles in these fields in Greek, English, and German.

Health Diplomacy

14

Elisavet Athanasia Alexiadou

Abstract

In today's increasingly interconnected and globalized world the goal of health protection cannot be achieved in isolation, namely by one country or an agency working alone, while no country can isolate itself from global health challenges and threats that transcend national boundaries and lay bare the restrictions of segmentation approaches. Without any doubt, the COVID-19 pandemic has vividly underscored how rapidly emerging infections can evolve, cost lives, adversely influence global travel and trade, and thus, the pressing need for the world to act together. It is within this context that health diplomacy could make a tangible contribution to securing and realizing global health as a global public good at all times and especially in the face of crises. In a changing global context, health diplomacy could serve as a bridge for building alliances on addressing health issues of common concern which require the cooperation of many countries and diverse actors and for ultimately promoting international cooperation for health. Against this backdrop, the chapter proposes a right to health approach to health diplomacy for identifying rights-based legal obligations within and beyond a State's national borders, reflecting the weight of collective and concerted actions and the need for a standard-setting in a world that is full of tensions and challenges that concern our common future as global citizens.

E. A. Alexiadou (✉)
International Hellenic University, Thessaloniki, Greece

Open University of Cyprus, Hellenic Open University, Patras, Greece

Aristotle University of Thessaloniki, Thessaloniki, Greece
e-mail: alexiadou.elisavet@ac.eap.gr

P. Naskou-Perraki (ed.), *Contemporary Diplomatic and Consular Relations*,
https://doi.org/10.1007/978-3-031-99243-8_14

14.1 Introduction: Setting the Scene

Health is a fundamental human right and a central condition for human well-being and good public health in turn constitutes one of the crucial means for driving sustainable development, growth, social justice and security.[1] More than seven decades ago, in 1946 the World Health Organization (WHO) defined health in the preamble of its Constitution as 'a state of complete physical, social and mental well-being, not merely the absence of disease or infirmity' while declaring that 'the enjoyment of the highest attainable standard of health is one of the fundamental rights of every human being without distinction of race, religion, political belief, economic or social condition'.[2] From this perspective, health goes beyond the medical realm and thus, is recognized as a right, determined to a large extent not only by biological factors, but also by environmental, cultural, social and economic factors, such as poverty and discrimination.[3] Accordingly, it is maintained that '... ill health is both a cause and a consequence of poverty: sick people are more likely to become poor and the poor are more vulnerable to disease and disability ... Good health is central to creating and sustaining the capabilities that poor people need to escape from poverty. A key asset of the poor, good health contributes to their greater economic security. Good health is not just an outcome of development: it is a way of achieving development'.[4] To this end, all individuals and people, whether in high- or low-income countries and on the basis of equality and non-discrimination, are entitled to a system of health protection against potential health-related risks and harms involving measures undertaken primarily by States to secure them from exposure to harm with detrimental effects on their health and well-being.[5]

Nevertheless, in today's increasingly interconnected and globalized world, with the Coronavirus disease 2019 (COVID-19) pandemic amply exemplifying how

[1] UN Committee on Economic, Social and Cultural Rights (CESCR), General Comment No. 14: The Right to the Highest Attainable Standard of Health, UN Doc. E/C.12/2000/4, 11 August 2000, para. 1. D. Fairman et al., Negotiating Public Health in a Globalized World: Global Health Diplomacy in Action, Springer, Dordrecht/Heidelberg/London/New York, 2012, p. 1.

[2] World Health Organization, Basic Documents: Forty-ninth Edition (including amendments adopted up to 31 May 2019), WHO, Geneva, 2020, p. 1.

[3] UN Committee on Economic, Social and Cultural Rights (CESCR), General Comment No. 14: The Right to the Highest Attainable Standard of Health, UN Doc. E/C.12/2000/4, 11 August 2000, paras. 9 and 11. I. Kickbusch and A. Liu, 'Global health diplomacy – reconstructing power and governance', The *Lancet* 2022, 399: 2156–2166, 2156.

[4] UN, The Right of Everyone to the Enjoyment of the Highest Attainable Standard of Physical and Mental Health: Report of the Special Rapporteur, Paul Hunt. UN ESCOR, Commission on Human Rights, 59th Sess., Agenda Item 10, UN Doc. E/CN.4/2003/58, 13 February 2003, paras. 45–46.

[5] UN Committee on Economic, Social and Cultural Rights (CESCR), General Comment No. 14: The Right to the Highest Attainable Standard of Health, UN Doc. E/C.12/2000/4, 11 August 2000, para. 8. World Health Organization, Glossary of Terms, WHO, Geneva, 1984, para. 30. See, e.g. B. C.A. Toebes, The Right to Health as a Human Right in International Law, Intersentia, Antwerp, 1999, p. 247. A. Hendriks, The Right to Health in National and International Jurisprudence, European Journal of Health Law 1998, 5, 389–408, p. 394.

rapidly emerging infections can evolve, spread, cost lives and reduce travel and trade activities among interdependent economies, the goal of health protection cannot be achieved in isolation, namely by one country or agency working alone, but rather in an internationally concerted way by means of international health cooperation.[6] Cognizant of the reality of interdependence even prior to the COVID-19 pandemic, the United Nations Committee on Economic, Social and Cultural Rights (UN CESCR), the oversight body for the implementation of the International Covenant on Economic, Social and Cultural Rights (ICESCR), explicitly underscored that for millions of people around the world, the full enjoyment of the right to health remains a distant goal in that 'formidable structural and other obstacles resulting from international and other factors beyond the control of States … impede the full realization of' the right to health recognized in Article 12 ICESCR.[7] In a similar vein, aligned with the repeated UN General Assembly resolutions calling for global solidarity and international assistance and cooperation in the COVID-19 response, the Director-General of WHO cautioned 'no one is safe until everyone is safe' amid the rapidly evolving pandemic situation and the varying government responses.[8] Notably, the reality of the increased interdependence in the world tends to advance understanding that health should be perceived and realized as a global public good (GPG) which all countries have a collective international responsibility for producing, sustaining, and securing for all in a rights-respecting manner for making the world safer and fairer.[9]

Even though it is generally accepted that in international law a State is the primary responsible for securing population health within its territory, yet in practice no country can isolate itself from global health challenges and threats that transcend not only national boundaries but also public–private divides, clearly laying bare the restrictions of segmentation approaches.[10] Admittedly, accelerated globalization of

[6]See generally, I. Kickbusch and C. Erk, Global Health Diplomacy: The New Recognition of Health in Foreign Policy in: A. Clapham & M. Robinson (ed.), Realizing the Right to Health, Rüffer and Rub, Zurich, 2009, p. 517–524, p. 519.

[7]UN Committee on Economic, Social and Cultural Rights (CESCR), General Comment No. 14: The Right to the Highest Attainable Standard of Health, UN Doc. E/C.12/2000/4, 11 August 2000, para. 5.

[8]UN General Assembly, Resolution 74/270. Global solidarity to fight the coronavirus disease 2019 (COVID-19), UN Doc. A/RES/74/270, 3 April 2020. UN General Assembly, Resolution 74/274. International cooperation to ensure global access to medicines, vaccines and medical equipment to face COVID-19, UN Doc. A/RES/74/274, 21 April 2020. UN General Assembly, Resolution 74/306. Comprehensive and coordinated response to the coronavirus disease (COVID-19) pandemic, UN Doc. A/RES/74/306, 15 September 2020. I. Kickbusch and A. Liu, Global health diplomacy – reconstructing power and governance, The Lancet 2022, 399: 2156–2166, p. 2156.

[9]I. Kickbusch and C. Erk, 'Global Health Diplomacy: The New Recognition of Health in Foreign Policy' in: A. Clapham & M. Robinson (ed.), Realizing the Right to Health, Rüffer and Rub, Zurich, 2009, p. 517–524, p. 519.

[10]Ch. R. Beitz, The Idea of Human Rights, Oxford University Press, Oxford, 2009, p. 114. See also, Convention on the Rights of the Child (CRC) (New York, 20 November 1989, entered into force 2 September 1990, 1577 UNTS 3) Article 2(1): 'States Parties shall respect and ensure the rights set

health concerns compounded with the proliferation of several unprecedented and interconnected crises, such as, climate crisis, migration crisis and health crisis, has generated considerable changes in diplomatic purposes and practices, while at the same time having major implications for persons' enjoyment of health rights and global health in general.[11] In this sense, addressing complex and pressing health-related challenges that pose a global and an immediate risk requires multistakeholder and multilevel diplomacy that engages a wide range of state and non-state actors, involving governments, international agencies, civil society, scientists, the media and the private sector, aligned with technical expertise, legal knowledge and negotiation skills, towards creating a global movement for health for all.[12] Essentially, in a changing global context, health diplomacy represents a significant forum for negotiations on addressing health issues of common concern which require the cooperation of many countries and diverse actors (not only professional diplomats), and involves processes that ultimately shape, influence and manage the global environment for health.[13] In literature, in an attempt to delineate the scope of health diplomacy seven dimensions are identified, as follows: (i) negotiating to foster health and well-being in the face of other interests (e.g. promote health interests instead of other interests, like geopolitical, economic and commercial interests); (ii) developing new governance mechanisms in support of health and well-being (e.g. UNAIDS, Gavi); (iii) establishing alliances in support of health and well-being outcomes (e.g. political or regional alliances); (iv) building and coordinating donor and stakeholder relations (e.g. developing relations with significant donors, which might be countries, private foundations and/or other organizations); (v) responding to public health crises; (vi) enhancing relations between countries through health and well-being (initiatives among countries such as supporting of health programmes, launching of vaccination programmes—the promotion of medical—vaccine

forth in the present Convention to each child within their jurisdiction …'. Economic and Social Council, Report of the High Commissioner for Human Rights on implementation of economic, social and cultural rights, UN DOC. E/2009/90, 8 June 2009, para. 34. I. Kickbusch and C. Erk, Global Health Diplomacy: The New Recognition of Health in Foreign Policy in: A. Clapham & M. Robinson (ed.), Realizing the Right to Health, Rüffer & Rub, Zurich, 2009, p. 517–524, p. 519. I. Kickbusch, H. Nikogosian, M. Kazatchkine, M. Kökény, A Guide to Global Health Diplomacy: Better health – improved global solidarity – more equity, Global Health Centre – Graduate Institute of International and Development Studies, Geneva, 2021, p. 14.

[11] R. Katz, S. Kornblet, G. Arnold, E. Lief and J. E. Fischer, Defining Health Diplomacy: Changing Demands in the Era of Globalization, The Milbank Quarterly 2011, 89(3), p. 503–523. M. Told, Capacity-building in global health diplomacy in Europe: experiences, challenges and lessons learned, in: I. Kickbusch, M. Kökény (eds.), Health diplomacy: European perspectives, WHO Regional Office for Europe, Denmark, 2017, p. 163–170, p. 163.

[12] R. Katz, S. Kornblet, G. Arnold, E. Lief and J. E. Fischer, Defining Health Diplomacy: Changing Demands in the Era of Globalization, The Milbank Quarterly 2011, 89(3), p. 503–523. I. Kickbusch and A. Liu, Global health diplomacy – reconstructing power and governance, The Lancet 2022, 399: 2156–2166, p. 2157.

[13] See, e.g. World Health Organization (WHO), Policy Brief on Health Diplomacy, WHO Regional Office of the Eastern Mediterranean 2014.

diplomacy) and (vii) contributing to peace and security (e.g. negotiating ceasefires to permit immunization campaigns).[14]

Not coincidentally the UN 2030 Agenda for Sustainable Development (the UN 2030 Agenda) whose adoption involved multistakeholder negotiations acknowledges global partnership as a crosscutting issue.[15] Of special note within the UN 2030 Agenda is the Sustainable Development Goal (SDG) 17 which focuses on strengthening the means of implementation and revitalizing the Global Partnership for Sustainable Development.[16] Obviously, the UN 2030 Agenda acknowledges the instrumental and catalytic role of global partnership in the development of societies as well as its driving force in achieving the SDGs, among which the goal of health for all, explicitly included in SDG 3 and closely interlinked with the other SDGs.[17] Within this context, it is argued that diplomacy, a core component of foreign policies, can provide significant tools to address the reality of interdependence; and in particular, health diplomacy, that covers a wide array of matters, ranging from health and health determinants to crucial foreign policy issues (i.e. national and international security, and trade), can align national interests with diplomatic realities of a globalized world while bringing together diplomatic negotiating skills with expertise and thus becoming an essential component of the system of global health governance.[18] Indeed, over the past two decades, health has begun to emerge as an integral issue in foreign policy agendas of most countries in relation to security, human rights, development and GPGs, with health diplomacy gaining increasing prominence in health governance at global and regional levels especially amid the COVID-19 pandemic, when multilateral cooperation was intensified, with its ensuing achievements and challenges, addressed within the framework of WHO.[19]

Against this backdrop, the chapter proceeds as follows. First, following this introductory section, Sect. 14.2 charts the history of health diplomacy within the

[14] I. Kickbusch and A. Liu Global health diplomacy – reconstructing power and governance, The Lancet 2022, 399: 2156–2166, p. 2157.

[15] UN General Assembly, Transforming our World: The 2030 Agenda for Sustainable Development, UN Doc. A/RES/70/1, 21 October 2015, preamble and para 39.

[16] Ibid., UN General Assembly 2015, p. 14.

[17] Ibid., UN General Assembly 2015, p. 10 (para. 39), 14 and 28 (paras. 60 and 62).

[18] See generally, C. Jönsson and M. Hall, Essence of Diplomacy, Palgrave Macmillan/Springer, N. Y., 2005. I. Kickbusch and C. Erk, Global Health Diplomacy: The New Recognition of Health in Foreign Policy in: A. Clapham & M. Robinson (ed.), Realizing the Right to Health, Rüffer and Rub, Zurich, 2009, p. 517–524, p. 519–520. Z. S. Takwa, Health Diplomacy and Africa: An Overview' in: H. N. Ndi, H. N. Bang, Z. S. Takwa, A. T. Mbu (eds.), Health Diplomacy in Africa: Trends, Challenges and Perspectives, Palgrave Macmillan/Springer, Switzerland, 2023, p. 35–55, p. 47.

[19] I. Kickbusch and A. Liu, 'Global health diplomacy – reconstructing power and governance', The *Lancet* 2022, 399: 2156–2166, p. 2157. Z. S. Takwa, Health Diplomacy and Africa: An Overview in: H. N. Ndi, H. N. Bang, Z. S. Takwa, A. T. Mbu (eds.), Health Diplomacy in Africa: Trends, Challenges and Perspectives, Palgrave Macmillan/Springer, Switzerland, 2023, p. 35–55, p. 47.

system of global health governance, whose critical component constitutes WHO from its inception. Subsequently, as the former UN Commissioner for Human Rights has pointedly noted 'human rights are the closest thing we have to a shared values system for the world',[20] in Sect. 14.3 the focus of attention shifts to examine health diplomacy through a right to health lens as constitutive part of the international obligation to cooperate and assist for advancing human health, reflecting the weight of collective and concerted actions and the need for a standard-setting in a world that is full of tensions and challenges. The chapter concludes with some final remarks that concern our common future as global citizens.

14.2 A Sense of History

The imperative of securing global health from health-related threats and harms that cross national borders by means of multilateral cooperation, involving diplomatic and foreign relations, can be traced back to the first international sanitary conferences which began in the 1850s, reflecting more than 170 years of collective efforts and actions in public health.[21] Notably, there was a growing concern at international level for establishing and maintaining health (quarantine) regulations in trade given that the spread of epidemics, like cholera, plague, and yellow fever, beyond national borders was perceived as a serious threat to international trade.[22] As a response to the urgent need to combat the spread of epidemics from one country to another and especially a yellow fever epidemic that spread rapidly along with international trade routes from South America into North America, in 1902 the First International Sanitary Convention of the American Republics, which was held in Washington, DC, established the first international public health intergovernmental agency, an International Sanitary Bureau, which was later renamed to Pan-American Sanitary Bureau (today called the Pan-American Health Organization).[23] Five years later, in 1907, the Office International d'Hygiène Publique (OIHP), based in Paris, was established with an agreement of 12 countries (Belgium, Brazil, Egypt, France, Italy, the Netherlands, Portugal, Russia, Spain, Switzerland, Great Britain and the United States of America). The primary functions of the OIHP

[20] M. Robinson, The value of a human rights perspective in health and foreign policy, Bulletin of the World Health Organization, 2007, 85(3), 241–242, p. 242.

[21] J. Tobin, The Right to Health in International Law, Oxford University Press, Oxford, 2012, p. 327. World Health Organization (WHO), The First Ten Years of the World Health Organization, WHO, Geneva, 1958, p. 3.

[22] H. Markel, Worldly approaches to global health: '1851 to the present', Public Health 2014, 128(2), 124–128, p. 125. Ibid., World Health Organization 1958, p.3 et seq. E. Riedel, The Human Right to Health: Conceptual Foundations, in: A. Clapham & M. Robinson (ed.), Realizing the Right to Health, Rüffer and Rub,Zurich,2009, p. 21–39, p. 21.

[23] Ibid., H. Markel 2014, p. 125. M.A. Espinal, 'The Pan American Health Organization': 120 years in the Americas hemisphere, The Lancet Regional Health - Americas 2023, 21: 10048. Ibid., World Health Organization 1958, p. 31.

involved the dissemination to Member States information of general public health interest and particularly in relation to the prevention and control of communicable diseases by applying international quarantine. Its work resulted in the International Sanitary Convention of 1926, a precursor to the International Health Regulations given that the OIHP undertook a more active role in international efforts to limit the spread of epidemics, involving the application of techniques of epidemiological surveillance, disease reporting and communications technologies (i.e. to disseminate information telegraphically).[24] With the creation of the League of Nations (LON) in 1919, a new phase of diplomatic endeavour to settle international disputes, achieve peace and security, and address concerns common to all on the basis of an 'institutionalized' approach to international affairs begun.[25] Health as one of the problems 'common to all' was considered to be central in the League's vision for a peaceful world.[26] Article 23 of the Covenant of the LON provided that Members would 'endeavour to take steps in matters of international concern for the prevention and control of disease', whereas Article 25 declared that 'the Members of the League agree to encourage and promote the establishment and cooperation of duly authorized voluntary national Red Cross organizations having as purposes the improvement of health, the prevention of disease and the mitigation of suffering throughout the world'.[27] Thus, under the auspices of the LON, the League of Nations Health Organization (LNHO) was established which was composed of high skilled personnel from Europe, the Americas, and Asia and became one of the League's successful operations in terms of its capacity for international collaboration and support in relation to public health issues.[28] Nevertheless, it is also argued that the activities at the LNHO were partly undermined due to the lack of support by a number of powerful nations, like the USA, which continued to work through the OIHP on quarantine issues, and the LNHO thus mainly functioned as a permanent epidemiological intelligence service to collect and disseminate data worldwide on the status of epidemic diseases of international importance as well as to establish

[24]Ibid., World Health Organization 1958, p. 17 and 28. Ibid., H. Markel 2014, p. 125–126. H. N. Ndi, 'Health in Diplomacy and Foreign Policy' in: H. N. Ndi, H. N. Bang, Z. S. Takwa, A. T. Mbu (eds.), Health Diplomacy in Africa: Trends, Challenges and Perspectives, Palgrave Macmillan/ Springer, Switzerland, 2023, p. 19–33, p. 26.

[25]I. Kickbusch and M. Ivanova, The History and Evolution of Global Health Diplomacy in: I. Kickbusch, G. Lister, M. Told, N. Drager (eds.) Global Health Diplomacy: Concepts, Issues, Actors, Instruments, Fora and Cases, Springer, New York/Heidelberg/Dordrecht/London, 2013, p. 11–26, p. 14.

[26]Ibid., I. Kickbusch and M. Ivanova 2013, p. 14. J. Tobin, The Right to Health in International Law, Oxford University Press, Oxford, 2012, p. 23.

[27]Ibid., J. Tobin 2012, p. 23. World Health Organization (WHO), The First Ten Years of the World Health Organization, WHO, Geneva, 1958, p. 21–22.

[28]Ibid., J. Tobin 2012, p. 24. P. G. Lauren, The Evolution of International Human Rights: Visions Seen, 2nd Ed University of Pennsylvania Press, Philadelphia, 2003, p. 116–117.

technical commissions on public health issues such as malaria, leprosy and typhus.[29]

The aftermath of Second World War saw the rise of multilateralism as countries united by their will to rebuild the world on firm foundations.[30] Due to the atrocities of the Second World War and the appalling state of health in war-ravaged countries States agreed upon the instrumental importance of health in maintaining world peace and security.[31] This understanding was evident in the wording of Article 55 of the UN Charter, in which the need to ensure the promotion of solutions of health problems was acknowledged among the required areas for international cooperation with a view to the creation of conditions of stability and well-being which are necessary for peaceful and friendly relations among nations.[32] Essentially, the idea whose conception was largely owed to the efforts of the Brazilian and Chinese delegations and which became central at the minds of the 46 delegations to the 1945 UN Conference in San Francisco establishing the UN, was the creation of a specialized health organization, namely an International Health Organization whose primary intentions would be to promote international health cooperation for peace and security among individuals and States.[33] In doing so, the creation of a single international institution as a UN specialized agency in 1948, within which all the prior obligations of OIHP and the LNHO were subsumed, manifested that WHO would play a key role for health diplomacy with its broad mandate for strategic leadership at an international level.[34] Notably, in the preamble of the WHO Constitution, the State parties acting in compliance with the UN Charter embraced the principle that 'the health of all peoples is fundamental to the attainment of peace and security and is dependent upon the fullest co-operation of individuals and States'.[35] Equally important, it is also declared in the preamble of the WHO Constitution that

[29] I. Kickbusch and M. Ivanova, The History and Evolution of Global Health Diplomacy in: I. Kickbusch, G. Lister, M. Told, N. Drager (eds.) Global Health Diplomacy: Concepts, Issues, Actors, Instruments, Fora and Cases, Springer, New York/Heidelberg/Dordrecht/London, 2013, p. 11–26, p. 15. H. Markel, Worldly approaches to global health: 1851 to the present, Public Health 2014, 128(2), 124–128, p. 126.

[30] Ibid., I. Kickbusch and M. Ivanova 2013, p. 15.

[31] J. Tobin, The Right to Health in International Law, Oxford University Press, Oxford, 2012, p. 27.

[32] United Nations, Charter of the United Nations, 1 UNTS XVI, 24 October 1945. Ibid, J. Tobin 2012, p. 27. World Health Organization (WHO), The First Ten Years of the World Health Organization, WHO, Geneva, 1958, p. 37–38.

[33] Ibid., World Health Organization 1958, p. 38. H. N. Ndi, Health in Diplomacy and Foreign Policy in: H. N. Ndi, H. N. Bang, Z. S. Takwa, A. T. Mbu (eds.), Health Diplomacy in Africa: Trends, Challenges and Perspectives, Palgrave Macmillan/Springer, Switzerland, 2023, p.19–33, p. 27. I. Kickbusch and M. Ivanova, The History and Evolution of Global Health Diplomacy in: I. Kickbusch, G. Lister, M. Told, N. Drager (eds.) Global Health Diplomacy: Concepts, Issues, Actors, Instruments, Fora and Cases, Springer, New York/Heidelberg/Dordrecht/London, 2013, p. 11–26, p. 15.

[34] Ibid., I. Kickbusch and M. Ivanova 2013, p. 15.

[35] World Health Organization, Basic Documents: Forty-ninth Edition (including amendments adopted up to 31 May 2019), WHO, Geneva, 2020, p.1.

unequal development in different countries in relation to health promotion and disease control, especially communicable disease, represents a common danger.[36]

From the moment of its inception, WHO, an intergovernmental organization with its various strengths and weaknesses, is considered to be the most ambitious multilateral attempt at global health cooperation to date, due to its hybrid functioning both as a technical and political organization in the field of global health governance, by keeping all nation-States jointly as member States with equal and direct representation (one country one vote) and gaining as such an increased level of formal legal legitimacy.[37] Although several multilateral venues for health have been developed, WHO still constitutes the norm-setting organization for health and has reinforced the adoption of multilateral health instruments with an extended scope, thus achieving global coverage.[38] Within this context, the earlier international sanitary conventions were replaced by the WHO International Health Regulations (IHRs), the first version of which was adopted in 1969 and later revised in 2005.[39] Meanwhile, the beginning of the Human Immunodeficiency Virus and Acquired Immunodeficiency Syndrome (HIV/AIDS) epidemics in the 1980s marked an important milestone for health diplomacy, placing health at the centre of the international political agendas as a concern of international development, while highlighting the weight of collective international action at a multilateral level, which resulted in the establishment of the Joint United Nations Programme on HIV/AIDS—UNAIDS—in 1996, when a wide array of actors, including UN programmes and agencies, civil society, governments and the private sector, were brought together.[40]

With the onset of the twenty-first century, health diplomacy came to the fore owed to WHO's strategic role in international politics and its standard-setting capacity in the field of global health governance, rendering thus WHO as a central

[36]Ibid.

[37]I. Kickbusch and M. Ivanova, The History and Evolution of Global Health Diplomacy in: I. Kickbusch, G. Lister, M. Told, N. Drager (eds.) Global Health Diplomacy: Concepts, Issues, Actors, Instruments, Fora and Cases, Springer, New York/Heidelberg/Dordrecht/London 2013, p. 11–26, p. 16–17. H. N. Ndi, 'Health in Diplomacy and Foreign Policy' in: H. N. Ndi, H. N. Bang, Z. S. Takwa, A. T. Mbu (eds.), Health Diplomacy in Africa: Trends, Challenges and Perspectives, Palgrave Macmillan/Springer, Switzerland, 2023, p. 19–33, p. 27. See generally, A. Bredimas, The World Health Organization and the Fight against Epidemics/Pandemics, Sakkoulas Publications, Athens/Thessaloniki, 2020.

[38]I. Kickbusch, H. Nikogosian, M. Kazatchkine, M. Kökény, A Guide to Global Health Diplomacy: Better health – improved global solidarity – more equity, Global Health Centre – Graduate Institute of International and Development Studies, Geneva, 2021, p. 19 and 85.

[39]Ibid., p. 85.

[40]I. Kickbusch and M. Ivanova, The History and Evolution of Global Health Diplomacy in: I. Kickbusch, G. Lister, M. Told, N. Drager (eds.) Global Health Diplomacy: Concepts, Issues, Actors, Instruments, Fora and Cases, Springer, New York/Heidelberg/Dordrecht/London: 2013, p. 11–26, p. 17–18. P. Piot, S. Timberlake, J. Sigurdson, Governance and the Response to AIDS: Lessons for Development and Human Rights in: A. Clapham & M. Robinson (ed.), Realizing the Right to Health, Rüffer & Rub, Zurich, 2009, p. 331–345, p. 336.

venue for global health negotiations and health diplomacy.[41] Accordingly, within the framework of WHO, in response to the globalization of the tobacco epidemic, the Framework Convention on Tobacco Control (FCTC), which regulates the production, sale and consumption of tobacco products, was adopted in 2003 under Article 19 of the WHO Constitution, while, following the severe acute respiratory syndrome (SARS) outbreak in 2002–2003, in 2005 the IHRs, which aim to prevent, protect against, control and provide a public health response to the international spread of disease, were revised.[42] Of further importance for multilevel cooperation as a way to address shared global challenges was the WHO Pandemic Influenza Preparedness (PIP) Framework. Following the 2006 outbreak of avian influenza A (H5N1), PIP Framework was adopted in 2011 after years of protracted negotiations at WHO, constituting the first international agreement that promotes the sharing of influenza viruses, access to vaccines and other benefits (i.e. technology transfers, influenza test kits).[43] Nevertheless, when the next disease outbreak hit the world in early 2014, namely the Ebola virus disease which began in West Africa, health diplomacy was confronted with the failure of countries and international agencies to respond effectively due to financial or political reasons, and thus the delayed response sparked a worldwide discussion on whether a separate agency for global health should be developed.[44] In fact, the growing need for reform of the health security system led health diplomats to call for a reinforcement of the IHRs, in conjunction with the development of a Contingency Fund and a global health emergency workforce to prevent future disease outbreaks.[45] By way of post-Ebola institutional and financial reforms new governance mechanisms and tools were established among which the WHO Health Emergencies Programme, the Contingency Fund

[41] I. Kickbusch and A. Liu, Global health diplomacy – reconstructing power and governance, The Lancet 2022, 399: 2156–2166, p. 2160. See generally, E. Renganathan, The World Health Organization as a Key Venue for Global Health Diplomacy in: I. Kickbusch, G. Lister, M. Told, N. Drager (eds.) Global Health Diplomacy: Concepts, Issues, Actors, Instruments, Fora and Cases, Springer, New York/Heidelberg/Dordrecht/London, 2013, p. 173–185.

[42] E. Renganathan, The World Health Organization as a Key Venue for Global Health Diplomacy in: I. Kickbusch, G. Lister, M. Told, N. Drager (eds.) Global Health Diplomacy: Concepts, Issues, Actors, Instruments, Fora and Cases, Springer, New York/Heidelberg/Dordrecht/London, 2013, p. 173–185, p. 182. World Health Organization, International Health Regulations (2005), 2nd Ed WHO, Geneva, 2008. WHO Framework Convention on Tobacco Control 2003, UNTS 2302, 166. World Health Organization, Basic Documents: Forty-ninth Edition (including amendments adopted up to 31 May 2019), WHO, Geneva, 2020, p. 7.

[43] I. Kickbusch and A. Liu, Global health diplomacy – reconstructing power and governance, The Lancet 2022, 399: 2156–2166, p. 2161.

[44] Ibid., p. 2161. I. Kickbusch, H. Nikogosian, M. Kazatchkine, M. Kökény, A Guide to Global Health Diplomacy: Better health – improved global solidarity – more equity, Global Health Centre – Graduate Institute of International and Development Studies, Geneva, 2021, p. 65 and 139.

[45] Ibid., I. Kickbusch, H. Nikogosian, M. Kazatchkine, M. Kökény 2021, p. 66.

for Emergencies, and the Joint External Evaluation to help countries evaluate their level of conformity with the IHRs.[46]

Meanwhile, during the COVID-19 outbreak a new phase of health diplomacy emerged owed to the proliferation of diplomatic activities on global health, engaging States, government actors (at all levels), scientists, international organizations and the private sector, within which several public health advocates expected a concerted international action against the COVID-19 to be undertaken.[47] Instead, the geopolitical tensions between China and the United States hampered the work of WHO, which had to coordinate the COVID-19 response globally by using limited resources.[48] Furthermore, amid the COVID-19 crisis in several countries increased isolationism, driven by nationalist goals, led some States to refuse to follow the scientific guidance of the WHO, thus neglecting their obligations for international assistance and cooperation and aggravating infection risks globally.[49] In addition, this neglect of global solidarity intensified during the development process of COVID-19 vaccines, given that high-income States moved expeditiously to store vaccine supplies to the detriment of the Global South.[50] In the face of these disturbing practices, the WHO Director-General sounded the alarm by stressing that: '[I]n a deadly pandemic, the right to health is the right to life. Every human has the right to be protected. But we need everyone protected as fast as possible—or else we all lose'.[51] In an attempt to overcome vaccine nationalism and realize global solidarity, political and global leaders prompted for a COVID-19 vaccine to be regarded as a GPG, as such being available and accessible to all.[52] Several vaccine diplomacy initiatives were developed under which the development, manufacture and delivery of vaccines were treated as GPGs. For instance, the alliance between several EU countries for pooled advanced purchase of vaccines required the pharmaceutical corporations with which the EU had a contract to make a portion of vaccine supplies available to low-income countries. Another notable example was the COVAX initiative, which brought together WHO, the Gavi, the Vaccine Alliance, the Coalition for Epidemic Preparedness Innovations (CEPI) and industry and allowed the participating countries to gather and share their resources to

[46] I. Kickbusch and A. Liu, Global health diplomacy – reconstructing power and governance, The Lancet 2022, 399: 2156–2166, p. 2161.

[47] Ibid., p. 2162.

[48] I. Kickbusch, H. Nikogosian, M. Kazatchkine, M. Kökény, A Guide to Global Health Diplomacy: Better health – improved global solidarity – more equity, Global Health Centre - Graduate Institute of International and Development Studies, Geneva, 2021, p.135.

[49] B. M. Meier, J. B. de Mesquita, and C. R. Williams, Global Obligations to Ensure the Right to Health: Strengthening Global Health Governance to Realise Human Rights in Global Health, Yearbook of Disaster Law Online 2022, 3(1), 3–34, p.13–14.

[50] Ibid., p. 15.

[51] T. A. Ghebreyesus, Vaccine Nationalism Harms Everyone and Protects No One, Foreign Policy 2021.

[52] I. Kickbusch, H. Nikogosian, M. Kazatchkine, M. Kökény, A Guide to Global Health Diplomacy: Better health – improved global solidarity – more equity, Global Health Centre - Graduate Institute of International and Development Studies, Geneva, 2021, p. 170.

develop a larger amount of vaccines, than any single country could succeed based exclusively on its own powers, and expand vaccine distribution.[53] All in all, the COVID-19 pandemic has clearly demonstrated how the rise in nationalist and isolationist practices throughout the world threatens the multilateral system, with multilateral institutions and global governance being entirely undermined and the context of health diplomacy being reshaped to effectively respond to new realities.[54] Last but not least, at the time of writing, another notable evolution in the multilateral sphere was the agreement of a package of critical amendments to the IHRs (2005) in tandem with the conducting of high level negotiations on a global Pandemic Agreement within the framework of WHO in an attempt for strengthening collective commitments for global health governance, security and equity within and between countries.[55]

14.3 Health Diplomacy Through a Right to Health Lens

The Vienna Declaration and Programme of Action, adopted in 1993 by the representatives of 171 States attending the World Conference on Human Rights, acknowledged that the promotion and protection of all human rights must be considered both as 'a legitimate concern of the international community' and as 'a priority objective' of the UN in conformity with its purposes and principles, in particular the purpose of international cooperation.[56] In view of the above it becomes clear that increased, sustained and collective engagement of multiple actors is required for securing health rights and fostering people's health and well-being across the world at all times. In principle, States, as duty-bearers, whether acting individually or collectively, have an obligation to ensure that all human beings throughout the world are entitled to equally enjoy a social and international order in which their human rights, including their health rights, can be fully realized.[57] For this reason, adjustments of political and economic relations are required both within States and between States towards implementing a basic social contract for a just,

[53] Ibid.

[54] Ibid., p. 107.

[55] World Health Organization, World Health Assembly agreement reached on wide-ranging, decisive package of amendments to improve the International Health Regulations (news release) 1 June 2024. Available at https://www.who.int/news/item/01-06-2024-world-health-assembly-agreement-reached-on-wide-ranging--decisive-package-of-amendments-to-improve-the-international-health-regulations--and-sets-date-for-finalizing-negotiations-on-a-proposed-pandemic-agreement

[56] Vienna Declaration and Programme of Action, UN Doc. A/CONF.157/23, 12 July 1993, para. 4 (section I).

[57] UN General Assembly, Universal Declaration of Human Rights 1948, G.A. Res. 217A (III), UN Doc. A/810, Articles 1 and 28. In relation to public health emergencies see, International Commission of Jurists and Global Health Consortium, Principles and Guidelines on Human Rights and Public Health Emergencies, 10 May 2023, p. 9.

sustainable and safer world.[58] Worldwide, 173 States in total are parties to the 1966 International Covenant on Economic, Social and Cultural Rights (ICESCR), the most prominent international legal document, which guarantees in Article 12 the right of everyone to the enjoyment of the highest attainable standard of physical and mental health ('right to health'), and are therefore legally obliged under Article 2(1) ICESCR 'to take steps, individually and through international assistance and cooperation, especially economic and technical' to progressively realize it, as envisaged in Articles 55–56 of the UN Charter.[59] As earlier mentioned, although international law primarily obliges the State to realize the right to health for its population within its jurisdiction, it is widely asserted that health is a global and shared responsibility.[60] Notably, the international obligation to cooperate for the purpose of securing health beyond a State's jurisdiction received increasing attention during the COVID-19 crisis.[61] The COVID-19 crisis has vividly manifested how political and global the field of health is, while at the same time underscoring the crucial role of health diplomacy as a means for ensuring that collective action can be undertaken.[62] Thus, today, in a world that is full of tensions and transnational challenges and threats involving global public health emergencies, such as the COVID-19 crisis, health negotiations are made increasingly political, diverse and multisectoral, rendering health a significant issue in foreign policy and diplomatic processes with implications for security, economic growth and social development.[63]

In light of this reality, overtime the UN CESCR has emphasized that States must 'recognize the essential role of international cooperation' and comply with their duty to take joint and separate action to achieve the full realization of the right to health 'through legislation and policies, including diplomatic and foreign relations' towards

[58] A. Eide, Obstacles and Goals to Be Pursued in: A. Eide et al. (ed), Economic, Social and Cultural Rights: A Textbook (2nd ed.,), Kluwer Law International, Dordrecht/Boston/London, 2001, p. 553–562, p. 553.

[59] International Covenant on Economic, Social and Cultural Rights 1966, 993 UNTS 3.

[60] J. Sellin, Access to medicines and the TRIPS agreement: Recognising extraterritorial human rights obligations in: M. Gibney, G. E. Türkelli, M. Krajewski, W. Vandenhole (eds.), The Routledge Handbook on Extraterritorial Human Rights Obligations, London, Routledge 2021, p. 339–350.

[61] Z. Nampewo, J. H. Mike, J. Wolff, 'Respecting, protecting and fulfilling the human right to health', International Journal for Equity in Health 2022, 21:36.

[62] I. Kickbusch, H. Nikogosian, M. Kazatchkine, M. Kökény, A Guide to Global Health Diplomacy: Better health – improved global solidarity – more equity, Global Health Centre - Graduate Institute of International and Development Studies, Geneva, 2021, p. 107.

[63] R. Khosla, P. Allotey, S. Gruskin, Reimagining human rights in global health: what will it take? BMJ Global Health 2022, doi:10.1136/bmjgh-2022-010373. See generally, I. Kickbusch, H. Nikogosian, M. Kazatchkine, M. Kökény, A Guide to Global Health Diplomacy: Better health – improved global solidarity – more equity, Global Health Centre - Graduate Institute of International and Development Studies, Geneva, 2021.

promoting an enabling global environment to the benefit of all people.[64] Within this context, a right to health approach to health diplomacy can help identify rights-based obligations to be realized beyond a State's national borders for advancing global health and thus transform moral and aspirational commitments into binding legal norms and collective international action in conformity with the duty to international cooperation. To this end, the Maastricht Principles on the Extraterritorial Obligations of States in the Area of Economic, Social and Cultural Rights (the Maastricht Principles on ETOs) issued in 2011 by international law and human rights experts from several diverse regions around the world, though legally non-binding, can constitute a useful interpretative source for framing the standards and principles that health diplomacy should reflect as constitutive part of the international duty to cooperate for realizing the right to health.[65] Pursuant to the Maastricht Principles on ETOs all States have obligations to respect, protect and fulfil human rights, including the right to health both within and beyond their national borders.[66] In essence, extraterritorial human rights obligations can offer a principal foundation for global health partnerships to realize the right to health by developing a normative framework for action on the basis of solidarity, equality and justice.[67] In parallel, in the General Comment No. 14 the UN CESCR provides an authoritative guidance on the States' obligations to realize the right to health, set out in Article 12 ICESCR, by delineating the legal obligations to respect, protect and fulfil the right to health both within and beyond a State's jurisdiction.[68] Thus, drawing primarily on these two authoritative sources and particularly, on the basis of this tripartite typology of legal obligations, we can discern a principle-based framework to inform and shape the scope of health diplomacy as a necessary bridge between principle and practice for realizing the international obligation to cooperate and assist for the purpose of securing the right to health throughout the world.

In particular, the UN CESCR established that the State obligation for international cooperation involves the duty 'to respect the enjoyment of the right to health in other countries'.[69] This international obligation to respect the right to health requires

[64] UN Committee on Economic, Social and Cultural Rights (CESCR), General Comment No. 14: The Right to the Highest Attainable Standard of Health, UN Doc. E/C.12/2000/4, 11 August 2000, para. 38. UN Committee on Economic, Social and Cultural Rights (CESCR), General comment No. 25 (2020) on science and economic, social and cultural rights (article 15 (1) (b), (2), (3) and (4) of the International Covenant on Economic, Social and Cultural Rights, UN Doc. E/C.12/GC/25, 30 April 2020, para. 77.

[65] Extraterritorial Obligations Consortium (ETO Consortium), Maastricht Principles on Extraterritorial Obligations of States in the Area of Economic, Social and Cultural Rights, January 2013.

[66] Ibid., Principle 3.

[67] B. M. Meier, J. B. de Mesquita, and C. R. Williams, Global Obligations to Ensure the Right to Health: Strengthening Global Health Governance to Realise Human Rights in Global Health, Yearbook of Disaster Law Online 2022, 3(1), 3–34, p. 18.

[68] UN Committee on Economic, Social and Cultural Rights (CESCR), General Comment No. 14: The Right to the Highest Attainable Standard of Health, UN Doc. E/C.12/2000/4, 11 August 2000.

[69] Ibid., UN Committee on Economic, Social and Cultural Rights (CESCR), General Comment No. 14, para. 39.

the States to refrain from any conduct which interferes (directly or indirectly) with or obstructs the enjoyment of the right to health in other countries.[70] Accordingly, the first UN Special Rapporteur on the right to health, Paul Hunt, affirmed in his report to the General Assembly that 'international assistance and cooperation require that all those in a position to assist should, first refrain from acts that make it more difficult for the poor to realize their right to health'.[71] This means that the level of the duty to respect would require States 'refrain at all times from imposing embargoes or similar measures restricting the supply of another State with adequate medicines and medical equipment. Restrictions on such goods should never be used as instruments of political and economic pressure'.[72] Alarmingly, especially at the onset of the COVID-19 pandemic, several countries imposed isolationist policies exposing long-standing structural obstacles, namely nationalist obstacles to global equity and global solidarity in global health governance with catastrophic implications for the right to health.[73] Particularly, in response to the high global shortages of personal protective equipment, medicines and other medical equipment, several countries imposed export restrictions so as to strengthen domestic supplies. Consequently, this highly disturbing situation made it extremely difficult for low- and middle-income countries (LMICs) that often struggle with severe resource constraints, to secure essential medical supplies and medications for combating the COVID-19 pandemic effectively.[74] Viewed in this light, health diplomacy should refrain from measures and activities that create barriers to global solidarity and equity and serve interests detrimental to people's welfare, while health should not be used as a political tool at the cost of the lives of people.[75] Indeed, from a right to health lens health diplomacy should serve as a bridge for peace, bringing important benefits to crisis situations,

[70] Extraterritorial Obligations Consortium (ETO Consortium), Maastricht Principles on Extraterritorial Obligations of States in the Area of Economic, Social and Cultural Rights, January 2013, Principles 19–22.

[71] UN, The Right of Everyone to the Enjoyment of the Highest Attainable Standard of Physical and Mental Health: Report of the Special Rapporteur, Paul Hunt, UN GA, 59th Sess., Agenda Item 105 (b), UN Doc A/59/422, 8 October 2004, para. 33.

[72] UN Committee on Economic, Social and Cultural Rights (CESCR), General Comment No. 14: The Right to the Highest Attainable Standard of Health, UN Doc. E/C.12/2000/4, 11 August 2000, para. 41.

[73] B. M. Meier, J. B. de Mesquita, and C. R. Williams, Global Obligations to Ensure the Right to Health: Strengthening Global Health Governance to Realise Human Rights in Global Health, Yearbook of Disaster Law Online 2022, 3(1), 3–34, p. 1, 13 and 24.

[74] J. Sellin, Access to medicines and the TRIPS agreement: Recognising extraterritorial human rights obligations in: M. Gibney, G. E. Türkelli, M. Krajewski, W. Vandenhole (eds.), The Routledge Handbook on Extraterritorial Human Rights Obligations, Routledge, London, 2021, p. 339–350, p.341–342. D. E. McMahon, G. A. Peters, L. C. Ivers, E. E. Freeman, Global resource shortages during COVID-19: Bad news for low-income countries, PLOS Neglected Tropical Diseases 2020, 14(7): e0008412, doi: 10.1371/journal.pntd.0008412.

[75] World Health Organization, Policy Brief on Health Diplomacy, WHO Regional Office of the Eastern Mediterranean 2014, p. 3.

diffusing tensions and helping to develop enabling environments for political dialogue and for building alliances and promoting international cooperation for health.[76]

At the same time, States have an international obligation to take action, separately, and jointly through international cooperation, including through bilateral or multilateral diplomatic means, to protect the right to health both within their territories and in other States.[77] Pursuant to the UN CESCR, this obligation requires States to prevent third parties (individuals, corporations) from violating this right in other countries.[78] Essentially, public health emergencies of international concern, such as the COVID-19 pandemic, vividly reveal the urgent need for (political, scientific and technical) international cooperation and regulation of private actors (e.g. pharmaceutical corporations) so as to ensure that vaccines, treatments and diagnostics are promptly developed and made equitably available and accessible for every country in the world.[79] Meanwhile, the CESCR has stressed that States as members of international organizations, involving the International Monetary Fund, the World Bank (WB), and regional development banks, should give due attention to the protection of the right to health in influencing the policies, agreements and international measures of these institutions.[80] To this end, health diplomacy has the potential to operationalize the international obligation to protect in that it can contribute to the fruitful interaction and global collaboration between States and other actors in global venues such as the WB, WHO or the World Trade Organization, while raising awareness that health is not just a national issue but has many global and transboundary dimensions with significant effects on global public goods and people's welfare across the world.[81] Notably, at the onset of the COVID-19 pandemic several new alliances were established to promptly work for the development of a vaccine in the fight against the pandemic. For instance, the Access to COVID-19 Tools (ACT) Accelerator, developed through the COVID-19 Vaccines Global Access (COVAX) initiative, represented a global collaboration of organizations and governments working to accelerate the development and

[76] Ibid., World Health Organization 2014, p. 3.

[77] Extraterritorial Obligations Consortium (ETO Consortium), Maastricht Principles on Extraterritorial Obligations of States in the Area of Economic, Social and Cultural Rights, January 2013, Principle 23.

[78] UN Committee on Economic, Social and Cultural Rights (CESCR), General Comment No. 14: The Right to the Highest Attainable Standard of Health, UN Doc. E/C.12/2000/4, 11 August 2000, para. 39.

[79] J. Sellin, Access to medicines and the TRIPS agreement: Recognising extraterritorial human rights obligations in: M. Gibney, G. E. Türkelli, M. Krajewski, W. Vandenhole (eds.), The Routledge Handbook on Extraterritorial Human Rights Obligations, Routledge, London, 2021, p. 339–350, p. 347.

[80] UN Committee on Economic, Social and Cultural Rights (CESCR), General Comment No. 14: The Right to the Highest Attainable Standard of Health, UN Doc. E/C.12/2000/4, 11 August 2000, para. 39.

[81] World Health Organization, Policy Brief on Health Diplomacy, WHO Regional Office of the Eastern Mediterranean 2014, p. 3.

manufacture of COVID-19 tests, treatments and vaccines and ensure equitable and fair access to essential medical supplies for every country across the world. Interestingly, this collaboration constitutes an illustrating example of multistakeholder health diplomacy in crisis times in which the Gavi, the Vaccine Alliance (a public-private global health partnership, including the WB, the UNICEF, civil society organizations), the Coalition for Epidemic Preparedness Innovations (CEPI) and the WHO worked together with industrial manufacturers, including those based in developing countries, to protect people's health across the world.[82]

At the same time, in addition to the obligation to protect, States must take action, separately, and jointly through international cooperation, to fulfil the right to health within their territories and extraterritorially by creating an international enabling environment with a particular focus on the health needs of marginalized and vulnerable people, who are in a greater danger of being severely affected in crisis situations than the general population.[83] Notably, this duty is more evident in the words of the Sustainable Development Goals in which health holds a centre place and especially in the SDG 3 ('ensure healthy lives and promote well-being for all at all ages') read in conjunction with SDG 17 ('strengthen the means of implementation and revitalize the Global Partnership for Sustainable Development'), as mentioned earlier.[84] Specifically, within the context of SDG3, Target 3.8 urges the achievement of universal health coverage, including financial risk protection, access to quality essential health-care services and access to safe, effective, quality and affordable essential medicines and vaccines for all, while a commitment 'to strengthen the capacity of all countries, in particular developing countries, for early warning, risk reduction and management of national and global health risks' is also indicated.[85] Equally important, for its part, the UN CESCR has clarified that States are under an international obligation to provide assistance in other States to facilitate (i.e. a sub-category of the duty to fulfil) access to essential health facilities, goods and services in other countries, wherever possible, and provide (i.e. a sub-category of the duty to fulfil) the necessary aid when required.[86] The UN CESCR went further by emphasizing that it is incumbent on States and other actors in a position to assist, to provide 'international assistance and cooperation, especially economic and technical' in accordance with Article 2(1) ICESCR which help

[82] I. Kickbusch, H. Nikogosian, M. Kazatchkine, M. Kökény, A Guide to Global Health Diplomacy: Better health – improved global solidarity – more equity, Global Health Centre - Graduate Institute of International and Development Studies, Geneva, 2021, p. 61.

[83] Extraterritorial Obligations Consortium (ETO Consortium), Maastricht Principles on Extraterritorial Obligations of States in the Area of Economic, Social and Cultural Rights, January 2013, Principle 28.

[84] UN General Assembly, Transforming our World: the 2030 Agenda for Sustainable Development, UN Doc. A/RES/70/1, 21 October 2015, p. 14.

[85] Ibid., p.16–17.

[86] UN Committee on Economic, Social and Cultural Rights (CESCR), General Comment No. 14: The Right to the Highest Attainable Standard of Health, UN Doc. E/C.12/2000/4, 11 August 2000, para. 39.

developing countries to fulfil their core and other right to health obligations.[87] In this sense, WHO as 'the directing and co-ordinating authority on international health work' with the political credibility to enforce cooperation can be viewed as a global institutional mechanism with the capacity to coordinate and operationalize the international obligation to fulfil the right to health for securing and advancing global health.[88] Indeed, on the basis of the WHO's constitutional framework a human rights mandate for its authority has been established to coordinate and steer global health efforts, involving funding efforts to strengthen the health capacity of all countries, especially of developing countries, and the negotiation of international agreements.[89] As earlier mentioned, the catalytic role of WHO in the complex global health landscape with its leading authority to keep countries jointly committed to enhance global health has been reaffirmed through the proposal to negotiate a pandemic treaty.[90]

From the perspective of the preceding discussion the following observations are made which altogether underscore why a right to health approach should hold a centre place in health diplomacy at all times and especially in crisis times like the COVID-19 crisis. Accordingly, a right to health lens on health diplomacy epitomizes the international obligation to cooperate for securing the right to health for all people, whether in high—or low income countries, on the basis of equality and non-discrimination, as a common human rights concern. In this way, collective commitment is strengthened and health interests become central in States' foreign and diplomatic policies not as charity, voluntarily upheld, but compulsorily in fulfilment of their international obligations to cooperate. Such an approach can generate significant advantages in that it offers a pathway with rules and behavioural norms through which multiple actors across borders can act together on common interests and solutions to effectively target the root causes of key health-related challenges of international concern and enhance synergies across multiple fragmented agendas for a healthier and more prosperous world.

[87] Ibid., UN Committee on Economic, Social and Cultural Rights (CESCR), General Comment No. 14, para. 45.

[88] World Health Organization, Basic Documents: Forty-ninth Edition (including amendments adopted up to 31 May 2019), Geneva: WHO 2020, p. 2, Article 2(a) of the WHO Constitution. B. M. Meier and A. M. Fox, International obligations through collective rights: moving from foreign health assistance to global health governance, Health and Human Rights Journal 2010, 12(1), 61–72, p. 67.

[89] B. M. Meier, J. B. de Mesquita, and C. R. Williams, Global Obligations to Ensure the Right to Health: Strengthening Global Health Governance to Realise Human Rights in Global Health, Yearbook of Disaster Law Online 2022, 3(1), 3–34, p. 7. B. M. Meier and A. M. Fox, International obligations through collective rights: moving from foreign health assistance to global health governance, Health and Human Rights Journal 2010, 12(1), 61–72, p. 67.

[90] I. Kickbusch and A. Liu, Global Health Diplomacy – Restructuring power and governance, The Lancet 2022, 399:2156–2166, p. 2156.

14.4 Conclusions

Without any doubt, the COVID-19 pandemic has vividly underscored the urgent need for the world to act together with global governance institutions in place, such as WHO, to coordinate a rights-based global health response to a shared global threat.[91] It is within this context that health diplomacy could make a tangible contribution to securing and realizing global health as a global public good at all times and especially in the face of unprecedented and interconnected crises by means of collective and coordinated international action, while overcoming fragmented policy competencies in national governance systems, isolationist policies, and geo-political, economic, national and commercial interests.[92] To this end, a right to health lens to health diplomacy offers comprehensive guidance for identifying rights-based legal obligations to respect, protect and fulfil within and beyond a State's national borders; for advancing global health through multistakeholder and multilevel cooperation; and for transforming moral shared commitments into binding legal norms and collective international action in conformity with the human rights responsibility of international cooperation and assistance in health. As the former WHO Director-General, Gro Harlem Brundtland, cautioned two decades ago '[i]t is now no longer a question of whether to make investment in global health an element of foreign policy. It is a question of how to turn policy into measurable results—and how to ensure the benefits reach future generations of world citizens'.[93]

Elisavet Athanasia Alexiadou, Ph.D. (Leiden University, NL), LL.M. (UK), LL.M. (GR), M.Sc. (GR), is an adjunct faculty member at the International Hellenic University, the Open University of Cyprus, the Aristotle University of Thessaloniki and the Hellenic Open University, as well as a lawyer at Greek Supreme Courts. She has conducted postdoctoral research in the fields of Corruption, Human Rights and Artificial Intelligence with a special focus on Healthcare at the Faculty of Law of the Aristotle University of Thessaloniki, which was funded with a two-year research grant from the Greek State Scholarships Foundation. She is a Research Fellow at the Social Administration Research Laboratory at the University of West Attica. She holds a Ph.D. in Law and Human Rights from the Faculty of Law of Leiden University (Institute of Public Law—Research Programme: Effective Protection of Fundamental Rights in a Pluralist World), an LL.M. in International and European Legal Studies with a specialization in Public International Law (with

[91] B. M. Meier, J. B. de Mesquita, and C. R. Williams, Global Obligations to Ensure the Right to Health: Strengthening Global Health Governance to Realise Human Rights in Global Health, Yearbook of Disaster Law Online 2022, 3(1), 3–34, p. 3.

[92] I. Kickbusch and C. Erk, Global Health Diplomacy: The New Recognition of Health in Foreign Policy in: A. Clapham & M. Robinson (ed.), Realizing the Right to Health, Rüffer and Rub, Zurich, 2009, p. 517–524, p. 519–520. Z. S. Takwa, Health Diplomacy and Africa: An Overview in: H. N. Ndi, H. N. Bang, Z. S. Takwa, A. T. Mbu (eds.), Health Diplomacy in Africa: Trends, Challenges and Perspectives, Palgrave Macmillan/Springer, Switzerland, 2023, p. 35–55, p. 47.

[93] F. Bustreo and C. F. J. Doebbler, 'Making health an imperative of foreign policy: the value of a human rights approach', Health and Human Rights Journal 2010, 12(1), 47–59, p. 52.

distinction) from the Aristotle University of Thessaloniki, an LL.M. in Medical Law from Northumbria University, and an M.Sc. in Healthcare Administration from the Hellenic Open University. She has published five monographs—books as well as several articles—papers in peer-reviewed scientific journals and chapters in collective volumes. She has presented her work at international conferences and seminars.

Economic and Entrepreneurial Diplomacy 15

Maria N. Bozoudi

Abstract

It is increasingly difficult to determine what is political in diplomacy and what is economic, and whether the dividing line between the two is real. The paper aims to explore the nuances of contemporary diplomatic practice involving the economy and trade, centering on the subject of diplomatic action. The U.S. Marshall Plan is one of the better known case studies of economic diplomacy carried out by government actors, while the era of globalization ushered in initiatives of entrepreneurial diplomacy carried out by business, in pursuit of corporate objectives. The twenty-first century, highlighted by the Eurozone crisis, has underlined the role of supranational institutions in policy- and rule-making negotiations and diplomatic consultations for global economic governance. At the same time, positive or negative economic sanctions and blockades, dating back to the Peloponnesian War, have become a distinct practice of contemporary diplomacy. Though one of the strongest forms of nonmilitary coercion, there is much debate about their effectiveness. In the end of the day, economic diplomacy may serve high politics, provided that measures are implemented with the full range of options in mind, and through a comprehensive strategy that engages state and non-state actors.

M. N. Bozoudi (✉)
Department of International and European Studies, University of Macedonia, Thessaloniki, Greece

P. Naskou-Perraki (ed.), *Contemporary Diplomatic and Consular Relations*,
https://doi.org/10.1007/978-3-031-99243-8_15

15.1 Diplomacy and the Economy

According to Ernest Satow, a highly distinguished British diplomat of the second half of the nineteenth century, diplomacy is the "application of knowledge, discretion, and acumen to the conduct of official relations between governments".[1] The word diplomacy itself derives from "diplomas," the folded credentials documents provided by kings, princes, and other leaders to those bearing them.[2] The purpose of the document was (and still is) to confer upon the carrier certain privileges and rights,[3] hence establishing diplomacy's integral relation to law.

Diplomacy took its modern form in 15th century Italy, though diplomatic actions were first recorded around 1300–1400 BC in Egypt, as evidenced by references in Pharaoh's correspondence on trade agreements with other empires.[4] During the Middle Ages, diplomacy aimed at securing peace between Christians, and during the Renaissance, it became a means of serving competing interests of European duchies, principalities, and other state-like entities.[5] Diplomats were tasked with making alliances, retrieving finances for wars, and even conducting wars. Gradually, the ad hoc character of diplomatic missions and delegations became permanent, just like the need for continuous management of foreign relations and monitoring non-domestic developments, and by the 16th century permanent diplomatic missions

[1] To this day, Satow's record of his own diplomatic experience, with references to diplomacy in general, the role of a diplomat, and international meetings, comprises one of the most comprehensive treatises on diplomacy and diplomatic practice. E. Satow (1917), A guide to diplomatic practice, in A. D. McNair (ed), Contributions to International Law and Diplomacy, Longmans, Green & Co, London, New York, Toronto, 1932, p. 1.

[2] In ancient Rome, the folded official document certifying Roman citizenship (and corresponding rights) was called a "duplus". The term "diploma", however, referred to more than a duplus, and was the official document brought by messengers (diplomarius) or official missions (embassies) outside Rome, to certify their purpose and rights.

[3] Satow (1917) in A. D. McNair, op. cit.

[4] The "Letters of Amarna", a set of 382 clay tablets discovered in the Tell-El-Amarna area of the Nile in 1887, are considered part of the international correspondence of Pharaoh Akhenaten, and include letters between the Pharaoh and other empires/powers of the time. Among other things, the topics covered include Egypt's foreign policy and matters of empire management, rules of trade with provinces and other kingdoms, geopolitical decision-making, various secret information, and Egypt's diplomacy in general. For the collection of letters, see, R. Cohen & Westbrook (eds), Amarna Diplomacy: The Beginnings of International Relations, Johns Hopkins University ty Press, Baltimore, 1992.

[5] G. Mattingly (Renaissance Diplomacy, Penguin Books, Baltimore, 1964) describes how three centuries of diplomatic relations between European states (fifteenth–seventeenth century) transformed the political idea of "the unity of Christendom", introducing the concept of sovereignty. More on this transition in C. H. Carter (ed), From the Renaissance to the Counter-Reformation: Essays in Honor of Garrett Mattingly, Random House, New York, 1965.

were engaging in what Armand Jean du Plessis, Cardinal of Louis XII and Duke of Richelieu,[6] called "perpetual negotiation" (negotiation continuelle).

Trade facilitation and security of trade routes—an intrinsic characteristic of modern diplomacy—was systematically pursued by states in the Italian north, particularly Milan and Venice. While the Byzantine Empire was collapsing and the Ottoman Empire was claiming its place at the gateway to Asia, European powers—France, Britain, Spain, Portugal, Genoa, and Venice—were embarking on a journey of overseas conquest and discovery. Competition amongst them began to shift: rather than pursuing domination over the Christian world, their ambitions now involved conquest of new lands and control of trade with them.[7] Aligned with new priorities, diplomatic missions did not only gather information, but also negotiated agreements for safe passage of goods, and worked to protect the privileges of the merchants they represented.

The importance of trade for diplomacy is best reflected in the way Ottomans handled diplomatic affairs with Europeans. The British ambassador was the first diplomat in Istanbul to be recognized as permanent representative of British merchants throughout the Empire, and, gradually, the status was granted to ambassadors of Venice, France, Portugal, and the Netherlands.[8] In addition, and even though at the time the concept of diplomatic immunity was perceived more in the context of social norms and hospitality, rather than a legal concept, trade missions, ships, goods, and crews of Europeans in the Mediterranean enjoyed Sultan's full protection against pirates and other bandits. A similar provision was made for transport of goods by land, with reciprocal security provisions made towards Ottoman merchants in Europe. It is also worth noting that ambassadors, consuls and specially recognized commercial agents were not subject to taxes.[9]

The whole of this interaction was first called "diplomacy" by Edmund Burke in 1796,[10] during a speech at the British Parliament. Diplomacy is since understood as

---

[6]More on Richelieu's conception of diplomatic theory, in G. R. Berridge, M. Keens-Soper & T.G. Otte, Diplomatic Theory from Machiavelli to Kissinger, Palgrave MacMillan, London, 2001, pp. 71–87.

[7]A. K. Smith, Creating a World Economy: Merchant Capital, Colonialism and World Trade, 1400–1825, Westview Press, Boulder, Colorado, 1991.

[8]For more on diplomatic practices between Ottomans and Europeans, see N. Yudrusev (ed), Ottoman diplomacy: conventional or unconventional?, Palgrave MacMillan, London, 2004. On concessions to Britain, see Chap. 2 (Arı, Bülent, Early Ottoman Diplomacy: Ad Hoc Period, pp. 36–65). As mentioned by A. Woods in A History of the Levant Company, Oxford University Press, Oxford, 1935 (p. 274), all British ambassadors to the Ottoman Empire between 1582 and 1805 were paid by the English Levant Company. The United States adopted a similar practice, combining the assignment of diplomatic and a commercial representation in the same role. More in D.M. Pletcher, The Diplomacy of Involvement: American Economic Expansion Across the Pacific, 1784–1900, University of Missouri Press, Columbia, 2001 (p. 365).

[9]N. Yurdusev, op. cit., pp. 42–43.

[10]Edmund Burke, speaking in the British Parliament in 1796, stated that "The only excuse for all our mendicant diplomacy is … that it has been founded on absolute necessity"—E. Burke, The Works of Edmund Burke in IX Volumes, Freeman & Bolles Printers, Boston, 1839, Vol. IX, p. 506.

communication between accredited state representatives aiming to promote foreign policy objectives through formal or informal agreements. As G. C. Berridge states, its main purpose is to "secure state interests without the use of force, or recourse to justice".[11]

15.2 Diplomacy and the Economy in the Twenty-First Century

Building on the direct relationship between diplomacy and the conduct of international economic relations, diplomacy can be used to exert power through economic pressure,[12] by employing knowledge of international political economy and business administration.[13] This is the result of an ever-increasing number of non-state actors shaping international economic relations, including business and nongovernmental organizations, and a multitude of transnational institutions that produce rules to regulate the global economy—such as the World Trade Organization (WTO), the International Monetary Fund (IMF), or the Bank of International Settlements (BIS). In other words, in practice "… it is increasingly difficult to distinguish between what is political in diplomacy and what is economic, and indeed, whether there is a dividing line between the two which has any validity at all … ."[14]

Modern economic diplomacy concerns all types of cross-border connections among people,[15] and is therefore not exclusive to central governments. It encompasses a wide range of activities carried out by state diplomatic missions, institutions (e.g., investment and export promotion agencies), or private sector bodies (e.g., chambers of commerce and other business associations). It is also carried by regional governments,[16] depending on region-specific competitive advantages they wish to promote (e.g., California in the ICT sector, or the Greek Cyclades Islands in the tourism sector). Depending on the main subject of diplomatic action, there is (a) commercial and economic diplomacy, originating from state actors (including regions); (b) entrepreneurial diplomacy, conducted by business; and (c) diplomacy for global economic governance, which involves policy- and rule-making negotiations and consultations under the auspices of global institutions.

[11] G. R. Berridge, Diplomacy: Theory and Practice, Palgrave-MacMillan, London, 2010, p. 1.

[12] More about using economic diplomacy to reflect power in D. A. Baldwin, Economic Statecraft, Princeton University Press, Princeton, 1985.

[13] See for example Lee & Hudson, The Old and new Significance of Political Economy in Diplomacy, Review of International Studies vol. 30, no. 3, 2004, pp. 343–360.

[14] From a speech by the British ambassador to the US in 1998, Christopher Meyer, as quoted by Dobson & Marsh (eds), Anglo-American Relations: Contemporary Perspectives, London & Marsh (eds), Anglo-American Relations, Routledge, New York, 2013, p. 113.

[15] J. R. Scholte, Globalization, Governance and Corporate Citizenship, in The Journal of Corporate Citizenship, no 1, 2000, pp. 15–23.

[16] R. Saner & L. Yiu, International Economic Diplomacy: Mutations in Post-modern Times, Discussion Papers in Diplomacy, Netherlands Institute of International Relations "Clingendael", Wassenaar/Hague, 2001.

15.2.1 Commercial and Economic Diplomacy

Commercial and economic diplomacy is a form of diplomatic relations increasingly used by states to enhance political leverage via trade, finance and investment. It involves the use of intergovernmental relations and state authority to promote international trade and investment relations of public and private sectors.[17] Economic diplomacy does not exist in a vacuum, is not independent of politics, and directly involves the use of economic incentives and disincentives to achieve political objectives.[18]

The US Marshall Plan for post-World War II aid to Western Europe comprises, to this day, the best example of making economic diplomacy a core pillar of foreign and security policy. In 1948–1951, approximately $13bn (over $130bn today) was made available to European countries, provided they agreed to adopt open market and democratic institutions. The terms were inextricably linked to the US strategy of containment versus the USSR,[19] as funding under the Marshall Plan was available to "free peoples who refuse to submit to armed minorities or external pressures."[20] US Foreign Secretary, George Marshall, considered economic aid as a tool that was not "against any one country or doctrine, but against hunger, poverty, destitution and chaos."[21] Economic support for Europe was meant to enhance growth, create jobs and increase income in the war-torn continent, ensure socio-economic stability, and thus help counter or avert Soviet attempts of political penetration.[22] In parallel, creating the Bretton Woods currency exchange regime system,[23] helped speed up the post-war return to a global economic and financial normality.

Four decades later, the fall of the Berlin Wall triggered the USA to design and implement a more comprehensive and meticulous economic diplomacy strategy, with the dual aim of facilitating post-communist transitions in Central and Eastern Europe, and Central Asia, and of boosting globalization.[24] Apart from securing

---

[17] S.J.V. Moons & R. de Boer, Economic Diplomacy, Product Characteristics and Level of Development, ETSG Conference 2004, p. 1.

[18] G.R. Berridge & A. James, A Dictionary of Diplomacy, Palgrave MacMillan, London, 2001, p. 81.

[19] X (George F. Kennan), The Sources of Soviet Conduct, Foreign Affairs, vol. 25, no 4, July 1947, as well as in his well-known telegram to the US Secretary of State, while still serving at the US Embassy in Moscow - Telegram, George Kennan to George Marshall [Long Telegram], February 22, 1946 in Harry S. Truman Administration File, Elsey Papers.

[20] Public Papers of the Presidents of the United States - Harry S. Truman, 1947 vol., US Government Printing Office, Washington DC, 1963, p. 178.

[21] G. Marshall, European Initiative Essential to Economic Recovery, Address at Commencement Exercises at Harvard University, June 5 1947, in US Department of State Bulletin, vol. 16, no 415, p. 1160.

[22] H. Kissinger, Diplomacy, Simon & Schuster, New York, 1994, p. 473.

[23] M. Daunton, The Economic Government of the World: 1933–2023, Farrar, Straus and Giroux, New York, 2023.

[24] More in National Research Councils, Transforming Post-Communist political Economies, The National Academies Press, Washington, DC, 1998.

market shares for US businesses in Asia and Eastern Europe, the USA also used national (e.g., the Federal Reserve) and international financial institutions, such as the World Bank and the European Bank for Reconstruction and Development (EBRD), to help transition economies finance their debts and deficits.[25]

Within the context of a globalized economy, and even more in today's shifting global dynamics, there is a growing need for diplomats with knowledge and understanding of international political economy, and finance and investment law, who can handle negotiations on bilateral or multilateral economic and technological agreements. All such negotiations are conducted by diplomats, who become catalysts of establishing and preserving practices, institutions and norms of conducting international economic relations.

Throughout history, economic diplomacy has centered on negotiations on tariffs and quotas, as reflected by the term "commercial diplomacy" that was initially used to describe it. In fact, due to an aristocratic lineage, many European diplomats considered the role of economic and commercial attachés inferior to that of a diplomat. Seeing trade as a middle-class affair, they refused to engage in such negotiations, or with commercial attachés, for the matter.[26] Today, "commercial diplomacy" refers primarily to the work of trade attachés. Though a part of economic diplomacy, commercial diplomacy comprises a distinct type of diplomatic activity, centered on trade and investment markets[27]—for example, it is the Department of Commerce Foreign Commercial Relations Service that bears such responsibilities in U.S. diplomatic missions.[28] Modern trade negotiations involve much more than tariffs and quotas, ranging from customs procedures, health and safety, and consumer protection, to environmental protection, accounting standards, transparency, competition, guarantees against political risk and taxation. As negotiations touch upon all aspects of economic activity, the term "economic diplomacy" better describes the picture.

Aiming to manage this broad span of negotiations on the economy, governments re-organize their diplomatic services to better coordinate political and economic diplomacy. For example, Canada, Australia, South Korea, Belgium—even Fiji and Mauritius—have merged responsibilities traditionally falling under separate Ministries for Foreign Affairs and Trade into a single Ministry. Another approach

---

[25] More in J. Roaf, R. Atoyan, B. Joshi, K. Krogulski & IMF staff team, 25 years of transition: post-communist Europe and the IMF, International Monetary Fund, Washington, D.C., 2014.

[26] More in D. Lee, R. Coolsaet, E. Potter & K. Rana, Policy Forum on Commercial and Economic Diplomacy, International Studies Perspectives, vol. 5, 2004, pp. 50–70.

[27] Companies wishing to enter or connect with foreign markets need access to information such as procedures for starting a business, taxation, rules for repatriating profits, labor market and work-force characteristics, banking system, trade law, incentives for FDI, potential risks, and so on. Special government agencies make such information public, but it can also collected by diplomatic missions and provided to interested parties back home. Gathering and updating this information usually too costly for individual companies, making it a service that diplomatic missions offer to businesses.

[28] Berridge & James, op. cit., pp. 39–40.

is that of the UK and the Czech Republic, which have set up Committees to coordinate the work of the two ministries.[29] In addition, consultation channels on trade, investment, and market issues, bringing together diplomatic authorities and the private sector, become permanent.

Economic diplomacy is also employed within the framework of global economic governance institutions, meaning intergovernmental organizations that regulate international economic relations. National delegations are tasked with managing negotiations and consultations taking place under their auspices, increasing demand for diplomatic staff with technical expertise.[30]

With regard to methods and practices, economic diplomacy adopts those of political diplomacy. It involves analysis, communication and negotiation on issues of commercial and investment interest, aiming at favorable agreements and arrangements. But, rather than political or military affairs, economic diplomacy aims to influence policies related to growth, trade, investment, and financial flows, either bilaterally or through multilateral economic platforms and fora.

15.2.2 Entrepreneurial or Corporate or Business Diplomacy

The difference between economic and business diplomacy lies in the actor: economic diplomacy is exercised by states and serves a broader foreign policy and diplomatic strategy. Business diplomacy is exercised by private sector entities, and the initiative lies with businesses themselves, driven by their investment and economic pursuits.

Admittedly, the nature of diplomacy as an art of representation, communication, and negotiation[31] makes it a particularly effective and useful tool for business. Export-oriented companies cooperate with diplomatic authorities of their home country abroad, while at the same time conducting most of their business through a direct relationship with government authorities in the host country. At the same time, they develop relationships with other companies, building a network of partners abroad, or disrupt such partnerships, by deciding to exit a market. All of the above fall within the spectrum of entrepreneurial diplomacy. Economic diplomacy may help mitigate the effects of business decisions and business diplomacy, but not prevent them from happening, at least not for long. For example, a private sector entity may choose to withdraw from a market due to shifts in its business strategy, or adherence to corporate responsibility principles. One such example is Google's Chinese market exit in 2010, citing widespread censorship. Such issues began soon after Google began its operations in China in 2005. The US State

[29] See government websites in each country.

[30] Saner & Yiu (ibid., p. 13) cite the example of Bern, where the presence of a large number of accredited officials in national delegations is noted, but not from the Ministries of Foreign Affairs.

[31] More on this in J. Melissen (ed), Innovation in Diplomatic Practice, Palgrave MacMillan, London, 1999.

Department remained informed throughout the build-up of tension, but, reportedly, the decision to exit was taken by the company.[32]

Though large enterprises can afford to develop their own diplomatic practices and channels, SMEs usually engage in business diplomacy through collective associations, such as exporters' associations or chambers of commerce, for instance through business delegations accompanying heads of state on formal visits abroad. There are, of course, MNCs with such a large economic footprint, that a nation's diplomatic apparatus may engage on their behalf. It is also often the case that a company's economic footprint, combined with its access to resources, may lead it to introduce dedicated corporate mechanisms and staff to manage its own foreign affairs, i.e., engage in corporate diplomacy. A corporate diplomat may be expected to negotiate with foreign authorities on legal issues, collect financial and other information, or assist in making corporate decisions or managing a crisis.[33] Admitedly, international executive roles rely not only on business acumen, but also on diplomatic skills.[34]

Business associations often develop twinning relations with counterparts in other countries, so as to help their corporate members identify partners and opportunities for business development, as well as to address problems with national authorities. The Turkish Foreign Economic Relations Board (DEIK) is an organization serving this dual purpose. Since 2014, DEIK is formally tasked with "conducting the foreign economic relations of the Turkish private sector" as a business diplomacy organization that works primarily through Business Councils. DEIK Business Councils are in essence joint partnerships with counterparts in 126 countries, and their objective is to study and discuss developments in each country, and help identify business opportunities, problems and best practices.[35]

In similar fashion, multinational business institutions voice policy concerns to governments, and form dialogue platforms to steer technical obstacles to doing business and trade. The World Economic Forum (WEF) is a platform for communication and negotiation—and thus diplomatic contact—between governments and the business community, and works on the co-design of global growth policies (e.g., cybersecurity, AI, climate change, health, smart cities, etc.).[36] The European Roundtable (ERT) is European industry's platform of dialogue with EU institutions.[37] As

[32] More in M. Forney & A. Kroeber, Google's Business Reason for Leaving China - of Reputation and Revenue, The Wall Street Journal, 06/04/2010 or B. Bosker, Google Shuts Down China Search, Redirects users to Hong-Kong (updated), Huffington Post, 23/03/2010 (22/05/2010). On the State Department's stance, see Reuters News, State Dept: Google China Announcement Likely, 22/3/2010.

[33] More on corporate diplomacy in Hofstede, Hofstede & Minkov, Cultures and Organizations: software of the mind, McGraw-Hill, London, 1991.

[34] More in Jennings & Hopkinson (eds.), Current Issues in International Diplomacy and Foreign Policy, vol. 1, HMSO/Wilton Park, London, 1999, pp. 243–54.

[35] More on the DEIK website - https://www.deik.org.tr/

[36] https://www.weforum.org

[37] https://www.ert.eu/

industry is ahead of governments in addressing climate change and the digital transition, and considering that challenges like job creation cannot be tackled by governments alone, B20 (Business 20)—G20s (Group 20)[38] private sector arm—has an increasingly important role in multilateral cooperation: representing over 6.7 m small, medium, and large enterprises, B20 voices the views and concerns of the global business community on energy efficiency, the digital economy, skills, etc.

15.2.3 Diplomacy for Global Economic Governance

In a 2010 speech, then European Central Bank President, Jean-Claude Trichet, described global economic governance as "the set of supra-national institutions and laws, as well as the international relations between countries that have an effect on cross-border economic and financial transactions."[39] In Trichet's speech, "supra-national" refers to the EU as a suis generis entity, to which states have ceded sovereign rights of policy making in key economic dimensions (e.g., trade policy).[40] The European Economic and Monetary Union (EMU) and its supporting system—European Central Bank, Eurosystem, Eurogroup, DG for Economic Affairs, European Stability Mechanism (ESM)—embody a unique modus operandi between diplomacy and European economic governance.

But how are global economic relations governed? Global economic governance is conducted by institutions created in the aftermath of World War II, focused on trade (WTO), development (World Bank) and exchange rate stability (IMF). The role and responsibilities of the three institutions are constantly transformed to meet shifts in global markets and global political economy, always according to the authority and power granted by governments. Management and use of this power is prescribed by international law, is integral for the pursuit of their mission, and requires what Satow described as "the application of knowledge, acumen and discretion to the conduct of official relations"[41]—in other words, diplomatic competence. Through their shared responsibility and role[42] to shape and secure rules and conditions for growth and prosperity, they engage in a series of negotiations and consultations—with states, business, the academic and scientific community, other international institutions, and civil society—employing diplomatic methods and practices. In the context of

[38]More on the B20 and G20 websites (https://www.b20coalition.org/ and http://www.g20.org/English). Although the spotlight falls on the Heads of State, G20 meetings are also attended by Central Bankers.

[39]J. C. Trichet, speech at the World Policy Conference in Marrakech, 16/10/2010. More on global economic governance in M. Moschella & C. Weaver (eds), Handbook of Global Economic Governance: players, power and paradigms, Routledge, London, 2014.

[40]Council of the European Union, Treaty on Stability, Coordination and Governance in the Economic and Monetary Union, Brussels, 02/03/2012.

[41]E. Satow, op. cit., p. 1.

[42]What J. Boughton & C. Bradford call "cooperative leadership", Global Governance: New Players, New Rules, Finance & Development, vol. 44, no. 4, December 2007.

"perpetual negotiation" that global markets create, their role as agents of diplomacy is to facilitate dialogue and communication.

The institutions' role is not limited to secretarial support for transnational consultations, but impacts policy, considering that their technical recommendations are, in fact, political acts, with political and policy implications. One only needs to recall how investors and markets reacted to sovereign credit ratings[43] or international financial institutions (IFIs) reports[44] during the financial crisis. Therefore, globalization and multiple economic crises since the 1970s[45] have turned international economic governance into a new field for employing diplomatic practices.

Navigating this diplomatic field requires corresponding diplomatic skills: IFIs executives are called upon to manage diverse political, economic, and social relationships in the course of their work, and especially during crises.[46] Executive officers at the World Bank, IMF, ECB, EBRD, and other multilateral development banks and finance institutions, engage in negotiations that call as much for technical expertise as for diplomatic vigilance. As a result, a new "hybrid" type diplomat has been on the rise: the "economic technocrat-diplomat" dedicated to global economic governance.

15.3 Diplomacy and Economic Sanctions

Sanctions comprise a distinct practice of economic diplomacy. The term is not strictly defined by law,[47] and refers primarily to economic measures, although sanctions can be political and military in nature, targeting states as much as companies, individuals, and all types of legal entities. Their character can be either negative, as in threats for penalties, aimed at deterring or reversing behavior, or positive, in the form of rewards, to encourage specific behavior and initiatives.[48] In

[43] More on the mechanisms of international markets in G. Caprio Jr. (ed), Handbook of Key Global Financial Markets, Institutions and Infrastructure, Elsevier, London, 2013; T. Sinclair, The New Masters of Capital: American Bond Rating Agencies and the Politics of Creditworthiness, Cornell University Press, Ithaca, 2008; L. J. White, Markets: the credit rating agencies, Journal of Economic Perspectives, vol. 24, no. 2, Spring 2010; G. Karp, Ratings game: power of S&P, other top credit agencies, grew from government action, Chicago Tribune, 14/08/2011.

[44] For instance, the IMF preliminary draft sustainability analysis of Greek debt—IMF, Greece: Preliminary Draft Sustainability Report, 26/06/2015.

[45] More on the economic crises of the last 30 years or so in J. E. Spero & J. A. Hart, The Politics of International Economic Relations, Wadsworth, Boston, 2010, pp. 224–240.

[46] More in E. Spero & J.A. Hart, op. cit.

[47] G.K Papastamkos, International Economic Sanctions: Theory and Practice, Ant. N. Sakkoula, Athens-Komotini, 1990, p. 34.

[48] Literature is more focused on negative sanctions, i.e., penalties or retaliation aimed at deterring behaviors that constitutes a danger to peace and human security. On positive sanctions see D. Baldwin, The Power of Positive Sanctions, World Politics, vol. 24, issue 01, October 1971, pp. 19–38.

either case, sanctions involve economic pressure or coercion as an instrument of foreign policy.

The practice of economic sanctions dates back to the Peloponnesian War, when Athenians decided to exclude Megareans from the Athenian Alliance market and ports.[49] US President Woodrow Wilson was an ardent supporter of the practice, seeing it as "the economic, peaceful, silent and deadly remedy" to maintain international order.[50] Indeed, the Institute of International Economics database records 170 cases of sanctions imposed by the USA after World War I. In fact, 50 of them started in the 1990s[51] (35 of which in 1993–96 alone[52]!), when the end of the Cold War made it possible to use the term "sanctions" in official international texts.

There is much debate about their effectiveness,[53] making it rather paradoxical that, despite doubts about their use for diplomatic pressure or influence, they are so often used. Their effectiveness depends on a number of factors, but is linked to committed application, and the nature and extent of disruption they cause. Disrupting existing economic flows and patterns may take the form of total economic exclusion from the global economic system (banking and financing, trade, etc.), except for emergency humanitarian aid (e.g., North Korea).[54] Disruption is meant to limit access to resources, either to hinder a specific threatening activity or behavior, or to trigger domestic reactions and calls for the desired change in international behavior.

Why are economic sanctions a diplomatic tool of preference? First, they allow a symmetrical form of response when important but not vital interests are threatened. Military threat or engagement is costly and disproportionate to the nature of non-vital threats. Second, sanctions formally communicate dissatisfaction or frustration on a particular action or policy, but allow room for communication and cooperation on other interests and priorities. Third, they appease public opinion calls to demonstrate power, without resorting to the use of force, and they also help

[49] Resolution on Megareans, in El. Venizelos (ed.), Thucydides Histories A, 2nd ed., Bookstore of Hestia, Athens, 1960, verse 139.

[50] M.S. Daoudi & M.S. Dajani, Economic Sanctions, Ideals and Experience, Routledge & Kegan Paul, London, 1983, p. 26.

[51] D. Baldwin, The Sanctions Debate and the Logic of Choice, International Security, vol. 24, no.3, Winter 1999/2000, p. 80.

[52] More in American Manufacturers Association—National Association of Manufacturers, A Catalog of New U.S. Unilateral Economic Sanctions for Foreign Policy Purposes, Washington, DC, 1997.

[53] For example, D. B. Kunz, Butter and Guns: America's Cold War Economic Diplomacy, Free Press, New York, 1997.

T. C. Morgan & V. L. Schwebach, Fools Suffer Gladly: The Use of Economic Sanctions in International Crises, International Studies Quarterly, vol. 41, no. 1, March 1997, pp. 27–50.

[54] In the case of North Korea, the UN Security Council has imposed sanctions on the country's nuclear program in resolutions 1718 (2006), 1874 (2009), 2087 (2013), 2094 (2013) and 2270 (2016). For example, Resolution 1718 (2006) prohibits the export of military equipment (tanks, combat vehicles, aircraft, helicopters, warships, missile systems) and luxury goods, and imposes controls on goods to and from the country, travel restrictions, and asset freezes.

reaffirm moral commitments, such as the protection of human freedoms. Fourth, and at least theoretically, economic sanctions signal strength versus transgressive behavior, and serve as a deterrent for aggression, highlighting the costs of noncompliance.

15.3.1 Imposing Economic Sanctions

Economic sanctions aim at inflicting economic harm, and can be applied in times of peace or war. Disruption of trade relations, transport and communications between belligerent parties fall under the law of war, and are the subject of a different discussion. During peacetime, sanctions are a legitimate response to threats to peace and security, and are consistent with UN Charter Article 51 (self-defense): they do not involve use of force, and comply with the principle of nonintervention and specific restraining clauses[55] under international law. There is a distinct difference between permissible economic pressure and unlawful coercion. On the one hand, pressure is exercised through permissible means and comprises acceptable form of influence. On the other, employing non-permissible means of economic pressure amounts to an aggression, or a form of violence, causing an existential threat for the state or entity subjected to them.

Economic sanctions, in general, are a response to an illegal act, making them a legal reaction to a preceding illegality. In addition to Article 51, their imposition may also be restricted by preexisting agreements between the parties involved. For example, there is an explicit commitment by WTO members to equal treatment, through the most favored nation clause (MFN). Sanctions among WTO members should be incompatible with the organization's charter, yet it is possible to get out of the MFN commitment and employ sanctions through referring to other safeguard or escape clauses, mostly on national security grounds.[56]

All forms of economic sanctions are aimed at deterring, coercing, warning and/or punishing[57] a state or other entity about the implementation or non- implementation of a legal or political commitment. Their ultimate aim is to restore a secure political and economic order, and avoid crossing red lines of military force. When a state or other actor fails to comply with international norms, rules and laws, or behaves in a way that disturbs and endangers stability, human security and peace, sanctions are used to deter threats such as the proliferation of nuclear weapons or weapons of mass destruction, or to protect human rights. Sanctions are applied by one or more states, following the decision of a competent international body. In this case, sanctions are institutional. Absent the authority of an international body, sanctions can still be

[55] G. K. Papastamkos, op. cit., p. 25.

[56] More in G. K. Papastamkos, op. cit., pp. 97–108.

[57] R. N. Haass, Economic Sanctions and American Diplomacy, Council on Foreign Relations, Washington, DC, 1998, p. 1.

imposed as a state's autonomous decision, falling within the framework of self-protection (self-help) measures.[58]

Economic sanctions might as well be included in the scope of trade agreements, serving as a legitimate response to policies and measures that do not comply with agreed rules. In this case, sanctions are authorized countermeasures or retaliatory measures to non-agreed trade and economic policies. For example, in January 2016, following a 7-year WTO dispute over EU tariffs on Chinese iron or steel screws imports, China was vindicated.[59] The dispute erupted when the EU adopted tariffs citing dumping by China. WTO regulations allow for antidumping measures,[60] such as import duties, to protect domestic production. Enforcement, however, is subject to very strict rules, and China claimed that these rules were not respected by the EU. WTO mediators sided with China, considering that EU actions caused disproportionate economic damage to Chinese industry.[61] The EU was asked to reduce tariffs, and not doing so would allow China to take further measures.[62]

In the EU context, economic sanctions are a measure of EU trade policy, and, as such, are an exclusive competence of Brussels.[63] Therefore, even if there is a WTO decision, as in this case, or a UN Security Council decision to impose or lift economic sanctions, EU member states can act only after an EU decision—as in the case of sanctions against Iran, because of its nuclear program, or against the Russian Federation, because of the conflict in Ukraine.

15.3.2 Forms of Economic Sanctions

The most common forms of economic sanctions are embargoes, trade blockades, and economic retaliation. They tend to focus on financial, monetary, and commercial-industrial relations,[64] with a growing emphasis on technology.[65]

[58] G. K. Papastamkos, op. cit., p. 23.

[59] More in T. Miles, EU loses WTO case, China could seek trade sanctions, Reuters, 19/01/2016.

[60] Exporting and selling products at a price lower (or even below cost) than in the domestic or international market in order to annihilate competitors.

[61] China's Ministry of Commerce claimed that the EU measures cost the economy approximately $1bn and about 100,000 lost jobs (Miles, op. cit.).

[62] Of course, the EU itself "bombarded" China with requests for an investigation into 22 antidumping cases, on products such as silicone, aspartame, biodiesel, various construction materials, solar panels, polyester threads, etc. - A. Rettman, Nuts and Bolts: WTO Ruling Helps China in EU Dumping Wars, EU Observer, 19/01/2016.

[63] This supranational competence derives from Article 113, Treaty on European Economic Community, Rome, 1957.

[64] More in M. P. Doxey, International Sanctions in Contemporary Perspective, London, MacMillan, 1996.

[65] More in E. Schmidt & J. Cohen, The New Digital Age: Reshaping the Future of People, Nations and Business, Hatchet UK, London, 2013.

Financial sanctions include restriction or suspension of credit facilities and other forms of financial assistance (development, investment), as well as freezing bank deposits and assets of the target actor or state. They are usually imposed in tandem with monetary policy measures aimed at pressuring the exchange rate, suspending the acceptance of government guarantees, affecting the cost of borrowing, or prohibiting funds transfer. These practices stress central banks by depleting their resources (esp. foreign exchange reserves), as well as private corporations, which have to limit international activities and suffer consequent losses.[66] This type of sanctions have evolved into a sophisticated diplomatic tool to deplete and deprive resources which are used to endanger security. For instance, by freezing most of Central Bank of Russia (BoR) assets in the USA, in response to the Ukraine invasion, the USA limited BoR's means to support the Ruble and imports, affecting Russia's capacity to finance the war, and increasing the risk of a central government default.[67]

Commercial and industrial sanctions involve measures such as increasing trade tariffs and quotas, lifting most favored nation status, and freezing joint business activities. An embargo,[68] or even a boycott, results in a partial or total prohibition or restriction of trade relations between two states, or between a state and a group of states. Embargoes are usually driven by governments, and focus on exports of specific types of goods and services (e.g., arms embargoes). Blockades involve (voluntary or involuntary) restrictions on private sector activities, affecting broader bilateral economic relations. In the case of the Ukrainian crisis, the US-EU embargo on Russia created shortages in imported components, and forced Uralvogonzavod, the largest tank manufacturer in Russia, to suspend production.[69] The aviation sector blockade, on the other hand, hammered aircraft construction and maintenance, production of spare parts, insurance and leasing of aircrafts to Russian and Belarusian airlines. It rendered the local sector unable to access spare parts and maintenance services, but also created costs for the global aviation industry: airlines

---

[66] One such example is the 2010–2015 US sanctions against Iran, which extended to the Iranian banking sector and all transactions in Iranian currency. Under US government's instructions in 2010, US banks were to stop trading in Iranian Rial, and the banking system was to exclude third country banks trading in that currency. Many Chinese banks risked losing access to the US financial markets because of their transactions with Iran, which was overcome by the adoption of the Chinese Yuan. But this simultaneously reduced demand for Rials, pushing the currency's exchange rate lower, and increased the cost of imports. More in China and Iran MacGyver a Way around US Sanctions, The American Interest, 09/05/2012.

[67] More in V. Pop, S. Fleming, J. Politi, Weaponization of Finance: How the West Unleashed Shock and Awe on Russia, Financial Times, 6/4/2022, and L. Benitez, Russia Credit Insurance Shows 99% Chance of Default Within Year, Bloomberg, 6/4/2022.

[68] The word origin is the Spanish verb "embargar", which means to prevent, stop, confiscate, seize, pledge. As a common law concept in seventeenth–nineteenth century, the term "embargo" was linked to the seizure and detention of merchant ships in order to exert pressure on the state whose flag they flew. Since the early twentieth century, the concept has mainly covered the prohibition of exports or imports (either as a whole or of specific goods or services).

[69] C. Hetzner, Russia's largest tank manufacturer may have run out of parts, Fortune, 3/22/2022.

have been forced to take longer routes to avoid the Russian and Belarussian airspaces, a large number of leased aircraft are stranded in Russia, while Western leasing companies are unable to collect leases and insurance premiums.[70]

Prohibiting or restricting exports of technological know-how is growingly acknowledged as an effective form of sanctions. It is a more defensive than offensive type of sanctions, usually adopted to protect domestic industry and gain a few years' technological lead. Excluding Russia from the semiconductors market as part of the technological sanctions imposed by 48 countries in response to the invasion of Ukraine[71] falls within this type of sanctions. Semiconductors are the cornerstone of modern technology, and global manufacturing firms have stopped selling microchips to Moscow. Although Russia can design microchips, it could not produce them, as sanctions also include sale of silicon foundries—either directly to Russia or through third party suppliers. It is estimated that a technology gap of at least two decades will be created: even if Russia commits resources to support domestic production, the processors it will be able produce by 2030, will be equivalent to those used in 2011.[72]

15.3.3 Applying Economic Sanctions: A Case Study

The 2015 agreement on Iran's nuclear program resulted from diplomatic negotiations which included comprehensive sanctions. Imposing them involved coordinating governments, businesses, and financial institutions to exert maximum economic pressure.

Iran's compliance with the rules of the International Atomic Energy Agency (IAEA) has been a source of concern for several years. After a series of warnings, UN members were asked to freeze assets of all individuals involved in Iran's nuclear program.[73] To implement UN Security Council resolutions, the P5 + 1 negotiating team[74] resorted to economic diplomacy practices.[75] In addition to Security Council resolutions that gradually called for collective sanctions, the USA and EU countries

[70] J. Freed, Explainer: How sanctions against Russia are battering the global aviation industry, Reuters, 8/3/2022.

[71] A. Fitri, International sanctions could cripple Russia's tech ambitions, Tech Monitor, 7/3/2022.

[72] T. Cibean, Russia plans to manufacture chips locally on a 28 nm node by 2030, Techspot, 16/4/2022.

[73] This was a series of Security Council resolutions that gradually broadened the scope of assets to freeze, starting with individuals working on the nuclear program and including state-owned companies—judgments 1696 (2006), 1737 (2006), 1747 (2007), 1803 (2008), 1835 (2008), and 1929 (2010).

[74] P5 is the five permanent members of the UN Security Council (France, UK, USA, China, Russia). The sixth member of the group is Germany. In Europe, this group is known as P3 + 3 (i.e., 3 European +3 non-European countries).

[75] I. R. A. Lakshmanan, If you can't do this deal, go back to Tehran: the inside story of the Obama administration's Iran diplomacy, Politico, 15/09/2015.

implemented their own measures, while, at the same time, businesses also acted in the same direction (United Against Nuclear Iran—UANI).[76]

Exit from the negotiating impasse began in 2008, when the USA returned to P5 + 1 group negotiations.[77] President Obama engaged in public diplomacy, through statements on "mutual respect,"[78] to indicate a new US approach. US economic diplomacy, however, remained in line with UN resolutions. In 2010, US oil industry was asked to drastically reduce imports from Iran, or risk losing access to the US banking system.[79] This decision sent a clear message to Iran's leadership, while also satisfying American public opinion, and space was created to work on channels of communication—soon found through Oman's mediation.[80]

The USA then turned to its own main economic partners, working with the largest importers of Iranian oil—China, India, and South Korea—to significantly reduce their imports. When China agreed to use its national currency in its dealings with Iran, Iran lost hard currency reserves.[81] This approach of expanded economic diplomacy grew to include the EU28, with a 2012 vote in favor of an oil embargo against Iran.[82] Pressure culminated with blocking the Iranian banking system out of the SWIFT network (Society for Worldwide Interbank Financial Telecommunication), a global first, freezing almost all Iranian international financial transactions for about 4 years.[83] By mid-2013, collective sanctions and intensifying US sanctions,[84] had cost Iran more than 50% of its export revenues (some $54bn),[85] while UANI's

[76] This coalition includes NGOs, trade unions and businesses.

[77] K. Katzman, Iran: Politics, Gulf Security, and U.S. Policy, Congressional Research Service, 2016, p. 23.

[78] T. Parsi, A Single Roll of the Dice: Obama's Diplomacy with Iran, Yale University Press, New Haven, 2012, p. 58.

[79] CISADA - Comprehensive Iran Sanctions, Accountability and Divestment Act - law signed on 01/07/2010 on the basis of Security Council Resolution 1929 (2010). K. Katzman, Iran Sanctions, Congressional Research Service, 2011.

[80] I. R. A. Lakshmanan, op. cit. (2015).

[81] For international reactions see for example in the international press: L. Horby, New Sanctions on Iran constrict trade flows to Asia, Reuters, 07/02/2012; The Hindu Business Line, India imposes more sanctions on Iran, 01/04/2011; India imposes more sanctions on Iran, The Hindu Business Line, 01/04/2011; Japan imposes new sanctions over nuclear program, BBC News, 03/09/2010; Ch. Sang-Hun, South Korea aims sanctions at Iran, New York Times, 08/09/2010. On China's stance in particular, see The American Interest, op. cit.

[82] Foreign Affairs Council Decision and subsequent Commission Regulation - Council Regulation (EU) No 267/2012 (24/03/2012).

[83] Excluding Iranian banks from the SWIFT network was ruled illegal by the European Court of Justice in February 2013 (J. Matonis, EU Court Strikes Down SWIFT's Blockade Against Iranian Banks, Forbes, 08/02/2013), but was lifted in early 2016 (Reuters, Iranian Banks Reconnect to SWIFT Network after 4-year Hiatus, 17/02/2016), and only for transactions with European banks.

[84] J. Calmes & R. Gladstone, Obama Imposes Freeze on Iran Property in US, New York Times, 06/02/2012.

[85] S. M. Peterson, Iran's Deteriorating Economy: An Analysis of the Economic Impact of Western Sanctions, ESIA International Affairs Review, 2012.

initiative led many businesses to sever their ties with Iran.[86] An embargo on Iranian ports,[87] in consultation with the EU and US shipping industry,[88] delivered the final blow. Within a year, Iran's GDP and currency collapsed, with inflation rocketing.[89] Iranian depositors and consumers panicked, creating parallel black markets. In a speech in April 2015, then US Treasury Secretary, Jack Liu, estimated that total costs of three years of sanctions on Iran amounted to more than $160bn in oil export revenues, while GDP fell by 9%.[90]

This sharp reduction in revenue made it impossible for Iran to continue developing its nuclear program at the previous pace. At that point, and in order to encourage political steps, the US released a small portion of Iran's $3bn of frozen assets,[91] as an incentive to continue working towards an agreement and indicating that sanctions would be lifted only on a quid pro quo basis. Eventually, the two sides agreed in late 2014, and the deal was implemented in July 2015. Sanctions were formally lifted in January 2016.[92]

15.4 Concluding Thoughts

Expressions of power involving the economy can create alternative ways of resolving a crisis, transform the context of political interactions, and even lead to policy re-prioritization. Economic diplomacy is the medium of expressing such power, and is therefore integral to the conduct of international relations, despite doubts about its effectiveness, especially in the form of sanctions and blockades—which comprise the strongest forms of nonmilitary coercion.

What makes twenty-first century economic diplomacy interesting is the broad array of actors involved, and this its flexibility and variety of measures it can employ, ranging from targeted trade tariffs and quotas, to sophisticated asset freezes, "hits" against Central Banks reserves, and disruptions of relationships of industrial interdependence—including technological interdependence, which is of crucial

[86] Such companies were Nexans, Safran, Porsche, Volvo, Grant Thornton, RSM, Crowe Horwath and Nexia, Fiat, and many others (full list: http://www2.unitedagainstnucleariran.com/our-initiatives/campaign-successes)

[87] I.R.A. Lakshmanan, EU Sanctions on Iran's Main Ports will Slash Trade if Enforced, Bloomberg, 10/02/2012.

[88] Some of the shipping companies that ceased operations in Iran include Evergreen (Taiwan), Yang Ming (Taiwan) and China Shipping Container Lines Co. (China). Ship certification companies also joined (Bureau Veritas, Germanischer Lloyd, Russian Maritime Register of Shipping, Class NK, Korean Register of Shipping, China Classification Society, Korean Register of Shipping (KR), etc.) - UANI, op. cit.

[89] S. M. Peterson, op. cit.

[90] J. J. Lew, Remarks of Treasury Secretary Jacob J. Lew to The Washington Institute, 29/04/2015.

[91] I.R.A. Lakshmanan, op. cit. (2015).

[92] D. E. Sanger, Iran Complies with Nuclear Deal; Sanctions are Lifted, New York Times, 01/16/2016.

importance in the Industry 4.0 and AI era. It has evolved into a form of "acupuncture" for international relations, with different dimensions of the economy being the pressure points. Exerting simultaneous pressure at multiple points allows economic diplomacy to serve high politics, provided that (a) it is exercised in accordance with international law, (b) it engages multiple state actors in applying different types and levels of economic pressure, (c) it achieves private sector commitment and engagement, (d) it includes well thought out financial dimensions, and (e) it is implemented in the context of a comprehensive strategy, with short-term and a long-term escalation and de-escalation options in mind.

Maria Bozoudi, PhD, Department of International and European Studies, University of Macedonia, Thessaloniki, GR. Dr Bozoudi bears extensive senior experience in transition environments, European integration, economic diplomacy and policy advocacy for growth and the digital economy. Among others, she has collaborated with the World Bank, the European Commission, OECD, OSCE, SECI and the Stability Pact for Southeastern Europe on flagship initiatives related to trade, transport, and investment facilitation, infrastructure development and PPPs, capacity building, skills, and regulatory reform. She has worked with leading think-tanks and NGOs in Greece, Germany, and the USA and has also taught courses on European integration, the Balkans, political economy, and international organizations. She has studied political science, diplomacy, international and European relations, and international trade policy, in Greece and the USA. She has additional training in project management, institutional organization, and leadership communication.

Judicial Diplomacy 16

Emmanouil Kalaintzis

Abstract

Judicial diplomacy, distinct from judicial communication, encapsulates the interactions and relations between domestic and foreign courts, fostering legal integration, trust-building, and the exchange of best practices. Despite the conventional separation of powers in liberal democracies, judicial diplomacy highlights the essential role of judges beyond their courtroom duties. Judges, guided by international legal instruments such as the UN Basic Principles on the Independence of the Judiciary and the Bangalore Principles, possess the right to freedom of expression and association while maintaining impartiality.

This chapter examines the evolution of judicial diplomacy through key institutions, both international and regional, that facilitate collaboration among judges. It explores organizations such as the International Association of Judges (IAJ), the International Association of Women Judges (IAWJ), and the European Judicial Training Network (EJTN), among others, highlighting their role in legal harmonization and strengthening judicial independence. Furthermore, it analyzes the relationship between judicial diplomacy and judicial cooperation, differentiating the former as a broader, strategic dialogue distinct from institutionalized cooperation mechanisms in criminal and civil justice.

E. Kalaintzis (✉)
Hellenic Court of Audit (Supreme Financial Court), Athens, Greece

P. Naskou-Perraki (ed.), *Contemporary Diplomatic and Consular Relations*,
https://doi.org/10.1007/978-3-031-99243-8_16

16.1 Introduction: Defining Judicial Diplomacy—The Right of a Judge to Associate

16.1.1 The Paradox of Diplomacy and Judiciary: A Theoretical Approach

Judicial diplomacy is usually confused with judicial communication, the method or technique to effectively communicate to the masses the outcome of an adjudication, shed some needed light to a judgment or simply inform the public on a topical issue within the remit of a court's competence. However, this chapter is dedicated to another meaning to the term, the one that more accurately depicts its true meaning. At first glance, the term is an oxymoron as there is an inherent conflict between politics and the judiciary. Diplomacy as per the classic definition of Ernest Satow is "the application of intelligence and tact to the conduct of official relations between government."[1] Headley Bull defined it as "the conduct of relations between states and other entities involved in world politics through official policies and peaceful means." Having in mind the separation of powers in contemporary liberal democracies, involving judges with politics seems antithetical and incompatible to their function. Nonetheless looking at the terminology of the word diplomacy we can clearly see what that assumption is wrong.

16.1.2 The Etymology and Evolution of Diplomacy

The word originates from the Greek word that means to fold which was used during the Roman times to signify the folded document that the emissaries used to prove their credentials. Over time, this concept evolved to encompass the broader field of international relations and negotiation. Consequently, literally the word stipulates an exchange of delegated messengers that were empowered gradually to negotiate and carry-on official exchanges among entities and/or states. Diplomacy hence should not be inextricably connected with external affairs and international relations of a state, it can obtain other meaning and can very well refer to the activities of a specific entity and the method employed to achieve outreach. Not as a goal but as a means to build closer ties, exchange of best practices, build trust and an *esprit de corps* among different national institutions.

16.1.3 The Role of Judges Beyond the Courtroom

Judges should speak through their judgments and rulings. However, should their influence extend beyond the courtroom? Absolutely! Judges are off the bench, but never off duty. The Judge may engage in activities to improve the Law, the Legal

[1] E. Satow, A Guide to Diplomatic Practice, Vol. 1, Cambridge University Press, 2011.

System and the Administration of Justice,[2] and this qualifies as the epitome of those activities. Judges enjoy the freedoms of expression, association, and peaceful assembly,[3] but the extend of which was not always very clear. This uncertainty stems from legal controversies and case law interpretations regarding judicial independence and impartiality. For instance, courts have sometimes ruled on whether judges' public statements or affiliations compromise their neutrality. Additionally, international legal instruments and national legislations impose restrictions on judicial expression to prevent potential conflicts with the right to a fair trial and public confidence in the judiciary. Rights are subject to limitations, and international instruments emphasize the importance of judicial independence and impartiality. Thus, the relationship between a judge's right to associate and express opinions and the public's right to an independent and impartial court warrants further scrutiny.

16.1.4 Judicial Independence and Impartiality in Democratic Systems

16.1.4.1 The International Legal Framework on Judicial Freedoms

Judicial impartiality and independence must not only be genuine but must also be perceived as such by the public, as "tribunals and courts must also appear to a reasonable observer to be impartial."[4] In 1985 the **General Assembly of the United Nations** adopted the *Basic Principles on the Independence of the Judiciary* confirming the right of members of the judiciary to the freedom of expression, belief, association, and assembly, in accordance with the Universal Declaration of Human Rights. Specifically, judges "shall be free to join associations of judges or other organizations to represent their interests, to promote their professional training and to protect their judicial independence."[5] The **UN Guidelines on the role of Prosecutors** (1990) provide that "Prosecutors like other citizens are entitled to freedom of expression, belief, association, and assembly. They shall have the right

---

[2] American Bar Association Code of Judicial Conduct, Canon 4 (1972). A Canon that was omitted in future versions of the Code of Judicial Conduct. See for example ABA Model Code of Judicial Conduct, February 2007, available: https://asbar.org/wp-content/uploads/attachments/ABA_MCJC_approved.authcheckdam.pdf (accessed 31.01.2024). See also A. Tate Jr., The Propriety of Off-Bench Judicial Writing or Speaking on Legal or Quasi – Legal Issues, University of Alabama, 1973, available at: https://www.law.ua.edu/resources/pubs/jlp_files/issues_files/vol03/vol03art03.pdf (accessed 31.01.2024).

[3] Universal Declaration articles 19 and 20 and article 10. International Covenant on Civil and Political Rights articles 14, 19, 21, and 22.

[4] Human Rights Committee, General Comment no. 32 (article 14: Right to equality before courts and tribunals and to a fair trial), UN Doc CCPR/C/GC/32 (2007), para 21.

[5] GA Res 40/146, Basic Principle on the Independence of the Judiciary, Seventh United Nations Congress on the Prevention of Crime and Treatment of Offenders held at Milan from 26 August to 6 September 1985 and endorsed by General Assembly resolutions 40/32 of 29 November 1985 and 40/146 of 13 December 1985, available at: https://www.ohchr.org/en/instruments-mechanisms/instruments/basic-principles-independence-judiciary (accessed at 20.01.2024).

to take part in public discussion of matters concerning the law, the administration of justice and the promotion and protection of human rights and to join or form local, national or international organizations and attend their meetings, without suffering professional disadvantage by reason of their lawful action or their membership in a lawful."[6] The International Association of Judges (ICJ) on the other hand, in its **Universal Charter of the Judge** (1999) makes reference only to professional associations and the right of a judge to be their member in order to permit them to be consulted especially "concerning the application of their statutes, ethical and otherwise, and the means of justice, and in order to permit them to defend their legitimate interests."[7]

"A judge like any other citizen, is entitled to freedom of expression, belief, association and assembly, but in exercising such rights, a judge shall always conduct himself or herself in such a manner as to preserve the dignity of the judicial office and the impartiality and independence of the judiciary" according to the seminal **Bangalore Principles** (2018).[8] A judge may speak out on matters that affect the judiciary or his/her personal integrity, a judge may also participate in a discussion of the law for educational purposes or to point out weaknesses in the law and such judicial commentary "should be made as part of a collective or institutionalized effort by the judiciary, not of an individual judge." There are also cases according to the **Bangalore principles** when a judge "as a human being with conscience, morals, feelings and values—considers it a moral duty to speak out" when the issues at hand concern the local or global community, in the same vein a judge may "write, lecture, teach and participate in activities concerning the law, appear at a public hearing, the legal system the administration of justice or related matters" and a "judge may form or join associations of judges or participate in other organizations representing the interests of judges."

16.1.4.2 The European Approach to Judicial Association

At a European level, initial approaches to judicial association were more restrictive. The Committee of Ministers of the Council of Europe in its Recommendation on the independence, efficiency, and role of judges (1994) with a different formulation that described the right to association of judges in more restricted terms,[9] specifying

[6]Guidelines on the Role of Prosecutors, Adopted by the Eighth United Nations Congress on the Prevention of Crime and the Treatment of Offenders, Havana, Cuba, 27 August to 7 September 1990, available at: https://www.ohchr.org/sites/default/files/prosecutors.pdf (accessed 20.01.2024).

[7]International Association of Judges, Universal Charter of the Judge, November 1999, available at: https://www.icj.org/wp-content/uploads/2014/03/IAJ-Universal-Charter-of-the-Judge-instruments-1989-eng.pdf (accessed at 20.01.2024).

[8]UNODC, The Bangalore Principles of Judicial Conduct, United Nations, 2018, available at: https://www.unodc.org/documents/ji/training/bangaloreprinciples.pdf (accessed 30.01.2024).

[9]CoE Committee of Ministers, Recommendation No. R (94) 12, on the independence, efficiency and role of judge, adopted on 13 October 1994, available at: https://www.ohchr.org/en/resources/educators/human-rights-education-training/12-recommendation-no-r-94-12-member-states-independence-efficiency-and-role-judges-1994 (accessed 30.01.2024).

that judges are "given the right to take collective action to safeguard their professional independence and protect their interests (… and) are free to form associations whose activities are confined to defending the independence and the interests of the profession." The **European Statute for Judges** (1998) provides for the right of judges to unionize, stating that "professional organizations set up by judges, and to which all judges may freely adhere, contribute notably to the defense of those rights which are conferred on them by their statute, in particular in relation to authorities and bodies which are involved in decision regarding them." Those associations should be consulted "over plans to modify their statute, and over the determination of the terms of their remuneration and of their social welfare."[10] Over time, the European perspective has shifted towards a more inclusive and progressive view. The **Magna Carta of the Consultative Council of European Judges** (CCJE) of the Council of Europe which is mainly a compilation of Opinions issued by the institution up until 2010, took a more progressive stance, asserting that "judges have the right to be members of national or international associations of judges, entrusted with the defense of the mission of the judiciary in the society."[11] In a similar manner the Committee of Ministers of the Council of Europe updated its original position and has underlined the freedom of any judge "to form and join professional organizations whose objectives are to safeguard their independence, protect their interests and promote the rule of law" in Recommendation (2010).[12] Going a step further, the Committee of Ministers explained that those associations should necessarily confine themselves to safeguarding judges "independence and protecting their professional interests, but also seek to uphold other principles of the justice system in the interest of individuals," drawing lessons from this diversification of forms of joint action by judges. It further stressed out that judges, performing their duties in an increasingly global society in an efficient manner necessitates "a better knowledge of the legal systems of other countries and a strengthening of mutual confidence"[13] therefore "exchanges among judges and judicial authorities should be promoted."[14] To achieve that, states "should provide courts with the appropriate means to (…)

[10]Working with associations such as the European Association of Judges (EAJ) and the European Association of Judges for Democracy and Freedom (MEDEL) the need for a proper framework on the Statute for Judges was expressed. Three experts were entrusted and in a multilateral meeting organized by the CoE in 1998 the European Charter on the Statute for Judges was adopted. European Charter on the statute for judges and Explanatory Memorandum, DAJ/DOC (98) 23, Strasbourg 8–10 July 1998, available at: https://rm.coe.int/09000016809293 4f#:~:text=GENERAL%20PRINCIPLES%201.1.,of%20his%20or%20her%20rights. (accessed 30.01.2024).

[11]CCJE, Magna Carta of Judges (Fundamental Principles), Strasbourg, 17 November 2010, CCJE (2010) 3, Final, available: https://rm.coe.int/CoERMPublicCommonSearchServices/DisplayDCTMContent?documentId=090000168063e431 (accessed 30.01.2024).

[12]Committee of Ministers, Judges: independence, efficiency and responsibilities, Recommendation CM/Rec (2010) 12 and explanatory memorandum, 17 November 2010, available at: https://rm.coe.int/16807096c1 (accessed at 30.01.2024).

[13]Ibid.

[14]Ibid.

support international co-operation and relations between judges."[15] The European Court of Human Rights (ECtHR) interpreting the above instruments confirmed not only the right but also the duty of the judge to express his/her opinion on legislative reforms affecting the judiciary.[16] Reiterating the duty of loyalty and discretion that is owed by civil servants, especially the judiciary any expression should be carried out with a moderation and propriety, but the judges are liable to strive to maintain their independence individually and as a corpus, endeavoring to enjoy public confidence. The UN Special Rapporteur on Independence of judges and lawyers has opined those relations with media should be carried out with circumspection and judges can express their views *sub judice* or in general with the condition of the respect of the fair trial, without creating prejudice to a certain adjudication.[17] As such the issue of judicial independence is of public interest in a democratic society and who is more legitimized to participate in the discourse other than a judge[18] and for those reasons they have the right to form and join professional organizations.[19] That is of course when they act in their personal capacity. There is also the chance that in this globalized and interconnected society courts themselves, especially supreme courts of the member states form and participate in judicial union, where judges participate in their official capacity representing their host institution to discuss topics of common interest and promote legal integration.

What is clear is that there is a complex balancing exercise at hand between the impartiality of a judge and the need and necessity to interact openly with colleagues from different legal orders. Judicial independence and impartiality must be balanced with a judge's freedom to participate in judicial diplomacy. While international legal instruments protect the right of judges to express opinions and associate with other judges, these rights are subject to limitations to avoid conflicts of interest. The UN Basic Principles on the Independence of the Judiciary emphasize that judges must exercise their rights in a manner that upholds the dignity of their office and does not compromise public trust in their impartiality. However, these rights are not absolute. The Principles clarify that judges must exercise their rights in a manner that preserves the dignity of their office and maintains public confidence in their impartiality and the integrity of the judiciary.

At the heart of modern jurisprudence lies a complex and increasingly vital balancing exercise: reconciling the absolute necessity of judicial independence and

[15] Ibid.

[16] ECtHR, Case of Baka v. Hungary, Application non. 20261/12, Judgment of 23 June 2016, available at: https://hudoc.echr.coe.int/fre#{%22itemid%22:[%22001-163113%22]} (available 14.01.2024).

[17] Human Rights Council, Independence of judges and lawyers, Report of the Special Rapporteur on the independence of judges and lawyers, A/HRC/41/48, 29 April 2019, available: https://documents.un.org/doc/undoc/gen/g19/118/68/pdf/g1911868.pdf?token=nDxsQ10yy11ON2ms7Q&fe=true (accessed 30.01.2024).

[18] ECtHR, Kudeshkina v. Russia, Application No. 29492/05, 26 February 2009 (available at 14.09.2009).

[19] Ibid.

impartiality with the growing need for judges to interact openly with colleagues across different legal orders. This tension creates a delicate tightrope that judiciaries worldwide must navigate with care. While judicial diplomacy is essential for the evolution of law and jurisprudence, the foundational principles of impartiality—both actual and perceived—must remain the unshakeable bedrock of public trust in the rule of law. The independence and impartiality of the judiciary are not mere aspirational goals; they are the sine qua non of a rule of law. Public confidence in the administration of justice depends entirely on the belief that judges will decide cases based solely on the facts presented and the applicable law, free from any external pressure or internal bias. This trust, however, is fragile. It is sustained by two distinct pillars: Actual Impartiality: This refers to the judge's true state of mind—a genuine absence of bias or prejudice toward any party and Perceived Impartiality: This relates to the external appearance of fairness. As the legal maxim states, justice must not only be done but must also be seen to be done. Courts must appear impartial to a "reasonable observer," a hypothetical, informed member of the public who would view the proceedings without suspicion of bias. A failure in perception can be as damaging to public trust as a failure in fact. In an interconnected world characterized by transnational crime, international trade, and universal human rights norms, judicial isolation is no longer viable. The active participation of judges in international dialogue, or "judicial diplomacy," offers indispensable benefits. This engagement allows for: (a) the cross-pollination of legal ideas and the sharing of best practices in court management and judicial ethics, (b) a deeper understanding and more consistent application of international law and treaties within domestic legal systems, (c) the harmonization of legal principles, particularly within integrated blocs like the European Union, where national courts function as EU courts, and finally (d) strengthening the global rule of law by building a community of judicial leaders committed to shared principles.

16.1.5 Judicial Diplomacy vs Judicial Cooperation

Following the preceding analysis and in an effort to reclaim and reframe the term diplomacy, apart from a method employed by states to further their agenda, diplomacy can be conceived in the context of the functioning of the judiciary as the necessary interactions and relations between domestic and foreign courts or collaborative action and communication among national courts, usually the highest judicial bodies, toward regional legal integration, the exchange of best practices or issues relevant to the status of a judge or any other contemporary legal matters. Judicial diplomacy, as defined above, typically occurs in forums where judges interact and discuss. These discussions often result in written outcomes, which depict common areas of progress, such as declarations. Judicial diplomacy is also utilized by apex regional courts (such as the Court of Justice of the European Union—CJEU and the European Court of Human Rights—ECtHR) as a form of an extra-forum dialogue with national courts aimed to further promoting understanding of the *modus operandi* of a multi-level system that necessitates active engagement and familiarity with evolving concepts to function properly. Judicial diplomacy is not to be confused with judicial cooperation. Judicial diplomacy should not be confused with judicial cooperation. While both involve collaboration between courts, judicial diplomacy refers to broader, strategic dialogues, whereas judicial cooperation focuses on formal, institutionalized frameworks. More specifically judicial cooperation connotes the institutionalized forms of collaboration among judicial authorities which is developed particularly in criminal and civil matters to facilitate free movement of persons and allow them to resolve disputes abroad or effectively trial crimes in cases with transnational elements. Judicial cooperation involves formal, legally binding agreements, such as mutual legal assistance treaties (MLATs) or frameworks for cross-border crime investigations. Judicial diplomacy, on the other hand, is not limited to formal agreements; it includes informal dialogues, conferences, and other activities that promote cross-border legal collaboration and understanding. In the context of the European Union, those forms include detention and transfer of prisoners, exchange of documents, taking evidence in another EU country, transfer of criminal proceedings, mutual legal assistance and extradition, cross-border access to electronic evidence, the European Arrest Warrant and mutual recognition of judgments. Networks and bodies supporting judicial cooperation include **Eurojust**, the **European Judicial Network** (EJN)[20] and the **European Public Prosecutor's Office** (EPPO).

This chapter will examine key institutions that constitute the foundation of judicial diplomacy, particularly those composed of judges. These institutions include self-standing nongovernmental organizations, international organizations of national judicial associations, and consultative bodies operating within international and regional frameworks. They play a vital role in fostering judicial collaboration, safeguarding judicial independence, and promoting legal integration across different jurisdictions. Given the diversity of these institutions, we have chosen a geographical criterion to categorize them and will focus on the most prominent organizations active at the time of writing. The below list is not to be considered exhaustive and wishes to show the diversity of those fora with a specific focus on international and European networks.

[20] The European Judicial Network (EJN) is a network of national contact points for the facilitation of judicial cooperation in criminal matters. The EJN was created by Joint Action 98/428 JHA of 29 June 1998 to fulfill Recommendation No. 21 of the Action Plan to Combat Organized Crime adopted by the Council on 28 April 1997. In December 2008, a new legal basis entered into force, Council Decision 2008/976/JHA of 16 December 2008 on the European Judicial Network (hereinafter the "EJN Decision"), which reinforced the legal status of the EJN, while maintaining the spirit of 1998. The EJN is composed of Contact Points in the Member States designated by each Member State among central authorities in charge of international judicial cooperation and the judicial authorities or other competent authorities with specific responsibilities in the field of international judicial cooperation.

16.2 International Level

16.2.1 INTOSAI: International Organization of Supreme Audit Institutions

Formally an autonomous, independent, and nonpolitical organization that operates as an umbrella organization for the external government audit community having consultative state with the Economic and Social Council (ECOSOC) of the United Nations founded in 1953. INTOSAI is not a judicial union per se, it is an organization bringing together the Supreme Audit Institutions (SAIs) addressing challenges related to national governance and promote accountability, transparency, and good governance, fostering the economy, effectiveness, and efficiency of government programs. It is included in the present analysis due to the model of auditing that certain jurisdictions utilize, certain SAIs have jurisdictional function [such as the *Cour de Comptes* (Royaume de Belgique—Koninkrijk België), *Cour des Comptes* (Republique Française), *Corte dei Conti* (República Italiaana), *Tribunal de Contas* (República Portuguesa), *Tribunal de Cuentas* (Reino de España), *Ελεγκτικό Συνέδριο—Elegktiko Sinedrio* (Ελληνική Δημοκρατία—Hellenic Republic)]. Therefore, judges are also participants in its activities representing the Courts that have also auditing competences or more accurately Supreme Audit Institutions with a judicial function.

INTOSAI has developed a series of professional Standards in order to support the effective functioning of SAIs in the public interest by providing, maintaining and advocating for internationally recognized professional principles, standards and guidance that promote the quality excellence, credibility and relevance of public sector audits. INTOSAI Professional Pronouncements are the formal and authoritative announcement or declarations addressed to its members included in the INTOSAI Framework of Professional Pronouncements (IFPP) which contains three categories:

- The **INTOSAI Principles** (INTOSAI–P), foundational concepts, mandates and ethical tenets.
- The **International Standards of Supreme Audit Institutions** (ISSAI), auditing standards applied by SAIs.
- The **INTOSAI Guidance** (GUID), practical guidance on the application of the above mentioned material[21].

These frameworks collectively promote accountability, transparency, and efficiency in government programs, ensuring effective public sector auditing.

[21] Documents relating to the INTOSA can be found here: https://www.intosai.org/documents/open-access.html (accessed 30.01.2024).

INTOSAI's evolving IFPP—backed by the 2025–2028 Strategic Development Plan—give Supreme Audit Institutions, including those with judicial competences, a coherent and increasingly user-friendly set of principles, standards, and guidance to drive high-quality, impactful public-sector audits worldwide. During the latest Strategic Development Plan (SDP) 2025–2028, the organization adopted five key initiatives (T - I - P - G - A): developing clear and consistent terminology of the IFPP, ensuring the clarity of the ISSAIs based on the results of the previous initiative, identifying and analyzing gaps and inconsistences in the INTOSAI Principles, developing a more effective approach to a structured communication around guidance documents and finally improving the accessibility to the pronouncements by making use of the opportunities provided by digitalization.

16.2.2 JURISAI (The International Organization of Supreme Audit Institutions with Jurisdictional Functions)

This organization is the principal forum for Supreme Audit Institutions with Jurisdictional powers, fostering collaboration, promoting shared principles, and strengthening a model of public audit rooted in the jurisdictional model of functioning. JURISAI, the International Organization of Supreme Audit Institutions with Jurisdictional Functions, is a specialized body uniting the distinct family of national audit institutions that operate as "Courts of Accounts." Formally established in 2024 as an evolution of a forum created in 2015, its history is rooted in the civil law tradition where public finance oversight is a judicial function. The nature of its member institutions is unique, possessing a dual authority: they not only conduct administrative and performance audits but also exercise judicial power. This allows their independent magistrates to issue legally binding judgments against officials for financial mismanagement, making accountability direct and enforceable. The core mission of JURISAI is to champion and strengthen this jurisdictional model of public audit on a global scale. This is achieved through several key objectives: fostering a rich dialogue and exchange of best practices via international congresses and seminars; developing and promoting shared principles and standards specifically tailored to the demands of judicial auditing; and, most critically, defending the institutional and individual independence of its members from any external pressure. By providing a unified platform, JURISAI empowers these courts to enhance their effectiveness and uphold their authority. Membership in JURISAI is exclusive to national Supreme Audit Institutions that are structured as courts and whose members are independent magistrates, ensuring a focused community of practice. The organization's ultimate significance lies in its role as a guardian of public trust. By ensuring that the management of state funds is not only reviewed but rigorously and impartially judged, JURISAI and its members reinforce the rule of law, provide a powerful mechanism against corruption, and affirm that those entrusted with the public purse are held to the highest legal and ethical standards.

16.2.3 International Association of Judges (IAJ)

The IAJ is a professional, nonpolitical international organization of national associations of judges founded in Salzburg in 1953 and has its headquarters in Rome. The association does not have any political or trade-union character, although its members are national association of judges from all member states (in total 93). The IAJ promotes the Rule of Law and the Independence of the Judiciary. The Association has consultative status with the United Nations (with specific reference to the International Labor Office and the U.N. Economic and Social Council) and with the Council of Europe. The Association has four Study Commissions, dealing respectively with judicial administration and status of the judiciary, civil law and procedure, criminal law and procedure, public and social law. These commissions are composed of delegates from national associations. They meet annually in the same location as the Central Council. Based on the national reports received, the members of the commissions study and discuss problems of common interest, pertaining to the justice process, on a comparative and transnational basis. The Association has four Regional Groups, the European Association of Judges (44 Countries); the African Group (20 Countries); the Iberoamerican Group (18 Countries); the Asian, North American and Oceanian Group (14 Countries).

According to its Statute the objectives of the IAJ are:

- *"To safeguard the independence of the judicial authority, as an essential requirement of the judicial function and guarantee of human rights and freedom.*
- *To safeguard the constitutional and moral standing of the judicial authority.*
- *To increase and perfect the knowledge and the understanding of Judges by putting them in touch with Judges of other countries, and by enabling them to become familiar with the nature and functioning of foreign organizations, with foreign laws and, in particular, with how those laws operate in practice.*
- *To study together judicial problems, whether these are of regional, national or universal interest, and to arrive at better solutions to them."*[22]

Those objectives are fulfilled through the organization of conferences, establishment of cultural relations, promoting and enhancing friendly relations between Judges and mutual assistance between national associations and groups.

The **International Association of Judges (IAJ) promotes** judicial independence and the rule of law through training programs, legal networking, and advocacy efforts at the United Nations and the Council of Europe.

[22]International Association of Judges, Constitution, 6th September 1953, Salzburg, available at: https://www.iaj-uim.org/statute/ (accessed 30.01.2024).

16.2.4 International Association of Tax Judges (IATJ)

The IATJ was established in 2010 in order to promote the exchange of views and experiences on matters submitted to Tax Judges around the work by collecting and sharing information on new legislation, best practices, procedures and policies on tax justice, reports on significant cases and analysis on tax jurisdictions.[23] The idea of the IATJ emerged during an Organization for the Economic Cooperation and Development (OECD) and International Fiscal Association (IFA) seminar for tax judges in 2009. The seat of the organization is in Amsterdam and 40+ jurisdictions are represented in the Association, across all continents. Its work is mainly performed by the General Assembly which meets annually and discusses the most current topics. The IATJ edits Commentaries published by the International Bureau of Fiscal Documentation (IBFD), which are regularly cited by national benches as comparative authority. The IATJ also drafts mode rules on issues of taxation, an example of which is the work that is underway regarding digital services taxation disputes.

16.2.5 International Association of Women Judges (IAWJ)

The International Association of Women Judges (IAWJ) founded in 1991 as a nonprofit, nongovernmental organization that brings together all kinds of judges from all levels of the judiciary worldwide united by their commitment to equal justice and the rule of law. Today, the IAWJ has grown into an organization with over 6500 judges in more than 100 countries and territories. The mission of the International Association of Women Judges is mainly focused on fighting discrimination against women and girls. IAWJ's mission is to reform judicial systems which fall short of ensuring women's equal access to justice, "promote and empower women judges who can help uproot gender bias, end discriminatory laws, advance gender-responsive courts, and promote human rights for all."[24] Its core mission is among other to: "*To promote women's access to the courts and advance women's rights to equal justice, To eliminate gender bias from judicial systems, To educate the public and the judiciary about human rights law and the role of the judiciary in implementing laws. which promote and protect the rights of women on an equal basis, To educate the public and policy makers on the importance of selecting judges who reflect the ideals of the rule of law, To study and educate the public about the role of the legal system in promoting and protecting the equal rights and interests of women and their role in society.*"[25]

[23] Statute of the International Association of Tax Judges, 01.01.2020, available at: https://iatj.net/Home/Statutes (accessed 30.01.2024).

[24] IAWJ Bylaws, Revised May 14, 2017, available at: https://www.iawj.org/content.aspx?page_id=22&club_id=882224&module_id=475491

[25] Ibid.

The activities of the IAWJ are truly noteworthy and are applied through a number of programs that are implemented at a local level by leveraging the engagement and leadership of women judges and include fight against sextortion, building enduring systems to end trafficking, strengthening judicial integrity, gender-based violence and LGBTI rights.

16.2.6 International Association of Refugee and Migration Judges (IARMJ)

The Association was founded in 1997 in Warsaw, Poland and is seated in Haaarlem, Netherlands. Building on the tremendous importance of the 1951 Geneva Convention relating the status of the refugee which has gained significant importance in recent years, the IARMJ seeks to enhance recognition "a. *that judges have a special role in determining issues involving refugee status, complementary protection (and rights and obligations arising from issues of migration law. In this role they are axiomatically required to consider core principles of the international rule of law including, international human rights law and practice, international humanitarian law and the concepts of human dignity and human security; b. that protection from being persecuted on account of race, religion, nationality, membership of a particular social group or political opinion is an individual right established under international law, and that the determination of refugee status and its cessation and exclusion should be subject to the international rule of law; c. that other international complementary protection issues, including non refoulement to the danger of arbitrary deprivation of life, torture, or cruel, inhuman or degrading treatment or punishment also involve rights protected by international human rights law and practices; d. that in this special role, judges often become involved in related issues, including: statelessness, deportation, extradition, detention, exceptional humanitarian circumstances, family unity and a wide ambit of international and domestic-based migration law and practices.*"[26] To achieve these ends, it pursues fostering judicial training, exchanging of information relevant, jurisprudence and legal framework. Individual judges or quasi-judicial officers are eligible to join the association; currently, more than 400 judges are members across four regional chapters (Europe, Americas, Africa, and Asia-Pacific). The association has issued valuable guidance papers (i.e., Guidance on Credibility Assessment in the EU) seeking to contribute to the need for continuing research on issues of common interest to achieve harmonious interpretations across jurisdictions. Another prime example of how the association employs judicial diplomacy is the convention of tripartite expert panels with representatives from the Court of Justice of the EU and

[26] Constitution of the International Association of Refugee and Migration Judges (IARMJ), Articles of Association, as endorsed by the General Meeting on 16 November 2018 and included in the formal notarial act of 7 March 2019, available at: https://www.iarmj.org/images/2019/constitution_2019/IARMJConstitution_English_Final_19March2019.pdf (accessed 30.01.2024).

the European Court of Human Rights to iron out doctrinal tensions. The IARMJ exemplifies how judges in a highly politicized, rapidly evolving field use specialist diplomacy to harmonize standards, build capacity, and inject judicial expertise into international policy debates.

16.3 Regional Level: Europe

16.3.1 Council of Europe (CoE)

There is significant work done within the context of the Council of Europe on the topic of justice. As an organization tasked with the promotion of human rights, rule of law and democracy the function and public service of justice lies at the heart of its mission. As witnessed by the Statute of the Council of Europe, the founders declared that the "pursuit of peace based upon justice and international co-operation is vital for the preservation of human society and civilization." Every aspiring member shall accept the principle of the rule of law and of the enjoyment by all persons within its jurisdiction of human rights and fundamental freedoms, to be admitted within the ranks of the organization.[27] To assist its operation on the matter there are a number of consultative bodies which will be examined below.

16.3.1.1 Commission for the Efficiency of Justice (CEPEJ)

One of the most important consultative bodies in the field of justice operating within the umbrella of the Council of Europe is the Commission for the efficiency of Justice (hereinafter CEPEJ). The CEPEJ aims to improve the efficiency and functioning of justice in the member States and the development of the implementation of the instruments adopted by the Council of Europe to this end. The Commission was established on 18 September 2002 with Resolution by the Committee of Ministers.[28] Its functions per its Statute include: "*a. identifying and developing indicators, collecting and analyzing quantitative and qualitative data, and defining measures and means of evaluation; b. drawing up reports, statistics, best practice surveys, guidelines, action plans, opinions and general comments; c. establishing links with research institutes and documentation and study centers; d. inviting to participate in its work, on a case-by-case basis, any qualified person, specialist or non-governmental organization active in its field of competence and capable of helping it in the fulfilment of its objectives, and holding hearings; e. creating networks of professionals involved in the justice area.*"[29]

[27] Statute of the Council of Europe, London 5.V.1949, European Treaty Series – No.1, available at: https://rm.coe.int/1680306052 (accessed 30.01.2024).

[28] Council of Europe, Committee of Ministers, Resolution Res (2002) 12 establishing the European Commission for the efficiency of justice (CEPEJ), Adopted on 18 September 2002.

[29] Ibid.

CEPEJ is composed of experts (including judges) from all 46 member states of the Council of Europe and observers states[30] and organizations[31] may be admitted to its work. CEPEJ according to its Rules of Procedure issues Recommendations on topical issues that pertain the functioning of the judicial systems of member states. The CEPEJ sets up several Working Groups that are tasked with the management of this process and the collecting of qualitative and quantitative data and discussions on focal areas.[32] Those discussions lead up to the drafting of recommendations, toolkits and databases on several areas including cyber-justice and artificial intelligence,[33] enforcement of judgments, mediation, quality of justice including digital transformation of the judiciary and the evaluation of judicial statistics. The concrete measures aim among other to optimize judicial time management and accompany the modernization efforts of judicial systems with the view to improve the quality of the public service of justice. The innovative measures that CEPEJ promotes include Guidelines on the role of the court-appointed experts in court-appointed experts in judicial proceedings;[34] on the creation of judicial maps to support access to justice, on the organization and accessibility of court premises, Checklist for promoting the quality of justice and of the courts,[35] Handbook for conducting satisfaction surveys aimed at court users.[36] Most notably at the request of the European Commission in the context of the rule of law annual report,[37] CEPEJ prepares a report on the judicial system of the Council of Europe member states.

[30] Holy See, Canada, Japan, Mexico, United States of America, Guatemala, Israel, Kazakhstan, Morocco, Tunisia.

[31] European Union, Council of the Bars and Law Societies of Europe (CCBE), Council of the Notariat of the European Union (CNUE), European Union of Recthspfleger and court Clerks (EUR), European networks of Council for the Judiciary (ENCJ), European Association of Judges EAJ), Association of European administrative judges (AEAJ), European judicial training Network (EJTN), European Expertise and Expert Institute (EEEI), International Union of Judicial Officers (UIHJ), Organization for Economic Co-Operation and Development (OECD), Magistrats européens pour la Démocratie et les Libertés (MEDEL), World Bank.

[32] CEPEJ – STAT is the database where the data are collected. It is a tool that facilitates the conduct of comparative studies that are led by the CEPEJ.

[33] The CEPEJ is supported in this field by the Artificial Intelligence Advisory Board (AIAB) provides expert advice on Artificial Intelligence (AI). It was established in 2022 to support the CEPEJ in monitoring the actual emergence of AI applications in the justice sector. Additional the European Cyberjustice Network (ECN) which operates in the same context allows the exchange of good practices supporting CEPEJ and its working groups.

[34] CEPEJ, Guidelines on the role of court-appointed experts in judicial proceedings of Council of Europe's Member States, 24th Plenary meeting, 11–12 December 2014, available at: https://rm.coe.int/168074827a (accessed 30.01.2024).

[35] CEPEJ, Checklist for promoting the quality of justice and the courts, adopted by the CEPEJ at its 11th plenary meeting, Strasbourg 2–3 July 2008, available at: https://rm.coe.int/european-commission-for-efficiencyof-justice-cepej-checklist-for-promo/16807475cf (accessed 20.01.2024).

[36] CEPEJ, Handbook for conducting satisfaction surveys aimed at court users in Council of Europe member states, adopted at the 28th plenary meeting of the CEPEJ on 7 December 2016, available at: https://rm.coe.int/168074816f (accessed 20.01.2024).

[37] An initiative that started in 2019.

CEPEJ is a pioneer in its work on issues relating to Artificial Intelligence (AI) and its use in judicial systems adopting in 2018 a Charter containing five basic principles upon which the use of AI can be integrated within the judicial systems of member states.[38] At the same time, it closely monitors that integration by mapping applications of AI in national justice systems.

The CEPEJ has played a crucial role in judicial diplomacy by developing guidelines for judicial efficiency and case management, influencing domestic legal reforms.

16.3.1.2 Superior Courts Network

The **Superior Courts Network** (SCN) aims to enrich the dialogue and foster the implementation of the **European Convention of Human Rights** (ECHR). The member states of the Council of Europe expressed their belief that the more faithful application of the Convention would be achieved through a more structured and effective dialogue between the Court and superior courts operating in their territories. The Declaration that was issued following the Brussels Conference[39] parties agreed to set-up "network facilitating information exchange on its judgements and decisions with national courts"[40] and has set up an IT portal accessed by all member courts. The Network began its operations in 2015 and now consists of 103 superior courts from 44 member States of the Council of Europe. It has opened its membership to accept as observer courts **the Court of Justice of the European Union** and the **Inter-American Court of Human Rights**.[41]

16.3.1.3 Consultative Council of European Judges (CCJE)

The CCJE is an advisory body of the Council of Europe on issues relating to the independence, impartiality and competence of judges and is exclusively composed by judges acting on their personal capacity, a unique feat at an international level. It aims to contribute to the implementation of the **Framework Global Action Plan for Judges in Europe** adopted by the Committee of Ministers in 2001. Particularly the CCJE aims to promote the implementation the right contained in article 6 of the

[38] See European Commission for the Efficiency of Justice (CEPEJ), European Ethical Charter on the Use of Artificial Intelligence in Judicial Systems and their environment, Adopted at the 31st plenary meeting of the CEPEJ, Strasbourg 3–4 December 2018, available at: https://rm.coe.int/ethical-charter-en-for-publication-4-december-2018/16808f699c (accessed 31.01.2024).

[39] High Level Conferences on the reform of the Convention system are being held at the initiative of the Chairmanship of the Committee of Ministers of the CoE on a regular basis in order to address potential shortcomings in the system.

[40] High-level Conference on the "Implementation of the European Convention on Human Rights, our shared responsibility", Brussels Declaration, 27 March 2015, available at: https://www.echr.coe.int/documents/d/echr/Brussels_Declaration_ENG (accessed 31.01.2024).

[41] Message from President O'Leary, Superior Courts Network (SCN), 30.01.2023, available: https://www.echr.coe.int/documents/d/echr/scn_message_president_oleary_eng?download=true (accessed 31.01.2024).

ECHR and more specifically the right to an independent and impartial court. Special focus is given on the status of judges and its influence on the quality of the justice system, the rule of law and the promotion and protection of human rights and fundamental freedoms. To fulfill its mission the CCJEU issues Opinions towards the Committee of Ministers and the member states. Those Opinions include the following:

- Opinion No. 26 (2023) "Moving forward: the use of assistive technology in the judiciary"
- Opinion No. 25 (2022) on freedom of expression of judges
- Opinion No. 24 (2021) on the evolution of the Councils for the Judiciary and their role in independent and impartial judicial systems
- Opinion No. 23 (2020) on the role of associations of judges in supporting judicial independence
- Opinion No. 22 (2019) on the role of judicial assistants
- Opinion No. 21 (2018) preventing corruption among judges
- Opinion No. 20 (2017) on the role of courts with respect to the uniform application of the law
- Opinion No. 19 (2016) on the role of court presidents
- Opinion No. 18 (2015) on the position of the judiciary and its relation with the other powers of state in a modern democracy
- Opinion No. 17 (2014) on the evaluation of judges' work, the quality of justice and respect for judicial independence
- Opinion No. 16 (2013) on the relations between judges and lawyers
- Opinion No. 15 (2012) on the specialization of judges
- Opinion No. 14 (2011) on justice and information technologies (IT)
- Opinion No. 13 (2010) on the role of judges in the enforcement of judicial decisions
- Opinion No. 12 (2009) on the relations between judges and prosecutors in a democratic society
- Opinion No. 11 (2008) on "the quality of judicial decisions"
- Opinion No. 10 (2007) on "Council for the Judiciary in the service of society"
- Opinion No. 9 (2006) on "the role of national judges in ensuring an effective application of international and European law"
- Opinion No. 8 (2006) on "the role of judges in the protection of the rule of law and human"
- Opinion No. 7 (2005) on "justice and society".
- Opinion No. 6 (2004) on fair trial with a reasonable time
- Opinion No. 5 (2003) on the law and practice of judicial appointments to the European court of human rights
- Opinion No. 4 (2003) on training for judges
- Opinion No. 3 (2002) on ethics and liability of judges
- Opinion No. 2 (2001) on the funding and management of courts
- Opinion No. 1 (2001) on standards concerning the independence of the judiciary and the irremovability of judges

The CCJE is particularly instructed to ensure the overall preservation and further promotion of relevant European standards related to the rule of law by elaborating opinions and other texts, advise the Committee of Ministers on issues pertinent to the independence, impartiality and competence of judges, as well as their status, career and effective exercise of judicial profession, hold exchanges with national counterparts, take due account of the following mainstreamed perspectives in the performance of its tasks: gender, youth, children's rights, rights of persons with disabilities, and Roma and Traveller issues, where relevant, contribute to building cohesive societies and to strengthening the role and meaningful participation of civil society in its work, contribute to the achievement of, and review progress towards, the UN 2030 Agenda for Sustainable Development, in particular with regards to Goal 5: Gender Equality and Goal 16: Peace, Justice and Strong institutions.

16.3.1.4 Consultative Council of European Judges (CCJE)

In little more than a decade, the World Conference on Constitutional Justice (WCCJ) has become the principal global forum through which constitutional and supreme courts conduct judicial diplomacy—the projection of authority, exchange of ideas, and coordination of action across borders by judges themselves rather than by executives or legislatures. By July 2025, the network comprised 122 courts and councils spread over every continent, giving it near universal reach within the community of constitutional adjudicators. The WCCJ illustrates how courts employ soft power: they neither issue binding orders to other states nor negotiate treaties, yet their collective declarations, peer support, and jurisprudential dialogue shape the behavior of governments and the evolution of constitutional norms. Judicial demand for a permanent dialogue platform crystallized during the First World Conference of Constitutional Courts in Cape Town (23–24 January 2009) under the theme "Influential Constitutional Justice: Its Influence on Society." Delegates agreed that occasional meetings were insufficient for the mounting transnational challenges—terrorism, economic crises, and human rights expansion—facing constitutional justice worldwide. Two years later, at Rio de Janeiro (2011), participants adopted a draft Statute that entered into force on 23 May 2011, formally creating the WCCJ as a standing organization. The Venice Commission of the Council of Europe was invited to host the permanent secretariat. Article 1 of the Statute defines the WCCJ's overarching purpose: "to promote constitutional justice—understood as constitutional review including human rights case law—through global judicial dialogue." Implementing this mandate revolves around three mutually reinforcing objectives: 1. Facilitating dialogue by convening triennial congresses and thematic workshops; 2. Fostering peer support for courts under political pressure, using public statements and private networks; and 3. Disseminating jurisprudence via databases such as CODICES, thus encouraging comparative reasoning and convergence of standards. The WCCJ is run by three main organs: (a) General Assembly where all member courts participate, (b) Bureau composed of chairs of ten regional/linguistic groups (e.g., CCJA for Africa, Ibero American Summit, and Conference of European Constitutional Courts) plus the host courts of the last and next congress, and (c) Secretariat housed in the Venice Commission, providing administrative support. With 122 courts by 2025 (latest entrants: the Supreme Court of the Maldives and the Federal Supreme Court of Ethiopia), the WCCJ's membership mirrors the geographic and legal system diversity of the United Nations itself. Accession is open to any court exercising constitutional jurisdiction, either directly or via one of the ten recognized regional groupings. Suspension is possible for "flagrant violations" of WCCJ principles (Statute Art. 8), although it has never been invoked—an indicator of both the peer pressure power and the political sensitivity surrounding expulsion.

16.3.1.5 Consultative Council of European Prosecutors (CCPE)

Created by the Committee of Ministers in 2005, this consultative body is comprised by high level prosecutors of all member States of the Council of Europe (all 46 plus observers) and is tasked to prepare opinions for the Committee of Ministers on issues related to the prosecution service, the role of public prosecution in the criminal justice system and to collect information about the functioning of prosecution services in Europe. Its creation mirrors the Consultative Council of European Judges along which it comprises the twin-pillar model. Its mission is in keeping with the implementation of Recommendation Rec (2000) 19 on the Role of Public Prosecution in the Criminal Justice System with the aim of developing common political and judicial instruments relating to the functioning and professional activities of prosecutors.[42] The CCPE adopts opinions, which are deeply routed in the Venice Commission Opinions and the work of GRECO, on topical issues regarding criminal justice and how prosecution should function in a democratic state under the rule of law the most prominent of which are the following:

- Opinion No. 19 (2024) Managing prosecution services to ensure their independence and impartiality
- Opinion No. 18 (2023) on councils of prosecutors as key bodies of prosecutorial self-governance
- Opinion No. 17 (2022) on the role of prosecutors in the protection of the environment
- Opinion No. 16 (2021) on implications of the decisions of international courts and treaty bodies as regards the practical independence of prosecutors
- Opinion No. 15 (2020) on the role of prosecutors in emergency situations, in particular when facing a pandemic
- Opinion No. 14 (2019) on the role of prosecutors in fighting corruption and related economic and financial crime
- Opinion No. 13 (2018) Independence, accountability and ethics of prosecutors
- Opinion No. 12 (2017) the role of prosecutors in relation to the rights of victims and witnesses in criminal proceedings

[42]Committee of Ministers, The Role of Public Prosecution in the Criminal Justice System, Recommendation Rec (2000) 19, adopted by the Committee of Ministers of the Council of Europe on 6 October 2000 and explanatory Memorandum, available at: https://rm.coe.int/CoERMPublicCommonSearchServices/DisplayDCTMContent?documentId=09000016804be55a (accessed 16.02.2024).

- Opinion No. 11 (2016) the quality and efficiency of the work of prosecutors, including hen fighting terrorism and serious and organized crime
- Opinion No. 10 (2015) the role of prosecutors in criminal investigations
- Opinion No. 9 (2014) European norms and principles concerning prosecutors
- Opinion No. 8 (2013) Relations between prosecutors and the media
- Opinion No. 7 (2012) The management of the means of prosecution services
- Opinion No. 6 (2011) The relationship between prosecutors and the prison administration
- Opinion No. 5 (2010) Public prosecution and juvenile justice
- Opinion No. 4 (2009) The relations between judges and prosecutors
- Opinion No. 3 (2008) The role of prosecution services outside the criminal law field
- Opinion No. 2 (2008) Alternatives to prosecution
- Opinion No. 1 (2007) Ways of improving international cooperation in the criminal justice field[43]

16.3.2 Self-Standing Associations

16.3.2.1 Association of European Administrative Judges (AEAJ)

The Association of European Administrative Judges (AEAJ) was founded in 2000. Its membership comprises national associations, representing administrative judges from the Member States of the European Union and the Council of Europe and individual members, being administrative judges from those countries in which such associations do not exist. The basis of the Association lies in different initiatives, followed by a meeting in October 1998 at the Academy of European Law (ERA) in Trier, which was devoted to comparative studies on the respective characteristics of administrative law in the respective Member States of the EU. The aim laid down in its Statute was to encourage the legal protection of the individual against public violence as well as the lawfulness of administrative actions and thus contribute to strengthening freedom and justice in Europe. On 25 March 2000, the representatives of Germany, Finland, France, Greece, Italy, and Austria founded the AEAJ as an international apex organization under German law. To date, national associations of administrative judges from 19 European countries have joined the Association. In addition, there are individual members from 15 other European countries, more than 4000 administrative judges are represented in the association. Its main goal is to promote effective legal redress against public authorities, foster legality of administrative action, strengthen the official position of administrative judges in Europe, and defend their interests vis-a-vis EU and the Council of Europe. Main organs are the General Assembly and the Board (President plus up to 12 members). The AEAJ

---

[43] CCPE, Opinions of the Consultative Council of European Prosecutors (CCPE), Collection of Opinions Nos. 1 to 18, (2007 – 2023), available at: https://rm.coe.int/ccpe-opinions-no-1-no-17-en-website-/1680a94b16 (accessed 30.01.2024).

main work is organized by four permanent working groups on (a) Independence & Efficiency, (b) Asylum & Migration, (c) Environmental Law, and (d) Taxation. The association is consulted by the Consultative Council of European Judges and has observer rights on Consultative Council of European Prosecutors; it cooperates regularly with the European Judicial Training Network and the ERA. Since 2021, a Rule of Law Officer coordinates rapid statements when member states threaten administrative court autonomy. The AEAJ wields significant soft power—often feeding doctrinal innovations in European and national courts through its working structures and publications.

16.3.2.2 Magistrats Européens pour la Démocratie et les Libertés (MEDEL)

The association was founded in June 1985 in Strasbourg and is seated in Paris by eight professional organizations (trade unions or associations) of judges and prosecutors. After the end of Cold War, MEDEL was strongly committed to supporting the establishment of independent judicial institutions that respect the rule of law in the new democracies that emerged in Eastern Europe. On this occasion, the association gradually expanded, welcoming new organizations of judges and prosecutors from Eastern and Southern Europe. The mission of the association is to guarantee the independence of the judiciary, the promotion of rule of law and the construction of a European judicial area based on the guarantee of fundamental rights, observing the situation in the different states. The associations have been contributing to the work of the Council of Europe, notably the drafting of the European Charter of Judges and holds the status of a consultative NGO with the Council of Europe.[44] In addition, MEDEL has gradually become a key player in the legal and judicial debate in the European area. Having contributed to the adoption of texts such as the European Charter of Judges or the recommendations of the Council of Europe on justice and the creation of new institutions such as the Consultative Council of European Judges and the Consultative Council of European Prosecutors, MEDEL has been a consultative NGO with the Council of Europe since 6 March 1995. The aims of the association are to promote the dialogue between judges from different countries in order to promote European integration, promotion and implementation of the civil, political and social rights necessary in a democratic society, independence of the judiciary, democratization of the judiciary, the freedom of assembly, association and expression of judges, transparency of the public judicial service, promotion of a democratic legal culture, defense of the rights of minorities, immigrants and the most disadvantaged.[45] MEDEL currently brings together

[44]The status of consultative NGOs is regulated by Resolution CM/Res (2016)3 by the Committee of Ministers, Participatory status for international nongovernmental organizations with the Council of Europe, 6 July 2016, available at: https://search.coe.int/cm/Pages/result_details.aspx?ObjectId=090000168068824c (accessed 30.01.2024).

[45]MEDEL, Statute, adopted in Strasbourg on 15 June 1985, available at: https://medelnet.eu/wp-content/uploads/2023/06/Statuts-MEDEL-2022-English.pdf (accessed 30.01.2024).

23 judge and prosecutor organizations, representing 18,000 judges from 16 European countries.

16.3.2.3 European Judicial Training Network (EJTN)

Founded in 2000 and registered in Brussels with the vision to bring together judicial training institutions, developing and implementing training and exchange activities for members of the European judiciary. These activities cover both initial and continuous training, and are delivered in close cooperation with our Members, Associate Members, Observers and Partners. The EJTN's mandate is to help build a genuine European area of justice and to promoted knowledge of legal systems and this involves analyzing training needs, designing programs and methods for collaborative training, developing exchanges, and disseminating experiences in the field of judicial training, coordinating programs and providing training expertise and know-how.

The EJTN is not formally a judicial union or association, hence it works closely with the European Commission (EC) and nearly 40 EU national judicial bodies (schools for the judiciary) which are its members, in organizing trainings, seminars, conferences, and exchanges for judges. Particularly according to the articles of association the objectives of the EJTN are the analysis and identification of the training needs of the judiciaries of member states, the exchange and dissemination of experience in the field of judicial training, the design of programs and methods for collaborative training, in particular using new technology, coordination of members' programs and activities in matters relating to European law and those which concern initiatives of the European Union, in collaboration with the Lisbon Network of the Council of Europe (where appropriate) to provide expertise and know-how to European, and other national and international institutions in order to promote the ideals inherent in an area of Freedom, Security and Justice, the promotion and advancement of the legal systems of candidate countries seeking accession to the European Union, the promotion of activities that are aimed at comparing and exchange of judicial practice, understanding of the judicial systems of Member States of the European Union, understanding of the means of judicial cooperation with the European Union, language skills, development of judicial skills and of those who are appointed to act as trainers within member states.[46] The European Judicial Training Network (EJTN) facilitates judicial exchanges among EU member states, helping judges understand different legal systems. These exchanges foster a shared legal culture and promote greater judicial cooperation. The IAJ's conferences offer judges a platform to discuss emerging legal trends, thereby contributing to the creation of a common legal understanding across borders.

[46] Reseau Européen de Formation Judiciaire – European Judicial Training Network, Amended by the General Assembly in Bucharest on 27–28 June 2019, available at: https://portal.ejtn.eu/Documents/Articles%20of%20Association%20and%20Rules%20of%20Procedure/AoA_EN.pdf (accessed 30.01.2024).

16.3.2.4 Association of European Competition Law Judges (AELCJ)[47]

The AECLJ is a group of judges (non-profit organization under Luxembourgish law—*association sans but lucratif*) situated at the Cour Supérieure de Justice of Luxembourg. The association aims to provide a forum where judges can exchange experiences, foster consistent application of EU & national competition law, organize trainings, run databases (EUCOJUD—open database of national competition-law judgements run in cooperation with the Luxembourg Centre for European Law—LCEL of the University of Luxembourg), and contribute to policymaking, who hear cases in their courts involving national and European competition law. The main aim of the Association is to promote policy and law issues throughout the respective judiciaries. The main purpose of the AECLJ is to provide a forum for the exchange of knowledge and experience in the field of competition law among the judiciary across the European Union and elsewhere in Europe thereby promoting a coherency and consistency of approach, particularly in the context of the modernization of the application of Articles 101 and 102 TFEU under EC Regulation 1/2003[48] and national implementing provisions.

16.3.2.5 European Association of Judges for Mediation—Groupement Européen des Magistrats pour la Médiation (GEMME)

GEMME is a French non-profit association with the purpose of bringing together judges wishing to utilize alternative dispute resolution methods (ADR) and "consider that effective and peace inducing justice involves promotion and development of these alternative methods, especially judicial mediation."[49] It was founded in 2003 with headquarters at Cour de Cassation de la République Francaise (Court of Cassation of the French Republic). It enlists around 800 judges, magistrates, and allied mediation professionals drawn from most European countries. There are also 17 fully-constituted sections (Belgium, Bulgaria, Croatia, France, Germany, Greece, Hungary, Ireland, Italy, Netherlands, Poland, Portugal, Romania, Spain, Switzerland, and the United Kingdom) and there national sections being currently formed (Finland, Latvia, Lithuania, Luxembourg, Slovakia, Sweden, and Ukraine). GEMME runs workshops for judges and clerks and partners often with EJTN and national schools for the judiciary. The association is governed by a Board of Directors composed of at least five members elected by the General Assembly, to which will be added a member appointed by each national section. The aims of the Association are "*to promote within each NMember State of the Union, as well as in the EFTA (European Free Trade Association-EFTA), the association of judges working to support mediation for the purpose of strengthening and improving the*

[47] More information can be obtained here: https://www.aeclj.com/

[48] Council Regulation (EC) No 1/2003 of December 2002 on the implementation of the rules on competition laid down in Articles 81 and 82 of the Treaty, available at: https://eur-lex.europa.eu/legal-content/EN/TXT/?uri=celex%3A32003R0001 (accessed 30.01.2024).

[49] Statute of the European Judges Group for Mediation (GEMME) as amended May 23, 2008, available at: https://gemmeeurope.org/en/about-us#etats (accessed 30.01.2024).

practice of mediation. - to promote the exchange of information within each member State of the Union and the EFTA concerning practices and experience in the area of mediation, conciliation or any other alternative method of dispute resolution. - to contribute to the development of mediation and alternative methods of dispute resolution, by participating in conferences and activities in the area of European institutions and those of EFTA, working to promote teaching of mediation and alternative methods of dispute resolution in the course of legal studies and training of judges and lawyers, familiarizing professionals and citizens with mediation and participating in defining training of collaborating mediators, - to use any means to assist judges with their individual steps to support mediation and encourage training for the purpose of relevant and effective practice of it, as for any other alternative method of dispute resolution that is legally permitted."[50]

16.3.2.6 EU Forum of Judges for the Environment (EUFJE)

The European Union Forum of Judges for the Environment (EUFJE) was created in Paris on May 2003, and is seated in Bruxelles as an international non-profit organization under Belgian law. It aims to raise awareness of judges of the key role of the judicial function in effectiveness of sustainable development and strengthen the effective application of European and international environmental law through networking, judicial training, comparative research, and policy dialogue. EUFJE members can be judges or courts of all jurisdictions (administrative, criminal, and civil) and all levels that are either experienced or interested in handling environmental cases. The Forum enumerates almost 150 members (judges and courts) in 43 countries. The EUFJE envisions to organize and offer trainings in the areas of environmental law and sustainable development, to exchange practices on the application of national, European, and international environmental law and to act as a platform for judicial networking, while sharing valuable consolidated input with policy-makers (i.e., European Commission).[51]

16.4 Conclusion

Judicial diplomacy holds great potential in strengthening the rule of law and improving the situation of the justice system in legal order that are need of reform. In post-conflict societies, such as those in the Balkans or Africa, judicial diplomacy has played a pivotal role in fostering judicial reforms and promoting the rule of law. In Bosnia and Herzegovina, the establishment of a special War Crimes Chamber within the state court involved both international and national judges working side-by-side. The international judges did not just adjudicate complex war crimes cases; they mentored their Bosnian colleagues in the intricacies of international

[50] Ibid article 2 par. 8.

[51] Forum des Juges de l'Union Europeene pour l'environnement, status coordonnées 14 Septembre 2019, available at: https://eufje.org/images/DocDivers/Bylaws2019.pdf (accessed 30.01.2024).

humanitarian law. This direct partnership was crucial for building local capacity, transferring knowledge, and ultimately enabling the domestic system to take full ownership of these sensitive prosecutions, thereby strengthening its legitimacy. The rise of constitutionalism across many African nations has been bolstered by judicial dialogue. Judges from countries like Kenya, Nigeria, and Ghana frequently engage with each other and with institutions like the South African Constitutional Court, which is globally renowned for its jurisprudence on socio-economic rights and transformative constitutionalism. This exchange has emboldened courts to make landmark rulings on electoral integrity, checks on presidential power, and fundamental human rights. Judicial diplomacy is not just a responsibility but an opportunity for judges to shape global legal standards, contribute to international legal frameworks, and uphold the rule of law on a global scale. As legal norms evolve in a transnational context, judges must actively engage in diplomacy to ensure the judiciary remains a pillar of democracy and justice. While the concept of judicial diplomacy sounds abstract, judicial diplomacy operates through several concrete channels: Judicial Networks and Associations: Organizations like the International Association of Judges (IAJ), the European Network of Councils for the Judiciary (ENCJ), or regional bodies serve as formal platforms. Through conferences, working groups, and publications, they allow judges to discuss common challenges, from court administration and digitalization to upholding judicial independence against political pressure. Bilateral and Multilateral Exchanges: These are often targeted programs where judges from an established judiciary visit or host judges from a system undergoing reform. For example, a senior German constitutional judge might spend time with their counterpart in a nascent democracy to share experiences on electoral law or human rights jurisprudence. These exchanges are often facilitated by international bodies like the UN, the Council of Europe (through its Venice Commission), or national development agencies. Jurisprudential Dialogue: This is a more subtle, yet powerful, form of diplomacy. When a high court in one country cites a landmark ruling from another country's court in its own decision, it is engaging in a dialogue. The Supreme Court of India might reference a decision from the South African Constitutional Court on social rights, or a Canadian court might look to UK precedents on privacy law. This cross-pollination of legal reasoning helps build a transnational consensus on fundamental principles. Contribution to "Soft Law": Judges play a key role in drafting and promoting non-binding international standards that shape judicial conduct globally. The Bangalore Principles of Judicial Conduct, for instance, were developed through extensive consultation among judges worldwide and have become a global benchmark for judicial ethics, even in countries that have not formally adopted them.

Senior District Judge Jed. S Rakoff once wrote very bluntly that "judges have to be neutral, but they don't have to be eunuchs." Despite the evident shock value of such a statement it indeed describes a valuable truth that is usually overlooked. The stance and position of a judge is valuable and much desired in a democratic society and his extrajudicial activities that unify and bring together different legal cultures and promote legal integration are of irreplicable value. A judge cannot be represented by any other than him/herself. Any interference in their work would be inappropriate, thus international relations on their field is carried by judges and magistrates as we attempted to illustrate above.

Judges need to self-restrict act with propriety and courtesy and live by example, they shall refrain from giving in the temptation to set broad policy, nonetheless they shall not turn a blind eye to societal calls, political advancements, both national and global and strive to focus on reimagining the position of justice within the ever-changing scenery. Serving justice is a responsibility with significant *gravitas* and a soul-searching task that necessitates trained reflexes. Envisioning justice in today's globalized scenery is inevitably an exertion that lacks borders as legal norms emerge in multiple levels and from different institutional actors. In conclusion judges shall be by default able to act as delegates of national judicial systems on their personal and professional capacity to benefit their service with the rich experience that the transnational confluence births, while guarding more effectively their independence and the rule of law against emerging threats.

As global legal challenges evolve, judicial diplomacy will play an increasingly vital role in addressing issues such as cybersecurity, AI governance, and transnational crime. Future efforts should focus on enhancing judicial networks, fostering digital judicial diplomacy, and ensuring judicial independence remains protected from undue political influence.

Emmanouil Kalaintzis is a Junior Judge at the Hellenic Court of Audit (Supreme Financial Court of Greece), a graduate of the National School of the Judiciary. He graduated from the Law School of the Aristotle University of Thessaloniki and holds three postgraduate degrees from the KU Leuven (Public European and Public International Law), the International Hellenic University (European and Transnational Commercial Law and Arbitration, Mediation and Energy Law) and the Democritus University of Thrace (Public International Law). He worked for 6 years in the European Parliament as a policy advisor and was an Expert at the European Economic and Social Committee. He was a Research Associate of the UNESCO Chair for Active Citizenship and Solidarity at the University of Macedonia for several years. He has published in Greek and foreign journals on issues of public international and European law.

Parliamentary Diplomacy: The Role of the Parliamentary Assembly of the Mediterranean

17

Stelio Campanale

Abstract

Parliamentary diplomacy is an increasingly important dimension of international affairs, reflecting a shift in how nations engage in diplomacy. Distinct from traditional diplomacy, which is typically carried out by government executives and foreign ministries, parliamentary diplomacy is defined as "the international relations of legislatures and legislators, conducted bilaterally and through multilateral forums."

17.1 Introduction

Parliamentary diplomacy is an increasingly important dimension of international affairs, reflecting a shift in how nations engage in diplomacy. Distinct from traditional diplomacy, which is typically carried out by government executives and foreign ministries, parliamentary diplomacy is defined as "the international relations of legislatures and legislators, conducted bilaterally and through multilateral forums." In this regard, the Parliamentary Assembly of the Mediterranean (PAM), established in 2005, emerges as a notable case study of regional parliamentary

---

Pursuant to information directly released to the author by PAM.

S. Campanale (✉)
International Law, Diplomatic and Consular Law and of International Trade Law, Libera Università Mediterranea-LUM Giuseppe Degennaro, Bari, Italy

Universiteti Katolik "Zoja e KëshillittëMirë", Tirana, Albania
e-mail: scampanale@campanalelawfirm.com

P. Naskou-Perraki (ed.), *Contemporary Diplomatic and Consular Relations*,
https://doi.org/10.1007/978-3-031-99243-8_17

diplomacy whereby the parliaments and parliamentarians of the Euro-Mediterranean and Gulf regions convene on the same platform to address regional challenges by engaging in regular exchanges and promoting cooperation.

17.2 Parliamentary Diplomacy: An Overview

17.2.1 The Role, Functions, and Impact of Parliamentary Diplomacy

Parliamentary diplomacy enables national legislative bodies to foster international cooperation by establishing and further strengthening dialogue among legislators from different nations. Through "inter-parliamentary assemblies," legislators engage in discussions and negotiations to address transnational issues, and pinpoint areas for collaboration.

In this regard, members of democratically elected parliament play a unique role in forming people-to-people connections, engaging with civil society organizations, and building relationships that may help bridge cultural and ideological divides. These connections are particularly valuable in conflict-prone regions, where parliamentary diplomacy is proven to bypass traditional avenues of diplomacy to help reduce tensions and foster peace-building initiatives. Through participation in international parliamentary organizations and assemblies, parliamentarians can additionally influence international policies, contribute to conflict resolution, and enhance regional cooperation.

Besides legislators, this path of diplomacy also allows for dialogue and negotiation through inter-parliamentary networks, aiming to promote mutual understanding and cooperation on a wide range of topics. As such, parliamentary diplomacy differs considerably from traditional diplomacy by operating with a "*soft power*" mechanism, focusing on dialogue, and relationship-building.

Predictably, parliamentary diplomacy is also a key driver in facilitating the harmonization of national laws and policies in response to global challenges. Issues ranging from international peace and security, climate change, to migration, human rights, and public health, often require coordinated international action and shared legislative frameworks. With parliamentary diplomacy, legislative bodies are able to share best practices, and collectively respond to pressing global challenges. Additionally, this type of diplomacy provides a platform for parliamentarians to advocate for internationally recognized norms and standards, advancing human rights, environmental sustainability, and other fundamental values.

Ultimately, the distinguishing factor of parliamentary diplomacy is not only its unique ability to complement traditional state-driven diplomacy, but also to bypass it, when necessary. Owing to the political immunities enjoyed by parliamentarians in carrying out their national duties and responsibilities, parliamentary diplomacy enables governments to utilize a separate path of diplomatic engagement that is not bound by national foreign policy doctrines. In other words, enabling parliamentarians to communicate across national boundaries effectively makes parliamentary diplomacy an alternative path to build trust, create mutual understanding, and address complex issues that may be difficult to resolve through executive-level diplomacy alone. This approach allows for greater inclusivity, as parliamentarians often represent a diverse spectrum of political and cultural perspectives, which can enhance the depth of diplomatic discussions. Furthermore, because parliamentary diplomacy operates outside executive government channels, it can achieve progress in areas where official negotiations have stalled.

17.3 Early Mediterranean Parliamentary Cooperation and the Founding of PAM

The roots of Mediterranean Parliamentary cooperation can be traced back to 1972, when Italian Prime Minister, Aldo Moro, proposed the integration of issues related to the Mediterranean into the broader context of the Conference on Security and Cooperation in Europe (CSCE). However, the initiative, while significant, initially received limited traction, as the Mediterranean dimension remained a secondary concern compared to broader European security discussions. The Helsinki Final Act of 1975 acknowledged Mediterranean considerations, yet they were largely marginalized, as the basin was ultimately not considered as a region, but described rather as the "Southern Flank" of the European continent.

A critical turning point occurred in 1990, when Italian and Spanish representatives put forth a proposal for the establishment of a Conference on Security and Cooperation in the Mediterranean and Middle East (CSCM). Although this initiative did not reach fruition in its original intergovernmental form, it sparked a series of parliamentary initiatives facilitated by the Inter-Parliamentary Union (IPU). This process culminated in four foundational conferences held between 1992 and 2005, which served as important steps toward more structured parliamentary cooperation in the region. These conferences highlighted the necessity for a collaborative framework that could address the unique geopolitical and socio-economic challenges facing Mediterranean countries.

The pressing need for sustained dialogue among Mediterranean nations ultimately led to the establishment of a permanent Parliamentary Assembly, solidifying regional cooperation on critical issues of peace, security, and development. This formalization was marked by the inaugural Plenary Session of the Parliamentary Assembly of the Mediterranean (PAM) in Amman in 2006, representing a historic step towards institutionalized parliamentary diplomacy in the region.

Unlike previous intermittent meetings, PAM arose directly from the determination and commitment of Mediterranean Parliaments to create a continuous, structured platform for collaboration. This commitment was fueled by a shared vision, namely, to foster an inclusive institution where Mediterranean nations could collectively address shared challenges, bridge cultural and political divides, and promote stability throughout the region.

17.4 PAM Institutional Architecture and Scope of Activities

PAM is the center of excellence for regional parliamentary diplomacy, and a unique forum whose membership is open to Euro-Mediterranean and Gulf countries, which are represented on equal footing. Each national delegation has up to five members with equal voting rights and decision-making powers.

This is also reflected in the composition of the Bureau and the alternating Presidency. The PAM Political Bureau is the executive body of the Organization. The President of the Assembly heads the meetings and may oversee liaison missions. Reflecting the Assembly's inclusivity and geographic equality, the eight elected Bureau members are equally divided between the North and the South. The presidency is rotating between both shore and the eight members are elected by the Assembly for a two-year rotating term.

PAM conducts the bulk of its work within three Standing Committees: (1) Political and Security-Related Cooperation; (2) Economic, Social, and Environmental Cooperation; and (3) Dialogue among Civilizations and Human Rights. The Assembly convenes annually in a Plenary Session. It may also set up Working Groups, ad-hoc Committees or Special Task Forces to tackle a particular topic (i.e., Counter-Terrorism, Confidence Building, Peace Support, Conflict Resolution, Middle East Peace Process, Mass Migration, Free Trade and Investments, Economic Integration, Climate Change, Energy, Human Rights, Dialogue of Civilizations, Gender issues).

Some of the operational and coordination instruments of PAM in these areas are initiatives such as the Economic Panel on Trade and Investments, the Academic Platform and the PAM Women Parliamentary Forum. However, central to these efforts are field missions, which are considered a key mediation mechanism to facilitate conflict resolution initiatives, promoting dialogue, and implementing trust-building measures. This proactive approach underscores the Assembly's commitment to fostering peace and stability in the Mediterranean and Gulf regions.

Furthermore, the Assembly regularly deploys Electoral Observation Missions to monitor elections in its Member States, and beyond, by invitation. Although the reports and resolutions adopted by PAM are not legally binding per se, they are a powerful soft diplomacy tool when dealing with parliaments, governments and civil society in the region. The PAM Secretariat is also entrusted with the parliamentary dimension of the 5+5 Western Mediterranean Forum and the MEDCOP.

Recently, PAM has also established the Permanent Parliamentary Observatory on AI and Emerging Technologies, with the aim to provide international community with state-of-the-art information on trends, developments, guiding principles and threats to democratic systems.

The international Secretariat, an autonomous, independent and decentralized body of the Assembly, assists and advises PAM President, PAM Bureau and all members in the execution of their mandate and is also responsible for the follow-up on the decisions taken by the Assembly providing coordination, assistance and support to the work of the Committees and all other bodies established under PAM. The Secretariat is led by the Secretary General, who is assisted by international and local staff, to coordinate and ensure the effective and timely execution of the activities of the Assembly. PAM Secretariat is also held responsible for interacting with national delegations, as well as with regional and international bodies sharing an interest in the PAM region. It has the mandate to stimulate the activities of the Assembly. Furthermore, it coordinates the awarding of the PAM Prize dedicated to individuals or institutions whose work is considered of great value for the PAM region.

PAM has a regional office in Naples, Italy, an International Study center, in the Republic of San Marino, and diplomatic representations in Geneva, New York and Vienna, as well as in Jerusalem, Bucharest, and Cairo.

PAM regularly organizes internship programs for university students from across the world in order for them to familiarize themselves with international affairs and the use of parliamentary diplomacy as an instrument to support peace, security, and regional integration.

17.5 Legislative Harmonization and International Cooperation

PAM emphasizes the implementation of international standards, ensuring that national legislation of its Member States aligns with United Nations Resolutions, the UN Charter and regional agreements. This alignment not only reinforces Member States' commitments to international norms but also fosters cooperation and best practices across the region.

In this regard, since its inception, the Parliamentary Assembly of the Mediterranean (PAM) has developed a very close, constructive, and fruitful cooperation with the United Nations system. On 16 December 2009, the UN General Assembly adopted resolution A/64/567, thereby granting PAM the Observer Status. Since then, PAM participates annually in the High-level Segment of the UNGA, at the UNHQ in New York.

On the issue of regional conflicts, PAM works with and in support of the UN and its specialized agencies, to ensure an effective cooperation among main stakeholders, at the executive level, to work towards peace and reconciliation. PAM also assists the efforts of the international community in facilitating the delivery of humanitarian aid and the negotiation of truces. In fact, the role of parliaments is crucial, especially when relations at the governmental level are absent or temporary suspended. Today, PAM is one of the very few international organizations, where, through the instrument of parliamentary diplomacy, politicians, and MPs from, inter alia, Israel, Palestine, Türkiye, Cyprus, Lebanon, and Syria continue to meet around the same table, with equal right, to openly discuss and engage to commit to concrete results. PAM acts as a respected and trustworthy channel of communication in its regions.

17.6 Crisis Response and Humanitarian Engagement

17.6.1 Field Initiatives

PAM's operational engagement extends beyond immediate crisis response to include long-term initiatives aimed at strengthening parliamentary systems and governance. Through technical support, PAM focuses on capacity building within parliaments, legislative framework development, and enhancement of administrative systems. These efforts are designed to promote sustainable governance and ensure that member states are equipped to address their own challenges.

Additionally, PAM is involved in humanitarian initiatives that facilitate aid delivery, coordinate civilian protection measures, and support relief operations in crisis-affected areas. This multifaceted approach reflects PAM's commitment to both immediate humanitarian needs and the long-term development of resilient parliamentary institutions.

17.7 Economic Cooperation and Development

17.7.1 Financial Partnership Framework

PAM plays a vital role in coordinating substantial economic initiatives, working closely with various international financial institutions. These collaborations are essential for addressing the economic challenges faced by Member States and fostering sustainable growth.

In addition to financial partnerships, PAM supports regional development programs that encompass infrastructure projects, economic reforms, and investment mobilization. These initiatives are designed to promote sustainable development and improve the quality of life for citizens across the Mediterranean, contributing to regional stability and prosperity.

17.7.2 Economic Diplomatic Engagement

Strategic economic cooperation initiatives are also central to PAM's mission. The Assembly actively promotes public-private partnerships by organizing economic fora, such as the annual PAM Economic Forum of Marrakech, and facilitating business dialogues. These efforts encourage collaboration between the public and private sectors, enhancing economic cooperation and driving development.

PAM's commitment to development coordination is marked in its efforts to align regional projects, mobilize resources, and monitor implementation. By fostering collaboration among Member States and stakeholders, PAM enhances the effectiveness of economic initiatives and promotes sustainable development throughout the region.

17.8 Conclusion

Over the past two decades, the Parliamentary Assembly of the Mediterranean (PAM) has diligently championed parliamentary diplomacy to foster political dialogue, regional stability, and prosperity. PAM's initiatives have been instrumental in advancing economic development and ensuring peace and security across the Mediterranean. This mission has gained even greater importance over the last ten years as the international security environment has deteriorated and conflicts have grown increasingly complex.

Prof. Avv. Stelio Campanale, Professor of International Law, Diplomatic and Consular Law and of International Trade Law (Libera Università Mediterranea-LUM Giuseppe Degennaro – Bari, IT). Visiting professor of International Markets Law (Universiteti Katolik "Zoja e KëshillittëMirë", Tirana). Lawyer and Auditor. Teacher of company management, corporate and compliance issues, international business contracts in many masters, PHD courses, business and management schools, in Italy and foreign countries. Visiting Professor UE Erasmus + at Universidad Publica de Navarra (ES) and Ecole Supérieure des Technologies et des Affaires (ESTA), Belfort (FR). For more than 30 years and in force, member of various Board of Directors and Compliance Supervisory Boards of Italian and foreign companies, including ones listed at New York Stock Exchange and Italian Stock Exchange. Author of books, chapters and articles in academic or professional journals on diplomatic and consular relations, international business and trade law, international law. Honorary Consul of Hellenic Republic in Bari, Italy. Member of the Board of Directors of the World Federation of Consular Corps and Associations (F.I.C.A.C.), NGO-UN ECOSOC, Brussel (Be). From 2016 to 2023, Co-Chairman of the Legal Committee and Co-Chairman of Security and Privileges Committee of F.I.C.A.C. From 2004 to 2020, President of Greek-Italian Business Chamber of Rome. From 2013 to 2016, Senior Advisor to the Secretary General of the Parliamentary Assembly of the Mediterranean (PAM), Malta/San Marino. Member of the Official Delegation of the Greek Government at the: signature of the Pact of Twinning between the Province of Rome and Nomarchia Attikis. Athens, (Gr) 27/5/2005; Meeting of Minister of Transportation of the European Corridor VIII countries. Bari, (It) 18/9/2003; Adriatic & Ionian Initiative. Bari, (It) 13/5/2003; Working table on economic reconstruction, development and cooperation of the stability pact for the Balkans. Bari, (It) 7–8/10/1999.

Annex

Aspects of Consular Relations Between Greece and the United Kingdom

Considering Consular Amenability to Local Jurisdiction in the Light of Customary International Law, the Consular Convention Between the United Kingdom and Greece and the Vienna Convention on Consular Relations

Opinion by Emerita Professor Kalliopi Koufa[1]

Introduction

The present article explores some issues of consular judicial immunity using the case study of a British vice-consul in Corfu, from 1958 to 1971 and permanent resident of Paleokastritsa, Corfu, since 1948, allegedly engaged in the publication of libels and defamatory statements against a British subject from 1968 to this day. The defendant having entered a plea to the jurisdiction of the court, contending that as British vice-consul he enjoyed immunity from civil jurisdiction under existing general and particular international law and, accordingly, that he was not amenable to the jurisdiction of the Greek courts, the following questions were put to the author for counsel: First, what are the rules, if any, of customary international law concerning the jurisdictional immunities of the consular officers? Second, under the circumstances, what is the relation of Article 13, paragraph 1, of the particular Consular Convention of 17 April 1953, between Greece and the United Kingdom, with general international law governing consular relations, as well as the provision of Article 43, paragraph 1, of the Vienna Convention of 24 April 1963 on Consular Relations, ratified by both countries? This is a study based on the original legal counsel answering these questions.

Underlying these questions, however, were issues going to the heart of consular law—such as, the nature of the consular functions and distinction of the consular legal status in international relations, the theoretical basis of consular immunities and

[1] Published by the Hellenic Review of International Relations Vol. 1, No. II (1980), σελ. 375–414).

P. Naskou-Perraki (ed.), *Contemporary Diplomatic and Consular Relations*,
https://doi.org/10.1007/978-3-031-99243-8

delimitation of their extent, the relationship between general and particular norms of customary and conventional international law governing the consular relations, and so on. While the consular functions and position have themselves been variable over the years, and modern developments have had their own important share in affecting changes in the traditional consular system, the fact that some basic features of the consular institution have still not really been altered does not weaken but rekindles interest in the discussion of the theoretical problems involved.

It is against that background then that the present article will attempt to treat systematically some of the issues involved in the problem of consular amenability to local jurisdiction. In particular, although the rationale for this analysis is the case study mentioned at the very beginning and will, on the whole, dominate the thinking and content of this article, a greater emphasis will be given to the theoretical elaboration and interpretation of the issues underlying the practical subject.

In consequence, the discussion proceeds in the sequence of a theoretical approach and development of the privileged position of the consul as organ for international relations (Part I), exploration of the legal framework providing for the jurisdictional immunity of the British consular officer in Greece (Part II), and a brief conclusion with the solution reached (Part III).

Chapter I: Legal Status of Consuls Under International Law

1. General

Under the rules of customary international law, the consul is not to be identified with the diplomat and hence does not enjoy the privileged diplomatic status. Even in those cases where the consul incidentally performs some functions which normally belong to the diplomatic representative, he will not for this reason enjoy the same privileges and immunities as the latter.[2]

In fact, there are occasions where the consular and diplomatic functions may be to some extent fused.[3] Or the consuls may even be assigned to perform diplomatic

[2]For a codification and reformulation of this principle, see Article 17 of the Vienna Convention of 24 April 1963 on Consular Relations, prepared by the International Law Commission and adopted by the United Nations Conference on Consular Relations. It may be noted that only in the oriental, non-Christian states the consuls of Christian states did enjoy the diplomatic privileges and immunities; see, among many other writers, J. Spyropoulos, Traité théorique et pratique du droit international public Athens, 1933, p. 222, (in Greek), H. Bonfils, Manuel de Droit international public, 4th ed., Paris, 1905, p. 418, L. Oppenheim, International Law-A Treatise, vol. I, 8th ed., London, 1967, pp. 831 and 845, C. Rousseau, Droit International Public, vol. IV (Les relations Internationales), Paris, 1980, pp. 246–247, L. Heffter, Das Europäische Völkerrecht der Gegenwart, Berlin, 1860, § 248.

[3]For, as is well known, sometimes it is very difficult to draw a definite boundary or completely separate the two functions; see, for example, L. Cavaré, Le Droit international public positif, vol. II, 3rd ed., Paris, 1969, p. 42 and, in particular, L.T. Lee, Consular Law and Practice, London, 1961, pp. 188–189.

duties. Sometimes too, in order to avoid the cost of establishing or maintaining a diplomatic mission, states may designate a consul to act as a diplomatic representative or commission a consul to engage in diplomatic activities.[4] According to both traditional theory and practice, even in those cases consuls cannot be transformed into diplomats, simply because they perform certain diplomatic functions, and will, therefore, not be entitled to such privileges and immunities as are conferred under customary international law to the diplomatic representatives[5]—unless of course such privileges and immunities have especially been agreed under a bilateral agreement between the state, appointing the consul and the state on whose territory the consul will discharge his duties, or under any other specific international convention.

This is why special emphasis is given by writers to the case where the consul can also be accredited as a diplomat, which means that in addition to his consular status he will be acquiring the diplomatic status as well.[6] For it is the fulfilment of the particular conditions of nomination as a diplomatic agent and the letter of credence that can give a consul the additional diplomatic character. It is, then, only in those cases where the consul has also been clothed with the diplomatic capacity that he can thereby enjoy all the privileges and immunities that have been accorded, from time immemorial, to the class of diplomatic envoys under generally accepted international law.[7]

2. Differentiation Between a Consular Officer and a Diplomatic Agent

While the position of consuls may have varied according to time and place, and it may be sometimes difficult to establish the definite borderline of power between a consular officer and a diplomatic agent; their differentiation is of upmost legal importance. In fact, an essential distinction of the status of the one in relation to the other seems to have a determinant significance in the attempt to understand the nature, assess the scope and delineate the extent of the privileges and immunities accorded, in any case, to both categories of state organs for international relations, under international law.

Thus, whereas the diplomatic agent is undoubtedly regarded as the state organ which represents all the political interests of the sending state abroad, the consul is

[4]Ibid., pp. 20–21, G. H. Hackworth, Digest of International Law, vol. IV, Washington, 1942, pp. 423 et seq., Oppenheim, op. cit., p. 831.

[5]Spyropoulos, op. cit., pp. 213–214, J. Irizarry y Puente, Traité sur les functions internationales des consuls, Paris, 1937, pp.15 et seq., 71 et seq., Bonfils, op. cit., p. 424, Oppenheim, op. cit., p. 840, C. Libera, "Le fondement juridique des privileges et immunitis consulaires", Revue Générale de Droit International Public, 1959, p. 444, Lee, op. cit., pp. 223–224, D. P. O'Connell, International Law, vol. II, 2nd ed., London, 1970, p. 918.

[6]See, for example, W. E. Hall, A Treatise on International Law, 8th ed., Oxford, 1924, p. 378, F. von Liszt, Das Völkerrecht systematisch dargestellt, 12th ed., Berlin, 1925, pp. 205, 207, Irizarry y Puente, op. cit., p. 20, Oppenheim, op. cit., p. 831, G. Schwarzenberger and E. D. Brown, A Manual of International Law, 6th ed., Milton, 1976, p. 68.

[7]O'Cormell, op. cit., p. 918.

especially considered as the organ which serves and defends certain local and specific rights and interests of the sending state in the country where he is stationed.[8] In other words, despite the variable range of activities and multifarious dealings exercised by the consular officer, it is generally admitted that the scope of consular duties is normally limited in space and matter. This means, in the first place, that his functions are local in nature and his powers do not extend beyond the territorial limits of a given area of the state to which he has been appointed (the so-called "circonscription consulaire" or consular district, which usually corresponds to a large city, a port, and maybe some wider administrative division of the receiving state). And, in the second place, that his attributions concern specific relations of the sending state, such as the promotion and protection of commerce and his country's mainly economic, local interests, as well as the interests of its nationals before the foreign local authorities, notwithstanding the performance of certain duties of an administrative or judicial nature.[9]

Accordingly, although it does not seem correct to contest the public character which a consul certainly possesses[10]—i.e. as a government agent mandatory of the appointing state—the character of his mandate is limited, owing to the very nature of the consular institution. More specifically, this means again that in contradistinction to the diplomat, who as the general delegate represents his state in the totality of its international relations with the country to which he has been accredited, the consular agent does not have a general representative character but acts as a delegate of his state up to a certain point and only within the limits of his special duties as a consul.[11] In other words, whereas the consul is in fact also a state organ for international relations, he officially represents his state within the framework of his attributions only.[12]

This particular legal situation of the consular agent is further evidenced by the fact that he cannot, as a rule, communicate directly but only through the superior

---

[8]See J. Zourek, "Le statut et les fonctions des consuls", Recueil de Cours de I'Académie de Droit International, 1962, If, pp. 433, 435, Rousseau, op. cit., p. 217, Oppenheim, op. cit., pp. 832–833 and 838–839, Irizarry y Puente, op. cit., pp. 12 et seq., Hall, op. cit., pp. 371–372.

[9]Spyropoulos, op. cit., p. 211, J. B. Starke, An Introduction to International Law, 7th ed., London, 1972, p. 390.

[10]Spyropoulos, op. cit., p. 214, Libera, op. cit., pp. 448 et seq., Zourek, op. cit., pp. 431–432, Oppenheim, op. cit., p. 840, Bonfils, op. cit., p. 423, Rousseau, op. cit., p. 217, A. Favre, Principes du droit des gens, Fribourg, 1974, pp. 613, 615, L. Marcantonatos, Les relations consulates aux termes de la Convention de Vienne du 24 avril 1963, Thessaloniki, 1974, p. 128.

[11]J. L. Brierly, The Law of Nations, 6th ed., Oxford, 1963, p. 264.

[12]In this sense see, for example, Zourek, op. cit., p. 432, Marcantonatos, op. cit., p. 128, P. Guggenheim, Traite de Droit international public, vol. I, Geneva, 1953, p. 512. See, however, Libera, op. cit., pp. 445 et seq. The particular legal position of the consul has, indeed, divided opinion as to whether a. consul really possesses a "representative" character; see, for example, among the authors contesting the representative character of the consul, Favre, op. cit., p. 615, Rousseau, op. cit., p. 218, Schwarzenberger and Brown, op. cit., p. 68, Irizarry y Puente, op. cit., pp. 12 et seq., Bonfils, op. cit., p. 424, Liszt, op. cit., p. 207, Hall, op. cit., p. 372.

diplomatic channels with the central services of the government of the state to which he has been appointed.[13]

3. Basis of Differential Legal Treatment

The legal protection, privileges and immunities, due to the organs of the foreign state which are committed to the management of its international relations is a logical consequence of their representative character as public agents, on the one hand, and of the discharge of their official function in the interest of their state abroad, on the other hand.

In substance, the international establishment of a system of legal protection of these state organs consists in the acceptance on the part of the receiving state to accord to them a privileged legal status, in compliance with the rules of international law concerning the granting of various privileges and immunities to the foreign representatives of state.[14] These international legal rules, already incorporated in the different municipal legislations or applied by the states as customary principles of international law,[15] limit their sovereign rights, in the sense that they impose on the

[13]Ibid., p. 207, Irizarry y Puente, op. cit., p. 18, Oppenheim, op. cit., p. 840, Zourek, op. cit., p. 435, Starke, op. cit., p. 391, Rousseau, op. cit., p. 219.

[14]See, however, Oppenheim, op. cit., pp. 787–788 and C. Wilson, Diplomatic Privileges and Immunities, Tucson, 1967, pp. 26 et seq.

[15]For example, concerning Greece see, in particular, Article 28, para. 1, of the Constitution actually in force (Greek Government Gazette, Fasc. A, No. Ill/June 9, 1975) which provides as follows:

"The generally accepted rules of international law, as well as international conventions from the time they are sanctioned by law and enter into force according to each one's own terms, shall be an integral part of internal Greek law, and they shall prevail over any contrary provision of law. The application of the rules of international law and of international conventions to aliens is always subject to the condition of reciprocity." Moreover, Article 2, para. 2, provides:

"Greece, adhering to the generally recognized rules of international law, seeks the strengthening of peace and justice, and the development of friendly relations among peoples and states."

Among the other Greek constitutional provisions concerning international law and relations, it is important in this context to point out Article 36, which is dealing with treaty-making, and refer, further, to the texts of Article 28, para. 3, and Article 100, para. 1 (f). Thus, according to Article 28, para. 3:

"Greece may freely proceed, by law voted by the absolute majority of the total number of members of Parliament, to limit the exercise of national sovereignty, if this is dictated by an important national interest, does not infringe upon human rights and the foundations of democratic government and is effected on the basis of the principles of equality and under the condition of reciprocity." And, finally, Article 100, para. 1 (f) provides the following:

"1. A Special Supreme Court shall be established the jurisdiction of which shall comprise:

...f) The settlement of controversy over the designation of rules of international law as generally accepted, according to article 28, paragraph I."

See generally on the provisions of the Greek Constitution of 1975 pertaining to international law, A. A. Fatouros, "International Law in the New Greek Constitution", American Journal of International Law, vol. 70(1976), pp. 492–506, whose English translation of the relevant articles has mainly been used here; and see especially on Article 28, para. 1, of the same Constitution, K. loannou, "The Application of Generally Accepted Rules of International Law in the Greek Legal Order" (in Greek), Armenopoulos, 1976, pp. 298–318. It may be of interest to recall that

states obligations of mutual commitments,[16] both in the direction of according enhanced legal protection to the foreign representatives of states, and in the direction of exempting them as well from the local jurisdiction of the receiving states. Thus construed, the international system of privileges and immunities is considered as the institution within the municipal legal order, of a particular legal regime governing the status of the foreign state organs committed to the management of international relations, by virtue of which these organs are differentially treated and placed in a privileged legal position compared to the other citizens or aliens residing within the boundaries of the state.

It obviously follows that any attempt to identify and correctly apply, within the municipal legal order, this privileged and differential regime, as it is instituted for each particular category of foreign state agents for international relations, basically depends on the foundation and justification of the international institution of privileges and immunities.[17] For it is equally clear that the very obligations under

under previous Greek Constitutions as well, and in the absence of express provisions, the principle that generally accepted rules of international law are part of the law of the land has long been established in Greek legal doctrine and judicial practice—ever since the Judgment of the Greek Court of Cassation in the Syrmou case (Areopagus No. 14/1896, Themis, 7, p. 179) clearly affirmed it, and created case-law. See also, Spyropoulos op. cit., pp. 21–22, Id., Public International Law (in Greek), 4th ed-, Athens, 1954, pp. 20–22, S. Calogeropoulos-Stratis, International Public Law (in Greek), Athens, 1946, pp. 19–20, G. Tenekides, Public International Law (in Greek), vol. I, 2nd ed., Athens, 1959, pp. 183 et seq., G. Zotiades, International Public Law (in Greek), vol. I, Athens, 1973, pp. 174–177, C. Efstathiadis, International Law (in Greek), vol. I, Athens, 1963, pp. 41–42, D. S. Konstantopoulos, International Public Law (in Greek), vol. Ill, 2nd ed., Thessaloniki, 1976, pp. 17–30. See also the Judgment No. 2626/1965 of the Athens Presidential Court of First Instance, Armenopoulos, 1965, p. 780: "...in conformity with the international convention of Vienna of 18 April 1961 on diplomatic relations, which, although it has not as yet been ratified by Greece, it is binding upon her, in as much as it contains rules of public international law in its articles which are relevant to the present case...".

For Greek legislation concerning immunity from jurisdiction see, in particular, Article 3, para. 2, of the Greek Code of Civil Procedure, exempting from Greek jurisdiction "the foreigners enjoying exterritoriality", except as regards immovable property in Greece (Article 29). Moreover, see Article 2 of the Greek Code of Criminal Procedure expressly referring to "conventions or international customs generally accepted" after having enumerated the categories of foreign state representatives, and persons residing with them, who are exempt from Greek criminal jurisdiction. See C. Economides, Inviolability and Exterritoriality of Diplomatic Agents-With Reference to Those of Consular Officers (An Analysis of the Vienna Conventions of 1961 and 1963), doctoral thesis (in Greek), Athens, 1975, pp. 101, 177 et seq., 221 et seq., G. Rammos, Elements of Greek Civil Procedure (in Greek), vol. I, 5th ed., Athens, 1961, pp. 148–150, Id., Manual of Civil Procedure, Athens, 1978, pp. 221–222, C. Fragistas, Civil Procedure (in Greek), Thessaloniki, pp. 114–118, S. Delicostopoulos - L. Sinaniotis, Commentary on the Code of Civil Procedure (in Greek), vol. I, Athens, 1968, pp. 42–44, C.D. Kerameus, Law of Civil Procedure (in Greek), vol. I, Thessaloniki, 1973, pp. 88–901. Zisiades, Criminal Procedure (in Greek), 3rd ed., vol. I, Thessaloniki, 1976, pp. 45–47, C. Vouyoukas, Law of Criminal Procedure (in Greek), vol. I, 5th ed., Thessaloniki, 1980, pp.101–102.

[16]Cf. Economides, op. cit., pp. 43 and 250; but see A.-B. Papacostas, The Exterritoriality of Diplomatic Representatives (in Greek), 2nd ed., Athens, 1971, pp. 10 and 54.

[17]But see Wilson, op. cit., p. 27.

international law to accord to all categories of foreign state organs committed to the management of its international relations a privileged legal regime in the receiving state never meant securing equal and identical legal protection for all these organs. On the contrary, it will be noted that the establishment of their international protection system was always proportional to their legal position and directly corresponding to their respective roles in inter-state relations.

In this sense, it is maintained that the establishment under international law of a regime of legal protection for both the diplomatic agents and the consular officers[18] does not in any way imply an obligation by the receiving states to secure equal protection within their municipal legal orders to those two—traditionally differentiated categories of foreign state agents for international relations.[19] In other words, it is submitted that both the nature and the extent of legal protection granted to each of these two specific categories of foreign state agents for international relations has always been conceived as parallel and in direct relation to their attributes and function (i.e. as diplomatic agents or consular officers). It is, furthermore, maintained that this theoretical position is evidenced and confirmed, in an irrefutable way, by the very attempt to construct and justify legally the international institution of protection, as it applies to each one of those two categories of state organs.

It is, therefore, deemed essential at this point to refer in a parallel manner to the theoretical premises which explain and justify not only the existence of the institution of diplomatic and consular privileges and immunities but also the problems that inevitably follow their establishment and implementation within the municipal legal order of states.

4. Theoretical Justification of Diplomatic and Consular Protection

Whereas the legal protection system afforded to the diplomatic agents because of their general representative character and their power to stand for their state in the totality of its political interests and international relations[20] could be based, from time immemorial,[21] on different versions of the "representational" theory, as

[18] In this sense see, for instance, Zourek, op. cit., pp. 439 et seq., Libera, op. cit., pp. 476–477, Guggenheim, op. cit., p. 514; contra, among others, Spyropoulos, op. cit., p. 203, Oppenheim, op. cit., pp. 840–841.

[19] Of course, they may do so and grant, for instance, under particular international agreements or by municipal legislation even more privileges than they are obliged under general international law. See, for example, also in this sense Article 73, para. 2, of the Vienna Convention of 24 April 1963 on Consular Relations providing that:

"Nothing in the present Convention shall preclude States from concluding international agreements confirming or supplementing or extending or amplifying the provisions thereof" (Emphasis supplied).

And see also Article 47, para.2, of the Vienna Convention of it April 1961 on Diplomatic Relations.

[20] In the sense discussed in section 2, ante.

[21] See, for example, Wilson, op. cit., pp. 1–2 referring also to ancient India.

developed through the ages, in accordance with historical conditions prevailing, and the corresponding political ideas and juristic theories on the state, the opposite is true as regards the consular agents—because again, of the locally and materially limited nature of their attributions and function.[22]

Thus, the special legal regime of protection governing the diplomatic representatives was initially founded on the theory of personal representation of the ruler. According to this conception, the diplomatic envoy is the personification and substitute of the sovereign, i.e. his alter ego in the host state, and, hence, invested with the same privileges and not amenable to the foreign jurisdiction.[23] On the contrary, as regards the consuls, they are certainly at the service of the sovereign, however they do not represent his personality but only the commercial interests and relations of his subjects. As a consequence, the legal position of consuls does not derive and is not protected by international law which, through the diplomatic representatives, prescribes the privileges and immunities to the sovereign himself.[24]

This explanation of privileges and immunities is obviously inadequate and outdated by the historical and political evolution itself. Moreover, it could not offer a solid theoretical basis for the international institution of any system of legal protection of foreign state organs within the municipal legal order of the host state, for the reason that it is logically inconsistent with the very foundation of international legal order on the existence of equal and independent states. In other words, among the various reasons against this doctrine, which have already been advanced,[25] it is pointed out that the theory of personal representation is, in essence, contradictory to the idea of state autonomy and the principles of non-intervention and legal equality of the states—i.e. to the delimitation of the sovereign political power and authority of each state within its own national boundaries.[26]

Anyway, it is important to emphasize here that, mainly as a result of this thesis of personal representation, it was widely adopted in doctrine and judicial practice, and to a certain extent it is still accepted today, that the consuls do not have a representative character and the proper capacity to defend the rights and interests of the sending state.[27]

Another explanation of the privileged legal regime enjoyed by the diplomatic representatives is based on the so-called theory of "exterritoriality" or

[22] See, for example, D. Anzilotti, Cows de droit international, vol. I, 3rd ed., French transl. by G. Gidel, Paris, 1929, pp. 271 etseq., J. Spyropoulos, Treatise on Public International Law (in Greek), Athens, 1933, pp. 213–214, Libera, op. cit., pp. 440–441, Zourek, op. cit., pp. 370 et seq.

[23] Cf. P. Cahier, Le droit diplomatique contemporain, 2nd ed., Geneve, 1964, pp. 184–186, Wilson, op. cit., pp. 1–5, Economides, op. cit., pp. 44–47, Papakostas, op. cit., pp. 20–21, Konstantopoulos, op. cit., vol. I, p. 331.

[24] Libera, op. cit., pp. 440–441, 445 et seq.

[25] For instance, see Wilson, op. cit., p. 4, Economides, op. cit., pp. 45–46, Papakostas, op. cit., p. 21.

[26] Cf. A. Fatouros, International Law of Development (in Greek)) Thessaloniki, 1977, p. 15.

[27] For example, see Rousseau, op.cit., pp. 218–219; and see also Lee, op. cit., pp. 59–60.

"extraterritoriality".[28] Originally formulated by H. Grotius,[29] this theory justifies the legal position of the diplomat by the legal fiction that he is deemed to be outside the territory of the host state and within the territory of his own state.

This thesis, which has influenced legal doctrine and judicial practice in most states until quite recently,[30] is now discredited and generally rejected. Apparently evading the major disadvantage of the previous theory of personal representation (i.e. the restriction of the sovereign rights of the receiving state in favour of the sending state) the fiction of exterritoriality leads to "absurd results if pressed to a logical conclusion".[31] In fact, by attempting to base the non-amenability to the local jurisdiction of the diplomatic representative on the fiction that he is deemed never to have left his state, or in any case to be outside the territory of the receiving state, this doctrine led from a fictitious exterritoriality to a real one.[32] In other words, it was only the logical consequence of this thinking to consider next, that the premises of the embassy constituted a part of the sending state within the territory of the receiving state.

It will be noted in contrast, as regards the juridical position of the consuls in the receiving state, that this question of evading the problem of limiting in their favour foreign sovereign rights did not arise in the first place, because they were not considered as "representatives" of their state.[33] In fact—except, of course, in the oriental non-Christian states in the early days[34]—consuls were subjected to the local law and jurisdiction and leading opinion and judicial practice in different countries had steadily rejected the application of "exterritoriality" to consular premises.[35]

In any event, this theory too is now repudiated and is, indeed, inadmissible to the extent that it is contrary to the international reality itself. For, on the one hand, it places the diplomatic agent above or completely outside the legal order of the host state—a fact which certainly is not always proved and does not fully correspond to

[28]Wilson, op. cit., pp. 5 et seq., Cahier, op. cit., pp. 186 et seq., Oppenheim, op. cit., pp. 792 et seq., O'Connell, op. cit., p. 888, Rousseau, op. cit., pp. 174 et seq., Konstantopoulos, op. cit., vol. I, p. 331, Efstathiadis, op. cit., vol. Ill, p. 14, Economides, op. cit., pp. 47 et seq., Papakostas, op. cit., pp. 18 et seq. And see, on different meanings of the words "exterritoriality" and "extraterritoriality", Lee. op. cit., pp. 205 et seq. and Wilson, op. cit., p. 12 and, in particular, note 67.

[29]De Jure Belli ac Pacis, II, XVIII, cited by Cahier, op. cit., p. 186. But the same passage states also that the diplomats "as if by a kind of fiction are considered to represent those who sent them"; see, in particular, Wilson, op. cit., p. 2 note 10.

[30]Oppenheim, op. cit., p. 793, Wilson, op. cit., p. 8, Rousseau, op. cit., p. 175. And see Economides, op. cit., p. 48 note 1 for Greek judicial practice.

[31]D. C. Holland, Diplomatic Immunity in English Law, Current Legal Problems, TV (1951), 92, as quoted in Wilson, op. cit., pp. 14–15, O'Connell, op. cit., p. 888.

[32]Cahier, op. cit., p. 186.

[33]For instance, see Libera, op. cit., p. 441.

[34]For instance, see Spyropoulos, op. cit., p. 222 and Wilson, op. cit., pp. 15–16. And see also Lee, op. cit., pp. 205 et seq., as well as note 1, ante.

[35]Irizarry y Puente, op. cit., p. 201, Lee, op. cit., p. .241, Rousseau, op. cit., p. 251.

international practice[36]—while, on the other hand, it creates, a lot of confusion as regards the consequences of admitting the existence of foreign territorial sections within the territorial boundaries of the state—a presumption which has frequently led to absurd judicial solutions and is not, in any case, confirmed by the practice of the different states.[37]

There is, finally, a third and more recent[38] explanation of the privileges and immunities of the foreign state organs for international relations, known as the theory of "function" or "functional necessity" (ut ne impediatur legatio).[39] This theory, which is the prevailing today, has also the great advantage of being able to explain the privileged legal regime which applies to both the diplomatic agents and the consular officers and which, at the same time, corresponds to their traditionally differentiated legal positions.

Thus, in fact, the theory of "function" bases the whole juridical construction of the privileged legal treatment granted to the one as well as to the other category of foreign state organs committed to the management of international relations on the collective interest associated with the unhampered exercise of their function—i.e. on the need to assure and protect the function of those state agents, because it is indispensable for international relations.[40] The protection under international law, according to this thesis, consists then in securing the privileges and immunities which are necessary to the efficient performance of the duties pertaining to these state agents for international relations and is not it any way aimed at benefiting them as individuals.[41]

This theory is generally accepted today in legal doctrine and judicial practice, not only because it can justify in a more satisfactory way than the other theories the basic reason for according legal protection to the diplomatic and consular representatives, but also because it is able to offer the essential measure for applying this legal protection to specific situations and, as a consequence, for successfully overcoming the difficult problems that very often arise in practice, from the implementation of the various privileges and immunities in the municipal legal order.

---

[36] Wilson, op. cit., pp. 10–11, Cahier, op. cit., p. 187.

[37] Ibid., Economides, op. cit., pp. 49–50.

[38] As a matter of fact, evidence of all three rival theories is found in various chronological periods and it should at least be mentioned here that there have been more than three legal theories attempting to explain the basis of obligation of diplomatic privileges and immunities. (See, for instance, Wilson, op. cit., p. 1 and Cahier, op. cit., p. 189). However, those are the basic and most important theories and, for our purposes, this traditional way of grouping and ordering them, according to their development in modern times, is sufficient.

[39] Konstantopoulos, op. cit., p. 332, Efstathiadis, op. cit., p. 14, Economides, op. cit., pp. 50 et seq., Cahier, op. cit., pp. 190 et seq., Wilson, op. cit., pp. 17 et seq., Rousseau op. cit., p. 176, O'Connell, op. cit., p. 889.

[40] Cf. Guggenheim, op. cit.. pp. 496–497.

[41] See, for example, preambles of the Vienna Conventions on Diplomatic Relations (18 April 1961) and on Consular Relations (24 April 1963). And see, among other authors,. Lee, op. cit., p. 223, Zourek, op. cit., p. 438, Cahier, op. cit., p. 191, Economides, op. cit., p. 51.

In particular, it is admitted that on the theoretical as well as on the practical level, the theory of functional necessity is the only thesis that can set within reasonable limits the privileged legal regime enjoyed by the diplomatic and consular representatives of state, both under international and municipal law. For in the field of international relations where, as a result of the inexistence of a supra-national legislator, it is the states themselves that set the limits of their own international jurisdiction, this doctrine of "function" provides an essential criterion for determining the extent of the privileges and immunities granted to these foreign state organs committed to the management of international relations—and this, moreover, in the framework of the reciprocal[42] interests of the sending and, in turn, of the receiving states as well. Thus, also, the regime of legal protection granted to these persons is no longer to be considered merely as an advantage, for its very scope corresponds to their necessary function in international relations, i.e. it is applied by the states to sefeguard the particular exercise and effective fulfilment of their respective duties as diplomatic or as consular organs.

Hence, however, the connection between the regime of legal protection granted and the specific function performed by the state organs for international relations becomes immediately apparent. And, furthermore, even the direct relation between their specific tasks and the limits of the legal protection afforded to each of these organs is also brought out in full relief.

In other words, it is submitted that we can also use the same legal basis—i.e. the criterion of functional necessity adhered to by the prevailing theory and practice—not just in the framework of each category, in order to determine in a satisfactory manner the scope of privileges and immunities accorded to that category, but also in the wider international framework, in order to differentiate as accurately as possible[43] between the categories—and especially at a time when there is a tendency to expand the authorised duties, as well as the privileges and immunities associated with the consular function.[44]

5. Significance and Utility of the Functional Criterion

As a matter of fact, despite the clear trend in contemporary conventional international law to approximate[45] the privileges and immunities accorded to the diplomatic and the consular agents, there can be no doubt that the legal protection afforded to

[42] Cf. Wilson, op. cit., p. 24.

[43] See section 1, ante and, in particular, note 2.

[44] Cf. L. Marcantonatos, "Les Nations Unies et les relations consulates", Thesaurus Acroasium, vol. II, Thessaloniki, 1976, p. 155, Eustathiades, op. cit., pp. 30 and 34.

[45] See, for instance, Article 34 of the Vienna Convention on Diplomatic Relations of 1961 and Article 49 of the Vienna Convention on Consular Relations of 1963; and see also Marcantonatos, op. cit., pp. 155–156 and Rousseau, op. cit., p. 261.

the latter is substantially more limited and, as a consequence, their legal position remains considerably inferior to that of the former.[46]

One of the main causes of the consolidation and improvement of the legal position of consuls in contemporary international law—and, moreover, of the expansion of privileged treatment granted not only to the consular officers but also to subordinate diplomatic personnel[47]—has, indeed, been the general endorsement of the concept of functional necessity in modern diplomatic and consular law. Accordingly, the two most recent and comprehensive multilateral international conventions on diplomatic and consular relations[48] have both expressly adopted the theory of "function" and based the privileges and immunities afforded to those two categories of foreign state organs for international relations, on the very same reason of functional necessity or interest of function,[49] as discussed above.

In particular, the Vienna Convention of 24 April 1963 on Consular Relations using almost the same terms in its preamble as the previous Vienna Convention of 18 April 1961 on Diplomatic Relations, has justified the privileges and immunities granted to consular officers by the "purpose" of states parties "to ensure the efficient performance of functions by consular posts on behalf of their respective states".[50]

It follows from this explicit recognition of the functional basis and of the representative character of consular posts in an international instrument of such importance, which does not only codify but develops as well[51] the international law governing consular relations, that the theoretical controversy on the legal status of the consuls is, at least under contemporary international law, solved. This means indeed that by accepting the long-time debated public and representative character[52]—i.e. in the very words of the Vienna Convention of 1963, "performance of" their "functions on behalf of their respective States"—which the consular officers also possess, these states are admittedly "realising" that it is equally in their interest to protect legally that function too. Thus, the same legal reason ("functional" basis) has come to be adopted for the consular privileges and immunities as well.

---

[46] Ibid., pp. 254 et seq. and 262–263.

[47] Wilson, op. cit., pp. 157 et seq. and, in particular, 161 et seq., Economides, op. cit., p. 251.

[48] For a historical account of the conclusion of the Vienna Convention on Diplomatic Relations see, for instance, Cahier, op. cit., pp. 35 et seq. and of the Vienna Convention on Consular Relations see, for instance, Marcantonatos, op. cit., pp. 131 et seq.

[49] Cf. Wilson, op. cit. pp. 19–20 and Economides, op. cit., p. 51.

[50] Whereas the Vienna Convention on Diplomatic Relations employs the words: "to ensure the efficient performance of the functions of diplomatic missions as representing States" (emphasis supplied).

[51] Cf., for example, Brierly, op. cit., p. 265 and L. Marcantonatos, Les relations consulaires aux termes de la Convention de Vienne du 24 avril 1963, Thessaloniki, 1974, pp. 291 et seq. And on the codification and progressive development of international law by the International Law Commission, see Art. 15 of the Statute of the I.L.C. and, for instance, see also D. Harris, Cases and Materials on international Law, 2nd ed., London, 1979, pp. 57–59.

[52] Zourek, op. cit., p. 438 and Marcantonatos, op. cit., p. 128.

From that point on, however, any further attempt which seeks to assimilate the legal regime of consuls to that of the diplomats is equally inadmissible under contemporary international law. For it is now the very foundation of the legal status of both these state organs for international relations upon the same reason of "function" or "functional necessity" that sets already the limit to their further legal assimilation. In other words, the basing also of the legal regime of the consular posts on the purpose to safeguard the efficient discharge of their specific tasks provides as well the measure of their differentiation from the diplomatic missions: that is the measure of their necessary functions in international relations determining, as already discussed, the extent of their privileged legal treatment in direct relation to the duties and objectives assigned to them.

It is, then, noteworthy that the same functional criterion relied upon to expand and improve the legal position of consular posts is, in an opposite direction, also relied upon to secure and restrict the limits of their privileged legal situation. Any attempt, therefore, to approximate further the regime of privileges and immunities granted to both the diplomatic and the consular organs—as distinct categories of state agents, differing by definition for their very attributions, tasks, and objectives in the field of international relations—is logically incompatible with the functional concept, as expressly accepted by modern diplomatic and consular law.

We can, thus, conclude that not only under general and customary international law but also under contemporary conventional international law, the legal assimilation of the privileges and immunities afforded to both these categories of foreign state organs committed to the management of international relations would be, in essence, contradictory to the very theoretical premises of the doctrine of "function".

Chapter II: Sources of the Jurisdictional Immunity of British Consuls in Greece

1. General

It is remarkable that any attempt towards a definition of the privileged legal regime accorded to the consular officials will resort to some kind of comparison with the privileged legal regime accorded to the diplomats. While it is much more ancient than the institution of permanent diplomatic missions,[53] the consular institution did not have a uniform and consistent development[54] as the former did. Accordingly, the controversial and precarious international legal status of the consular officers was mostly having its effect on the very practical issue of their legal treatment which—

[53]E. Stowell, International Law: A Restatement of Principles in Conformity with Actual Practice, London, 1931, p. 220, Zourek, op. cit., p. 367, Lee, op. cit., p. 3. On the evolution of the institution of permanent diplomatic missions see, in particular, Cahier, op. cit., pp. 8 et seq.

[54]On the evolution of the consular institution see, among others, Bonfils, op. cit., pp. 416 et seq., Zourek, op. cit., pp. 370 et seq.. Lee, op. cit., pp. 3 et seq. These also include valuable and abundant bibliography on the matter.

except for the "(C)onsuls in states not within the pale of international law enjoy(ing) by treaty exceptional privileges for the protection of their countrymen"[55]—was in all cases inferior to the consistent and uncompromised privileged legal treatment enjoyed by the diplomatic agents in the host state.

It is obvious then that a substantive and unambiguous distinction of the consular legal status, as well as a justification of the system of their legal protection are, in essence, key issues in any discussion of their privileges and immunities under international law. Thus, these matters were dealt with in the first part of the present analysis.

But, furthermore, it is submitted that a clear conception of the consular privileges and immunities under international law, provides an adequate and satisfactory basis for the correct interpretation and implementation, in the concrete case, of the specific privilege or immunity in the municipal legal order. For, as already developed above,[56] the international institution of privileges and immunities of the foreign state organs committed to the management of international relations consists, in fact, in the establishment under international law, by mutual commitments of the states, of a legal regime of enhanced protection and exemption from the local jurisdiction, for these foreign organs, depending on their position and their role in international relations.

It follows that the privileged legal treatment of the consuls too, as foreign state organs for international relations, consists in the fulfilment by the states of the rules of international law relating to the granting of certain legal protection and exemption from the local jurisdiction of the receiving state to the consuls also, in accordance with their particular position and role in international relations. Yet, whereas the customary origin of the diplomatic privileges and immunities is not even debated, the same cannot be held with regard to the consular privileges and immunities. In fact, the legal source of the international regime of consular privileges and immunities is, like so many other issues concerning the consular institution, highly controversial.

According to one school of thought, the international regime of consular privileges and immunities is conventional and particular.[57] This means that the consular legal protection is solely regulated by the consular conventions, or any other international agreements that expressly provide for the granting of consular privileges and immunities. According, then, to this opinion, in contradistinction to the case of the diplomatic representatives, whose privileged legal regime derives from the general and customary rules of international law, the privileged legal regime of the consular officers eventually derives from specific conventional rules of international law. In the absence of such rules, the privileged legal treatment of the consuls can be based either on the good will of the states or on international courtesy

[55] Hall, op. cit., p. 378. And see also notes 1 and 33, ante.

[56] Part I, section 3, ante.

[57] For instance, see Economides, op. cit., p. 30, Cavare, op. cit., p. 45, Libera, op. cit., p. 436, P. Reuter, Institutions Internationales, Paris, 1963, p. 131.

or on comity or even on the principle of reciprocity.[58] In other terms, in the absence of an explicit conventional will on the part of the states, the granting of certain privileges and immunities to consuls does not correspond to any obligation under international law and may, therefore, be revoked at any time.[59]

It may readily be seen that this view—which is obviously connected closely with the doctrine already examined[60] that denies the representative and even the public character of the consular organ—is certainly incorrect, in at least as much as it disavows[61] or, at best, ignores[62] the customary origin also of the consular privileges and immunities, for the discharge of their proper functions under international law, both customary and conventional.

It is submitted, on the contrary, that the international system of consular legal protection is not only based on conventional and particular international law but derives also from customary and general international law[63] and, in any case, it is not founded on the good will, courtesy, etc. of the states. This viewpoint[64] is concordant with and is further buttressed by the argumentation employed earlier[65] about the consular privileges and immunities being, in principle, analogous to the consular function in international relations[66]—i.e. in direct relation and proportional to the specific tasks performed by the consul, as state organ for international relations, in accordance with customary and/or conventional international law.

Thus, since it is admitted in principle,[67] that the legal protection afforded to the consular officials corresponds in degree and is related to their function under conventional and/or customary international law, it inevitably follows that whenever the particular conventional provisions do not fully determine (or to the extent, at least, that they do not define) the consular duties, and the legal protection afforded to ensure their efficient discharge, these are subject to the customary and general rules of international law. In other terms, to the extent that consular duties are inferred from customary international law, this law determines also the limits of the legal protection afforded.

[58] Spyropoulos, op. cit., p. 215, Oppenheim, op. cit., p. 841.

[59] Cf. Libera, op. cit., p. 437.

[60] Part I, section 2, ante.

[61] E.g. Spyropoulos, op. cit., p. 215.

[62] E.g. Oppenheim, op. cit., p. 841.

[63] For an elaboration of the interplay of general and particular international law, although in the different context of particularism vis-à-vis universalism, see K. Koufa, "The U.N. and regional international organisation", Jus Gentium, No. 16, Thessaloniki, 1976, pp. 19–21.

[64] See, in particular, Libera, op. cit., pp. 476–477, Zourek, op. cit., pp. 451 et seq.

[65] Part I, section 3, ante.

[66] See pp. 382 and 388–389 ante.

[67] For, it should, however, be noted as a minor point, that there are privileges or benefits (e.g. financial) that could also find a good practical justification elsewhere; see, in particular, Lee, op. cit., pp. 226 et seq.; and see also Economides, op. cit., pp. 52–53, although for the case of diplomatic privileges.

In support of this view, it may also be pointed out that the privilege of judicial immunity accorded to the consular officials by various consular and other international conventions is frequently granted explicitly "in respect of acts…falling within the functions of a consular officer under international law".[68] Such a formulation amounts, in essence, to an unequivocal, though indirect, reference by particular conventional international law to general customary international law for the ultimate determination of the scope of consular judicial immunity.[69]

We may, accordingly, conclude that where there exist particular conventional stipulations, fully defining the functions and the respective privileges and immunities of the consular officers, it goes without saying that these particular conventional rules of international law will necessarily apply. In the absence, however, of particular conventional provisions or, eventually, to the extent that the existing particular provisions of consular or other international agreements do not fully cover the functions and the corresponding legal protection of the consular organs, then there can be little doubt indeed that the rules of general customary international law will be applicable. Finally, the general customary rules of international law will certainly apply a fortiori, whenever the consular or other international treaty itself is expressly referring to "international law or practice",[70] for an ultimate determination of the consular functions, upon which the consular regime of legal protection is based, in principle, as already indicated.

Thus, we are led to the inference that the international institution of consular privileges and immunities is based on both conventional and customary international law. This latter, in fact, despite the existence and expansion of conventional international regulation on consular relations, unequivocally retains, as will be shown below,[71] its practical significance, especially in the matter of the functions and the related privileged legal regime attached to the consular office. Hence, the great importance of devoting attention to clarifying and describing the legal source and the specific international rules governing the exemption from local jurisdiction of the consular organ in the relevant case study, becomes immediately apparent.

2. The Legal Framework for Judicial Immunity

The legal framework for the judicial immunity accorded to foreign consular officers who perform their functions in Greece would consequently be, on the one hand, conventional international law and, on the other hand, customary international law.

---

[68] Article 13, para. 1 (emphasis supplied) of the Consular Convention of April 17,1953, between Greece and the United Kingdom. And see also Libera, op. cit., pp. 474–475.

[69] See also sections 2(i) and 2(ii) post.

[70] Article 33, para. 1(a), of the Consular Convention of 1953 between Greece and the United Kingdom; see also Libera, op. cit., pp. 472–473; and see also note 66, ante.

[71] In sections 2(i), 2(ii), and 2(iii) post.

Greece, like other countries, has concluded at times, various consular and other international treaties governing its consular relations with most of the states.[72] To the extent, however, that there are no particular conventional stipulations or where the existing stipulations either do not fully determine the consular functions and the related jurisdictional immunity or expressly refer to international law for their determination, it goes without saying that the relevant rules of general customary international law will, according to what has already been said, be applicable in these matters, in Greece also. Indeed, the very fact that customary international law preserves its significance and validity, despite the conclusion of numerous bilateral and multilateral consular and other treaties to which Greece is a party, is considered so important that it is emphasized once again.

In particular, we may accordingly delimit the regime of legal protection afforded to the British consular officers in Greece by (i) the Consular Convention between Greece and the United Kingdom, signed in Athens, on 17 April 1953, and ratified by the Greek Legislative Decree No. 2619 of 17 September–9 November 1953;[73] (ii) the Vienna Convention of 24 April 1963 on Consular Relations, ratified by the Greek Act of Parliament No. 90 of 23 July 1975;[74] and (iii) the relevant rules of customary international law to the extent that, following what has already been developed above, the conventional rules under (i) and (ii) will eventually allow some margins for its application.

Within that legal framework, then, of consular relations between Greece and the United Kingdom, it is now deemed necessary to proceed next to an examination of the particular rules applying to the specific case of the British vice-consul sued for libel and disclaiming his liability on account of his consular status (i.e. contending that, owing to his official capacity, he is immune from suit in Greek courts).[75]

[72] See, for instance, Economides, op. cit., pp. 30–32, note 1.

[73] Greek Government Gazette, Fasc. A, No. 310 (1953); the text is also printed in Codex Nomikou Vematos, 1953, pp. 890–899 and 1042–1052. Ratifications with the United Kingdom were exchanged on 15 January 1954, and the Convention entered into force on 14 February 1954.

[74] Greek Government Gazette, Fasc. A, No. 150 (1975). The United Kingdom instrument of ratification of the Convention and the Optional Protocol concerning the Compulsory Settlement of Disputes was deposited on 9 May 1972, and the Convention and Optional Protocol entered into force for the United Kingdom on 8 June 1972.

[75] It is evident that the present analysis will be solely concerned with the international facet of the case. An examination also of the Greek municipal legislation in the matter of judicial immunity (e.g. the relevant provisions of the Greek civil procedure) would by far exceed the scope of the present essay. Anyway, since judicial immunity according to our thesis (see Part I, section 3 and Part II section I, ante) and according to the Greek municipal legal system (see, for instance, Article 3, para. 2, of the Greek Code of Civil Procedure and Article 2 of the Greek Code of Criminal Procedure, and see, in particular, note 14, ante) basically depends on international law for a determination of the limits of the exemption from the local jurisdiction, the international aspect is deemed to be the determining factor motivating the court in the concrete case study.

2. (i) The Consular Convention of 17 April 1953

The regime of privileged legal treatment afforded to consular officers under the Consular Convention of 1953 between Greece and the United Kingdom is contained in Part III, Articles 9–14 (Legal Rights and Immunities) and Part IV, Articles 15–17 (Financial Privileges) of the Convention. Of these, Articles 13 and 14 pertain respectively to judicial immunity and to personal immunity or inviolability.

In particular, the text of Article 13, paragraph 1, reads as follows:[76]

> A consular officer or employee shall not be liable, in proceedings in the courts of the receiving state, in respect of acts performed in his official capacity, falling within the functions of a consular officer under international law, unless the sending state requests or assents to the proceedings through its diplomatic representative.[77]

Whereas Article 14, on the other hand, provides:

> Except at the request or with the consent of the sending state a career consular officer shall not be subjected in any territory of the receiving state to detention in custody pending trial, in respect of acts performed otherwise than in his official capacity, unless he is accused of a grave offence as defined in Article 2 (9) of this Convention.[78]

The provisions pertaining to consular functions are contained in Articles 18–32 (Parts V.—General Consular Functions, VI.—Estates and Transfers of Property, VII.—Shipping) while, finally, Article 33, paragraph 1 (of Part VIII.—General Provisions relating to Consular Functions) stipulates the following:

> The provisions of Articles 18 to 32 relating to the functions which a consular officer may perform are not exhaustive. A consular officer shall also be permitted to perform other functions, provided that—
>
> (a) they are in accordance with international law or practice relating to consular officers as recognised in the territory; or
> (b) they involve no conflict with the laws of the territory and the authorities of the territory raise no objection to them.[79]

It is manifest from the language of Article 13, paragraph 1, that under the Convention of 1953, judicial immunity is afforded to the consular officers not just

---

[76] The English text of the Convention used here is the official (Treaty Series, No. 38 (1958), Her Majesty's Stationery Office, London). The author wishes to express her thanks to the British consul general in Thessaloniki, Mr. M. Ward, for kindly providing this text.

[77] Emphasis supplied. See also note 66, ante.

[78] Emphasis supplied. Article 2, para. (9), of this Convention defines "grave offence", in the case of the United Kingdom by reference to the duration of penalty (imprisonment for five years or over) whereas in the case of Greece by reference to the classification of "crime" under Greek law (see Article 18 of the Greek Criminal Code).

[79] Emphasis supplied. See also note 68, ante.

for "acts" done in their "official capacity" but, moreover, for "acts" done in the exercise of an official "function(s)...under international law". In other words, consular exemption from the local jurisdiction of the receiving state is only granted for the official acts of the consular organs if these official acts partake of consular duties in accordance with international law. The two conditions (or necessary requirements) which may, at first sight, be understood as restricting the application of judicial immunity in the terms of this clause are then, on the one hand, the official character of the act of the consular organ and, on the other hand, its connection with the consular functions under international law.[80]

The view that consular non-amenability to local jurisdiction, under the Convention of 1953, is basically dependent on the act being done in an official capacity and, moreover, within the scope of the consular functions under international law, is further supported by Article 33, paragraph 1. In fact, this provision is also clarifying what rules of international law determine as well the manifold consular duties which, as already indicated above,[81] are directly and logically related to the consular function in international relations and to the regime of legal protection afforded to the consular organs by the receiving state.

Thus, in the language of Article 33, paragraph 1, the enumeration of the consular functions in the provisions of Articles 18–32 of the Convention (constituting the particular conventional rules of international law between the two contracting states) is only indicative, and express reference is further made to "international law and practice" (i.e. to the general and customary rules of international law, as developed above)[82] for "other" consular functions that "may" eventually "also" be performed—provided, of course, that they are recognised, or do not conflict with the legislation of and are not objected to by one of the contracting parties (Article 33, paragraph l(a) and (b)). In other words, these provisions must be consistently read and understood to mean that the Consular Convention of 1953, presuming no doubt the direct relevance and relation between consular function (consular duties under international law) and privileged legal regime (application of judicial immunity) is simply willing to refer the rest of the matter to the relevant rules of generally accepted international law.

It is submitted then that (although resulting in an indirect manner) the net and irrefutable effect of Article 13, paragraph 1, along with Article 33, paragraph 1, is to make the determination and application of judicial immunity for the acts of the consular organs, not solely dependent on the particular conventional stipulations of the consular agreement between the two parties, but also, in a more general way, subject to the rules of general international law on consular relations. Which means, however, in essence, that it is the very rules of general international law on consular relations that ultimately determine the extent (or the limits) of consular exemption

[80]On the problem, however, of what acts are "official" in border-line situations see, in particular, Lee, op. at., pp. 253 et seq. and Irizarry y Puente, op. cit., pp. 153 et seq. and 165 et seq.

[81]See Part I, sections 2 and 5, ante.

[82]See pp. 392–393 ante.

from local jurisdiction as stipulated by Article 13, paragraph 1, of the Convention of 1953.

It accordingly follows, moreover, that whereas in the language of Article 13, paragraph 1, consular non-amenability to the local jurisdiction of the receiving state is nonetheless conditioned, as already noted,[83] by the "official" character as well of the act performed, it is primarily the other necessary requirement, namely that this act must "fall within" the consular "functions under international law" that is critically crucial for the judicial immunity to be applied. In other terms, the formal nature or "official" character of the act performed (which, in any event, must necessarily partake of consular functions in accordance with general or particular international law) is logically following and subsidiary to the other requirement or condition of application of judicial immunity. Primary requirement for the exemption is rather the direct relation of the "act" to the exercise of some consular function under the particular or the general rules of international law, while the second requirement (that the "act" should be performed in the official consular capacity) is, actually, resulting to an even greater contraction of "acts" justifying the application of judicial immunity for the consular organs, in concrete instances.

As a consequence, it is admitted that the stipulation of Article 13, paragraph 1, of the Convention of 1953, essentially restricts consular exemption from local jurisdiction to the official acts done in the exercise of consular functions, in accordance with international law. Stated another way, judicial immunity covers the official performance of consular functions under international law.

It follows, on the contrary, that for the unofficial or private acts or acts exceeding the consular authority, as well as for the acts that are irrelevant or even contrary to the consular functions under (particular or general) international law, consular officers are, no doubt, amenable to local jurisdiction under the provision of Article 13, paragraph 1. With respect to these acts, it may, furthermore, be argued that, far from being excluded by the Convention of 1953, the competence of the courts of the receiving state can, in fact, also be derived from some other stipulations therein.

Thus, in the first place, according to the terms of the first clause of Article 13, paragraph 2,[84] "it is understood" that the privilege of judicial immunity may not be invoked and the consular organ is amenable to the local civil courts for contracts privately concluded and "not expressly as agent for his government". And, in the second place, according to the characteristic formulation of Article 14,[85] which provides for the privilege of inviolability (or personal immunity) of the "career" consular officers, in respect of private acts or acts that bear no relation to their official or consular capacity, unless there is "a grave offence", as defined

[83] Pp. 395–396, ante.

[84] Article 13, para. 2, states:

"It is understood that the provisions of paragraph (1) of this Article do not preclude a consular officer or employee from being held liable in a civil action arising out of a contract concluded by him in which he did not expressly contract as agent for his government and in which the other party looked to him personally for performance..." (emphasis supplied).

[85] See the text of Article 14 at p. 395, ante.

elsewhere in the Convention.[86] To be more specific, whereas in the words of Article 13, paragraph 1, concerning the judicial immunity: "(a) consular officer …shall not be liable, in proceedings in the courts of the receiving state, in respect of acts performed in his official capacity, falling within the functions of a consular officer under international law…", on the contrary, the stipulation of Article 14, concerning the personal immunity, uses the words: "…a career consular officer shall not be subjected in any territory of the receiving state to detention in custody pending trial, in respect of acts performed otherwise than in his official capacity…".

Finally, in support of the argumentation already used, it seems appropriate to invoke the two relevant fundamental principles of international law, as defined and consolidated in international judicial and arbitral practice concerning the interpretation of international agreements.[87] According to the first, the text of a treaty should be considered as a whole and the meaning of particular phrases should not be detached from the context.[88] For, "words must be interpreted in the sense which they would normally have in their context, unless such interpretation would lead to something unreasonable…".[89] According to the second, "restrictions or limitations upon the exercise of sovereignty…must be construed as restrictively as possible" unless, of course, the restrictive interpretation would be contrary to the plain terms of the agreement or if it conflicts with other obligations under international law.[90] That even reciprocal undertakings, whereby exemption from the local jurisdiction is granted, would constitute limitations upon the exercise of national sovereignty, cannot seriously be denied.[91]

With respect, therefore, to the analytical and systematic examination of the relevant stipulations of the Consular Convention of 1953 between Greece and the United Kingdom, and the help of the above mentioned general principles of interpretation, there can be little doubt indeed that, notwithstanding his consular status, the British vice-consul in Corfu would be amenable to the jurisdiction of the Greek courts for any private, illegal, or bearing no relation to his consular functions, acts

[86] See note 77, ante.

[87] Spyropoulos, op. cit., pp. 247–248, Efstathiadis, op. cit., vol. III, p. 58, Tenekidis, op. cit., pp. 328–330, O'Connell, op. cit.,vol. I, p. 261. Cf., however, also Guggenheim, op. cit., pp. 132 et seq., Favre, op. cit., pp. 251–253, Oppenheim, op. cit., pp. 950–957.

[88] See P.C.I.J., Series B, Advisory Opinion No. 2, August 22, 1922, Competence of the International Labor Organization with respect to Agricultural Labor, as reported in M.O. Hudson, World Court Reports, vol. I, Washington, 1934, p. 128.

[89] P.C.I.J., Series B, Advisory Opinion No. 11, May 16,1925, Postal Service in Danzig, as reported in Hudson, op. cit., p. 466. And cf. also Article 31 of the Vienna Convention of 1969 on the Law of Treaties.

[90] P.C.I.J., Series A, Judgment No. 1, August 17, 1923, The S.S. "Wimbledon", as reported in Hudson, op. cit., p. 175. But see Harris, op. cit., pp. 623–624, citing the relevant objections and skepticism expressed by Lord McNair.

[91] See pp. 379–381, ante, and see Schwarzenberger, op. cit., p. 78, classifying immunities under "Limitations of State Jurisdiction…" It is another matter, however, that "every treaty obligation limits the sovereign powers of a State", according to the authoritative formulation of Lord McNair, as quoted in Harris, op. cit., p. 624.

performed. For, in such a case, the privilege of judicial immunity does not apply and, as a consequence, the competence of the local Greek court in which the British vice-consul was sued, may not in any way be excluded.

2. (ii) The Vienna Convention on Consular Relations of 1963

Based on the draft Articles adopted in 1961 by the International Law Commission, the United Nations Conference on Consular Relations elaborated, in Vienna, in 1963, the final text of a Convention on Consular Relations, bearing the characteristics of a general legislation codifying and developing progressively the international law on consular relations.[92]

This most important multilateral international agreement was adopted and signed, in Vienna, on 24 April 1963, and entered into force on 19 March 1967, in accordance with the terms of its Article 77, paragraph 1, which stipulates as follows:

> The present Convention shall enter into force on the thirtieth day following the date of deposit of the twenty-second instrument of ratification or accession with the Secretary-General of the United Nations.

Furthermore, the provision of Article 77, paragraph 2, of the same Convention states the following:

> For each State ratifying or acceding to the Convention after the deposit of the twenty-second instrument of ratification or accession, the Convention shall enter into force on the thirtieth day after deposit by such State of its instrument of ratification or accession.

In conformity then with these stipulations, the United Kingdom deposited its instrument of ratification on 9 May 1972, and the Vienna Convention entered into force for the United Kingdom on 8 June 1972, whereas Greece deposited its instrument of ratification on 14 October 1975, and the Vienna Convention became operative for Greece too, on 13 November 1975.[93]

With regard to the scope of application of the Vienna Convention on Consular Relations and its relationship with other international agreements already concluded, it is stated by Article 73, paragraph 1:

> The provisions of the present Convention shall not affect other international agreements in force as between States parties to them.

This explicit clarification, that the existing bilateral consular and other international agreements are not abrogated by the Vienna Convention of 1963 but will, on

[92] See U.N. Doc. A/Conf. 25/6, Draft articles on consular relations adopted by the I.L.C. at its thirteenth session; U.N. Doc. A/Conf. 25/12, Vienna Convention on Consular Relations; and see U.N. Doc. A/Conf. 25/16 and U.N. Doc. A/Conf. 25/16/Add. 1, Official Records, U.N. Conference on Consular Relations.

[93] See also note 73, ante.

the contrary, maintain their force, is even further emphasized by the express stipulation in the next paragraph of Article 73, whereby the subsequent conclusion of other agreements "confirming or supplementing or extending or amplifying" the provisions on the same subject in the future, is by no means prevented by the Convention.[94]

That the consular agreement of 17 April 1953 between Greece and the United Kingdom continues then to regulate the consular relations of the two contracting states, and is in no way replaced by the Vienna Convention of 24 April 1963, is no doubt already very clear. The very language of Article 73, paragraph 1, seems, prima facie, to render unnecessary whatever margin of usefulness might have been found in the examination of the corresponding provisions of the Vienna Convention, in the matter of judicial immunity relevant in the concrete case. Moreover, the above mentioned provision of Article 77, concerning the entry into force of the Vienna Convention, and the established facts of the present case (i.e. acts performed by the British vice-consul in 1968, and even until his suit in the Greek court, whereas his consular status was terminated in 1971, date at which the Vienna Convention was anyway still inoperative for both Greece and the United Kingdom, according to the terms of its Article 77, paragraph 2) point again, at first approach, to the same direction, that further recourse to the Vienna Convention is useless here.

However, at a deeper, more comprehensive level, the failure (in view of the above provisions) to take a closer look at the Vienna Convention—i.e. explore the relevance of its stipulations on judicial immunity to the concrete case—would not only constitute a serious omission but a legal mistake, given the indisputably codifying character of the Convention.

In fact, as already noted,[95] although the Vienna Convention on Consular Relations has incorporated new elements of a purely conventional nature, that advance and develop the international regulation of consular relations, it basically remains a codifying text which reflects, reaffirms and consolidates existing practice, principles and customary rules of international law on consular relations.[96] This two-sided nature of the Vienna Convention, borne in mind, there may accordingly be cogent reasons for investigating the customary or conventional character of its specific provisions in concrete situations. For, to the extent that these are incorporating customary law, their particular significance as declaratory rules of existing international law is conspicuous. Considering, therefore, that the Consular Convention of 1953 between Greece and the United Kingdom, as already discussed,[97] is expressly referring to "international law or practice" on consular

[94]See the full text of Article 73, para. 2, in note 18, ante. And see also the commentary on the corresponding Article 65 (First tart) of the LL.C. Draft in Yearbook of the I.L.C. 1960, vol. H, pp. 178–179.

[95]See pp. 387–388, and 399, ante.

[96]Cf., in particular, Lee, op. cit., p. 325, Zourek, op. cit., pp. 457–458, 477–478 and U.N. Doc. A/4425, Report of the I.L.C. covering the work of its twelfth session (25 April–1 July 1960), Ch. II, para. 23.

[97]See pp. 396–397, ante.

relations, it is submitted that the essentially mixed nature of the Vienna Convention on Consular Relations may not a fortiori be disregarded here. As a consequence, the exploration of its provisions relating to judicial immunity (in order to ascertain their relevance and possible application in the concrete case) is considered, in the last analysis, as being imposed in the very terms of the Consular Convention of 1953.

Considering then the Vienna Convention on Consular Relations in this legal context (as a conventional codifying instrument) it is apparently necessary to explore its provisions relating to judicial immunity, in order to establish their customary or conventional provenance.

Thus, if these provisions are (or to the extent that these are) conventional and developing the law on consular relations, it is well understood that they cannot be taken into further consideration. On the contrary, if these provisions are (or to the extent that these are) customary and declaratory of existing consular law, it is then necessary (before even taking them, eventually, into consideration) to establish further their scope of application and relevance to the concrete situation (i.e. because of Article 73, paragraph 1, of the Vienna Convention of 1963 and of Article 13, paragraph 1, along with Article 33, paragraph 1, of the Consular Convention of 1953). In other words, it will then have to be established if (and to what extent) the judicial immunity afforded under the (general international) law of the Vienna Convention on Consular Relations is differing from that afforded under the (particular international) law of the Consular Convention between Greece and the United Kingdom, as already analysed.[98]

In particular, the Vienna Convention on Consular Relations contains two Articles concerning judicial immunity. Of these, one (Article 43) is generally dealing with the privilege of immunity from the jurisdiction of the receiving state, as well as with the exceptions provided, while the other (Article 71) is especially referring to the consular officers who are nationals or permanent residents of the receiving state. According then to the terms of Article 43, paragraph 1, it is stipulated:

> Consular officers and consular employees shall not be amenable to the jurisdiction of the judicial or administrative authorities of the receiving State in respect of acts performed in the exercise of consular functions.[99]

And the text of the relevant part of Article 71, paragraph 1, reads:

> Except in so far as additional facilities, privileges and immunities may be granted by the receiving State, consular officers who are nationals of or permanently resident in the receiving State shall enjoy only immunity from jurisdiction and personal inviolability in respect of official acts performed in the exercise of their functions….[100]

---

[98] See also pp. 392–393 and 396–397, ante.

[99] Emphasis supplied.

[100] Emphasis supplied.

It is, thus, in the very terms of the above provisions that the following positions may readily be acknowledged, with regard to the privilege of judicial immunity afforded under the Vienna Convention:

The consular officers are not amenable to the local courts in respect of acts done in the exercise of consular functions. Conversely, the consular officers are amenable to the local courts in respect of all their other acts—i.e. which are not done in the exercise of consular functions. If, however, the consular officers happen to be nationals or permanent residents of the receiving state, then that set of acts which was covered by the privilege of judicial immunity—i.e. acts done in the exercise of consular functions—is even further compressed. That is to say, it is no longer sufficient for the granting of judicial immunity that the acts were done in the exercise of consular functions, but it is additionally required that they (the acts done in the exercise of consular functions) were "official" as well. It is then well understood that in respect of all their other acts—i.e. that were not done officially and, therefore, were private—the consular officers who are nationals or permanent residents of the receiving state are amenable to the local courts, even if these acts were performed in the frame of their consular functions.

Concerning the customary or conventional provenance of the above stipulations of the Vienna Convention (in view of their possible application and relevance to the present case, in the terms of Article 13, paragraph 1, of the Consular Convention between Greece and the United Kingdom, on the basis of the foregoing discussion) the following should be outlined:

In the first place, the rule laid down in Article 43, paragraph 1, of the Vienna Convention (i.e. that consular officers are amenable to the local courts of the receiving state, except for acts that were performed in the exercise of their consular duties) is undoubtedly part of customary international law.[101] In fact, this is a fundamental rule, to be found in almost every consular convention and in the legislation of states, and which the prevailing school of thought—based, precisely, on the voluminous evidence of custom—has unequivocally recognised as a universally accepted principle governing the consular relations.[102] The incorporation of this rule in the Vienna Convention is considered by the International Law Commission, in its reports and commentaries on the privilege of consular jurisdictional immunity (finally formulated under Article 43) as a confirmation and consecration of the principle "almost universally admitted" that "unlike members of the diplomatic staff", consuls are "in principle subject to the jurisdiction of the receiving State in respect of all their private acts" or acts that are "not performed in the exercise of their consular function…except as otherwise provided by treaty".[103] With respect,

[101] Zourek, op. cit., p. 454.

[102] Ibii., Lse, op. cit., p. 223, Libera, op. cit., pp. 448 et seq; see also U.N. Doc. A/CN. 4/131, Second report by J. Zourek, Special Rapporteur, Part I, Sec. II, including abundant bibliography. Contra Spyropoulos, op. cit., p. 215.

[103] Yearbook of the I.L.C., 1960, vol. II, pp. 11 and 170; and Yearbook of the I.L.C., 1961, vol. II, p. 117.

however, to acts performed in the exercise of their functions, consular officers are exempted from the local jurisdiction of the receiving state, this exemption corresponding, in essence, to the "immunity which the sending State is recognized as possessing in respect of acts which are those of a sovereign State".[104] Such acts are by their very nature (i.e. official acts of a sovereign state) outside the jurisdiction of the receiving state, in contradistinction to the private acts or acts that extend beyond consular duties or bear no relation to them—and, as a consequence, cannot be attributable to the sending state. For, with respect to the latter acts, consular officers are, no doubt, amenable to the local courts.

Secondly, the more restrictive rule (as regards the scope of application of judicial immunity) set out in the first sentence of Article 71, paragraph 1—i.e. that consular officers who are nationals or permanent residents of the receiving state are amenable to the local courts of that state, even for acts performed in the exercise of their functions, unless such acts are official—appears to establish, in fact, the double safeguard against consular exemption from the local jurisdiction—i.e. the two conditions or necessary requirements for the application of judicial immunity—already examined previously, in the framework of the Consular Convention of 1953.[105]

Yet, this stipulation does not codify a pre-existing rule of customary international law.[106] Originally, the International Law Commission draft on consular intercourse and immunities, proposed the granting of jurisdictional immunity (and inviolability) only to the consular officers who are nationals of the receiving state, and in its commentary, was expressly referring to the need "to define the legal status" of these officials also.[107] In this, it was admittedly[108] copying previous experience with the Vienna Conference on Diplomatic Relations of 1961, where its proposal to accord jurisdictional immunity (and inviolability) to diplomatic agents, nationals of the receiving state, was finally expanded to include, as well, those diplomatic agents who were permanently residing in the receiving state.[109]

Anyway, since it is evident by now that the provision of Article 71, paragraph 1, of the Vienna Convention of 1963 no doubt belongs to the "progressive development" of the law on consular relations, it cannot here be further specified or taken into consideration—notwithstanding interest, perhaps, in a comparison with the different formulation used in Article 13, paragraph 1, of the Consular Convention of 1953, and, of course, the fact that the British vice-consul, of our case study, is a permanent resident of Paleokastritsa, Corfu, ever since 1948.

---

[104] Ibid., Economides, op. cit., pp. 190–191.

[105] Part II, section 2(i) ante.

[106] Zourek, op. cit., p. 476.

[107] See U.N. Doc. A/4843, Report of the I.L.C. covering the work of its thirteenth session (1 May–7 July 1961), commentary on Article 69, para. 1.

[108] See Zourek, op. cit., pp. 476–477.

[109] See Article 38, para. 1, of the Vienna Convention on Diplomatic Relations of 18 April 1961 (U.N. Doc. A/Conf. 20/13).

It is already clear then that the problem, previously referred to,[110] of an eventual comparison of the relevant to judicial immunity provisions of the Vienna Convention with the stipulation in Article 13, paragraph 1, of the particular consular agreement between Greece and the United Kingdom, could possibly arise, only in respect of the general provision of Article 43, paragraph 1, of the Vienna Convention incorporating, in the very words of the International Law Commission, "part of customary international law".[111]

And yet, a simple reading (and contrast) of the words used in these two Articles is sufficient to show prima facie, that the provision of Article 43, paragraph 1, of the Vienna Convention is broader, regarding the formulation of restrictive conditions (necessary requirements) for applying the privilege of consular judicial immunity. In fact, it becomes quite obvious that, while the Vienna Convention accords judicial immunity for the acts done "in the exercise of consular functions", the Consular Convention of 1953, in the terms of its Article 13, paragraph 1, does not accord judicial immunity for the acts done "within the functions of a consular officer under international law", unless such acts were also done in "his official capacity". As a consequence, since the granting of judicial immunity under the particular consular agreement between Greece and the United Kingdom seems to be envisaged in terms definitely more restrictive than those laid down in the general codification of the Vienna Convention on Consular Relations, there is no more ground either for considering also the provision of Article 43, paragraph.1, any further in this context.

However, it is another matter if (and to what extent) the provision of Article 43, paragraph 1, having an established customary character is, in essence, as broad as a first approach seems to indicate. It is submitted that the answer must unequivocally be no; and, accordingly, it will be necessary to return to this point below, in the final stage of discussing customary international law, in terms of the express reference to it by—the Consular Convention of 1953, as already noted.[112] At this stage, the mere fact that the provision of Article 13, paragraph 1, of the particular Consular Convention of 1953 contains a more specific and restrictive formulation of the privilege of judicial immunity, suffices to exclude any possibility of application of Article 43, paragraph 1, of the Vienna Convention in the present context.

2. (iii) The Rules of Customary International Law

Since the particular consular agreement of 1953 between Greece and the United Kingdom expressly refers to international law and practice, for the ultimate determination of the consular functions (which are, as already explained, directly and logically related with the privilege of consular judicial immunity[113]) it is necessary by now to investigate whatever margin of exemption (of the British vice-consul)

[110] See pp. 401–402, ante.

[111] See commentary on Article 43 (UN. Doc. A/4843).

[112] See p. 395, ante.

[113] See pp. 391 and 396, ante.

from the "proceedings in the courts"[114] (of Greece) might have been entrusted, by the foregoing particular conventional regulation, to the general rules of customary international law.

In other terms, since it is submitted that the net effect of the provision of Article 13, paragraph 1, along with the provision of Article 33, paragraph l(a), of the Consular Convention of 1953, is to make general and customary international law the determining factor for the ultimate delimitation of consular judicial immunity, the systematic analysis would, certainly, be incomplete without an examination of whether the rules of general and customary international law may still justify the non-amenability of the British vice-consul in the Greek court, by including, eventually, the specific acts, allegedly performed, among "the functions of a consular officer under international law".[115] For these acts are certainly not covered by the (admittedly "not exhaustive"[116]) enumeration of the consular functions laid down in the provisions of Articles 18–32 of the Consular Convention of 1953. Arguably, this is the only reasoning left to make out the meaning of the reference of Article 13, paragraph 1, to general international law in the concrete situation.

Thus, to be more specific, it has been admitted that the express reference, in the various bilateral consular and other international agreements, to international law or practice in the matter of consular functions (or acts falling within the functions or duties of consuls) cannot logically, and therefore persuasively, mean anything else but that the contracting parties recognize (beyond and next to their own conventional arrangements) the existence of rules of international law (general and customary) on consular functions.[117] Once this syllogistic is accepted as underlying these express references to international law—notwithstanding the comprehensiveness or detailed regulations of the treaty—there may be, on reflection, only two more possibilities of applying the privilege of judicial immunity, as afforded by Article 13, paragraph 1, of the Consular Convention of 1953, in the concrete case study: Either if, despite its comprehensive enumeration of consular functions, this Convention has still omitted some consular act or duty, "falling" however "within the functions of a consular officer under international law"; or, for whatever other reason, extraneous to the Consular Convention of 1953, and yet in conformity with international law[118] and the very nature of the consular function in international relations.

It is submitted that the consequent discussion of these issues may even give some additional insight into the controversial reference of Article 13, paragraph 1 (and the

[114] Article 13, para. 1, of the Consular Convention of 19S3; and see the text of this Article at p. 395, ante.

[115] Ibid.

[116] Article 33, para, l. of the Consular Convention of 1953; for the text see p. 395, ante; and see also p. 396, ante.

[117] Cf. Libera, op. cit., pp. 460–461, Zourek, op. cit., pp. 386–387; and see also p. 392, ante.

[118] Cf. U.N. Legislative Series, v. VII, p. 134, the memorandum annexed to the note of 9 April 1956, by the permanent representative of Greece to the U.N., recognizing the subsidiary application of the rules of international law in the regulation of consular immunities, as reported in Libera, op. cit., p. 460.

like references in similar treaties) to international law. It is, therefore, along those lines that the following points will still be made.

It is well known that under general and customary international law, the duties of consuls include the protection of the rights and interests of the sending state and of its nationals, the promotion of trade, and the rendering of services and any assistance (professional, moral and material) to nationals of the sending state, some most important maritime functions and powers with regard to ships and crews having the nationality of the sending state, as well as certain notarial, registration and even judicial functions.[119] It is, furthermore, also well known that these time-honoured categories of consular functions, generally accepted through the conclusion of series of treaties and regulations of like nature, and repeated state practice on the national and international level, have been expanding in the course of time, on the basis of the "most-favoured-nation clause" and the principle of reciprocity.[120]

In any case, there can be no doubt that all acts justifying the application of consular judicial immunity must, accordingly, fall within the above categories of functions. That is to say, must bear a direct and logical relation to some duty or assignment partaking of the exercise of any of the above groups of consular functions established under international law.

And yet, a perusal of the provisions of Articles 18–32 of the Consular Convention of 1953 between Greece and the United Kingdom shows no doubt that the consular functions included therein coincide in general with the above mentioned groups or categories of functions of a consular officer under international law. Moreover, it should definitely be stressed, at this stage, that the Consular Convention of 1953 is, in fact, one of those typical examples of bilateral consular treaties that regulate, in a most considerate and comprehensive way, the matters relating to the duties and the treatment of consular officials.[121]

Thus, since admittedly the provisions of Articles 18–32 concern and regulate, as adequately and completely as possible, the same consular duties and assignments with those that are already established under international law, it is obviously in another direction that the inquiry as to the practical importance and significance of the clause "acts…falling within the functions of a consular officer under international law" should definitely now be turned. For, evidently here, it cannot anyway concern an omission by the consular agreement to include another function which, yet under the rules of international law, could still justify the non-amenability to court of the British vice-consul of this case study, in respect of his concrete actions.

In fact, while the consular duties recognised by traditional international law are so varied and expanding that it may be even difficult, sometimes, to exactly define their

[119] For instance, see Spyropoulos, op. cit., pp. 215–217, Efstathiadis, op. cit., pp. 26–27, Stowell op. cit., pp. 222–223, Oppenheim, op. cit., pp. 837–839, Zourek, op. cit., pp. 387 et seq.. Lee, op. cit., pp. 59 et seq.

[120] Cf. Libera, op. cit., p. 472, Lee, op. cit., p. 7, Efstathiadis, op. cit., p. 23, Economides, op. cit., pp. 31–32 note.

[121] Cf. Lee, op. cit., pp. 307–308.

scope,[122] it is well understood that their exercise in the interest of (at best, without detriment to) the sending state and its nationals constitutes the core of the consular function. It may be, accordingly, maintained that the defence and protection of the rights and interests of the sending state and of its nationals is, no doubt, the essential element (a common denominator, perhaps) of the manifold consular functions and assignments. From the legal angle, this essential common feature, underlying the consular official acts, is an all-important by-product of certain basic principles gradually developed in the course of the long evolution of consular law.

Thus, in particular, although as already shown at the beginning of this essay,[123] consuls do not have a right of general representation of the sending state (e.g. as the diplomatic agents, that represent their state in the totality of its international relations) they do, however, represent the sending state in the exercise of the particular functions they are entitled to do, within the limited sphere of the consular district.[124] It follows that the powers and authority enjoyed by the consular officials—as public organs and not as private persons are, in the last analysis, those of the sending state, which is also responsible for their (consular) activities. Accordingly, consular activities and acts are, in essence, activities and acts of the state (attributable to the sending state which is officially represented by its consular officer) and the institution of legal proceedings against this officer, in respect of such acts, would amount to an institution of legal proceedings against the sending state.[125]

As a first consequence of the above, we may then note the well-established rule that consular activity should not, in any event, conflict with the laws and regulations of the receiving state, which consular officials no doubt are bound to respect.[126]

On the other hand, the protection of the nationals of the sending state is, indeed, a sovereign right of that state, and the consular officers attend to it and exercise it not as private mandatories, but as official state organs.[127] This protection of the rights and interests of nationals derives, in fact, from the very logic of the consular function in international relations (i.e. the very reason of the institution of consuls, right from the start) and is, therefore, the cornerstone of consular functions, recognised by international law even in some cases where such rights and interests are simply endangered or just menaced.[128]

[122] Cf. Talleyrand, as quoted in Zourek, op. cit., p. 366:

"Après avoir ete un Ministre habile, que de choses il faut encore savoir pour être un bon Consul; car les attributions d'un Consul sont variées a l'infini: elles sont d'un genre tout différent de celles des autres employés des Affaires étrangèeres. Elles exigent une foule de connaissances pratiques pour lesquelles une éducation particulière est nécessaire".

And see also Lee, op. cit., pp. 59 and 187–188.

[123] Part I, section 2, ante.

[124] Stowell, op. cit., p. 222, Zourek, op. cit., p. 454.

[125] Cf. Economides, op. cit., p. 190 and Yearbook of the I.L.C., 1960, vol. II, p. 10.

[126] Zourek, op. cit., p. 428, Efstathiadis, op. cit., p. 33.

[127] Zourek, op. cit., p. 432; and see Part I, section 2, ante.

[128] Cf. Zourek, op. cit., p. 389.

And yet, it is well understood that this consular protection of rights and interests may not, in any way, justify an eventual non-compliance with the laws and regulations or interference in the domestic affairs of the receiving state.[129] Obviously then there might be a problem of relationship between the duty to act in the interest of the sending state and of its nationals, and the duty to respect the laws and regulations and not interfere in the domestic affairs of the receiving state.

However, it has been noted more than once that the legal position and the whole system of privileged treatment afforded to the consular officials in the receiving state is squarely based on the necessity to secure the unhampered discharge of their functions.[130] The submission was, moreover, that the whole legal regime of consular privileges and immunities can only find its rational and satisfactory theoretical and practical justification through the criterion of "function" providing, on the one hand, the necessary freedom and security in the exercise of consular duties and, on the other hand, the essential measure for delimiting the extent of this legal protection, within the legal order of the receiving state.[131]

As a second consequence, then, of the above, we may already retain the basic differentiation in international law between acts falling within the consular functions and covered by judicial immunity, and acts outside the consular functions for which consular officers are personally responsible under local law. Stated another way, the ratio decidendi of whether a certain act performed by the consular officer would involve his personal responsibility under local law is the departure of his act from what he is required to perform in his official capacity (i.e. as a consul) under international law.

It is accordingly submitted that, in the first place, a delimitation of consular functions under international law (conventional and/or customary, particular and/or general[132]) in the concrete context and, in the second place, the evaluation of the causal link between the concrete act performed and the consular functions (under applicable international law) are of determinant significance.

Thus, it is manifest by now that any act of a consular officer which is harmful to the rights or interests of the sending state or of its nationals, is evidently outside the consular functions, for the very reason that it runs counter—at best, it is alien—to all consular duties and assignments under international law. Consequently, all acts performed by the British vice-consul in Corfu, in violation of his basic obligation of protection and defence of the rights or interests of his nationals would definitely depart substantially from his consular functions and, therefore, in case of an

[129] Cf. Article 33, para. l(b), of the Consular Convention of 1953 between Greece and the Uni ted Kingdom and Article 55, para. 1, of the Vienna Convention on Consular Relations. And see also Yearbook of the I.L.C. 1960, vol. II, p. 30.

[130] But see note 66, ante.

[131] See Part I, section 5, ante.

[132] For an attempt to assess and explain the dialectical tension between general and particular international law, see K. Koufa, Regional Organisation of International Society, doctoral thesis (in Greek), Thessaloniki, 1975, pp. 51–63 and 154–155.

infringement on the Greek law, would no doubt involve his personal liability (civil or/and criminal).

It is worth noting, moreover, that an application of the theory of "functional offence" (délit fonctionnel), as it is known in traditional consular law,[133] would just lead to the same conclusion.

Thus, according to this doctrine, consular judicial immunity for acts falling within the exercise of consular duties means, in essence, that the consular officer would be exempted from the local jurisdiction of the receiving state, even in respect of his acts that violate the laws and regulations of the receiving state, if such acts are done in the performance of his consular duties.[134] "Functional" is, however, only the unlawful act or offence which derives exclusively from (and certainly not outside) the exercise of consular functions according to international law. Consequently, a consular officer is not responsible and will not be liable in civil or criminal proceedings in the courts of the receiving state for the "functional offences" committed—as these can only involve the responsibility of the sending state. Conversely, the consular officer is personally responsible and, therefore, liable in civil or criminal proceedings in the local courts, in respect of his unlawful acts or offences that bear no connection with, or do not flow from, the exercise of his consular duties. For these latter are not part of consular functions and, thus, not attributable to the sending state.[135]

Finally, it may also be appropriate, in this connection, to note the relevant formulation of Article 55, paragraph 1, concerning consular respect for the laws and the regulations of the receiving state, of the Vienna Convention on Consular Relations, in the terms of which:

> Without prejudice to their privileges and immunities, it is the duty of all persons enjoying such privileges and immunities to respect the laws and regulations of the receiving State. They also have a duty not to interfere in the internal affairs of that State.[136]

According to both the International Law Commission draft and its commentary, on the one hand, this provision reserves the granted regime of privileges and immunities, from the obligation to comply with the laws and regulations of the receiving state, while, on the other hand, it should not be interpreted as an interference in the domestic affairs of the receiving state, when consular officials make representations for the purpose of protecting and defending the interests of their state or its nationals in conformity with international law.[137]

Before drawing the major arguments of this discussion to a conclusion, there remains one final point to be made with respect to the problématique of qualifying and determining, under traditional customary international law, what acts properly

[133] Sew, in particular, Irizarry y Puente, op. cit., pp. 165 et seq.

[134] Ibid., Zourek, op. cit., p. 455; and cf. also Yearbook of the I.L.C., 1960, vol. I, p. 307.

[135] Ibid.

[136] Emphasis supplied.

[137] See Yearbook of the I.L.C., 1960, vol. II. pp. 30 and 176.

partake of the exercise of consular functions—and are, therefore, covered by judicial immunity. It involves consideration of the final formulation of Article 43, paragraph 1, on immunity from, jurisdiction, of the Vienna Convention on Consular Relations. For, it has been stated that this provision incorporates a rule of customary international law[138] and the submission, in the previous section, was that despite its broad formulation the underlying concept of jurisdictional immunity might not be, in the last analysis, as broad as a first reading of Article 43, paragraph 1, seems to indicate.[139]

In fact, there is a clearly discernible tendency, in both the relevant Report and the commentaries by the International Law Commission, in regard of jurisdictional immunity, to confuse[140] or, at best, refuse to draw a line[141] between "acts performed in the exercise of (consular) functions" and "official acts" of consuls. This position, however, simply reflects the dominant opinion in the thinking and practice of traditional consular law.[142] Thus, to quote a highly authoritative formulation of consular jurisdictional immunity:

> A receiving state shall exempt a person from liability and from its judicial and administrative jurisdiction for an act done by him while he was a consul in the performance of consular functions which he was entitled to exercise....[143]

The fact that during discussions and in the final formulation of Article 43, paragraph 1, the proposal to add the adjective "official" in front of "acts" was rejected, is justified in the commentary as necessary, in the interest not to weaken the position of consuls.[144] What should really be stressed, however, is the overall clear impression resulting from the final discussion by the International Law Commission on the provision of that Article: namely, that the content of jurisdictional immunity, in respect of acts performed in the exercise of consular functions, is already firmly established and well known in municipal law and international practice, so that courts may reasonably decide in case of doubt.[145]

---

[138] Yearbook of the I.L.C.,1960, vol. II, pp. 10 and 170; cf. also Part II, section 2(ii), ante.

[139] See p. 405, ante.

[140] U.N. Doc. A/CN. 4/131, op. cit., section II, para. 44.

[141] U.N. Doc. A/4425, op. cit., commentary on Article 41, and U.N. Doc. A/4843, op. cit., commentary on Article 43.

[142] See, in particular, Lee, op. cit., pp. 246 et seq.

[143] Emphasis supplied; see Draft Convention on the Legal Position and Functions of Consuls, prepared by the Harvard Law School committee, Article 21, as reported in M. Whiteman, Digest of International Law, vol. 7, Washington, 1970, p. 770.

[144] See note 140 ante; and see also Yearbook of the I.L.C., 1960, vol. I, p. 307.

[145] See Yearbook of the I.L.C., 1961, vol. I, pp. 119–121.

Conclusion

The incidence of a British vice-consul's amenability to the local Greek jurisdiction, for injurious activity against a British national, done in Greece and infringing upon the Greek laws, has been at the background of this essay on jurisdictional immunity under customary international law, the Vienna Convention on Consular Relations and the Consular Convention of 1953 between Greece and the United Kingdom. Resuming the major points of the discussion seems to allow for the following concluding comments and solution.

Essential element in the differentiation between the diplomatic and the consular jurisdictional immunity is, indeed, that this privilege is afforded to the latter category of foreign state organs as an exception rather than as a rule. This exception unequivocally derives from (and is a part of) general customary international law. That consular officers are amenable to the local jurisdiction of the receiving state, except in respect of their acts partaking of the (official) consular function—i.e. duties under (conventional and/or customary) international law—is, in any case, a fundamental rule that, despite varying formulations in the consular conventions, in doctrine and judicial practice, has retained a well-established content and usage. Consequently, there might be more of a terminology problem to it, rather than one of substance.

The indissoluble logical connection between consular judicial immunity and consular functions, according to international law, underlies any attempt to assess the lack of competence of the local courts with respect to the concrete acts performed by the consular officer. Thus, it is the same criterion used to protect the (indispensable in international relations) consular function, that is relied upon to secure the state's (unavoidable and omnipresent) "title to exercise jurisdiction" without "overstep(ping) the limits which international law places upon (this) jurisdiction".[146]

If the general criterion for the determination of whether concrete acts partake of the exercise of official (consular) functions lies within the frame of a demarcation of these functions under international law, it is, further, well understood that, in the concrete incidence, the acts of the British vice-consul may not even be considered as touching on the borderland of his official and unofficial function.

Thus, when the very content of the act performed by a consular official, either does not bear whatever relation to his consular functions or, even, is in conflict with these, judicial immunity may not be afforded. In the latter case, it is, moreover, possible to argue that, since the whole system of legal protection afforded to the consular organs is founded on the essential need to safeguard their functions under international law, it would be unthinkable to afford the legal protection for trespassing against them.

[146] P.C.I.J., Series A, Judgment No. 9, September 7,1927, The S.S. "Lotus", as reported in Hudson, op. cit., p. 35.

As a consequence, it is submitted that for any act conflicting in essence with what, in the last analysis, the consular function in international relations stands for—i.e. attending to and protecting the rights and interests of the sending state and of its nationals—cannot justify, in fact, any disrespect of or non-compliance with the local law, and the consular organ should, no doubt, be amenable to the local jurisdiction of the receiving state.

Bibliography

Addo, M. K. (1999). Vienna Convention on Consular Relations (Paraguay v United States of America) and Lagrand, applications for provisional measure. *International and Comparative Law Quarterly, 48*(3), 673–681.

Alharbi, F. R., & Csala, D. (2021). Gulf Cooperation Council Countries' Climate change mitigation challenges and exploration of solar and wind energy resource potential. *Applied Sciences, 11*(6), 2648.

Allport, G. W. (1954). *The nature of prejudice*. Addison-Wesley.

Alvarez, J. E. (2006). *International organizations as lawmakers*. Oxford University Press.

Alvarez, D. (1980). *Bureaucracy and Cold war Diplomacy. The USA and Turkey, 1943-1946* (p. 190). Institute of Balkan Studies.

Anagnostopoulou, D. (2014). The enhancement of the rights of the European citizen. In T. Skouteris & M. Vagias (Eds.), *International organizations and the protection of human Rights, Essays in honour of Professor Paroula Naskou-Perraki* (pp. 153–172). Themis N. A. Sakkoulas.

Anderson, M. S. (1993). *The rise of modern diplomacy, 1450-1919*. Longman.

Andrew, M. C. (2018). *Energy security and climate change: A national security perspective*. Harvard University Press.

Ang, I., Isar, Y. R., & Mar, P. (2015). Cultural diplomacy: Beyond the national interest? *International Journal of Cultural Policy, 21*(4), 364–381.

Ant, B. (2020). *The World Health Organization and the fight against epidemics/pandemics*. Sakkoulas. (in Greek).

Ant, B. (2021). *International Law and Diplomacy in the years of the Revolution of 1821*. Sakkoulas. (in Greek).

Antonopoulos, K. (2007). *The resolution of disputes by the International Court of Justice of the United Nations, Case-Law & Practice* (2nd ed.). Ant N. Sakkoulas. (in Greek).

Antonopoulos, K., & Magliveras, K. (2022). *The Law of International Society* (4th ed.). Nomiki Bibliothiki. (in Greek).

Arndt, F., Inter-Parliamentary Union (IPU), & Wolfrum, R. (Eds.). (2009). *Max Planck Encyclopedia of Public International Law*. Oxford University Press.

Arnold, P., & Οι, Ο. Α. (1983). *Αθήνα 1896 - Σεούλ 1988*. Αθηναϊκές Εκδόσεις. (in Greek).

Aust, A. (1986). The theory and practice of informal international instruments. *International & Comparative Law Quarterly, 35*.

Austermann, F. (2012). Towards embassies for Europe? EU delegations in the Union's Diplomatic System', Jean Monnet Multilateral Research Network on 'The Diplomatic System of the European Union'. *Policy Paper, 8*, 1–4.

Awungshi, Y., & Khashimwo, P. (2023). Mapping India-Nigeria relations: Bringing energy sector into focus. *Journal of Advance Research in Social Science & Humanities, 9*(9).

Babcock, S. (2002). The role of international law in United States death penalty cases. *LJIL, 15*(1), 367–387.

P. Naskou-Perraki (ed.), *Contemporary Diplomatic and Consular Relations*, https://doi.org/10.1007/978-3-031-99243-8

Baetens, F. (2019, July 18). *The International Court of Justice renders its judgement in the Jadhav case (India v. Pakistan)*. EJIL: Talk!.
Bailey, S. D. (1964). *The general assembly of the United Nations: A study of procedure and practice* (rev. edn), Praeger.
Bailey, T. (1968). Advice for the diplomat. In *The art of diplomacy – The American Enterprise* (p. 5). Appleton-Century-Crofts.
Bakri, N. (2011, July 11). Crowds in Syria attack U.S. and French embassies. *New York Times*.
Baldwin, D. A. (1971, October). The power of positive sanctions. *World Politics, 24*(1).
Baldwin, D. A. (1985). *Economic state craft*. Princeton University Press.
Baldwin, D. A. (1999, Winter). The sanctions debate and the logic of choice. *International Security, 24*(3).
Ballesteros, A. (1995). *Diplomacia y relaciones internacionales* (3rd ed.). Ministerio de Asuntos Exteriores.
Barkin, J. S. (2023). *International organizations: Theories and institutions* (2nd ed.). Palgrave Macmillan.
Barston, R. P. (1997). *Modern diplomacy* (2nd ed.). Longman.
Basdevant, J. (Ed.). (1966). *Dictionnaire de la terminologie du droit international*. Sirey.
Beitz, C. R. (2009). *The idea of human rights*. Oxford University Press.
Bellou, F. (2015). Tackling the internal and external security nexus and the role of the European External Action Service. In D. Anagnostopoulou (Ed.), *Challenges and developments in the EU area of freedom, security and justice, Proceedings of the Conference in memory of Dimitrios Evrigenis*. Publications of the University of Macedonia. (in Greek).
Benitez, L. (2022, April 6). *Russia credit insurance shows 99% chance of default within year*. Bloomberg Tax.
Berridge, G. R. (2005). *Diplomacy. Theory and practice* (3rd ed.). Palgrave.
Berridge, G. R. (2010). *Diplomacy: Theory and practice*. Palgrave-MacMillan.
Berridge, G. R., & James, A. (2001). *A dictionary of diplomacy*. Palgrave-MacMillan.
Berridge, G. R., Keens-Soper, M., & Otte, T. (2001). *Diplomatic theory from Machiavelli to Kissinger* (Studies in diplomacy). Palgrave.
Besson, S. (2006). Deliberative democracy in the European Union: Towards the deterritorialization of democracy. In S. Besson & J. L. Martí (Eds.), *Deliberative democracy and its discontents* (p. 181). Ashgate.
Bettati, M. (1998). Création et personnalité juridique des organisations internationales. In R. J. Dupuy (Ed.), *Manuel sur les organisations internationales/A Handbook of International Organisations* (2nd ed.). Martinus Nijhoff.
Biad, A. (1997). A strategy for conflict prevention and management in the Mediterranean. *Revista, CIDOB d'Afers Internacionals, 37*, 53–63.
Bloomefield, L. M., & FitzGerlad, G. F. (1975). *Crimes against internationally protected persons: Prevention and punishment. An analysis of the UN Convention*. Praeger.
Bodansky, D. (1993). The United nations framework convention on climate change: A commentary. *Yale Journal of International Law, 18*, 451.
Boissier, L. (1955). *L'Union interparlementaire et sa contribution au développement du droit international et à l'établissement de la paix* (Vol. 88, p. 174). Recueil des Cours 159.
Bonfils, H. (1905). *Manuel de Droit international public* (4th ed.). Librairie nouvelle de droit et de jurisprudence.
Bos, A., & Siblesz, H. (Eds.). (1986). *Realism in law-making – Essays in honour of Willem Riphagen*. Martinus Nijhoff.
Boşilcă, R. L. (2014, March). The European Union – A 'Sui Generis' International Diplomatic Actor: Challenges posed to the international diplomatic law. *Romanian Journal of European Affairs, 14*(1), 19 and 22.
Bosker, B. (2010, March 23–May 22).*Google shuts down China search, redirects users to Hong-Kong (updated)*. Huffington Post.

Boughton, J. M., & Bradford, C. I., Jr. (2007, December). Global governance: New players, new rules. *Finance & Development, 44*(4).

Brownlie, I. (1980). Parliamentary control over foreign policy in the United Kingdom. In A. Cassese (Ed.), *Parliamentary control over foreign policy* (pp. 1–10). Sijthoff and Noordhoff.

Brownlie, I., & Goodwin-Gill, G. S. (1999, 5 October). *Joint opinion on the international legal personality of the IPU, its status as an International Organisation in International Law and the Legal implications of such status for IPU's relations with governments and other international organisations, Reform of the Interparliamentary Union, Doc No. IPU-Dok.EX/229/9-Inf. 1.*

Buarque, D. (2017). The tainted spotlight: how crisis overshadowed Brazil's public diplomacy bet in hosting sports events and led to a downgrade of the country's reputation. *Trama Interdisciplinar, 8*(3), 71–92.

Buchan, R., & Navarrete, I. (2019, August 8). *The Jadhav judgement: Espionage, carve-outs and customary exceptions*. EJIL: Talk!.

Burke, E. D. (1839). *The works of Edmund Burke (in 9 volumes)* (Vol. 4). Freeman & Bolles Printers.

Burns, F. J. (2008, April 7). *Protests of China make Olympic torch relay an obstacle course*. New York Times.

Bustreo, F., & Doebbler, C. F. J. (2010). Making health an imperative of foreign policy: The value of a human rights approach. *Health and Human Rights Journal, 12*(1), 47–59.

Caflisch, L., & Cuny, L. (1998). The OSCE Court of Conciliation and Arbitration: Current problems. In Institut für Friedensforschung und Sicherheitspolitik (Ed.), *OSCE yearbook 1997* (pp. 347–355).

Cahier, P. (1964). *La droite diplomatique contemporaine*. Droz, Publications de l'Institut Universitaire de Hautes Etudes Internationales No 40.

Calmes, J., & Gladstone, R. (2012, June 02). *Obama imposes freeze on Iran property in US*. New York Times.

Calvet de Magalhães, J. (2001). *Manual diplomático: direito diplomático, práticadiplomática* (4th ed.). Ed. Bizâncio. (Coleção documentos 8).

Caprio, G., Jr. (Ed.). (2013). *Handbook of key global financial markets, institutions and infrastructure*. Elsevier.

Carroll, E., & Mackie, K. (2000). *International mediation: The art of business diplomacy*. Kluwer Law International.

Carter, C. H. (Ed.). (1965). *From the renaissance to the counter-reformation: Essays in Honor of Garrett Mattingly*. Random House.

Causevic, A. (2017). Facing an unpredictable threat: Is NATO ideally placed to manage climate change as a non-traditional threat multiplier? *Connections: The Quarterly Journal, 16*(2), 59–80.

Cavaré, L. (1969). *Le Droit international public positif* (Vol. II, 3rd ed.). Wentworth Press.

Cheatham, A., & Roy, D. (2023). *Venezuela: The rise and fall of a Petrostate* (Council on Foreign Relations). Retrieved June 25, 2024, from https://www.cfr.org/backgrounder/venezuela-crisis

Christianos, V. (Ed.). (2012). *EU Treaty & TFEU. Article interpretation*. Nomiki Bibliothiki. (in Greek).

Christodoulides, T.-A. (1985). *Structure and operation of international organizations*. Ant. N. Sakkoulas. (in Greek).

Chrysogonos, C. H. (2022). *Constitutional Law* (3rd ed.). Sakkoulas. (in Greek).

Cibean, T. (2022, April 16). *Russia plans to manufacture chips locally on a 28 nm node by 2030*. Techspot.

Coghlan, J. (1990). *Sport and British politics since 1960*. The Falmer Press.

Cohen, R., & Westbrook, R. (Eds.). (1992). *Amarna diplomacy: The beginnings of international relations*. Johns Hopkins University Press.

Cooper, A. F., & Frechette, L. (2015). *Celebrity diplomacy*. Routledge.

Couloumbis, T., & Wolfe, J. H. (1990). *Introduction to international relations: Power and justice*. Prentice Hall.

Crawford, J., Pellet, A., & Olleson, S. (Eds.). (2010). *The law of international responsibility*. Oxford University Press.
Crocker, C. A., Osler, H. F., & Aall, P. (Eds.). (2021). *Diplomacy and the future of world order*. Georgetown University Press.
Croft, S. (2005). South Asia arms control process: Cricket diplomacy and the composite dialogue. *International Affairs, 81*(5), 1039–1060.
Daoudi, M. S., & Dajani, M. S. (1983). *Economic sanctions, ideals and experience*. Routledge & Kegan Paul.
Dash, S. (2023). India-Nigeria Oil Partnership. *Indian Journal of African Studies, 84*.
Daunton, M. (2023). *The economic government of the world: 1933-2023*. Farrar, Straus and Giroux.
Davis, C. (2023). *Discriminatory clubs: The geopolitics of international organizations*. Princeton University Press.
de MagalhãesJ, C., & Pereira, B. F. (1988). *The pure concept of diplomacy*. Greenwood Press.
De Puig, L. M. (2008). *International parliaments*. CoE Publications.
de Tocqueville, A. (2010). *Democracy in America*. Liberty Fund.
Deese, D. A., & Nye, J. S. (1981). *Energy and security, Book: Report of Harvard's Energy and Security Research Project*.
Denza, E. (2016). *Diplomatic law – Commentary on the Vienna Convention of Diplomatic Relations* (4th ed.). Oxford University Press.
Dikaios, G. (2024). *EU climate diplomacy towards the IMO and ICAO: Normative without power*. Palgrave Macmillan.
Dimier, V., & McGeever, M. (2006, September). Diplomats without a flag. The institutionalisation of the delegations of the commission in Africa, Caribbean and Pacific Countries. *Journal of Common Market Studies, 44*(09).
Dipla, X. (2003). *The International Court of Justice of the United Nations. His position in the International Judiciary and his contribution to the modern law of the sea* (Vol. I). Ant. N. Sakkoulas. (in Greek).
Dipla, X., & Doussis, E. (2001). *The International Court of Justice of the United Nations, Summary of Cases 1980-2000* (Vol. II). Ant. N. Sakkoulas. (in Greek).
Do Nascimento e Silva, G. E. (1972). *Diplomatic Law – Commentary to the Vienna Convention on Diplomatic Relations*. A. W. Sijthoff.
Dobson, A. P., & Marsh, S. (Eds.). (2013). *Anglo-American relations: Contemporary perspectives*. Routledge.
Doussis, E. (2010). Seal the deal: A new approach to climate change. In S. Dalis (Ed.), *From Bush to Obama* (pp. 240–256). Papazisis. (in Greek).
Doussis, E. (2012). The international system of environmental protection. In A. Kontis & C. Tsardanidis (Eds.), *International political economy: Theory, structure and challenges of global economy* (2nd ed., pp. 871–896). Papazisis. (in Greek).
Doussis, E. (2014). *Environmental governance in crisis: Rio+20: Promises with doubtful implementation*. Papazisis.
Doussis, E. (2017). *Climate change*. Papadopoulos. (in Greek).
Doussis, E. (2020). *International law and diplomacy of climate change*. Nomiki Bibliothiki. (in Greek).
Doxey, M. P. (1996). *International sanctions in contemporary perspective*. Palgrave MacMillan.
Dunn, F. S. (1929). *The practice and procedure of international conferences*. The Johns Hopkins Press.
Dupuy, J. R. *International Law, Quesais-je?, No 131*.
Earsom, J., & Delreux, T. (2021). Evaluating EU responsiveness to the evolution of the international regime complex on climate change. *International Environmental Agreements: Politics, Law and Economics, 21*(4), 711–728.
Economides, K. P. (1975). *Inviolability and immunity of diplomatic officials with reference to the detainee's consular officers*. Sakkoulas. (in Greek).

Economides, K. P. (1988). Bringing an end the hostilities with Albania. *International Law and International Policy, 16*, 46.
Economides, K. P. (1989). *Public International Law*. Ant. N. Sakkoulas. (in Greek).
Economides, K. P. (1991). *Introduction to Diplomatic and Consular Law, The Institutions of the State in International Relations*. Ant. N. Sakkoulas. (in Greek).
Edwards, H. (1984). Sport politics - Los Angeles 1984: The Olympic tradition continues. *Journal of Sociology of Sports, 1*, 172–183.
Edwards, A., & Ferstaman, C. (Eds.). (2010). *Human security and non-citizens: Law, policy and international affairs*. Cambridge University Press.
Efstathiadis, K. T. (1977). *International Law, I*. Ant. N. Sakkoulas. (in Greek).
Eide, A. (2001). Obstacles and goals to be pursued. In A. Eide et al. (Eds.), *Economic, social and cultural rights: A textbook* (2nd ed., pp. 553–562). Kluwer Law International.
Eilts, F. H. (1979). Diplomacy - Contemporary practice, (Lecture, US Army War College, Carlisle Barracks, Pennsylvania, August 31, 1973). In E. Plischke (Ed.), *Modern diplomacy – The art and the artisans* (pp. 3–18). American Enterprise Institute for Public Policy Research.
Elder, M. (2007). *Putin lands a deal for Turkmen Gas*. The Moscow Times. Retrieved June 25, 2024, from https://www.themoscowtimes.com/archive/putin-lands-a-deal-for-turkmen-gas
Erbach, G. (1984, July 07–10). On the character and contents of sport and of international sporting activities at present and in the future. In M. llmirinen (Ed.), *The Proceedings of the Congress Sport and International Understanding, Helsinki*, Springer.
Espinal, M. A. (2023). The Pan American Health Organization: 120 years in the Americas hemisphere. *Lancet Regional Health Americas, 21*, 100488.
Espy, R. (1979). *The politics of the Olympic Games*. University of California Press.
Evrigenis, D. (1992). *On diplomatic and legislative reciprocity. Contribution to the jurisprudence of the law of international relations, Armenopoulos 1959, p. 757 et seq.* (as republished in Annales – Periodical of the Department of Law of the School of Law and Economics, Volume Three, Papers of Dimitrios I. Evrigenis, Issue Two, Thessaloniki, 1992, p. 877 et seq.) (in Greek).
Fairman, D., et al. (2012). *Negotiating public health in a globalized world: Global health diplomacy in action*. Springer.
Falk, R. A. (1971). The United Nations: Variety systems of operation. In L. Gordenker (Ed.), *The United Nations in international politics* (p. 184). Princeton University Press.
Falk, R. A., & Strauss, A. (2001). Toward global parliament. *Foreign Affairs, 80*, 212.
Fassbender, B. (2009). *The United Nations Charter as the Constitution of the International Community*. Martinus Nijhoff.
Fatouros, A. (1986). *The role of Congress in the Foreign Policy of the United States of America* (p. 45). Kouloubis-Konstas. (in Greek).
Faupin, H. (1998). Les problèmes juridiques posés par la circulation automobile des diplomates. *AFDI, 44*, 167–186.
Feltham, R. G. (1998). *Diplomatic handbook* (7th ed.). Longman.
Finch, G. A. (1916). The Bryan Peace Treaties. *American Journal of International Law, 10*, 882–890.
Finn, H. K. (2003, November). The case for cultural diplomacy. Engaging foreign audiences. *Foreign Affairs, 82*(6), 15–20.
Fitri, A. (2022, March 7). *International sanctions could cripple Russia's tech ambitions*. Tech Monitor.
Fleischauer, A., & See, C. (1985). The United Nations and the progressive development and codification of international law. *International Journal of Innovation and Learning, 25*(1), 2.
Fodella, A. (2009). Structural and institutional aspects of non-compliance mechanisms. In T. Treves et al. (Eds.), *Non-compliance procedures and mechanisms and the effectiveness of international environmental agreements* (pp. 355–373). TMC Asser Press.
Forney, M., & Kroeber, A. (2010, April 06). Google's business reason for leaving China – of reputation and revenue. *The Wall Street Journal*.

Francioni, F. (2007). Des biens culturels au patrimoine culturel: l'évolution dynamique d'un concept et de son extension. In A. A. Yusuf (Ed.), *Elaboration de règles internationales sur l'éducation, la science et la culture* (Vol. I, pp. 239–241). Editions UNESCO/Martinus Nijhoff Publishers.

Freeman, W. (2012). *Physical education, exercise, and sport science in a changing society* (7th ed.). Jones & Bartlett.

Gangas, D. (2021). *Olympic movement and international politics: A confrontational coexistence over time*. International Olympic Academy.

Gargalianos, D. (1992). *The new European Sports Charter*. Pandektis. (in Greek).

Gary, H., & Alistair, P. (2012). *Environmentalism since 1945*. Routledge.

Gerani, S. (2019). *Small states in regional conflicts: The cases of Kuwait and Cyprus*. Thesis, University of Macedonia.

Giannaras, C. (2001). *Cultural diplomacy*. Ikaros Publications. (in Greek).

Giatsis, S. (1991). *Contemporary Olympic Games, University lectures*. Department of Physical Education & Sport Science, Aristotle University of Thessaloniki.

Gienow-Hecht, J. C. E., & Donfried, M. C. (Eds.). (2013). *Searching for a cultural diplomacy*. Berghahn Books.

Glencross, A. (2014). *The politics of European Integration: Political union or a house divided?* Wiley-Black Well.

Goldthau, A. (2014). Rethinking the governance of energy infrastructure: Scale, Decentralization and Polycentrism. *Energy Research & Social Science, 8*, 203.

Gosalbo, B. R. (2011). The organisation of the external relations of the European Union in the Treaty of Lisbon. In P. Koutrakos (Ed.), *The European Union's external relations a year after Lisbon, Centre for the Law of EU External Relations, CLEER Working Papers no. 3* (p. 13).

Gottlieb, G. (1972). The nature of international law: Toward a second concept of law. In C. E. Black & R. A. Falk (Eds.), *The future of the international legal order, Volume 4: The structure of the international environment* (p. 331). Princeton University Press.

Graaf, T. (2013). *The politics and institutions of global energy governance*. Palgrave Macmillan.

Gramsci, A. (1971). *Selections from the prison notebooks of Antonio Gramsci*. International Publishers.

Gross, L. (1948). The Peace of Westphalia, 1648-1948. *The American Journal of International Law, 42*(1), 20–41.

Guarascio, F. (2022, April 8). *EU slashes 10% of Russian imports with new sweeping sanctions*. Reuters.

Gutner, T. (2017). *International organization in world politics*. Sage.

Haass, R. (1998). *Economic sanctions and American Diplomacy*. Council on Foreign Relations.

Hadjikonstantinou, K., Apostolidis, C., & Sarigiannidis, M. (2014). *Fundamental concepts in international public law* (2nd ed.). Sakkoulas. (in Greek).

Hambro, E. (1972). Some notes on parliamentary diplomacy. In W. Friedmann, L. Henkin, & O. Lissitzyn (Eds.), *Transnational law in a changing society: Essays in Honor of Philip C. Jessup* (p. 280). Columbia University Press.

Hamilton, K., & Langhorne, R. (1995, 2011). *The practice of diplomacy: Its evolution, theory and administration*. Routledge.

Han, H., & Ahn, S. W. (2020). Youth mobilization to stop global climate change. *Sustainability, 12*, 4127.

Happel, D., & Kramer, R. (1984). The objectives of sport and international understanding. In M. llmirinen (Ed.), *The Proceedings of the Congress "Sport and International Understanding"*, pp. 108–110, Helsinki, 7–10.7.82. Springer.

Heffter, L. (1860). *Das Europäische Völkerrecht der Gegenwart* (p. 248, 246–247). Verlag von E. H. Schröder.

Hendriks, A. (1998). The right to health in national and international jurisprudence. *European Journal of Health Law, 5*, 389–408.

Henkin, L. (1996). *Foreign affairs and the United States Constitution*. Oxford University Press.

Hetzner, C. (2022, March 22). *Russia's largest tank manufacturer may have run out of parts.* Fortune.

Hofstede, G., & Minkov, M. (1991). *Cultures and organizations: Software of the mind.* McGraw-Hill.

Holland, D. C. (1951). Diplomatic immunity in English Law. *Current Legal Problems, 4*, 106.

Horby, L. (2012, February 07). *New sanctions on Iran constrict trade flows to Asia.* Reuters.

Houlihan, B. (1994). *Sport and international politics.* Harvester Wheatsheaf.

Hübner, P. (1970). Interparlamentarische Union. In H. Röhring & K. Sontheimer (Eds.), *Handbuch des deutschen Parlamentarismus: DAS Regierungssystem der Bundesrepublik in 270 Stichworten* (p. 218). R. Piper.

Huntington, S. (1996). *The clash of civilizations and the remaking of world order.* Simon & Schuster.

Iakovidis, I. (2021). *Jurisdictional immunities and human rights, Human Rights Studies 3.* Nomiki Bibliothiki. (in Greek).

Ioannou, K., Economidis, K., Rozakis, C., & Arg, F. (1991). *Public International Law.* Ant. N. Sakkoulas. (in Greek).

Irizarry y Puente, J. (1937). *Traité sur les functions internationales des consuls.* Cambridge University Press.

Isar, Y. R. (2014). *Engaging the world: Towards global cultural citizenship, final report.* European Union.

Isar, Y. R. (2015). Culture in EE external relations: An idea whose time has come? *International Journal of Cultural Policy, 21*(4), 494–508.

Iwata, H., & Okada, K. (2014). Greenhouse gas emissions and the role of the Kyoto Protocol. *Environmental Economics and Policy Studies, 16*(4), 325–342.

James, A. (2016). Diplomatic relations between states. In C. M. Constantinou, P. Kerr, & P. Shaer (Eds.), *The SAGE handbook of diplomacy* (pp. 257–267). Sage.

Jara, R. E. (2013, March). Diplomacy. In R. Wolfrum (Ed.), *Max Planck Encyclopedia of Public International Law.* Oxford University Press.

Jennings, C., & Hopkinson, N. (Eds.). (1999). *Current issues in international diplomacy and foreign policy* (Vol. 1). HMSO/Wilton Park.

Jessup, P. C. (1956). Parliamentary diplomacy: An examination of the legal quality of the rules of procedure of organizations of the United Nations. *Recueil des Cours, 89*, 181.

Jons, R. E. (1979). *Principles of foreign policy.* St. Martin's Press.

Jönsson, C., & Hall, M. (2005). *Essence of diplomacy.* Palgrave Macmillan/Springer.

Kalpyris, E., & Hatzantonakis, I. (1999). *Guide to the examinations of the Ministry of Foreign Affairs.* Ant. N. Sakkoulas. (in Greek).

Karabarbounis, X. (1998). The Hellenic Parliament and Foreign Policy: An Institutional Approach. *Thesis: A Journal of Foreign Policy Issues, II*(1), 3. (in Greek).

Karabarbounis, X. (2004). Parliament of the Greeks and Foreign Policy. In S. Perrakis, A. Bredimas, & X. Karabarbounis (Eds.), *Parliamentary diplomacy & the Hellenic Parliament.* Ant. N. Sakkoulas. (in Greek).

Karaitidis, D. (2014). Diplomacy a complex function. In T. Karvounarakis (Ed.), *Diplomacy in the 21st century, Proceedings of the Conference 23–24 May 2013* (p. 27 et seq). University of Macedonia Publications. (in Greek).

Karns, M. P., & Mingst, K. A. (2013). International organizations and diplomacy. In A. Cooper et al. (Eds.), *The Oxford handbook of modern diplomacy* (pp. 142–159). Oxford University Press.

Karp, G. (2011, August 14). *Ratings game: Power of S&P, other top credit agencies, grew from government action.* Chicago Tribune.

Karvounarakis, T. (2013). *The art of diplomacy and its Artisans.* Thyrathen. (in Greek).

Karvounarakis, T. (2014). *Diplomacy in the 21st century, Proceedings of Conference 23–24 May 2013.* University of Macedonia Publications. (in Greek).

Karvounarakis, T. (Ed.). (2018). *The University of Macedonia Master's in International Public Administration Book. Essays on the functioning of the world community.* University of Macedonia Publications.

Katz, R., Kornblet, S., Arnold, G., Lief, E., & Fischer, J. E. (2011). Defining health diplomacy: Changing demands in the era of globalization. *The Milbank Quarterly, 89*(3), 503–523.

Katzman, K. (2016). *Iran: Politics, Gulf Security, and U.S. Policy.* Congressional Research Service.

Kaufmann, J. (1988). *Conference diplomacy* (2nd ed.). Martinus-Nijhoff.

Kennan, G. F. (1946, February 22). *Telegram by George Kennan to George Marshall [Long Telegram].* Harry S. Truman Administration File, Elsey Papers.

Kennan, G. F. (1947, July). The sources of Soviet conduct. *Foreign Affairs, 25*(4).

Kennan, G. F. (1951). *American Diplomacy, 1990-1950.* University of Chicago Press.

Kennelly, M., & Toohey, K. (2007). Terrorism and the Olympics: The Games have gone on. *Sporting Traditions, 24*(1–2), 1–22.

Khosla, R., Allotey, P., & Gruskin, S. (2022). Reimagining human rights in global health: what will it take? *BMJ Global Health.*

Kickbusch, I., & Erk, C. (2009). Global health diplomacy: The new recognition of health in foreign policy. In A. Clapham & M. Robinson (Eds.), *Realizing the right to health* (pp. 517–524). Rüffer & Rub.

Kickbusch, I., & Ivanova, M. (2013). The history and evolution of global health diplomacy. In I. Kickbusch, G. Lister, M. Told, & N. Drager (Eds.), *Global health diplomacy: Concepts, issues, actors, instruments, fora and cases* (pp. 11–26). Springer.

Kickbusch, I., & Liu, A. (2022). Global health diplomacy—Reconstructing power and governance. *The Lancet.*

Kickbusch, I., Nikogosian, H., Kazatchkine, M., & Kökény, M. (2021). *A guide to global health diplomacy: Better health – Improved global solidarity – More equity.* Global Health Centre - Graduate Institute of International and Development Studies.

Kirgis, F. (2003, June). *Diplomatic immunities in Iraq,* The American Society of International Law – ASIL Insights. (In Greek).

Kirkey, C., Paquin, S., & Roussel, S. (2016). Charting Quebec's engagement with the international community. *American Review of Canadian Studies, 46,* 135–148.

Kissinger, H. (1994). *Diplomacy.* Simon & Schuster.

Kissinger, H. (2011). *Years of upheaval.* Simon & Schuster.

Kissling, C. (2011). *The legal and political status of international parliamentary institutions.* Committee for a Democratic UN.

Koller, P. (2009). International Law and Global Justice. In L. H. Meyer (Ed.), *Legitimacy, justice and public international law.* Cambridge University Press.

Konstantopoulos, D. S. (1986). *Public International Law, I. Introduction – General Principles – Human Rights – UN* (4th ed.). Sakkoulas. (in Greek).

Konstantopoulos, D. S. (1992). *The explosion of the war between Germany and Greece (1941) and the protection of their interests by their respective protectors, Greece and the war in the Balkans (1940-41)* (Vol. 245, pp. 119–161). Institute for Balkan Studies.

Konstas, D. (1986). The Parliament exercise external policy. In T. Kouloubis & D. Konstas (Eds.), *The Hellenic Parliament in Foreign Policy 1974-1984.* Ant. N. Sakkoulas. (in Greek).

Konstas, D. (2002). *Diplomacy and politics.* Livani. (in Greek).

Kontochristou, M. (2018). Building Europe. Cultural policies in the European Union. In M. Kontochristou (Ed.), *Culture in the international. Challenges and policies.* Sideris. (in Greek).

Koops, J., & Macaj, G. (2015). *The European Union as a diplomatic actor.* Palgrave Macmillan.

Koptsidis, G. Historical elements of the structure and operation of the Ministry of Foreign Affairs. In T. Karvounarakis (Ed.) *Diplomacy in 21st century* (p. 11 et seq) (In Greek)

Koufa, K. (1976). *The U.N. and regional international organisation* (Vol. 16, pp. 19–21). Jus Gentium.

Koufa, K. (1980). Aspects of consular relations between Greece and the United Kingdom: Considering consular amenability to local jurisdiction in the light of customary international law, the Consular Convention between the United Kingdom and Greece and the Vienna Convention on Consular Relations. *Hellenic Review of International Relations, I*(II).

Koufa, K. (1986). Evolution of International Law: International Legislation though the United Nations. In *Thesaurus Acroasium Vol. XVi – The evolution of International Law since the Creation of the U.N. with Special Emphasis on Human Right* (pp. 263–286). Institute of International Public Law and International Relations of Thessaloniki.

Kouskouvelis, I. (1997). *Decision making – Judgement – Negotiation, theory and practice*. Papazisis. (in Greek).

Kozymka, I. (2014). *The diplomacy of culture: The role of UNESCO in sustaining cultural diversity*. Palgrave Macmillan.

Kunz, D. B. (1997). *Butter and Guns: America's Cold War economic diplomacy*. Free Press.

Laksmanan, I. R. A. (2012, February 10). *EU sanctions on Iran's main ports will slash trade if enforced*. Bloomberg.

Laksmanan, I. R. A. (2015, September 15). *If you can't do this deal, go back to Tehran: The inside story of the Obama administration's Iran diplomacy*. Politico.

Lapaš, D. (2016). Controversial subjects of contemporary international law: IGO-like entities as participants in international legal relations – Do we need a 'Reparation Case II'? In M. S. Wolfrum & T. M. Sošič (Eds.), *Contemporary developments in international law: Essays in Honour of Budislav Vukas* (pp. 56–86). Martinus Nijhoff.

Lapchick, R. E. (1975). *The politics of race and international sport*. Greenwood Press.

Lasswell, H. D. (1950). *National security and individual freedom*. McGraw-Hill.

Laudy, P. (1989). *Les parlements dans le monde contemporain: Modes d'élection – fonctionnement – Structures*. Payot.

Lauren, P. G. (2003). *The evolution of international human rights: Visions seen* (2nd ed.). University of Pennsylvania Press.

Lee, L. T. (1966). *Vienna convention on consular relations*. A. W. Sijthoff.

Lee, D., & Hudson, D. (2004). The old and new significance of political economy in diplomacy. *Review of International Studies, 30*(3).

Lee, L. T., & Quigley, J. (2008). *Consular law and practice* (3rd ed.). Oxford University Press.

Lee, D., Coolsaet, R., Potter, E., & Rana, K. (2004). Policy forum on commercial and economic diplomacy. *International Studies Perspectives, 5*.

Lew, J. (2015, April 29). *Remarks of Treasury Secretary Jacob J. Lew to The Washington Institute*. Washington Institute.

Libera, C. (1959). Le fondement juridique des privileges et immunitis consulaires. *Revue Générale de Droit International Public*, 444.

Loannou, K. (1976). The application of generally accepted rules of international law in the Greek Legal Order. *Armenopoulos*, 298–318. (in Greek).

Lobanov, S. A., & Surkhayeva, Y. J. (2024). International legal approach to understanding energy diplomacy. *Moscow Journal of International Law*.

Longhorne, R. (1992). The regulation of diplomatic practice: The beginnings to the Vienna Convention on Diplomatic Relations 1961. *Review of International Studies, 18*, 3–17.

Lorenz, K. (1966). *On aggression*. MJF Books.

Lucas, J. (1992). *Future of the Olympic Games*. Human Kinetics.

Lütz, S., Leeg, T., Otto, D., & Dreher, V. W. (2021). *The European Union as a global actor: Trade, finance and climate policy*. Springer.

MacAloon, J. (1991). The turn of two centuries: sport and the politics of international relations. In F. Landry, M. Landry, & M. Yerles (Eds.), *"Sport…The Third Millennium", International Symposium, Quebec City, Canada, 21–25.05.1990*. Les Presses De L'Université Laval.

MacDonald, R. S. J. (2000). The Charter of the United Nations as a World Constitution. In M. N. Schmitt (Ed.), *International law Across the Spectrum of Conflict: Essays in Honor of Professor L. C. Green on the occasion of his eightieth birthday* (p. 263). Naval War College.

Magliveras, K. (2004). The Interparliamentary Union and the Hellenic Parliament. In S. Perrakis, A. Bredimas, & H. Karabarbounis (Eds.), *Parliamentary diplomacy and the Hellenic Parliament* (pp. 289–331). Ant. N. Sakkoulas. (in Greek).

Magliveras, K. (2017). *The Law of international society* (3rd ed., pp. 65–78). Nomiki Bibliothiki.

Magliveras, K. (2020). Organization' and 'International organizations: A discourse on synthesis. In L. Boisson de Chazournes et al. (Eds.), *Liber Amicorum a l'honneur de H. Dipla - Enjeux et Perspectives, A* (pp. 513–531). Pedone.

Magliveras, K. (2021a). The implications of African Union Law: conceptual analysis with emphasis on the institutional consequences. In F. Amao, M. Olivier, & K. Magliveras (Eds.), *The emergent African Union Law: Conceptualization, delimitation, and application* (pp. 30–44). Oxford University Press.

Magliveras, K. (2021b). *The role of international organisations as promoters, enforcers and exporters of democratic ideals and the rule of law in European Center for Research and Training of Human Rights and Humanitarian Action, Safeguarding Democratic Institutions within a Europe in Crisis: Challenges and responses, Proceedings of the International Conference, Nafplion, 11–12 May 2018* (pp. 85–106). Sideris.

Magliveras, K., & Bourantonis, D. (2003). Rescinding the signature of an international treaty as a means for opposing it: The case of the United States and the Rome statute establishing the International Criminal Court. *Diplomacy and Statecraft, 14*, 21–49.

Magliveras, K., & Naldi, G. (2021). *Association of South-East Asian Nations (ASEAN)*. Wolters Kluwer.

Magliveras, K., & Naldi, G. (2023a). *The African Union (AU)* (3rd ed.). Wolters Kluwer.

Magliveras, K., & Naldi, G. (2023b). The state of Palestine as a Sovereign actor in the international community: implications for its legal status. In S. Abidde (Ed.), *Palestine, Taiwan, and Western Sahara: Statehood, sovereignty, and the international system* (pp. 93–118). Rowman & Littlefield/Lexington Books.

Malone, G. (1988). *Political advocacy and cultural communication: Organizing the nation's public diplomacy*. University Press of America/Miller Center University of Virginia.

Mandela, N. (2000). *Address to the 1st Laureus World Sports Award*. https://www.un.org/development/desa/disabilities/wp-content/uploads/sites/15/2019/12/Adam-UN-slides.pdf

Manfredi Sanchez, J. L., & Pérez, F. S. (2020). Climate change begins at home: City diplomacy in the age of the Anthropocene. In P. Surowiec & I. Manor (Eds.), *Public diplomacy and the politics of uncertainty* (pp. 57–81). Palgrave Macmillan.

Marcantonatos, L. G. (1974). *Les Relations consulaires aux termes de la Convention de Vienne du 24 Avril 1963*. Institute of International Public Law and International Relations, Scientific Publications/Directorate: D.S. Konstantopoulos.

Marek, K. (1977). *Reflections on contemporary law-making in international law*. International Relations in a Changing World I.U.H.E.I.

Mark, S. L. (2009, April). *A greater role for cultural diplomacy, discussion papers in diplomacy*. Netherlands Institute of International Relations 'Clingendael'.

Mark, S. L. (2010). Rethinking cultural diplomacy: The cultural diplomacy of New Zealand, the Canadian Federation and Quebec. *Political Science, 62*(1), 62–83.

Markel, H. (2014). Worldly approaches to global health: 1851 to the present. *Public Health, 128*(2), 124–128.

Markezinis, B. (1974). The sovereign immunity of states in private and public international law. *Court Case, 5*, 603.

Marshall, G. (1947, June 5). European initiative essential to economic recovery - Address at commencement exercises at Harvard University. *US Department of State Bulletin, 16*(415).

Martinez, M. (1991). *European security and threats outside Europe - The organisation of peace and security in the Mediterranean region and the Middle East*. Parliamentary Assembly of the Western European Union.

Matonis, J. (2013, February 08). *EU court strikes down SWIFT's blockade against Iranian Banks*. Forbes.

Mattingly, G. (1964). *Renaissance diplomacy*. Penguin Books.

Maurer, A. W. W. (Ed.). (2001). *National Parliaments on their ways to Europe losers or latecomers?* Nomos.

McLaren, R. H. (2016). *The independent person. 2nd Report*. World Anti-Doping Agency. https://www.wada-ama.org/sites/default/files/resources/files/mclaren_report_part_ii_2.pdf

McMahon, D. E., Peters, G. A., Ivers, L. C., & Freeman, E. E. (2020). Global resource shortages during COVID-19: Bad news for low-income countries. *PLoS Neglected Tropical Diseases, 14*(7).

McNair, A. D. (Ed.). (1932). *Contributions to international law and diplomacy*. Longmans.

Meier, B. M., & Fox, A. M. (2010). International obligations through collective rights: Moving from foreign health assistance to global health governance. *Health and Human Rights Journal, 12*(1), 61–72.

Meier, B. M., de Mesquita, J. B., & Williams, C. R. (2022). Global obligations to ensure the right to health: Strengthening global health governance to realise human rights in global health. *Yearbook of International Disaster Law Online, 3*(1), 3–34.

Melissen, J. (Ed.). (1999). *Innovation in diplomatic practice*. MacMillan.

Melissen, J. (Ed.). (2005). *The new public diplomacy. Soft Power in international relations*. Palgrave Macmillan.

Mennecke, M. (2001). Towards the humanization of the Vienna Convention of Consular Rights: The LaGrand case before the International Court of Justice. *GYIL, 44*, 430–468.

Miller, R. (2020). Qatar, energy security, and strategic vision in a small state. *Journal of Arabian Studies, 10*, 122–138.

Mitchell, J. M. (1986). *International cultural relations*. Allen & Unwin.

Moons, S. J. V., & de Boer, R. (2004). Economic diplomacy, product characteristics and level of development. *ETSG Conference*.

Morgan, T. C., & Schwebach, V. L. (1997, March). Fools suffer gladly: The use of economic sanctions in international crises. *International Studies Quarterly, 41*(1).

Moschella, M., & Weaver, C. (Eds.). (2014). *Handbook of global economic governance: Players, power and paradigms*. Routledge.

Murray, S. (2018). *Sports diplomacy: Origins, theory, and practice*. Routledge.

Murray, S., & Pigman, P. A. (2014). Mapping the relationship between international sport and diplomacy. *Sport in Society, 17*(9), 1098–1118.

Murray, S., & Price, G. (2020). *Towards a Welsh sports diplomacy strategy*. Commissioned by British Council Wales.

Murty, B. S. (1989). *The international law of diplomacy: The diplomatic instrument and world public order*. Martinus Nijhoff.

Nafziger, J. (1991). *International sports law*. Hatzikonstantinou (translation), Paratiritis.

Nahlik, S. E. (1990). Development of Diplomatic Law. *Recueil des Cours de l'Académie de Droit International de la Haye, 222*.

Naldi, G., & Magliveras, K. (2023). The East mediterranean gas forum: A regional institution struggling in the mire of energy insecurities. *International Organizations Law Review, 20*, 194–227.

Nampewo, J. H., & Mike, J. W. (2022). Respecting, protecting and fulfilling the human right to health. *International Journal for Equity in Health*.

Naskou-Perraki, P., & Bachtsevanidou, D. (Eds.). (2008). *UNESCO Conventions*. Ant. N. Sakkoulas.

Naskou-Perraki, P., & Giannopoulos, P. (2000). *Provisional measures at the international court of justice of The Hague, Library of International Economic Law, CIEEL*. Ant. N. Sakkoulas. (in Greek).

Naskou-Perraki, P., & Zaikos, N. (2022). *Diplomatic and consular law, parliamentary, cultural and economic diplomacy, with the contribution of Anagnostopoulou D, Sarigiannidis M., Zervaki A., Bozoudi M* (2nd ed.). Sakkoulas. (in Greek).

Naskou-Perraki, P., Zaikos, N., & Chainoglou, K. (2010). *Diplomatic and consular law, texts of international practice*. Ant. N. Sakkoulas. (in Greek).

Naskou-Perraki, P., Antonopoulos, K., & Sarigiannidis, M. (2024). *International organisations* (3rd ed.). Sakkoulas. (in Greek).

Nicholson, H. (1939). *Diplomacy*. Thornton Butterworth.

Nicholson, H. (1966). *The evolution of diplomacy*. Collier Books.

Nijman, J. E. (2004). *International legal personality - An inquiry into the history and theory of international law*. TMC Asser Press.

Nussbaum, M. C. (2011). *Creating capabilities. The human development approach*. The Belknap Press.

Nye, J. S. (2004). *Soft power: The means to success in world politics*. Public Affairs Books.

O'Connell, D. P. (1970). *International Law* (Vol. II, 2nd ed.). Stevens.

O'Neill, J., & Terzi, A. *Changing trade patterns, unchanging European and global governance*. Bruegel Working Paper 2014/02.

Olafson, G., & Brown-John, C. (1986). Canadian international sport policy: A public policy analysis. In G. Redmond (Ed.), *The 1984 Olympic Scientific Congress Proceedings* (Human Kinetics Publishers) (Vol. 7, pp. 69–76).

Olson, D. M. (1994). *Democratic legislative institutions: A comparative view*. M. E. Sharpe.

Oppenheim, L. (1955). *International law, A treatise, Vol. 1, Peace* (8th ed.). Longman.

Oppenheim, L. (1967). *International law - A treatise* (Vol. I, 8th ed.). Longmans.

Ottinger, R. L. (2010). Copenhagen Climate Conference–Success or failure? *Pace Environmental Law Review, 27*, 411–419.

Pancracio, J.-P. (1998). *Dictionnaire de la Diplomatie*. Microbuss.

Papakostas, A.-B. (1971a). *The immunity of diplomatic representatives* (2nd ed.) (in Greek).

PapaKostas, A.-B. (1971b). *The exterritoriality of diplomatic representatives* (2nd ed.) (in Greek).

Papakostas, A.-B. (1989). *The law of diplomatic and consular relations*. Ant. N. Sakkoulas. (in Greek).

Papastamkos, G. K. (1990). *International economic sanctions: Theory and practice*. Ant. N. Sakkoula. (in Greek).

Park, S.-J. (1991). *The Seoul Olympics: The inside story*. Bellew Publishing.

Parsi, T. (2012). *A single roll of the dice: Obama's diplomacy with Iran*. Yale University Press.

Paust, J. J. (1998). Breard and treaty-based rights under the Consular Convention. *AJIL, 92*(4), 691–697.

Perez de Cuellar, J. (1997). *Manuel de derecho diplomático* (Politica y derecho). Fondo de Cultra Económica.

Pergantis, V. (2017). *The human dimension of diplomatic protection, nature and delimitation of the Institution*. Sakkoulas. (in Greek).

Perrakis, S. (2001). *The International Court of Justice of the United Nations, Detections of a judicial route in the peaceful resolution of international disputes*. Ant. N. Sakkoulas. (in Greek).

Perrakis, S., Bredimas, A., & Karabarbounis, C. (Eds.). (2004). *Parliamentary diplomacy and the Hellenic Parliament*. Ant. N. Sakkoulas. (in Greek).

Peters, A. (2009). Dual democracy. In J. Klabbers, A. Peters, & G. Ulfstein (Eds.), *The constitutionalization of international law* (pp. 323–327). EJIL: Talk!.

Peters, A. (2011). The constitutionalisation of international organisations. In N. Walker, J. Shaw, & S. Tierney (Eds.), *Europe's Constitutional Mosaic*. Hart.

Peters, A. (2012). Are we moving towards constitutionalisation of the world community? In Cassese (Ed.), *Realising utopia: The future of international law* (p. 118). Oxford University Press.

Petersmann, E. U. (1997). Constitutionalism and international organisations. *Northwestern Journal of International Law & Business, 17*, 398.

Peterson, S. M. (2012). Iran's deteriorating economy: An analysis of the economic impact of Western Sanctions. *ESIA International Affairs Review*.

Philips, L. (2011, May 3). EU wins new powers at UN, transforming global body. *EU Observer*.

Piot, P., Timberlake, S., & Sigurdson, J. (2009). Governance and the response to AIDS: Lessons for development and human rights. In A. Clapham & M. Robinson (Eds.), *Realizing the right to health* (pp. 331–345). Rüffer & Rub.

Plantey, A. (2000). *Principes de Diplomatie*. Pedone.

Pletcher, D. M. (2001). *The diplomacy of involvement: American Economic Expansion across the Pacific, 1784-1900*. University of Missouri Press.

Plischke, E. (1978). Microstates: Lilliputs in world affairs. *The Futurist, 12* (February 1978), 19–25, as republished in Plischke E. (Ed.), *Modern diplomacy – The art and the artisans*. American Enterprise Institute for Public Policy Research, 1979, p. 92 et seq.

Plischke, E. (Ed.). (1979). *Modern diplomacy – The art and the artisans*. American Enterprise Institute for Public Policy Research.

Pomeroy, S. B., Burstein, S. M., Donlan, W., & Tolber-Roberts, J. (2014). *Ancient Greece: A political, social, and cultural history* (3rd ed.). Oxford University Press.

Pop, V., Fleming, S., & Politi, J. (2022, April 6). Weaponization of finance: How the west unleashed shock and awe on Russia. *Financial Times*.

Pound, R. (1994). *Five rings over Korea: The secret negotiations behind the 1988 Olympic Games in Seoul*. Little, Brown & Company.

Prevots, N. (1998). *Dance for export: Cultural diplomacy and the cold war*. Wesleyan University Press.

Psychogiopoulou, E. (2018). European cultural policy: The cultural mainstreaming clause of article 167 par. 4 of the Treaty on the functioning of the European Union and its implementation. In M. Kontochristou (Ed.), *Culture in the international. Challenges and policies* (pp. 59–78). I. Sideris. (in Greek).

Qingmin, Z. (2013). Sports diplomacy: The Chinese experience and perspective. *The Hague Journal of Diplomacy, 8*(3–4), 211–233.

Quigley, J., Aceves, W. J., & Adela Shank, S. (2000). *The law of consular access, A documentary guide*. Routledge.

Rasmussen, S. B. (2010). The messages and practices of the European Union's public diplomacy. *The Hague Journal of Diplomacy, 5*(3).

Renganathan, E. (2013). The World Health Organization as a key venue for global health diplomacy. In I. Kickbusch, G. Lister, M. Told, & N. Drager (Eds.), *Global health diplomacy: Concepts, issues, actors, instruments, fora and cases* (pp. 173–185). Springer.

Rettman, A. (2016, January 19). Nuts and bolts: WTO ruling helps China in EU dumping wars. *EU Observer*.

Riedel, E. (2009). The human right to health: Conceptual foundations. In A. Clapham & M. Robinson (Eds.), *Realizing the right to health* (pp. 21–39). Rüffer & Rub.

Rinke, A. (2022, April 8). *Germany could end Russian oil imports this year – Scholz*. Reuters.

Ripple, J. W., Wolf, C., Gregg, J. W., Rockström, J., Newsome, T. M., Law, B. E., Marques, L., Lenton, T. M., Xu, C., Hug, S., Simons, L., & King, S. D. A. (2023). The 2023 state of the climate report: Entering uncharted territory. *BioScience*. https://doi.org/10.1093/biosci/biad080

Rivera, T. (2015). *Distinguishing cultural relations from cultural diplomacy: The British Council's relationship with her Majesty's government*. Figueroa Press.

Roaf, J., Atoyan, R., Bikas, J., Krogulski, K., & IMF staff team. (2014). *25 years of transition: post-communist Europe and the IMF*. International Monetary Fund.

Roberts, I. (Ed.). (2009). *Satow's diplomatic practice* (6th ed.). Oxford University Press.

Robinson, M. (2007). The value of a human rights perspective in health and foreign policy'. *Bulletin of the World Health Organization, 85*(3), 241–242.

Rockower, P. (2014). The state of gastrodiplomacy. *Public Diplomacy, 11*, 13–17.

Rofe, J. S. (Ed.). (2018). *Sport and diplomacy: Games within games*. Manchester University Press.

Rosen, A. (2015). The wrong solution at the right time: The failure of the Kyoto Protocol on climate change. *Policy & Politics, 43*(1), 30–58.

Roucounas, E. (1996). Grèce. In P. M. Eisemann (Ed.), *The integration of international and European Community Law into the National Legal Order: A study of the practice in Europe*. Kluwer Law International.

Roucounas, E. (1998). *Diplomatie et Démocratie, Boutros Boutros-Ghali Amicorum Discipulorumque Liber, t. 2*. UNESCO.

Roucounas, E. (2019). *A landscape of contemporary theories of international law*. Brill Nijhoff.

Roucounas, E. (2021). *Public International Law* (4th ed.). Nomiki Bibliothiki. (in Greek).

Rousseau, C. (1980). *Droit International Public, Vol. IV (Les relations Internationales)*. Sirey.

Rozakis, C. (1985). *International politics – Introductory courses* (Vol. I). Ant. N. Sakkoulas. (in Greek).

Rozenberg, O., & Hefftler, C. (2015). Introduction. In C. Hefftler, C. Neuhold, & O. Rozenberg (Eds.), *The Palgrave handbook of national parliaments and the European Union*. Palgrave.

Rusk, D. (1955). Parliamentary diplomacy – Debate v. Negotiation. *World Affairs Interpreter, 26*(2).

Šabič, Z. (2008). Building democratic and responsible global governance: The role of international parliamentary institutions. *Parliamentary Affairs, 61*.

Said, E. W. (1994). *Culture and imperialism*. Vintage Books.

Sailes, G. (1898). *L institution des consulats, son origine, son developpement au Moyen Age chez les different peulpes*. Leroux.

Salmon, J. (1994). *Manuel de Droit Diplomatique, Bruylant, Précis de la Faculté de Droit*. Univesrité Libre de Bruxelles.

Samaranch, J. A. (1984, March). *Olympic Review*, 156.

Saner, R., & Yiu, L. (2001). *International economic diplomacy: Mutations in post-modern times, discussion papers in diplomacy*. Netherlands Institute of International Relations "Clingendael".

Sanger, D. E. (2016, January 16). Iran complies with nuclear deal - Sanctions are lifted. *New York Times*.

Sasse, C. (1980). The control of the National Parliaments of the nine over European affairs. In A. Cassese (Ed.), *Parliamentary control over foreign policy* (p. 137). Sijthoff & Noordhoff.

Satow, E. (1932). (1917), A guide to diplomatic practice. In A. D. McNair (Ed.), *Contributions to international law and diplomacy* (p. 1). Longmans.

Satow, E. (2011). *A guide to diplomatic practice* (Vol. I). Cambridge University Press.

Satow, E. (2012). *Diplomatic practice* (6th ed.). Oxford University Press.

Schmidt, E., & Cohen, J. (2013). *The new digital age: Reshaping the future of people, nations and business*. John Murray.

Scholte, J. A. (2000). Globalization, governance and corporate citizenship. *The Journal of Corporate Citizenship, 1*.

Schultze, C. *Jurisprudence of the International Court of Justice: Order issued in the case concerning the Vienna Convention on Consular Relations (Paraguay v. United States of America)*.

Schwarzenberger, G. (1941). *Power politics – An introduction to the study of international relations and post-war planning*. Jonathan Cape.

Scovazzi, T. (2007). *Le patrimoine culturel de l'humanité, Académie de Droit International de la Haye, Centre d'Etude et de Recherche de Droit International et des Relations Internationales*. Martinus Nijhoff Publishers.

Seferiadis, S. (1925). *Lessons of international public law, Book A, The Peaceful International Public Law*. Athens. (in Greek).

Segrave, J., & Chu, D. (Eds.). (1988). *The Olympic games in transition*. Human Kinetics.

Seidl-Hohenveldern, I., & Loibl, G. (2000). *Das Recht der Internationalen Organisationen einschließlich der Supranationalen Gemeinschaften*. Heymanns.

Sellin, J. (2021). Access to medicines and the TRIPS agreement: Recognising extraterritorial human rights obligations. In M. Gibney, G. E. Türkelli, M. Krajewski, & W. Vandenhole (Eds.), *The Routledge handbook on extraterritorial human rights obligations* (pp. 339–350). Routledge.

Sen, A. (May 22, 1979). *Equality of what? The Tanner lecture on human values*. Delivered at Stanford University.

Sen, B. (1988). *A diplomat's handbook on international law and practice* (3rd ed.). Martinus Nijhoff Publishers.

Shamwell, H. F., Jr. (1983). Implementing the convention on the prevention and punishment of crimes against internationally protected persons, including diplomatic agents. *Terrorism, 6*(4), 529–543.

Shazia, R. (2015). Parliamentary track 1 ½ diplomacy: An effective tool for peace-making. *Strategic Studies, 35*(2), 71–88.

Shelton, D. (2015). *Remedies in international human rights law*. Oxford University Press.

Sicilianos, L.-A. (2024). *The human dimension of international law interactions between general international law and human rights* (2nd ed.). Nomiki Bibliothiki. (in Greek).

Signitzer, B. H. (2008). Public relations and public diplomacy. In A. Zerfass, B. van Ruler, & Sriramesh (Eds.), *Public relations research* (pp. 205–220). VS Verlag für Sozialwissenschaften.

Simri, U. (1982). The situation of the international sports movement at the beginning of the 1980s. *International Journal of Physical Education, XIX*(1), 1st Quarter.

Sinclair, T. J. (2008). *The new masters of capital: American Bond rating agencies and the politics of creditworthiness*. Cornell University Press.

Skaltsas, K. I. (1972). *The diplomatic representatives in the context of international relations and international law*. Sakkoulas. (in Greek).

Skouris, V. (Ed.). (2003). *Interpretation of EU and EC Treaties*. Ant. N. Sakkoulas. (in Greek).

Slaughter, A. M. (2004). *A new world order*. Princeton University Press.

Smith, A. K. (1991). *Creating a world economy: Merchant capital, colonialism and world trade, 1400-1825*. Westview Press Boulder.

Smith, J. (2020, March). *Energy diplomacy in the middle east: Challenges and opportunities*. International Conference on Energy Policy.

Snow, N., & Taylor, P. (Eds.). (2009). *Routledge handbook on public diplomacy*. Routledge.

Sovacool, B. K., & Brown, M. A. (2010). Competing dimensions of energy security: An international perspective. *Annual Review of Environment and Resources, 35*, 77–108.

Spero, J. E., & Hart, J. A. (2010). *The politics of international economic relations*. Routledge.

Spyropoulos, I. (1933). *Public international law, System of the theory and practice of public international law*. Athens. (in Greek).

Stamatoudi, I. A. (2011). *Cultural property law and restitution: A commentary to international conventions and European Union Law*. Edward Elgar.

Stavridis, S. (2021). Parliamentary diplomacy: A review article. *International Journal of Parliamentary Studies*.

Stowell, E. (1931). *International law: A restatement of principles in conformity with actual practice*. Holt.

Strenk, A. (1980). Diplomats in track suits: The role of sports in the foreign policy of the German Democratic Republic. *Journal of Sport & Social Issues, 4*(1), 34–45.

Tachiaos, N. (2015). Byzantine legacy to the slav world: Approach and dialectic process. *Cyrillomethodianum, XIX*, 5–23.

Takwa, Z. S. (2023). Health diplomacy and Africa: An overview. In H. N. Ndi, H. N. Bang, Z. S. Takwa, & A. T. Mbu (Eds.), *Health diplomacy in Africa: Trends, challenges and perspectives* (pp. 35–55). Palgrave Macmillan/Springer.

Tate, A., Jr. (1973). *The propriety of off-bench judicial writing or speaking on legal or quasi – Legal issues*. University of Alabama. https://www.law.ua.edu/resources/pubs/jlp_files/issues_files/vol03/vol03art03.pdf

Taylor, T. (1988). Politics and the Seoul Olympics. *The Pacific Review, 1*(2), 190–195.

Tenekidis, G. K. (1975). *Public international law, General theory of public international law/Sources of international law* (4th ed.). Papazisis. (in Greek).

Theodoropoulos, V. (1990). *Foreign policy – Diplomacy – Diplomats*. O Typos. (in Greek).

Thompson, K. W. (1965). *The new diplomacy and the quest for peace*. International Organisation.

Tinta, M. F. *Due process and the right to life in the context of the Vienna Convention on Consular Relations: Arguing the LaGrand case.*

Tissot, C. (1863). *Des proxenies grecques et de leur analogie avec les institutions consulaires modernes*. Dijon.

Tobin, J. (2012). *The right to health in international law*. Oxford University Press.

Toebes, B. C. A. (1999). *The right to health as a human right in international law*. Intersentia.

Told, M. (2017). Capacity-building in global health diplomacy in Europe: Experiences, challenges and lessons learned. In I. Kickbusch & M. Kökény (Eds.), *Health diplomacy: European perspectives* (pp. 163–170). WHO Regional Office for Europe.

Toohey, K. (1986). The politics of the 1984 Los Angeles Olympics. In G. Redmond (Ed.), *The 1984 Olympic Scientific Congress Proceedings* (Vol. 7, pp. 161–170). Human Kinetics Publishers.

Topić, M., & Rodin, S. (Eds.). (2012). *Cultural diplomacy and cultural imperialism. European perspectives*. Peter Lang.

Trichet, J. C. (2010, October 16). *Speech at the World Policy Conference in Marrakech.*

Trova, E. (2018). *The cultural heritage of Europe, Concept and content*. Sakkoulas. (in Greek).

Tsatsos, D. T. (1981). *Constitutional law* (Vol. A). Ant. N. Sakkoulas. (in Greek).

Vagias, M., & Dib, M. (2021). If he so requests? The Jadhav Judgement and Article 36(1)b of the Vienna Convention on Consular Relations. *EvrYIEL, 3*, 87–108.

Van Kessel, T. (2016). *Foreign cultural policy in the Interbellum. The Italian Dante Alighieri Society and the British Council Contesting the Mediterranean*. Amsterdam University Press.

Varouxakis, S. (1987). *International organizations, Vol. 2, Legal theory of international organizations*. Papazisi. (in Greek).

Varouxakis, S. (2011). *The diplomacy of mediterranean*. Sakkoulas. (in Greek).

Vasileiadis, N., & Mpoutsiouki, S. (2015). *Cultural diplomacy. Greek and International dimensions*. SEAB. (in Greek).

Venizelos, E. (1986). Executive power relations and parliament in the exercise of foreign policy. In Kouloubis-Konstas (Ed.), *The Hellenic Parliament in Foreign Policy 1974-1984* (p. 180). Ant. N. Sakkoulas. (in Greek).

Venizelos, E. (2021). *Lectures on constitutional law*. Sakkoulas.

Venizelos, E. (Ed.). *Thucydides Histories volumes I–II* (2nd ed.). Bookstore of Estia. (in Greek).

Verbeek, B. (2009). Leadership of international organizations. In J. Kane et al. (Eds.), *Dispersed democratic leadership: Origins, dynamics, and implications* (pp. 235–254). Oxford University Press.

Virmani, A. (2011). *Global economic governance: IMF Quota Reform, IMF Working Paper WP/11/208.*

von Bogdandy, A., & Bast, J. (Eds.). (2010). *Principles of European Constitutional Law*. Hart.

von Liszt, F. (1925). *Das Völkerrecht systematisch dargestellt* (12th ed.). Gale.

Wählisch, M. (2016). Human security. In *Max Planck Encyclopedia of international law*. Oxford University Press.

Watson, A. (2004). *Diplomacy: The dialogue between states*. Routledge.

Weisglas, F. W., & de Boer, G. (2007). Parliamentary diplomacy. *The Hague Journal of Diplomacy, 2*, 93–97.

Wessel, R. A., & Van Vooren, B. (2013). The EEAS's diplomatic dreams and the reality of European and International law. *Journal of European Public Policy.*

White, L. J. (2010). Markets: The credit rating agencies. *Journal of Economic Perspectives, 24*(2).

Wivel, A., & Paul, T. V. (Eds.). (2019). *International institutions and power politics*. Georgetown University Press.

Wolfers, A. (1952). National security as an ambiguous symbol. *Political Science Quarterly, 67*(4), 481–502.

Woods, A. C. (1935). *A history of the Levant Company*. Oxford University Press.

Wouters, J., & Duquet, S. (2011, May). *The EU, EEAS and Union Delegations and International Diplomatic Law: New Horizons?* Leuven Centre for Global Governance Studies, Working Paper No. 62.

Wouters, J., & Duquet, S. (2019). Diplomatic and consular relations. In S. Chesterman, M. D. Malone, & S. Villalpando (Eds.), *The Oxford Handbook of United Nations Treaties*. Oxford University Press.

Yergin, D. (2011). *The prize: The epic quest for oil, money & power*. Simon & Schuster.

Yudrusev, N. A. (Ed.). (2004). *Ottoman diplomacy: Conventional or unconventional?* Palgrave MacMillan.

Yusuf, A. A. (Ed.). (2007). *Elaboration de règles internationales sur l'éducation, la science et la culture* (Vol. I). Editions UNESCO/Martinus Nijhoff Publishers.

Zacharias, D. (2008). The UNESCO Regime for the protection of World Heritage as prototype of an autonomy gaining institution. *German Law Review, 9*(11), 1833–1864.

Zaikos, N. (2002). *United Nations International Law Commission – Contribution to the Study of the codification and progressive development of international Law* (p. 124). Sakkoulas/Institute of International Public Law and International Relations (Contemporary Studies of International Law and International Relations 3/Directorate: Professor K. Koufa). (in Greek).

Zaikos, N. (2006). *International Law and cooperation with the enemy. The legal nature of the "dummy" governments of the Second World War from the point of view of international Law* (p. 35 et seq). Stamouli. (in Greek).

Zaikos, N. (2012). Considerations on the international legal regulation of war in the post-Cold War world. In K. Kentrotis (Ed.), *Twenty years after the fall of the Berlin Wall: Assessments and prospects* (p. 165 et seq). I. Sideris.

Zengerling, C. (2013). *Greening international jurisprudence: Environmental NGOs before international courts, tribunals and compliance committees*. Martinus Nijhoff Publishers.

Zervaki, A. (2010). *The concept of the cultural and natural heritage of humanity: the contribution of UNESCO*. Ant. N. Sakkoula. (in Greek).

Zervaki, A. (2018a). Culture and sustainability: Yet another challenge for the United Nations. In X. Dipla (Ed.), *The United Nations and the new challenges for the international system* (pp. 183–202). Sakkoulas. (in Greek).

Zervaki, A. (2018b). Culture and international organization: UNESCO's contribution to contemporary international cultural relations and governance. In M. Kontochristou (Ed.), *Culture in the international. challenges and policies* (pp. 79–99). I. Sideris. (in Greek).

Zhiznin, S (2005). *International energy politics and diplomacy*

Zhiznin, S. (2007). *Energy diplomacy: Russia and the World Wang*. East Brook Publishing Company.

Zhiznin, S., & Xu, H. Q. (2022). *An introduction to energy diplomacy: China's perspective*. Springer Nature.

Zoras, K. L., & Gikas, V. D. (2002). *The institutional set-up of Greek foreign policy* (Studies of International and European Affairs 2). Ant. N. Sakkoulas. (in Greek).

Zourek, I. (1962). Le statut et les fonctions des consuls. *Recueil de Cours de l' Académie de Droit International*, 433 et seq.

Online Sources

Barber, L. (2020). *China's response to Sudan's political transition*. US Institute of Peace. Retrieved June 25, 2024, from http://www.jstor.org/stable/resrep24904

Council on Foreign Relations. (1850–2023). *Oil dependence and U.S. Foreign Policy*. Retrieved June 25, 2024, from https://www.cfr.org/timeline/oil-dependence-and-us-foreign-policy

European Commission. *Ending energy isolation - Project of common interest "EuroAsia Interconnector"*. Retrieved June 25, 2024., from https://commission.europa.eu/projects/ending-energy-isolation-project-common-interest-euroasia-interconnector_en

European Commission. (2021a). *EU energy policy: Engaging with partners beyond our borders*. Retrieved June 25, 2024, from https://ec.europa.eu/energy

European Commission. (2021b). *EU-Morocco Green partnership*. Retrieved June 25, 2024, from https://climate.ec.europa.eu/news-your-voice/news/eu-and-morocco-form-green-partnership-energy-climate-and-environment-ahead-cop-26-2021-06-28_en

European Union. (2020). *The European Green Deal*. Retrieved June 25, 2024, from https://eur-lex.europa.eu/legal-content/EN/TXT/?uri=CELEX%3A52019DC0640

Global Commission on the Geopolitics of Energy Transformation. (2019). *A new world: The geopolitics of the energy transformation*. Retrieved June 25, 2024, from https://www.irena.org/publications/2019/Jan/A-New-World-The-Geopolitics-of-the-Energy-Transformation

IEA. (2022). *Energy security in energy transitions*. https://www.iea.org/reports/world-energy-outlook-2022/energy-secutiry-in-energy-transitions

International Energy Agency (IEA). (2020a). *World Energy Outlook 2020*.

International Energy Agency (IEA). (2020b). *Power systems in transition*. Retrieved June 25, 2024, from https://www.iea.org/reports/power-systems-in-transition

International Energy Agency (IEA). *Energy security in energy transitions*. Retrieved June 25, 2024., from https://www.iea.org/reports/world-energy-outlook-2022/energy-security-in-energy-transitions

International Monetary Fund. (2002). *The commonwealth of independent states' troubled energy sectors*. Retrieved June 25, 2024, from https://www.imf.org/external/pubs/ft/fandd/2002/09/mathieu.htm

Minerals Security Partnership. Retrieved June 25, 2024., from https://www.state.gov/minerals-security-partnership/

North Sea Wind Power Hub. (2021). *Programme overview* Retrieved June 25, 2024, from https://northseawindpowerhub.eu/knowledge/towards-the-first-hub-and-spoke-project

Spalding, J. (2023). *The deal that keeps the oil flowing*. Epicenter, Weatherhead Center for International Affairs, Harvard University. Retrieved June 25, 2024, from https://epicenter.wcfia.harvard.edu/blog/deal-keeps-oil-flowing

The Moscow Times. (2007). *Putin lands a deal for Turkmen gas*. Retrieved June 25, 2024, from https://www.themoscowtimes.com/archive/putin-lands-a-deal-for-turkmen-gas

United Nations Framework Convention on Climate Change (UNFCCC). (2015). *Paris Agreement*. Retrieved June 25, 2024, from https://www.irena.org/publications/2024/Apr/Geopolitics-of-the-energy-transition-Energy-security

United States Department of Energy. (2020). *Energy diplomacy*. Retrieved June 25, 2024, from https://www.energy.gov/diplomacy

MIX
Papier aus verantwortungsvollen Quellen
Paper from responsible sources
FSC® C105338

If you have any concerns about our products,
you can contact us on
ProductSafety@springernature.com

In case Publisher is established outside the EU,
the EU authorized representative is:
Springer Nature Customer Service Center GmbH
Europaplatz 3, 69115 Heidelberg, Germany

Printed by Libri Plureos GmbH
in Hamburg, Germany